Multilingual
Illustrated Dictionary

English | IsiZulu | Sesotho | IsiXhosa | Setswana | Afrikaans | Sepedi

Multilingual
Illustrated Dictionary

| English | IsiZulu | Sesotho | IsiXhosa | Setswana | Afrikaans | Sepedi |

Dictionary   Isichazimazwi   Bukantswe

Isichazi-magama   Bukafoko   Woordeboek

Pukuntšu

John Bennett ○ Nthuseng Tsoeu

**Thabisile Buthelezi • Tuelo Mpolokeng • Monyamane Shai
Zalisile Mkhontwana • Liesbet van Wyk**

PHAROS • JUTA GARIEP

First edition published in 2006 by
Pharos Dictionaries,
a division of NB Publishers,
40 Heerengracht, Cape Town, South Africa

Edited by Jimmy Ntombela, Mahlomola Mosomothane, Bhelekazi Gqokoma, Idah Mogotsi,
Alison Arrison and Brenda Bopape.
Proofread by Sizakele Ncoko, Tsietsi Mohapi, Monde Mfanekiso, Godfrey Mareme,
Alison Arrison and Malesela Masenya.
Second proofreading by Nogwaja Zulu, Porcia Nokaneng, Tozi Buthelezi, Eileen Poee,
Berlyn Ntusikazi, Iolanda Steadman, Jana Luther and Fred Pheiffer.

Cover design by John Bennett and Flame Design
Layout and typesetting by John Bennett and Deon Schutte
Illustrated by Pandora Alberts, John Bennett, Stuart Dumville, Bennie Krüger,
Robyn Minter, Anthony Riley and Jiggs Snaddon-Wood
Reproduction by Castle Graphics
Printed and bound by Mills Litho, Cape Town

First edition, first impression 2006
Second impression 2007

ISBN: 978-07021-6712-6

Acknowledgements

The authors and publishers thank PictureNet SA for the permission
to reproduce the photograph on page 281.

The authors thank all the translators, editors, proofreaders and illustrators for their valuable
contribution to produce this dictionary. We also thank family and friends for your support.
And lastly, we thank Sportsmans Warehouse Tokai branch for allowing us the opportunity to
photograph sport merchandise.

We dedicate this dictionary to all South Africans.
We can all learn to understand and speak one another's language.

Contents Okuqukethwe Dikahare Isiqulatho Diteng Inhoud Diteng

How to use this dictionary

This dictionary is illustrated throughout for easy reference and labelled in seven different languages: English, IsiZulu, Sesotho, IsiXhosa, Setswana, Afrikaans and Sepedi. Each one is colour-coded and in the same order throughout the dictionary. The language colours are:

English
IsiZulu
Sesotho
IsiXhosa
Setswana
Afrikaans
Sepedi

This dictionary is made up of 12 themes, a basic grammar section and an index for each language. To find what a word means in another language, you must turn to the index at the back of the dictionary. Remember, each language has its own index and the words are listed in alphabetical order. Let's try it out!

1 Look for the word *apple* in the English index.

2 Turn to the page reference given.

3 There you will find the word in the seven languages.

appendicitis 95
applause 277
apple 230
apple pie 247
apricot 230

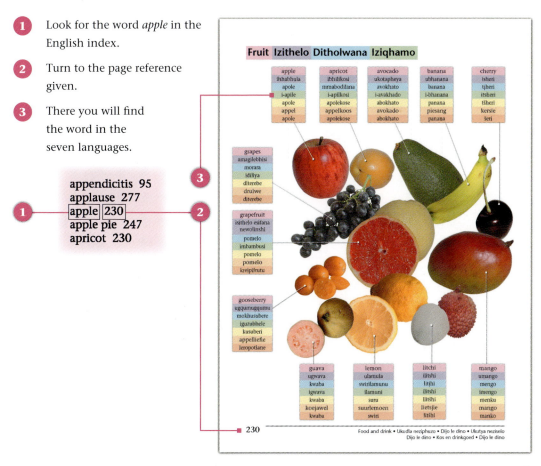

Fruit	Izithelo	Ditholwana	Iziqhamo

apple	apricot	avocado	banana	cherry
ihhabbula	ibhilikosi	ukotapheya	ubhanana	isheri
apole	mmabodilana	avokhato	banana	tjheri
i-apile	i-apilkosi	i-avakhado	i-bhanana	itsheri
apole	apolekose	abokhato	panana	tšheri
appel	appelkoos	avokado	piesang	kersie
apole	apolekose	abokhato	panana	šeri

grapes
amagilebhisi
morara
idiliya
diterebe
druiwe
diterebe

grapefruit
isithelo esifana newolinshi
pomelo
imhambusi
pomelo
pomelo
kreipifrutu

gooseberry
ugqumugqumu
mokhusubere
iguzubhele
kusuberi
appelliefie
leropotlane

guava	lemon	litchi	mango
ugwava	ulamula	ilitshi	umango
kwaba	swirilamunu	litjhi	mengo
igwava	ilamuni	ilitshi	imengo
kwaba	suru	llitšhi	menku
koejawel	suurlemoen	lietsjie	mango
kwaba	swiri	litši	manko

230

Food and drink • Ukudla neziphuzo • Dijo le dino • Ukutya neziselo
Dijo le dino • Kos en drinkgoed • Dijo le dino

5

Indlela yokusebenzisa lesi sichazimazwi

Lesi sichazimazwi sihlelwe ngendlela enezithombe ezinamabalabala ukwenza kube lula ukusisebenzisa. Sihlelwe ngezilimi eziyisikhombisa ezahlukene isiNgisi, isiZulu, isiSuthu, isiXhosa, isiTswana, isiBhulu nesiPedi. Izilimi zihlukaniswe ngemibala kodwa zilandela uhla olulodwa kuso sonke isichazimazwi. Imibala yezilimi yilena:

IsiNgisi
IsiZulu
IsiSuthu
IsiXhosa
IsiTswana
IsiBhunu
IsiPedi

Lesi sichazimazwi sakhiwe ngezindikimba eziyishumi elinesibili, isigaba sohlelo kanye nohla lwamagama lwalolo nalolo limi. Ukuthola ukuthi igama lichazani kolunye ulimi, kufanele uvule uhlu lwamagama ngemuva kwesichazimazwi. Khumbula ukuthi ulimi nolimi lunoluhlu lwamagama kanti namagama ahlelwe ngokulandelelana kwezinhlamvu. Ake sizame!

1. Bheka igama elithi *apple* ohlwini lwamagama lwesiNgisi.

2. Vula ekhasini olunikeziwe.

3. Lapho uzothola leli gama ngezilimi eziyisikhombisa

```
appendicitis  95
applause  277
apple  230
apple pie  247
apricot  230
```

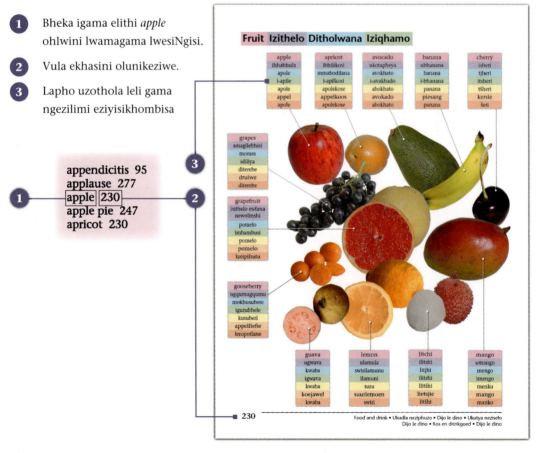

O ka sebedisa bukantswe ena jwang

Bukantswe ena e kgabile ka ditshwantsho tse mebalabala tse bobebe mme e hlophisitswe ka dipuo tse supileng tse fapaneng e leng: Senyesemane, SeZulu, Sesotho, SeQhotsa, Setswana, Seburu le Sepedi. Puo ka nngwe e na le mmala o ikgethang ho tse ding ho fihlela pheletsong ya bukantswe ena. Mebala ya dipuo tse fapaneng e bonahala tjena:

| Senyesemane |
| SeZulu |
| Sesotho |
| SeQhotsa |
| Setswana |
| Seburu |
| SePedi |

Bukantswe ena e na le dikarolo tse leshome le metso e mmedi, karolwana ya hlakiso ya puo le tshupiso ya puo ka nngwe. Hore o fumane moelelo wa puo e nngwe, phetla leqepheng la tshupiso le pheletsong ya buka ena. Hopola hore puo ka nngwe e na le tshupiso ya yona mme mantswe a ngotswe ho ya ka tatelano ya ditlhaku tsa nteterwane. A re lekeng tjena:

1. Sheba lentswe *apple* tshupisong ya Senyesemane.

2. Phetla leqepheng leo o le neilweng.

3. Ha se moo he! O tla fumana lentswe leo ka dipuo tse supileng.

appendicitis 95
applause 277
apple 230
apple pie 247
apricot 230

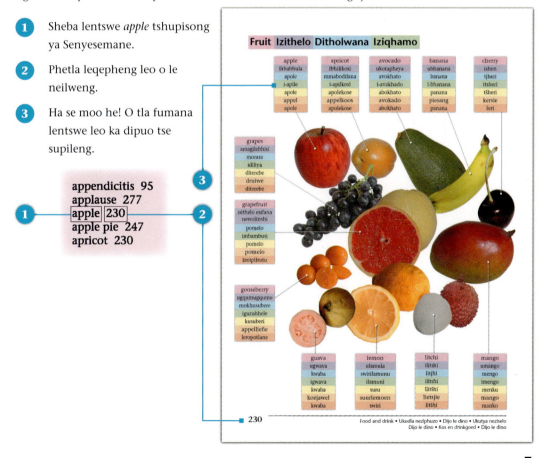

Indlela yokusebenzisa esi sichazi-magama

Esi sichazi-magama sibonisa ngendlela enemifanekiso eqaqambileyo, inguqulelo elula echazwe ngeelwimi ezisixhenxe ezi zezi, isiNgesi, isiZulu, isiSuthu, isiXhosa, isiTswana, isiBhulu kunye nesiPedi. Ulwimi ngalunye lubonakaliswe ngombala owodwa kwisichazi-magama siphela. Ulwimi ngalunye luboniswe ngale mibala ilandelayo:

IsiNgesi
IsiZulu
IsiSuthu
IsiXhosa
IsiTswana
IsiBhulu
IsiPedi

Esi sichazi-magama sinemixholo elishumi elinesibini, icandelo lemigaqo-ntetho, nesalathiso solwimi ngalunye. Ukufumana intsingiselo yegama kolunye ulwimi, vula kwisalathiso esingemva kwisichazi-magama. Khumbula, ulwimi ngalunye lunesalathiso salo kwaye amagama alandelelaniswe ngokokulandelelana koonobumba. Make sizame!

1 Khangela igama *apple* kwisalathiso sesiNgesi.

2 Yiya kwiphepha elichazwe kwisalathiso

3 Apho uyakufumana intsingiselo yegama elo lichazwe ngeelwimi ezisixhenxe.

appendicitis 95
applause 277
apple | 230 |
apple pie 247
apricot 230

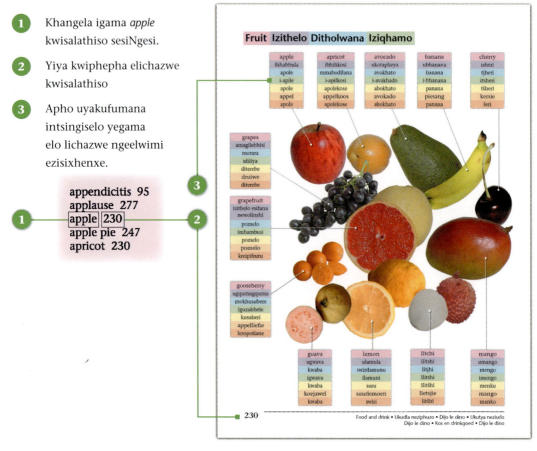

Tsela ya go dirisa bukafoko e

Bukafoko eno e tlhalositswe sentle go go supetsa motlhofo e bile e kwadilwe ka dipuo tse di farologaneng di le supa: Seesimane, SeZulu, Sesotho, SeXhosa, Setswana, Seaferikanse le Sepedi. E nngwe le e nngwe e dirilwe ka mebala le ka thulaganyo e e tshwanang ya bukafoko. Mebala ya puo ke:

Seesimane
SeZulu
Sesotho
SeXhosa
Setswana
Seaferikanse
Sepedi

Bukafoko eno e dirilwe ka dithitokgang di le lesomepedi (12) karolo ya theo ya thutapuo le tshupane ya puo nngwe le nngwe. Fa o batla go itse bokao jwa lefoko lengwe mo puong e nngwe, o tshwanetse go ya kwa tshupane kwa lemoragong la bukafoko. Gakologelwa, puo nngwe le nngwe e na le tshupane ya yona le mafoko a kwadile ka tatelano. A re lekeng!

1. Batla lefoko *apple* mo tshupaneng ya Seesimane.

2. Bula tshupane ya tsebe e e neilweng.

3. O tla bona lefoko mo dipuong di le supa.

appendicitis 95
applause 277
apple 230
apple pie 247
apricot 230

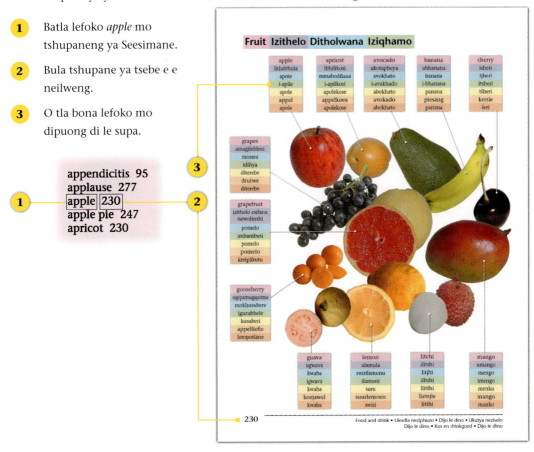

Fruit Izithelo Ditholwana Iziqhamo

apple	apricot	avocado	banana	cherry
ihhabhula	ibhilikosi	ukotapheya	ubhanana	isheri
apole	mnabodilana	avokhato	banana	tjheri
i-apile	i-apilkosi	i-avakhado	i-bhanana	itsheri
apole	apolekose	abokhato	panana	tšheri
appel	appelkoos	avokado	piesang	kersie
apole	apolekose	abokhato	panana	šeri

grapes
amagilebhisi
morara
idiliya
diterebe
druiwe
diterebe

grapefruit
isithelo esifana newolinshi
pomelo
imbambusi
pomelo
pomelo
kreipifrutu

gooseberry
ugqumuguqumu
mokhusubere
iguzubhele
kusuberi
appeltiefie
leropotiane

guava	lemon	litchi	mango
ugwava	ulamula	ilitshi	umango
kwaba	swirilamunu	litjhi	mengo
igwava	ilamuni	ilitshi	imengo
kwaba	suru	llitshi	menku
koejawel	suurlemoen	lietsjie	mango
kwaba	swiri	litši	manko

230

Food and drink • Ukudla neziphuzo • Dijo le dino • Ukutya neziselo
Dijo le dino • Kos en drinkgoed • Dijo le dino

9

Hoe om hierdie woordeboek te gebruik

Hierdie woordeboek is volledig geïllustreer en het byskrifte in sewe verskillende tale: Engels, Zoeloe, Suid-Sotho, Xhosa, Tswana, Afrikaans en Noord-Sotho. Elke taal het sy eie kleur en vaste volgorde in die boek. Die kleure en volgorde van die verskillende tale is:

Engels
Zoeloe
Suid-Sotho
Xhosa
Tswana
Afrikaans
Noord-Sotho

Die woordeboek is in 12 temas verdeel. Daar is ook 'n basiese grammatika-gedeelte en indeks vir elke taal. Om uit te vind wat 'n woord in 'n ander taal beteken, sal jy eerste in die indeks agter in die boek moet kyk. Onthou, elke taal het 'n indeks, en die woorde is in alfabetiese volgorde. Dit werk so:

1 Soek die woord *apple* in die Engelse indeks.

2 Blaai nou na die bladsynommer.

3 Hier sal jy die woord in al sewe tale vind.

appendicitis 95
applause 277
apple 230
apple pie 247
apricot 230

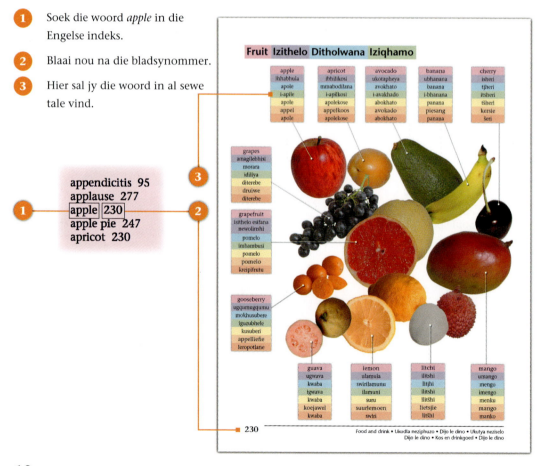

Pukuntšu ye e šomišwa bjang

Pukuntšu ye ka moka ga yona e na le diswantšho go kgonagatša go e diriša gabonolo mme e arogantšwe ka dipolelo tše šupago: Seisemane, Sezulu, Sesotho, Sethosa, Setswana Seafrikanse le Sepedi. Polelo ye nngwe le ye nngwe e filwe mmala wa yona mme di latelana ka tsela e tee mo pukuntšung ka moka. Mebala ya dipolelo tšeo ke ye:

Seisimane
Sezulu
Sesotho
Sethosa
Setswana
Seafrikanse
Sepedi

Pukuntšu ye e na le ditabakgolo tše lesomepedi (12) karolo ya motheo ya popopolelo le tšhupane ya polelo ye nngwe le ye nngwe. Go tseba gore tlhalošo ya lentšu le itšeng ke efe ka polelo ye nngwe, o swanetše go ya go tšhupane ka mafelelong a pukuntšu. Elelwa, polelo ye nngwe le ye nngwe e na le tšhupane ya yona mme mantšu a latelelana ka alfabete. A re itekeng:

1 Nyaka lentšu *apple* mo tšhupaneng ya Seisimane.

2 Eya letlakaleng la tšhupetšo le filwego.

3 Fao o tla hwetša tlhalošo ya lentšu leo ka dipolelo tše šupago.

appendicitis 95
applause 277
apple 230
apple pie 247
apricot 230

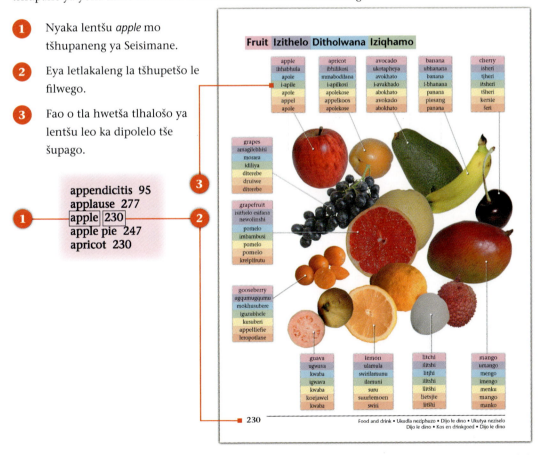

1

My body

Umzimba wami

Mmele wa ka

Umzimba wam

Mmele wa me

My liggaam

Mmele wa ka

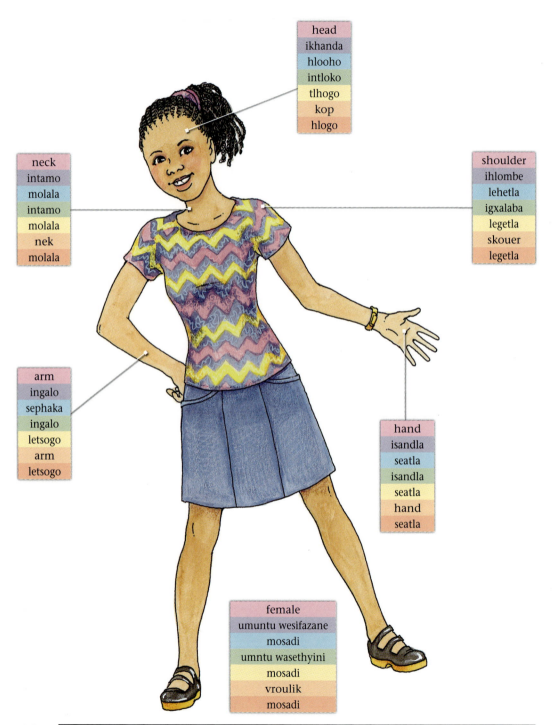

head
ikhanda
hlooho
intloko
tlhogo
kop
hlogo

neck
intamo
molala
intamo
molala
nek
molala

shoulder
ihlombe
lehetla
igxalaba
legetla
skouer
legetla

arm
ingalo
sephaka
ingalo
letsogo
arm
letsogo

hand
isandla
seatla
isandla
seatla
hand
seatla

female
umuntu wesifazane
mosadi
umntu wasethyini
mosadi
vroulik
mosadi

Die liggaam Mmele

chest
isifuba
sefuba
isifuba
sehuba
bors
kgara

waist
ukhalo
letheka
isinqe
letheka
middel
letheka

abdomen
isisu
mpa
isisu
mpa
maag
mpa

foot
unyawo
leoto
unyawo
lonao
voet
lenao

leg
umlenze
tlhafu
umlenze
leoto
been
leoto

male
umuntu wesilisa
monna
indoda
monna
manlik
monna

My body • Umzimba wami • Mmele wa ka • Umzimba wam • Mmele wa me • My liggaam • Mmele wa ka

15

Face Ubuso Sefahleho Ubuso Sefatlhego

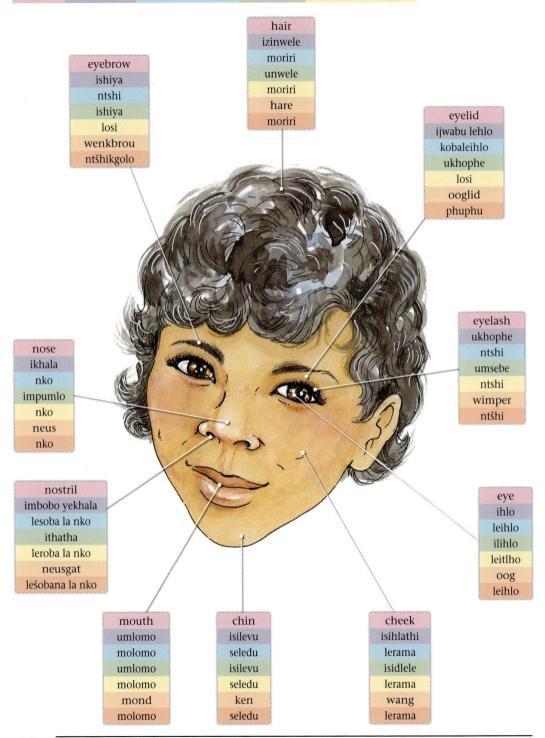

hair
izinwele
moriri
unwele
moriri
hare
moriri

eyebrow
ishiya
ntshi
ishiya
losi
wenkbrou
ntšhikgolo

eyelid
ijwabu lehlo
kobaleihlo
ukhophe
losi
ooglid
phuphu

nose
ikhala
nko
impumlo
nko
neus
nko

eyelash
ukhophe
ntshi
umsebe
ntshi
wimper
ntšhi

nostril
imbobo yekhala
lesoba la nko
ithatha
leroba la nko
neusgat
lešobana la nko

eye
ihlo
leihlo
ilihlo
leitlho
oog
leihlo

mouth
umlomo
molomo
umlomo
molomo
mond
molomo

chin
isilevu
seledu
isilevu
seledu
ken
seledu

cheek
isihlathi
lerama
isidlele
lerama
wang
lerama

16   My body • Umzimba wami • Mmele wa ka • Umzimba wam • Mmele wa me • My liggaam • Mmele wa ka

Gesig Sefahlego

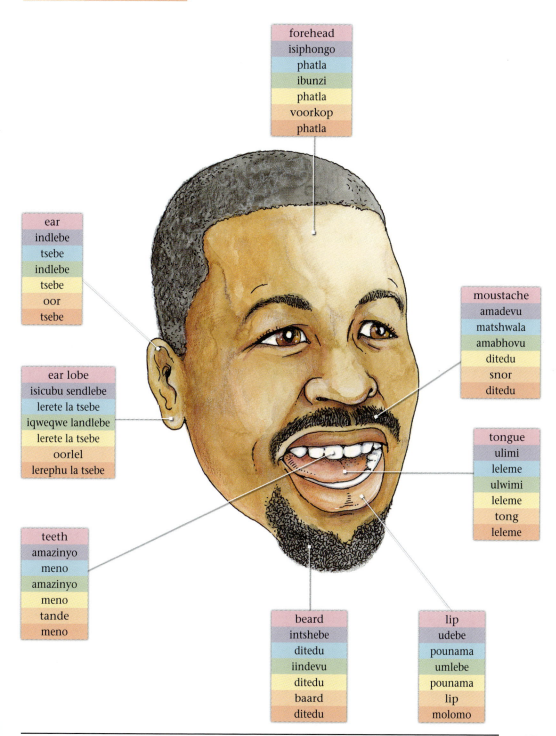

forehead
isiphongo
phatla
ibunzi
phatla
voorkop
phatla

ear
indlebe
tsebe
indlebe
tsebe
oor
tsebe

moustache
amadevu
matshwala
amabhovu
ditedu
snor
ditedu

ear lobe
isicubu sendlebe
lerete la tsebe
iqweqwe landlebe
lerete la tsebe
oorlel
lerephu la tsebe

tongue
ulimi
leleme
ulwimi
leleme
tong
leleme

teeth
amazinyo
meno
amazinyo
meno
tande
meno

beard
intshebe
ditedu
iindevu
ditedu
baard
ditedu

lip
udebe
pounama
umlebe
pounama
lip
molomo

Upper body	Umzimba ongenhla	Mmele o ka hodimo	Umzimba ongentla	Mmele kwa godimo
Bolyf	Bogodimo bja mmele			

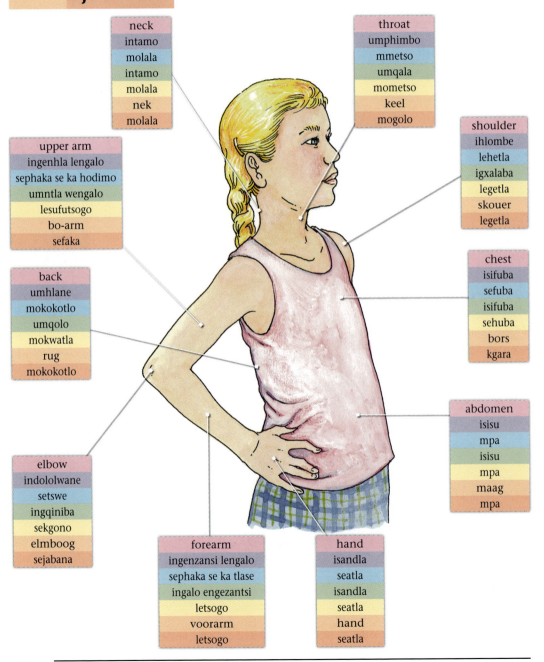

neck
intamo
molala
intamo
molala
nek
molala

throat
umphimbo
mmetso
umqala
mometso
keel
mogolo

shoulder
ihlombe
lehetla
igxalaba
legetla
skouer
legetla

upper arm
ingenhla lengalo
sephaka se ka hodimo
umntla wengalo
lesufutsogo
bo-arm
sefaka

chest
isifuba
sefuba
isifuba
sehuba
bors
kgara

back
umhlane
mokokotlo
umqolo
mokwatla
rug
mokokotlo

abdomen
isisu
mpa
isisu
mpa
maag
mpa

elbow
indololwane
setswe
ingqiniba
sekgono
elmboog
sejabana

forearm
ingenzansi lengalo
sephaka se ka tlase
ingalo engezantsi
letsogo
voorarm
letsogo

hand
isandla
seatla
isandla
seatla
hand
seatla

Lower body	Umzimba ongezansi	Mmele o ka tlase	Umzimba ongezantsi
Mmele kwa tlase	Onderlyf	Botlase bja mmele	

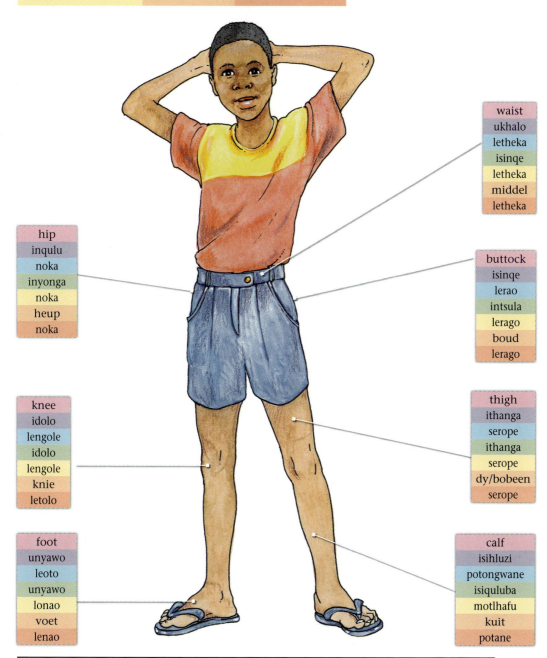

waist
ukhalo
letheka
isinqe
letheka
middel
letheka

hip
inqulu
noka
inyonga
noka
heup
noka

buttock
isinqe
lerao
intsula
lerago
boud
lerago

knee
idolo
lengole
idolo
lengole
knie
letolo

thigh
ithanga
serope
ithanga
serope
dy/bobeen
serope

foot
unyawo
leoto
unyawo
lonao
voet
lenao

calf
isihluzi
potongwane
isiquluba
motlhafu
kuit
potane

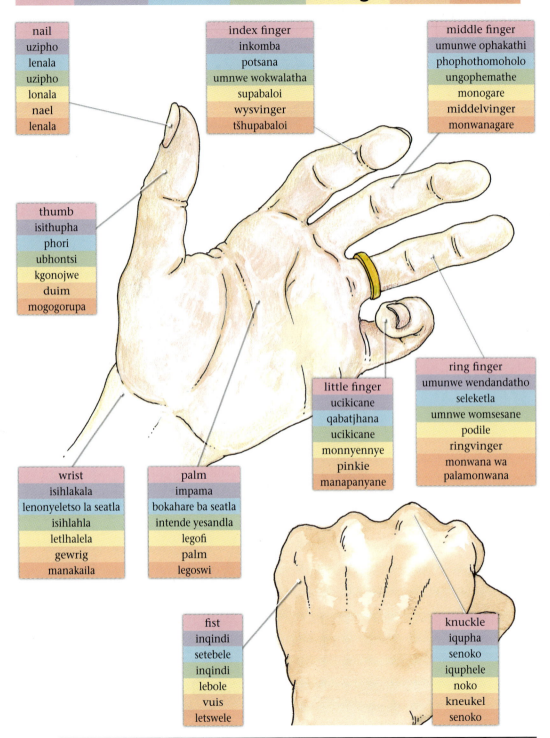

nail
uzipho
lenala
uzipho
lonala
nael
lenala

index finger
inkomba
potsana
umnwe wokwalatha
supabaloi
wysvinger
tšhupabaloi

middle finger
umunwe ophakathi
phophothomoholo
ungophemathe
monogare
middelvinger
monwanagare

thumb
isithupha
phori
ubhontsi
kgonojwe
duim
mogogorupa

ring finger
umunwe wendandatho
seleketla
umnwe womsesane
podile
ringvinger
monwana wa palamonwana

little finger
ucikicane
qabatjhana
ucikicane
monnyennye
pinkie
manapanyane

wrist
isihlakala
lenonyeletso la seatla
isihlahla
letlhalela
gewrig
manakaila

palm
impama
bokahare ba seatla
intende yesandla
legofi
palm
legoswi

fist
inqindi
setebele
inqindi
lebole
vuis
letswele

knuckle
iqupha
senoko
iquphele
noko
kneukel
senoko

Foot Unyawo Leoto Unyawo Lonao Voet Lenao

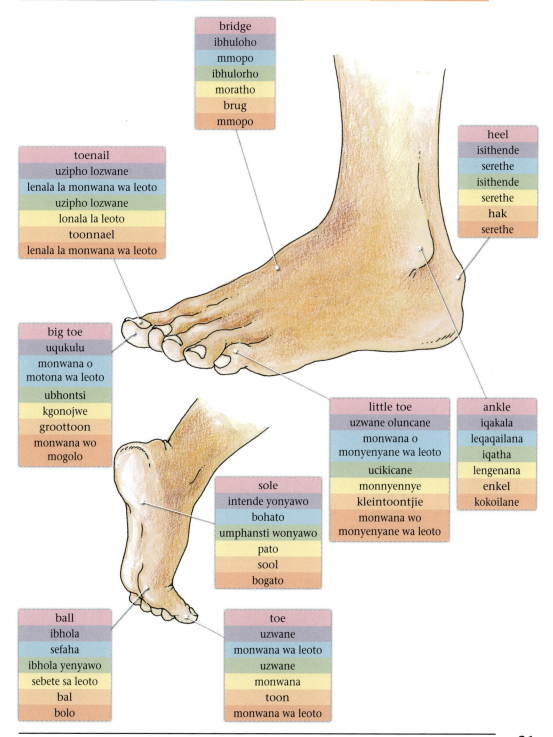

bridge
ibhuloho
mmopo
ibhulorho
moratho
brug
mmopo

heel
isithende
serethe
isithende
serethe
hak
serethe

toenail
uzipho lozwane
lenala la monwana wa leoto
uzipho lozwane
lonala la leoto
toonnael
lenala la monwana wa leoto

big toe
uqukulu
monwana o motona wa leoto
ubhontsi
kgonojwe
groottoon
monwana wo mogolo

little toe
uzwane oluncane
monwana o monyenyane wa leoto
ucikicane
monnyennye
kleintoontjie
monwana wo monyenyane wa leoto

ankle
iqakala
leqaqailana
iqatha
lengenana
enkel
kokoilane

sole
intende yonyawo
bohato
umphansti wonyawo
pato
sool
bogato

ball
ibhola
sefaha
ibhola yenyawo
sebete sa leoto
bal
bolo

toe
uzwane
monwana wa leoto
uzwane
monwana
toon
monwana wa leoto

The skin Isikhumba Letlalo Ulusu Letlalo Die vel Letlalo

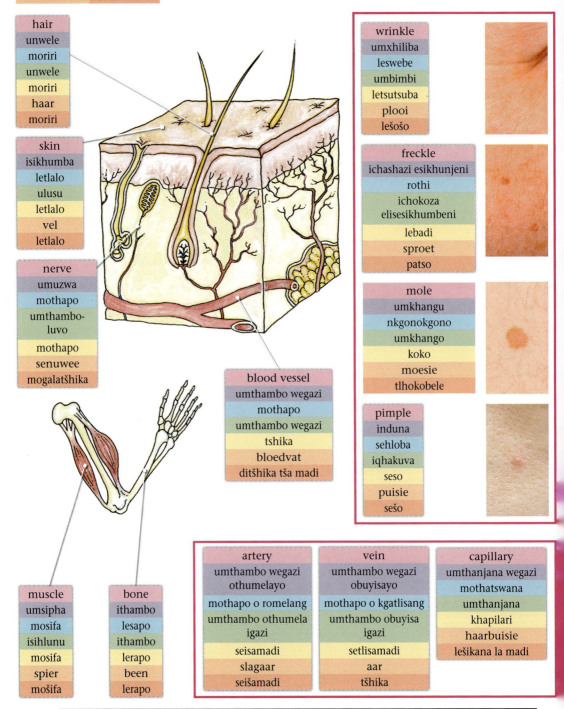

hair
unwele
moriri
unwele
moriri
haar
moriri

skin
isikhumba
letlalo
ulusu
letlalo
vel
letlalo

nerve
umuzwa
mothapo
umthambo-luvo
mothapo
senuwee
mogalatšhika

blood vessel
umthambo wegazi
mothapo
umthambo wegazi
tshika
bloedvat
ditšhika tša madi

muscle
umsipha
mosifa
isihlunu
mosifa
spier
mošifa

bone
ithambo
lesapo
ithambo
lerapo
been
lerapo

wrinkle
umxhiliba
leswebe
umbimbi
letsutsuba
plooi
lešošo

freckle
ichashazi esikhunjeni
rothi
ichokoza elisesikhumbeni
lebadi
sproet
patso

mole
umkhangu
nkgonokgono
umkhango
koko
moesie
tlhokobele

pimple
induna
sehloba
iqhakuva
seso
puisie
sešo

artery	vein	capillary
umthambo wegazi othumelayo	umthambo wegazi obuyisayo	umthanjana wegazi
mothapo o romelang	mothapo o kgatlisang	mothatswana
umthambo othumela igazi	umthambo obuyisa igazi	umthanjana
seisamadi	setlisamadi	khapilari
slagaar	aar	haarbuisie
seišamadi	tšhika	lešikana la madi

Inside the body Ingaphakathi lomzimba
Bokahare ba mmele Okungaphakathi emzimbeni
Mmele mo gare In die liggaam Ka gare ga mmele

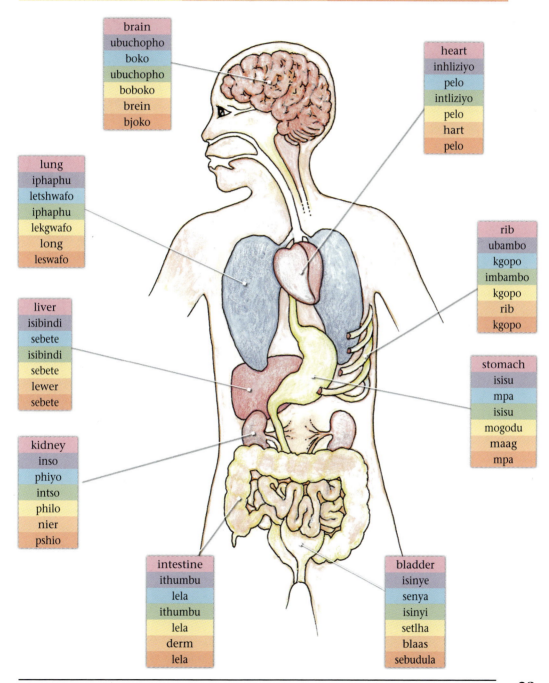

brain
ubuchopho
boko
ubuchopho
boboko
brein
bjoko

heart
inhliziyo
pelo
intliziyo
pelo
hart
pelo

lung
iphaphu
letshwafo
iphaphu
lekgwafo
long
leswafo

rib
ubambo
kgopo
imbambo
kgopo
rib
kgopo

liver
isibindi
sebete
isibindi
sebete
lewer
sebete

stomach
isisu
mpa
isisu
mogodu
maag
mpa

kidney
inso
phiyo
intso
philo
nier
pshio

intestine
ithumbu
lela
ithumbu
lela
derm
lela

bladder
isinye
senya
isinyi
setlha
blaas
sebudula

Feelings Imizwa Maikutlo Iimvakalelo Maikutlo

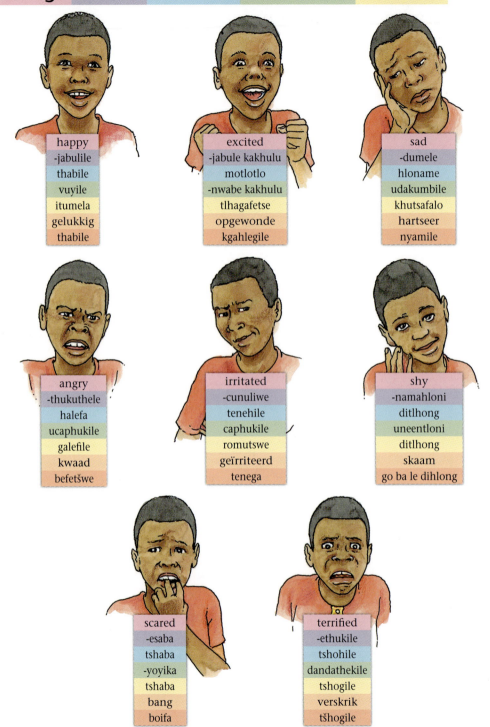

happy
-jabulile
thabile
vuyile
itumela
gelukkig
thabile

excited
-jabule kakhulu
motlotlo
-nwabe kakhulu
tlhagafetse
opgewonde
kgahlegile

sad
-dumele
hloname
udakumbile
khutsafalo
hartseer
nyamile

angry
-thukuthele
halefa
ucaphukile
galefile
kwaad
befetšwe

irritated
-cunuliwe
tenehile
caphukile
romutswe
geïrriteerd
tenega

shy
-namahloni
ditlhong
uneentloni
ditlhong
skaam
go ba le dihlong

scared
-esaba
tshaba
-yoyika
tshaba
bang
boifa

terrified
-ethukile
tshohile
dandathekile
tshogile
verskrik
tšhogile

Gevoelens Maikutlo

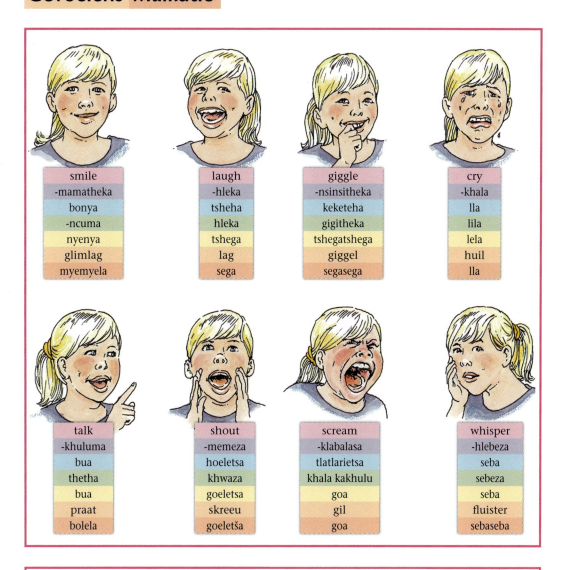

smile	laugh	giggle	cry
-mamatheka	-hleka	-nsinsitheka	-khala
bonya	tsheha	keketeha	lla
-ncuma	hleka	gigitheka	lila
nyenya	tshega	tshegatshega	lela
glimlag	lag	giggel	huil
myemyela	sega	segasega	lla

talk	shout	scream	whisper
-khuluma	-memeza	-klabalasa	-hlebeza
bua	hoeletsa	tlatlarietsa	seba
thetha	khwaza	khala kakhulu	sebeza
bua	goeletsa	goa	seba
praat	skreeu	gil	fluister
bolela	goeletša	goa	sebaseba

Senses Imizwa Dikutlo Izivo Kutlo Sintuie Dikwi

sight	hearing	taste	touch	smell
ukubona	ukuzwa	ukunambitha	ukuthinta	ukunuka
pono	kutlo	tatso	kamo	monko
ukubona	ukuva	ukungcamla	ukuphatha	ukunukisa
pono	kutlo	tatso	tshwara	monkgo
gesig	gehoor	smaak	tas	reuk
pono	go kwa	tatso	kgoma	monkgo

Phrases	Amabinzana	Dipolelwana	Amabinzana
Hello.	Sawubona.	Dumela.	Molo.
How are you?	Unjani?	O phela jwang?	Unjani?
I am well thank you.	Ngikhona, ngiyabonga.	Ke phetse, ke a leboha.	Ndiphilile, enkosi.
What's your name?	Ungubani igama lakho?	O mang lebitso la hao?	Ungubani igama lakho?
My name is …	Igama lami ngingu …	Lebitso la ka ke …	Igama lam ngu…
I am pleased to meet you.	Ngiyajabula ukukwazi.	Ke thabela ho o tseba.	Ndinovuyo ukudibana nawe.
What's your surname?	Ungubani isibongo sakho, ungowakwabani?	Fane ya hao ke mang?	Ungubani ifani yakho?
My surname is …	Isibongo sami ngingowakwa …	Fane ya ka ke …	Ifani yam ngu…
Where do you live?	Uhlalaphi?	O dula kae?	Uhlala phi?
I live at …	Ngihlala e…	Ke dula …	Ndihlala e…
What is your home language?	Ukhuluma luphi ulimi lwebele?	Le bua puo efe lapeng?	Loluphi ulwimi lwakokwenu?
My home language is …	Ulimi lwami lwebele i…	Lapeng re bua …	Ulwimi lwasekhaya sisi…
Would you like to learn more languages?	Uyathanda ukufunda ezinye izilimi?	Na o batla ho ithuta dipuo tse ngata?	Ungathanda ukufunda ezinye iilwimi?
That would be great, thanks!	Kungaba kuhle kakhulu. Ngiyabonga.	Nka thaba haholo, ke a leboha!	Kungaba kuhle oko, enkosi!
How are you feeling today?	Uzizwa unjani namuhla?	O ikutlwa jwang kajeno?	Uziva njani namhlanje?
I am happy/excited/angry/sad/afraid.	Ngiyajabula/ngijabule kakhulu/ngithukuthele/ngidumele/ngiyesaba.	Ke thabile/motlotlo/halefile/hloname/tshohile.	Ndiyavuya/ndonwabile/ndichulumancile/ndinomsindo/ndidakumbile/ndiyoyika.
I am not feeling well.	Angiphathekile kahle.	Ha ke ikutlwe monate.	Andiziva mnandi.
Why, what is wrong?	Kungani kwenzekeni embi?	Molato ke eng?	Kutheni? Yintoni embi?
I have a sore stomach.	Ngiphethwe yisisu.	Ke opelwa ke mala.	Ndinesisu esibuhlungu.

Dikapolelo	Frases	Dikafoko
Dumela.	Hallo.	Dumela.
O kae?	Hoe gaan dit met jou?	O kae?
Ke teng, ga go na molato.	Dit gaan goed, dankie.	Ke gona, ke a leboga.
Leina la gago ke mang?	Wat is jou naam?	Leina la gago o mang?
Leina la me ke …	My naam is …	Leina la ka ke …
Ke itumelela ga go itse.	Aangename kennis.	Ke thabela go go tseba.
Sefane sa gago ke mang?	Wat is jou van?	Sefane sa gago ke sefe?
Sefane sa me ke …	My van is …	Sefane sa ka ke …
O nna/dula kae?	Waar woon jy?	O dula kae?
Ke nna/dula kwa …	Ek woon in …	Ke dula …
Puo ya gago ya kwa gae ke efe?	Wat is jou huistaal?	Polelo ya gago ya gae ke efe?
Puo ya me ya kwa gae ke …	My huistaal is …	Polelo ya ka ya gae ke …
A o batla go ithuta dipuo tse dingwe?	Wil jy graag meer tale aanleer?	O rata go ithuta dipolelo tše dintši?
Go ka e ntumedisa, ke a leboga!	Dit sal wonderlik wees, dankie!	Nka thabela seo, ke a leboga!
O ikutlwa jang gompieno?	Hoe voel jy vandag?	A o ikwa bjang lehono?
Ke itumetse/tlhagafetse/galefile/hutsafetse/tshogile.	Ek is gelukkig/opgewonde/kwaad/hartseer/bang.	Ke thabile/kgahlegile/befetšwe/nyamile/tšhogile.
Ga ke ikutlwe sentle.	Ek voel nie lekker nie.	Ga ke ikwe botse.
Goreng, molato ke eng?	Hoekom, wat makeer?	Ka lebaka la eng, molato ke eng?
Mala a me a botlhoko/Ke bolawa ke mala.	My maag is seer.	Ke longwa ke mala.

Family and friends

Umndeni kanye nabangani

Lelapa le metswalle

Usapho nezihlobo

Balelapa le ditsala

Familie en vriende

Lapa le bagwera

Family and friends • Umndeni kanye nabangani • Lelapa le metswalle • Usapho nezihlobo
Balelapa le ditsala • Familie en vriende • Lapa le bagwera

29

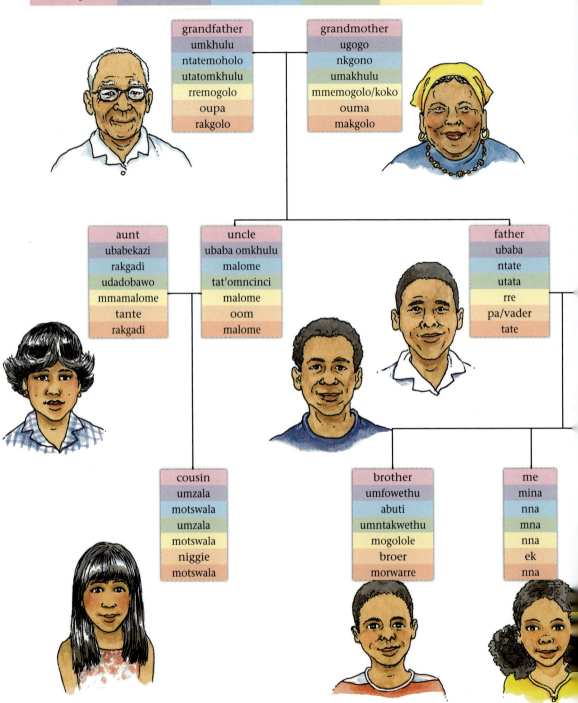

grandfather
umkhulu
ntatemoholo
utatomkhulu
rremogolo
oupa
rakgolo

grandmother
ugogo
nkgono
umakhulu
mmemogolo/koko
ouma
makgolo

aunt
ubabekazi
rakgadi
udadobawo
mmamalome
tante
rakgadi

uncle
ubaba omkhulu
malome
tat'omncinci
malome
oom
malome

father
ubaba
ntate
utata
rre
pa/vader
tate

cousin
umzala
motswala
umzala
motswala
niggie
motswala

brother
umfowethu
abuti
umntakwethu
mogolole
broer
morwarre

me
mina
nna
mna
nna
ek
nna

Family and friends • Umndeni kanye nabangani • Lelapa le metswalle • Usapho nezihlobo
Balelapa le ditsala • Familie en vriende • Lapa le bagwera

grandmother	grandfather
ugogo	umkhulu
nkgono	ntatemoholo
umakhulu	utatomkhulu
mmemogolo/koko	rremogolo
ouma	oupa
makgolo	rakgolo

mother	aunt	uncle
umama	umama omkhulu	umalume
mme	rakgadi	malome
umama	umakazi	umalume
mme	mmamalome	rangwane
ma/moeder	tante	oom
mma	rakgadi	malome

sister	cousin
udadewethu	umzala
ausi	motswala
udade	umzala
kgaitsadi	motswala
suster	neef
kgaetšedi	motswala

Family and friends • Umndeni kanye nabangani • Lelapa le metswalle • Usapho nezihlobo
Balelapa le ditsala • Familie en vriende • Lapa le bagwera

31

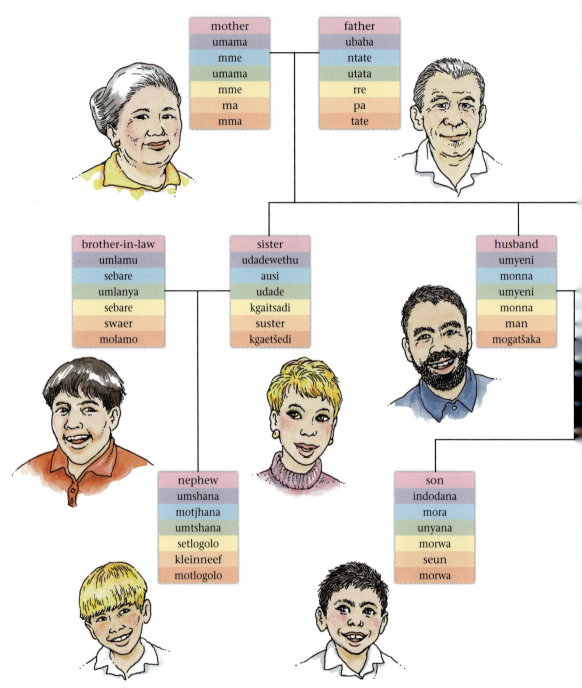

mother	father
umama	ubaba
mme	ntate
umama	utata
mme	rre
ma	pa
mma	tate

brother-in-law	sister	husband
umlamu	udadewethu	umyeni
sebare	ausi	monna
umlanya	udade	umyeni
sebare	kgaitsadi	monna
swaer	suster	man
molamo	kgaetšedi	mogatšaka

nephew	son
umshana	indodana
motjhana	mora
umtshana	unyana
setlogolo	morwa
kleinneef	seun
motlogolo	morwa

Family and friends • Umndeni kanye nabangani • Lelapa le metswalle • Usapho nezihlobo
Balelapa le ditsala • Familie en vriende • Lapa le bagwera

mother-in-law	father-in-law
umkhwekazi	umukhwe
matsale	ratsale
umazala	utatazala
mmatswale	ratswale
skoonma	skoonpa
mmatswale	ratswale

wife	brother	sister-in-law
umkami	umfowethu	umlamu
mosadi	abuti	molamo
unkosikazi	umnakwe	indodakazi
mosadi	morwarre	mogatsa-mogolole
vrou	broer	skoonsuster
mogatšaka	morwarre	mogadibo

daughter	niece
indodakazi	umshana
moradi	motjhana
intombi	umtshana
morwadi	setlogolo
dogter	kleinniggie
morwedi	motlogolo

Family and friends • Umndeni kanye nabangani • Lelapa le metswalle • Usapho nezihlobo
Balelapa le ditsala • Familie en vriende • Lapa le bagwera

33

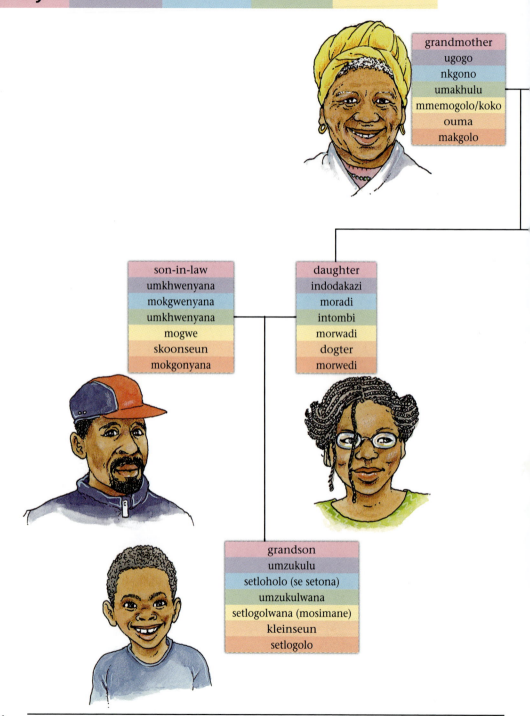

grandmother
ugogo
nkgono
umakhulu
mmemogolo/koko
ouma
makgolo

son-in-law
umkhwenyana
mokgwenyana
umkhwenyana
mogwe
skoonseun
mokgonyana

daughter
indodakazi
moradi
intombi
morwadi
dogter
morwedi

grandson
umzukulu
setloholo (se setona)
umzukulwana
setlogolwana (mosimane)
kleinseun
setlogolo

Family and friends • Umndeni kanye nabangani • Lelapa le metswalle • Usapho nezihlobo
Balelapa le ditsala • Familie en vriende • Lapa le bagwera

My familie 3 | Lapa la ka 3

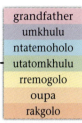

grandfather
umkhulu
ntatemoholo
utatomkhulu
rremogolo
oupa
rakgolo

Titles Izethulo zabantu Dihlooho Iitayitile Ditlhogo Titels Dithaetlele	

Mr	Mrs
Mnu.	Nkk.
Mong.	Mof.
Mnu.	Nkosikazi/Nksk.
Rre	Mme
Mnr.	Mev.
Morena	Mohumagadi

Miss	Ms
Nksz.	Nksz.
Mofumahatsana (Mof)	mofumahatsana
Nksz.	Nksz.
Mohumagatsana	Mohumagatsana
Mej.	Me.
Mohumagatšana	Mohumagatšana

Dr	Prof.
Dkt.	Prof.
ngaka	moporofesara
Gqr.	Njinga.
Ngaka	Moporofesara
Dr.	Prof.
ngk	Prof

Sir	Madam
Mnu	Nkk.
mohl.	mof.
Mhle.	Nksz.
Rra	Mma
Meneer	Mevrou
Morena	Mohumagadi

son	daughter-in-law
indodana	umakoti
mora	ngwetsi
unyana	umolokazana
morwa	ngwetsi
seun	skoondogter
morwa	ngwetši

granddaughter
umzukulu
setloholo (se setshehadi)
umzukulwana
setlogolwana (mosetsana)
kleindogter
setlogolo

Family and friends • Umndeni kanye nabangani • Lelapa le metswalle • Usapho nezihlobo
Balelapa le ditsala • Familie en vriende • Lapa le bagwera

Extended family Umndeni Ba leloko Izalamane

parent
umzali
motswadi
umzali
motsadi
ouer
motswadi

godparent
umzali ongummeleli womntwana
moemedi kerekeng
ummeli ecaweni
mogologolwane
peetouer
motswadikemedi

child
ingane
ngwana
umtwana
ngwana
kind
ngwana

grandchild
umzukulu
setloholo
umzukulwana
setlogolwana
kleinkind
setlogolwana

grandparent
umkhulu
moholoholo
umawokhulu
mogolwagolwane
grootouer
khukhu

stepmother
umame omusha
mmangwane
umama kumtshato omtsha
mme-ka-nyalo
stiefma
mmangwane

stepfather
ubaba ongangizali
rangwane
utata kumtshato omtsha
rre-ka-nyalo
stiefpa
tate

stepson
indodana engeyona eyakho
mora
unyana kumtshato wangaphambili
morwa-ka-nyalo
stiefseun
morwa ka kgoro

stepdaughter
indodakazi engeyona eyakho
moradi
intombi kumtshato wangaphambili
morwadi-ka-nyalo
stiefdogter
morwedi ka kgoro

stepbrother
umfowethu womunye wabazali
abuti
umnakwethu kumtshato wangaphambili
nkgonne-ka-nyalo
stiefbroer
morwarre ka kgoro

Family and friends • Umndeni kanye nabangani • Lelapa le metswalle • Usapho nezihlobo
Balelapa le ditsala • Familie en vriende • Lapa le bagwera

Balosika Uitgebreide familie Leloko

stepsister	twin	triplet
udade wokutholwa	iwele	amaphahla abantwana abathathu
ausi	lefahla	mafahla a mararo
udade kumtshato wangaphambili	iwele	amawele amathathu
kgaitsadi-ka-nyalo	mawelana	bana ba batshotsweng ba le bararo
stiefsuster	tweeling	drieling
kgaetšedi ka kgoro	lefahla	mafahla a moraro

oldest	middle child	youngest
izibulo	umntwana ophakathi	uthunjana
letsibolo	ngwana ya mahareng	kgorula
izibulo	umntwana ophakathi	untondo
leitibolo	ngwanagare	gofejane
oudste	middelkind	jongste
leitšibolo	ngwana wa magareng	phejane

only child	relative	orphan	friend
uzinyobulala	isihlobo	intandane	umngane
ngwana ya mong	leloko	kgutsana	motswalle
umntwana ekuphela kwakhe	isizalwana	inkedama	umhlobo
monosi	losika	khutsana	tsala
enigste kind	familielid	weeskind	vriend/vriendin
monoši	leloko	tšhuana	mokgotse

Family and friends • Umndeni kanye nabangani • Lelapa le metswalle • Usapho nezihlobo
Balelapa le ditsala • Familie en vriende • Lapa le bagwera

Stages of life Izigaba zokukhula Mehato ya bophelo
Amanqanaba obomi Dikgato tsa botshelo
Lewenstadiums Dikgato tša bophelo

baby
usana
lesea
usana
lesea
baba
lesea

child
ingane
ngwana
umntwana
ngwana
kind
ngwana

Marriage	Umshado	Lenyalo
Umtshato	Lenyalo	Huwelik
Lenyalo		

bride
umakoti
monyaduwa
umtshakazi
monyadiwa
bruid
monyadiwa

bridegroom
umkhwenyana
monyadi
umyeni
monyadi
bruidegom
monyadi

boy
umfana
moshemane
inkwenkwe
mosimane
seun
mošemane

girl
intombazane
ngwanana
intombazana
mosetsana
dogter
mosetsana

teenager
intsha
motjha
umntu omtsha
mošwa
tiener
mofsa

bridesmaid
impelesi
moetsana
impelesi
moetsana
strooimeisie
lekgetla

best man
impelesi yomkhwenyana
moemedi wa monyadi
umpheleki womyeni
motshwari
strooijonker
lekgetla

adult
umuntu omdala
moholo
umntu omkhulu
mogolo
volwassene
mogolo

man
indoda
monna
indoda
monna
man
monna

woman
inkosikazi
mosadi
umfazi
mosadi
vrou
mosadi

Family and friends • Umndeni kanye nabangani • Lelapa le metswalle • Usapho nezihlobo
Balelapa le ditsala • Familie en vriende • Lapa le bagwera

Family events Izehlo emndenini Mekete ya lelapa
Iziganeko zekhaya Ditiro tsa lelapa
Familiegebeurtenisse Ditiragalo tša selapa

birth	christening	birthday	initiation
ukuzalwa	ukubhabhadiswa	usuku lokuzalwa	ukusoka
tswalo	kolobetso	letsatsi la tswalo	lebollo
ukuzala	uphehlelelo	umhla wokuzalwa	ulwaluko
botsalo	kolobetso	letsatsi la matsalo	bogwera
geboorte	doop	verjaarsdag	inisiasie
matswalo	kolobetšo	letšatši la matswalo	koma

education	engagement
imfundo	umethembiso
thuto	peheletso
imfundo	ingeji
thuto	peelelo
opvoeding	verlowing
thuto	go thiba sefero

wedding	divorce	funeral
umshado	isehlukaniso	umngcwabo
lenyalo	tlhalano	lepato
umtshato	uqhawulo-mtshato	umngcwabo
lenyalo	tlhalo	phitlho
bruilof/troue	egskeiding	begrafnis
lenyalo	tlhalo	poloko

Family and friends • Umndeni kanye nabangani • Lelapa le metswalle • Usapho nezihlobo
Balelapa le ditsala • Familie en vriende • Lapa le bagwera

39

Phrases	Amabinzana	Dipolelwana	Amabinzana
How many brothers and sisters do you have?	Bangaki abafowenu nodadewenu?	O na le baholwane le dikgaitsedi tse kae?	Bangaphi abanakwenu noodade wenu?
I have … brothers and … sisters.	Nginabafowethu aba … kanye nodadewethu aba …	Ke na le baholwane le dikgaitsedi tse …	Ndinabantakwethu aba… noodade wethu aba…
What is your clan name?	Ubani isithakazelo sakini?	O mang seboko sa hao?	Ungumni isiduko sakho?
My clan name is …	Isithakazelo sakithi ngu…	Seboko sa ka ke …	Isiduko sam ngu…
Where do your grandparents live?	Bahlalaphi omkhulu nogogo wakho?	Baholoholo ba hao ba dula kae?	Bahlala phi oomawomkhulu bakho?
My grandparents live in …	Omkhulu nogogo bahlala …	Baholoholo ba ka ba dula …	Oomawomkhulu bam bahlala …
Where were you born?	Wazalelwaphi?	O hlahetse kae?	Wazalelwa phi?
I was born in …	Ngazalelwa e …	Ke hlahetse …	Ndazalelwa e…
When is your birthday?	Lunini usuku lwakho lokuzalwa?	Letsatsi la hao la tswalo le neng?	Lunini usuku lokuzalwa kwakho?
My birthday is on …	Usuku lwami lokuzalwa lungomhla wama-…	Letsatsi la ka la tswalo le …	Usuku lokuzalwa kwam lungowama …
Happy birthday!	Usuku lokuzalwa olumnandi!	Mahlohonolo a letsatsi la tswalo!	Mini emnandi kuwe!
How old are you?	Uneminyaka emingaki?	Dilemo tsa hao di kae?	Mingaphi iminyaka yakho?
I am 14 years old.	Ngineminyaka eyishumi nane.	Ke na le dilemo tse leshome le metso e mene/14.	Ndineminyaka eli-14.
Congratulations on your engagement!	Ngiyakuhalalisela ngomethembiso wakho!	Re thabisana le wena ka letsatsi la tumellano ya hao ya lenyalo!	Ndiyavuyisana nawe ngokunge jwa!
When is the wedding?	Unini umshado?	Lenyalo le neng?	Unini umtshato wakho?
The wedding will happen on …	Umshado uyokuba ngomhla wa …/we…	Lenyalo le tla ba ka …	Umtshato woba ngomhla we…/wama…
Happy wedding anniversary!	Usuku lokukhumbula umshado wenu olumnandi!	Re thabisana le wena ka sehopotso sa lenyalo la hao!	Mini emnandi yesikhumbuzo somnyaka nitshatile!

Family and friends • Umndeni kanye nabangani • Lelapa le metswalle • Usapho nezihlobo
Balelapa le ditsala • Familie en vriende • Lapa le bagwera

Dikapolelo	Frases	Dikafoko
O na le bomorwarraago le bokgaitsadio ba le kae?	Hoeveel broers en susters het jy?	O na le barwarre le dikgaetšedi tše kae?
Ke na le bomorwarre ba le ... le bokgaitsadi ba le ...	Ek het ... broers en ... susters.	Ke na le barwarre ba... le dikgaetšedi tše ...
Leina la kgoro ya gago ke mang?	Wat is jou stamnaam?	Leina la kgoro ya geno ke lefe?
Leina la kgoro ya me ke ...	My stamnaam is ...	Leina la kgoro ya gešo ke ...
Bagolwagolwane ba gago ba nna/dula kae?	Waar woon jou grootouers?	Rakgolo le makgolo wa gago ba dula kae?
Bagolwagolwane ba me ba nna/dula kwa ...	My grootouers woon in ...	Rakgolo le makgolo ba dula ...
O tsholetswe kae?	Waar is jy gebore?	O belegetšwe kae?
Ke tsholetswe kwa ...	Ek is in ... gebore.	Ke belegetšwe ...
Letsatsi la gago la matsalo ke leng?	Wanneer verjaar jy?	Letšatši la gago la matswalo le neng?
Letsatsi la me la matsalo ke ...	Ek verjaar die ...	Letšatši la ka la matswalo ke di ...
Nna le letsatsi la matsalo le le monate!	Veels geluk met jou verjaarsdag!	A e be lethabo letšatšing la gago la matswalo!
O na le dingwaga di le kae?	Hoe oud is jy?	O na le mengwaga ye mekae?
Ke na le dingwaga di le somenne.	Ek is 14 jaar oud.	Ke na le mengwaga ye 14.
Masego le katlego mo letsatsing la gago la go beelediwa!	Veels geluk met jou verlowing!	Ditebogišo ge o thibile sefero.
Letsatsi la lenyalo ke e leng?	Wanneer trou jy?	Lenyalo le neng?
Lenyalo le tla nna ka ...	Die troue vind op ... plaas.	Lenyalo le tla ba ka ...
Re itumela le wena ka segopotso sa lenyalo la gago!	Gelukkige troudag-herdenking!	A e be lethabo segopotšong sa lenyalo!

Family and friends • Umndeni kanye nabangani • Lelapa le metswalle • Usapho nezihlobo
Balelapa le ditsala • Familie en vriende • Lapa le bagwera

Clothing

Izingubo

Diaparo

Izinxibo

Diaparo

Klere

Diaparo

Men's clothes | Izingubo zabesilisa | Diaparo tsa banna | Impahla yamadoda

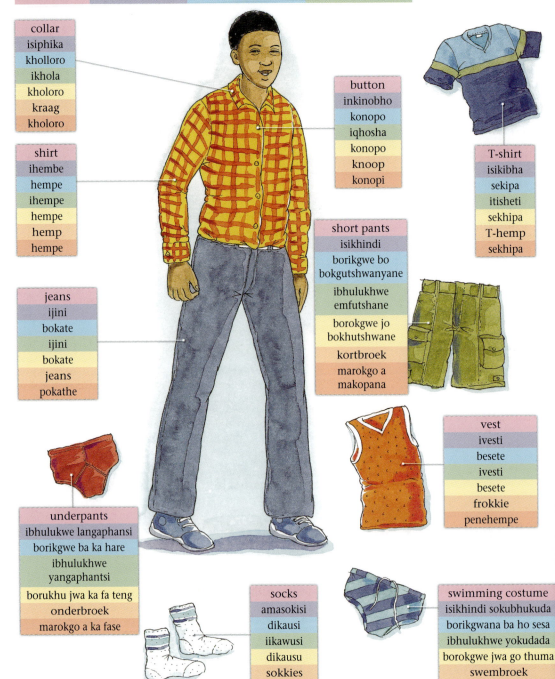

collar
isiphika
kholloro
ikhola
kholoro
kraag
kholoro

shirt
ihembe
hempe
ihempe
hempe
hemp
hempe

jeans
ijini
bokate
ijini
bokate
jeans
pokathe

underpants
ibhulukwe langaphansi
borikgwe ba ka hare
ibhulukhwe yangaphantsi
borukhu jwa ka fa teng
onderbroek
marokgo a ka fase

button
inkinobho
konopo
iqhosha
konopo
knoop
konopi

short pants
isikhindi
borikgwe bo bokgutshwanyane
ibhulukhwe emfutshane
borokgwe jo bokhutshwane
kortbroek
marokgo a makopana

T-shirt
isikibha
sekipa
itisheti
sekhipa
T-hemp
sekhipa

vest
ivesti
besete
ivesti
besete
frokkie
penehempe

socks
amasokisi
dikausi
iikawusi
dikausu
sokkies
masokisi

swimming costume
isikhindi sokubhukuda
borikgwana ba ho sesa
ibhulukhwe yokudada
borokgwe jwa go thuma
swembroek
seaparo sa go rutha

Diaparo tsa banna   Mansklere   Diaparo tša banna

windbreaker
ijakedi evikela emoyeni
baki e futhumatsang
isilamba
sesireletsaphefo
windjekker
paki ya phefo

buttonhole
imbobo yenkinobho
lesoba la konopo
intunja yeqhosha
phatlha ya konopo
knoopsgat
lešoba la konope

tie
uthayi
tae
iqhina
thai
das
thai

suit
isudu
sutu
isuti
sutu
pak klere
sutu

trousers
ibhulukwe
borikgwe
ibhulukhwe
borokgwe
langbroek
borokgo bjo botelele

waistcoat
intolibhantshi
bakana ya ka hare
i-ondulubhatyi
onorobaki
onderbaadjie
onoropaki

tuxedo
isudu yomcimbi yabesilisa
thakesito
isuti enxitywa ngexesha lesidlo
thakisido
aandpak
paki ya letena

jersey
ijezi
jesi
ijezi
jesi
trui
jeresi

jacket
ibhantshi
baki
ibhatyi
baki
baadjie
paki

pyjamas
amaphijama
dipijama
iipijama
dipejama
pajamas
ditšwarwamalaong

tracksuit
itrekisudi
terekesutu
itreksuti
terekesutu
sweetpak
sutu ya boitšhidullo

shoe
isicathulo
seeta
isihlangu
ditlhako
skoen
seeta

blouse
ibhulawozi
bolaose
ibhlawuzi
bolaose
bloes
polaose

sleeve
umkhono
letsoho la seaparo
umkhono
letsogo la seaparo
mou
letsogo la seaparo

stocking
amasokisi
kausu
iikawusi
molentse
kous
kauso

suit
isudu
sutu
isuti
sutu
pakkie
sutu

skirt
isiketi
sekethe
isiketi
sekhete
romp
sekhethe

petticoat
ipitikoti
onoroko
unondilokhwe
onoroko
onderrok
onoroko

ball gown/evening gown
ingubo yomcimbi wasebusuku
mose wa tantshi
ilokhwe yokudanisa yasebusuku
mosese wa tanse
aandrok
roko ya go tansa

Diaparo tsa basadi Vroueklere Diaparo tša basadi

bikini
ibhigini
bikini
ibhikini
bikini
bikini
pikini

dress
ingubo yokugqoka
mose
ilokhwe
mosese
rok
roko

swimming costume
ikhosishumi yokubhukuda
khosetjhumo ya ho sesa
isinxibo sokuqubha
seaparo sa go thuma
baaikostuum
seaparo sa go rutha

trousers
ibhulukwe
borikgwe
ibhulukhwe
borokgwe
langbroek
borokgo bjo botelele

zip
uziphu
setjhiri
iziphu
sipi
rits
sengamedi

pyjamas
amaphijama
dipijama
iipijama
dipejama
pajamas
ditšwarwamalaong

nightgown
igawuni yasebusuku
gauno
igawuni
mosese wa go robala
nagrok
roko ya go robala

tights
ithayithi
thaethe
uthayithi
thaete
spanbroek
diswinedi

bra
ubhodisi
boti
ibhodi
bodisi
bra
semabejane

panty
idilozi
penti
ipenti
phenti
broekie
phenthi

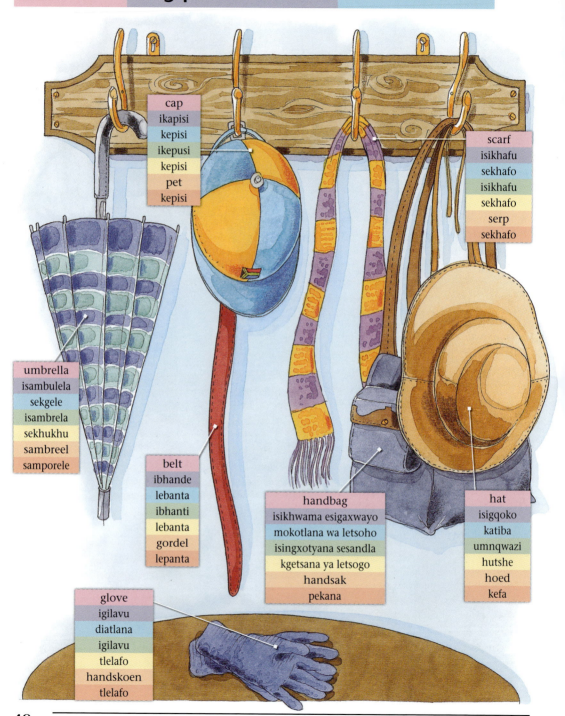

cap
ikapisi
kepisi
ikepusi
kepisi
pet
kepisi

scarf
isikhafu
sekhafo
isikhafu
sekhafo
serp
sekhafo

umbrella
isambulela
sekgele
isambrela
sekhukhu
sambreel
samporele

belt
ibhande
lebanta
ibhanti
lebanta
gordel
lepanta

handbag
isikhwama esigaxwayo
mokotlana wa letsoho
isingxotyana sesandla
kgetsana ya letsogo
handsak
pekana

hat
isigqoko
katiba
umnqwazi
hutshe
hoed
kefa

glove
igilavu
diatlana
igilavu
tlelafo
handskoen
tlelafo

Izinto zehombo	Didiriswa tse dingwe	Bykomstighede	Ditlabakelo

purse	wallet	briefcase
isikhwama semali	iwalethi	isikhwama sezincwadi
sepatjhe	sepatjhe	borifikheisi
isipaji	iwalethi	ibrifkhesi
sekgwama	sepatšhe	kgetsana ya dibuka
beursie	notebeurs	aktetas
sekhwama	sepatšhe	kheisi ya dipuku

Jewellery Okokuhloba Mabenyane Ubucwebe-cebe Dibenya
Juweliersware Tšewelare

earring	necklace
icici	umgexo
lesale	sefaha
icici	intsimbi yomqala
lengena	nekeleise
oorbel	halssnoer
lengena	palamolala

ring	chain
indandatho	umgexo
lesale la monwana	sefaha sa ketane
umsesane	itsheyina
palamonwana	sebaga sa ketane
ring	ketting
palamonwana	ketane

bangle	watch
ibhengela	iwashi
bengele	watjhe
isacholo	iwotshi
bengele	tshupanako
armband	horlosie
bengele	sešupanako

Shoes Izicathulo Dieta Izihlangu

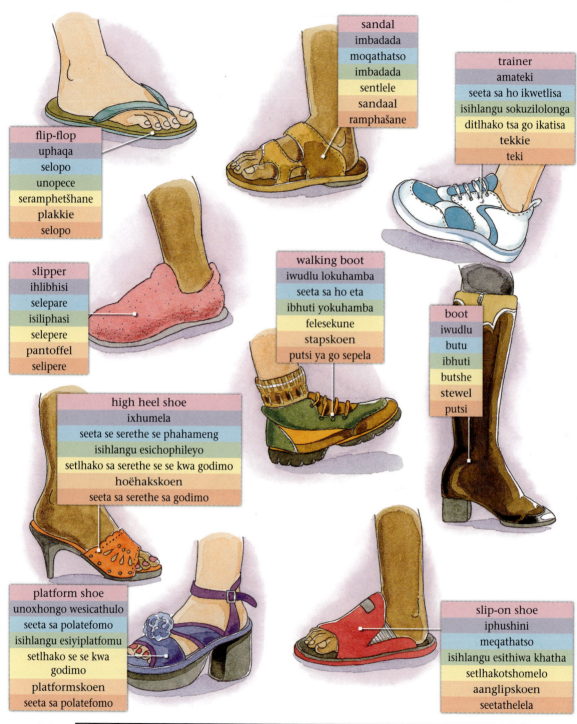

sandal
imbadada
moqathatso
imbadada
sentlele
sandaal
ramphašane

trainer
amateki
seeta sa ho ikwetlisa
isihlangu sokuzilolonga
ditlhako tsa go ikatisa
tekkie
teki

flip-flop
uphaqa
selopo
unopece
seramphetšhane
plakkie
selopo

slipper
ihlibhisi
selepare
isiliphasi
selepere
pantoffel
selipere

walking boot
iwudlu lokuhamba
seeta sa ho eta
ibhuti yokuhamba
felesekune
stapskoen
putsi ya go sepela

boot
iwudlu
butu
ibhuti
butshe
stewel
putsi

high heel shoe
ixhumela
seeta se serethe se phahameng
isihlangu esichophileyo
setlhako sa serethe se se kwa godimo
hoëhakskoen
seeta sa serethe sa godimo

platform shoe
unoxhongo wesicathulo
seeta sa polatefomo
isihlangu esiyiplatfomu
setlhako se se kwa godimo
platformskoen
seeta sa polatefomo

slip-on shoe
iphushini
meqathatso
isihlangu esithiwa khatha
setlhakotshomelo
aanglipskoen
seetathelela

Ditlhako Skoene Dieta

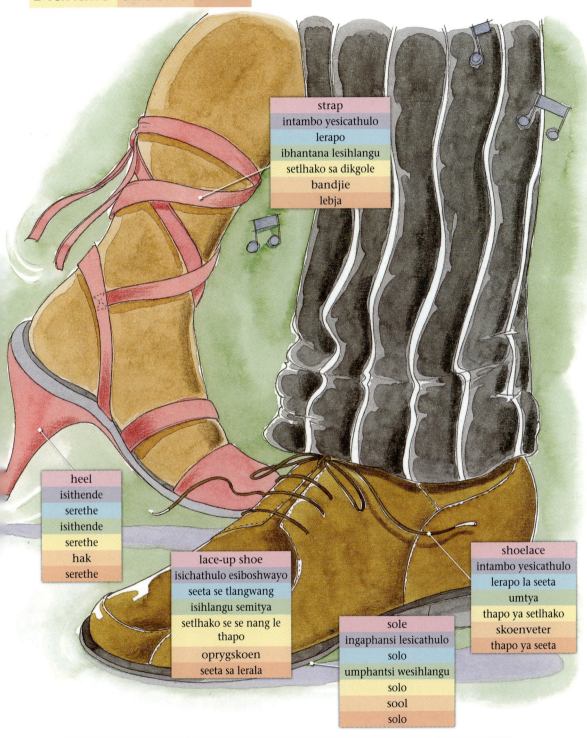

strap
intambo yesicathulo
lerapo
ibhantana lesihlangu
setlhako sa dikgole
bandjie
lebja

heel
isithende
serethe
isithende
serethe
hak
serethe

lace-up shoe
isichathulo esiboshwayo
seeta se tlangwang
isihlangu semitya
setlhako se se nang le thapo
oprygskoen
seeta sa lerala

sole
ingaphansi lesicathulo
solo
umphantsi wesihlangu
solo
sool
solo

shoelace
intambo yesicathulo
lerapo la seeta
umtya
thapo ya setlhako
skoenveter
thapo ya seeta

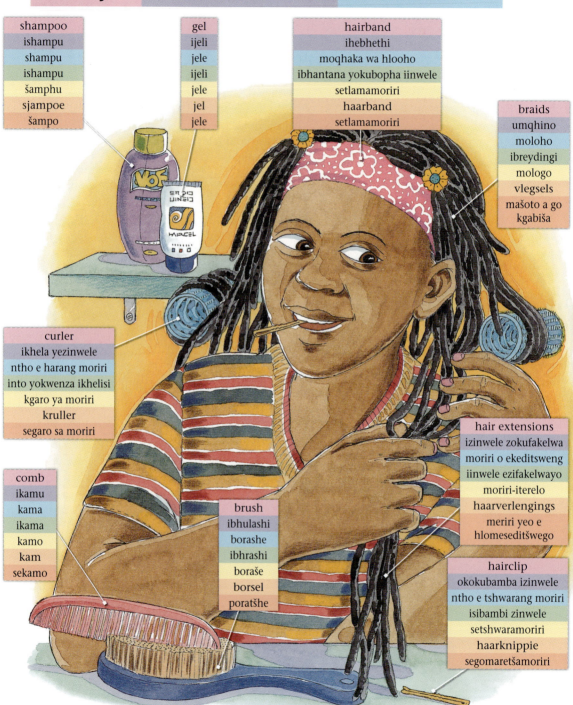

shampoo
ishampu
shampu
ishampu
šamphu
sjampoe
šampo

gel
ijeli
jele
ijeli
jele
jel
jele

hairband
ihebhethi
moqhaka wa hlooho
ibhantana yokubopha iinwele
setlamamoriri
haarband
setlamamoriri

braids
umqhino
moloho
ibreydingi
mologo
vlegsels
mašoto a go kgabiša

curler
ikhela yezinwele
ntho e harang moriri
into yokwenza ikhelisi
kgaro ya moriri
kruller
segaro sa moriri

comb
ikamu
kama
ikama
kamo
kam
sekamo

brush
ibhulashi
borashe
ibhrashi
boraše
borsel
poratšhe

hair extensions
izinwele zokufakelwa
moriri o ekeditsweng
iinwele ezifakelwayo
moriri-iterelo
haarverlengings
meriri yeo e hlomeseditšwego

hairclip
okokubamba izinwele
ntho e tshwarang moriri
isibambi zinwele
setshwaramoriri
haarknippie
segomaretšamoriri

Make-up Uphawuda wasebusweni Ho ipenta sefahleho Ukuhombisa ubuso
Ditlolo tsa letlalo Grimering Matamafosa

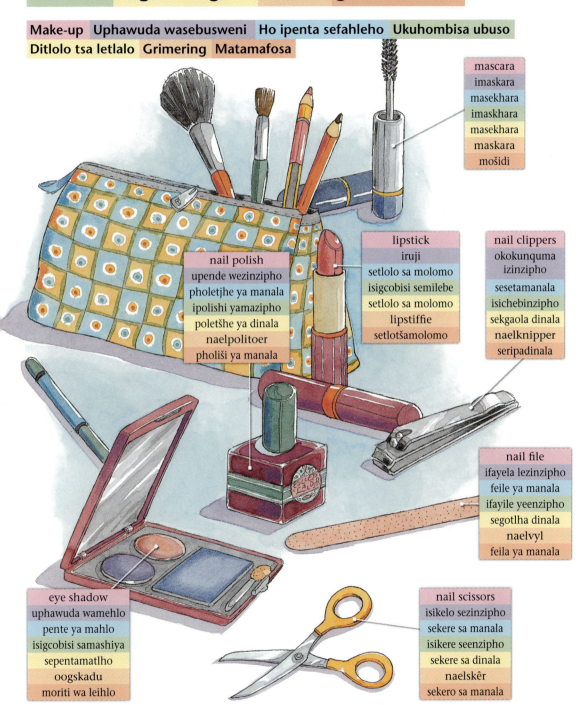

mascara
imaskara
masekhara
imaskhara
masekhara
maskara
mošidi

nail polish
upende wezinzipho
pholetjhe ya manala
ipolishi yamazipho
poletšhe ya dinala
naelpolitoer
pholiši ya manala

lipstick
iruji
setlolo sa molomo
isigcobisi semilebe
setlolo sa molomo
lipstiffie
setlotšamolomo

nail clippers
okokunquma izinzipho
sesetamanala
isichebinzipho
sekgaola dinala
naelknipper
seripadinala

nail file
ifayela lezinzipho
feile ya manala
ifayile yeenzipho
segotlha dinala
naelvyl
feila ya manala

eye shadow
uphawuda wamehlo
pente ya mahlo
isigcobisi samashiya
sepentamatlho
oogskadu
moriti wa leihlo

nail scissors
isikelo sezinzipho
sekere sa manala
isikere seenzipho
sekere sa dinala
naelskêr
sekero sa manala

Clothes of South Africa	Izingubo zase-Ningizimu Afrika	Diaparo tsa Afrika Borwa	Izinxibo zo-Mzantsi Afrika

cape
isibhaceko
kheipi
ikheyiphu
kheipi
mantel
kheipi

headdress
isicholo
tuku
iqhiya
hutshekgolo
hooftooisel
seaparo sa hlogo

headscarf
isikhafu sekhanda
sekhafo
isikhafu
sekhafo sa tlhogo
kopdoek
sekhafo sa hlogo

necklace
umgexo
sefaha sa molala
intsimbi yomqala
nekeleise
halssnoer
pheta

earring
icici
lesale
icici
lengena
oorbel
lengena

bracelet
isikhono
sefaha sa letsoho
isacholo
mofiri
armband
leseka

beads
ubuhlalu
difaha
amaso
dibaga
krale
dipheta

blanket
ingubo
kobo
ingubo
kobo
kombers
lepai

54

Diaparo tsa Aforikaborwa   Klere van Suid-Afrika   Diaparo tša Afrika Borwa

turban
umshuqulo wasekhanda wama-Arabhi
tuku ya ma-Arab
iqhiya yama-Arabhu
tuku ya banna ba Ma-Arab
tulband
thopene

fez
isigqoko esingumbhoshongo samaSulumane
katiba ya maMoseleme
umnqwazi wama-Islam
tlhoro ya banna ba Mamoseleme
fes
fese

yarmulke
isigqoko sabesilisa bamaJuda
katiba ya Baheberu
umqwazana wamaYuda
tlhoro ya Majuta
jarmoelka
yamoke

skirt
isiketi
sekhethe
isiketi
sekhete
romp
sekhethe

belt
ibhande
lebanta
ibhanti
lebanta
gordel
lepanta

ankle bracelet
iketango laseqakaleni
sefaha sa leqaqailana
isacholo seqatha
mofiri wa leoto
enkelband
leseka la kokoilane

thong sandal
amaphaqaphaqa
moqathatso
imbadada
raphatšhane
toonsandaal
sentlele

bonnet
ibhonethe
bonete
isankwana
bonete
kappie
ponete

sari
ingubo ethandelwa emzimbeni yowesifazane weNdiya
sari
ilokhwe yamaNdiya
sari
sari
sari

Phrases	Amabinzana	Dipolelwana	Amabinzana
I would like to buy a shirt.	Ngicela ukuthenga ihembe.	Ke batla ho reka hempe.	Ndingathanda ukuthenga ihempe.
What sort of shirt would you like?	Ufuna ihembe elinjani?	O batla hempe e jwang?	Ingaba uthanda ihempe enjani?
A T-shirt with a collar please.	Ngicela isikibha esinesiphika.	Sekipa se nang le kholloro hle!	Ihentshana enekhola.
How may I help you?	Ngingakusiza ngani?	Nka o thusa ka eng?	Ndingakunceda ngantoni?
I am looking for a pair of trainers.	Ngifuna amateki.	Ke batla para ya dieta tsa ho ikwetlisa.	Ndifuna izihlangu zokubaleka.
What is your shoe size?	Ugqoka muphi usayizi?	Saese ya hao ke efe?	Unxiba eyiphi isayizi?
My shoe size is size 5.	Usayizi wami wu-5.	Seeta sa ka ke saese 5.	Ndinxiba isi-5.
Try this pair.	Ake ulinganise lezi.	Ako itekanye ka tsena.	Linganisa ezi.
These do not fit me. Do you have a bigger size?	Azingilingani lezi. Unawo usayizi omkhulu kuna lona?	Dieta tsena ha di ntekane. Na o na le saese e kgolwanyane?	Ezi azindilingani. Ingaba unazo ezinkulwana?
Do you like these trousers?	Uyalithanda leli bhulukwe?	Na o rata borikgwe boo?	Uyayithanda le bhulukhwe?
You are wearing a beautiful skirt.	Ugqoke isiketi esihle.	O tenne sekhethe se setle.	Unxibe isiketi esihle.
Where did you buy that blouse?	Walithengaphi leli bhulawozi?	Bolaose boo o bo rekile kae?	Uyithenge phi le bhlawuzi?
How much does this blanket cost?	Ibiza malini le ngubo?	Kobo yee ke bokae?	Yimalini le ngubo?
Let's go swimming tomorrow. Bring your swimming costume along.	Asihambe siyobhukuda kusasa. Ubophatha isikhindi sakho sokubhukuda.	Ha re yo sesa hosane. O tle le khosetjhumu ya ho sesa.	Masiye kuqubha ngomso,uze nempahla yakho yokuqubha.
That is a cool idea! May I borrow a towel?	Umbono omuhle lowo! Ngicela ungiboleke ithawula?	O nahanne hantle! A ko nkadime thaole?	Licebo elihle elo. Ungandiboleka itawuli yakho?

Dikapolelo	Frases	Dikafoko
Ke batla go reka hempe.	Ek wil graag 'n hemp koop.	Ke nyaka go reka hempe.
O batla hempe ya mofuta mang?	Watter soort hemp wil jy hê?	O nyaka mohuta ofe wa hempe?
Sekipa se se nang le kholoro.	'n T-hemp met 'n kraag, asseblief.	Sekhipa sa go ba le kholoro.
Nka go thusa ka eng?	Kan ek help?	Nka go thusa?
Ke batla ditlhako tsa go ikatisa.	Ek is op soek na 'n paar tekkies.	Ke nyaka diteki.
O rwala bokae?	Watter grootte skoen dra jy?	Saese ya seeta sa gago ke efe?
Ke rwala 5.	Ek dra 'n nommer 5.	Ke rwala saese 5.
Lekeletsa para e.	Pas hierdie paar aan.	Leka tše.
Tseno ga di ntekane. A o na le nomoro e kgolwanyane?	Hierdie tekkies pas my nie. Het julle 'n groter nommer?	Tše ga di ntekane. A o na le saese ye kgolwana?
A o rata marokgwe ano?	Hou jy van hierdie langbroek?	A o rata marokgo a?
O apere sekhete se sentle.	Jy het 'n pragtige romp aan.	O apere sekhethe se sebotse.
O rekile kae bolaose joo?	Waar het jy daardie bloes gekoop?	O e rekile kae polause yeo?
Kobo eno ke bokae?	Hoeveel kos hierdie kombers?	Lepai le le bitša bokae?
A re yeng go thuma ka moso. Le tle le diaparo tsa lona tsa go thuma.	Kom ons gaan môre swem. Bring jou swembroek saam.	A re ye go rutha gosasa. O tle le seaparo sa gago sa go rutha.
Ke kakanyo e ntle. A nka adima toulo?	Dis 'n goeie plan! Kan ek 'n handdoek leen?	Ke kgopolo ye botse! A o ka nkadima toulo?

4

Ikhaya

Legae

My huis

Legae

flat
ifulethi
folete
iflethi
folete
woonstel
folete

house
indlu
ntlo
umzi
ntlo
huis
ngwako

cottage
ikhotheji
kotase
indlwana
ntlwana
kothuis
ngwakwana

bungalow
indlu engenasitezi
ntlo ya mapolanka
indlu engena-apsteyizi
ntlo ya mapolanka
bungalow
ngwako wa lebatofase

shack
umkhukhu
mokhukhu
ityotyombe
mokhukhu
pondok
mokhukhu

BAYVIEW FLATS

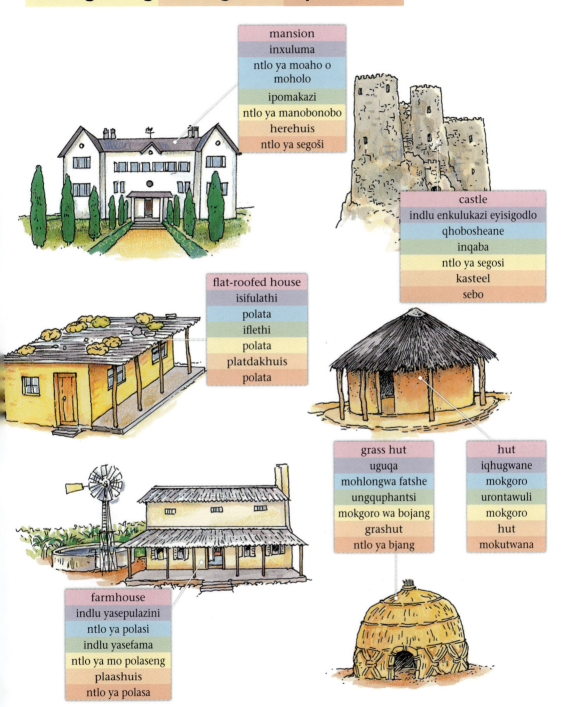

mansion
inxuluma
ntlo ya moaho o moholo
ipomakazi
ntlo ya manobonobo
herehuis
ntlo ya segoši

castle
indlu enkulukazi eyisigodlo
qhobosheane
inqaba
ntlo ya segosi
kasteel
sebo

flat-roofed house
isifulathi
polata
iflethi
polata
platdakhuis
polata

grass hut
uguqa
mohlongwa fatshe
ungquphantsi
mokgoro wa bojang
grashut
ntlo ya bjang

hut
iqhugwane
mokgoro
urontawuli
mokgoro
hut
mokutwana

farmhouse
indlu yasepulazini
ntlo ya polasi
indlu yasefama
ntlo ya mo polaseng
plaashuis
ntlo ya polasa

Parts of a home	Izingxenye zekhaya	Dibaka tse fapaneng tsa lelapa

ceiling
usilingi
siling
isilingi
siling
plafon
siling

chimney
ushimula
tjhemene
itshimini
tšhemele
skoorsteen
setupamuši

window frame
izinhlaka zefasitela
foreimi ya fensetere
isakhelo se festile
foreime ya letlhabaphefo
vensterraam
foreimi ya lefasetere

window latch
isiqhebeza sefasitela
leketleketle
isibambo sefestile
matshwaro a letlhabaphefo
vensterknip
sekgonyo sa lefasetere

roof
uphahla lwendlu
marulelo
uphahla
marulelo
dak
tlhaka

wall
udonga
lebota
udonga
lebota
muur
lebota

door
umnyango
lemati
ucango
setswalo
deur
lebati

keyhole
imbobo kakhiye
lesoba la senotlolo
umngxunya wesitshixo
thobasenotlolo
sleutelgat
nthobana ya senotlelo

door handle
isibambo somnyango
setshwaro sa lemati
isiphatho socango
matshwaro a setswalo
deurknop
setshwaro sa lebati

key
ukhiye
senotlolo
isitshixo
senotlolo
sleutel
senotlelo

step
isitebhisi
mohato
isitepsi
serepudi
trap
setepisi

room
igumbi
phaposi
igumbi
phaposi
kamer
phapoši

burglar bar
izinsimbi ezivimbela abagqekezi
ditshepe tsa monyako
isikhuseli bagqekezi
lebatitshipi
diefwering
sethibelalehodu

verandah
uveranda
mathuleng a ntlo
iveranda
mathudi
stoep
mathudi

window
ifasitela
fensetere
ifestile
letlhabaphefo
venster
lefasetere

| Building materials | Izinto zokwakha | Dintho tsa ho aha | Izixhobo zokwakha | Didiriswa tsa kago |
| Boumateriaal | Dikgerekgere tša go aga | | | |

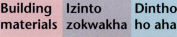

corrugated iron	glass	brick	wood
ukhetho	igilasi	isitini	ukhuni
lasenke	kgalase	setene	mapolanka
izinki	iglasi	isitena	umthi
senke e e makokoma	galase	setena	logong
sinkplaat	glas	baksteen	hout
lesenke	galase	setena	kota

window sill
unqenqema lwefasitela
mmotomoto
isithala esiphansti kwefestile
sili ya letlhabaphefo
vensterbank
botlase bja lefasetere

roof tile	tile	metal	mud
isitini sokufulela uphahla lwendlu	ithayela laphansi	okusansimbi	udaka
thaele ya ho rulela	thaele	tshepe	seretse
ithayile yophahla	ithayile	isinyithi	udaka
thaele ya marulelo	thaele	tshipi	seretse
dakteël	teël	metaal	modder
tlhaka ya thaele	thaele	metale	leraga

plastic	nail	plank	thatching grass
ipulasitiki	isipikili	ipulangwe	utshani bokufulela
polasetiki	sepekere	lepolanka	jwang ba ho rulela
iplastiki	isikhonkwane	iplanga	ingca yokufulela
polasetiki	sepekere	polanka	marulelo a bojang
plastiek	spyker	plank	dekgras
plastiki	sepikiri	lepolanka	bjang bja go rulela

floor
phansi endlini
mokato
umgangatho
bodilo
vloer
lebato

wall
uthango
lebota
udonga
lebota
muur
lebota

home
ikhaya
lelapa
ikhaya
legae
tuiste
gae

garage
igalaji
karatjhe
igaraji
karatšhe
motorhuis
karatšhe

driveway
umgwaqwana ongenela ekhaya
tselana ya koloi
umgaqwana wokungena imoto
mokgothana wa dikoloi
oprit
mokgothana wa koloi

garden
ingadi
lekgwakgwa
isitiya
tshingwana
tuin
serapa

fence
uthango
terata
ucingo
legora
heining
legora

gate
isango
heke
isango
heke
hek
sefero

vegetable garden
ingadi yemifino
serapa sa meroho
isitiya semifuno
tshingwana ya merogo
groentetuin
serapa sa merogo

swimming pool
ichibi lokubhukuda
letamo la ho sesa
idama lokuqubha
letangwana la go thumela
swembad
bodibaruthelo

Legae botshabelo   Oos wes, tuis bes   Gae ga mahlako

yard	bathroom	bedroom	storeroom
igceke	igumbi lokugezela	igumbi lokulala	igumbi lokugcina impahla
jarete	phaposi ya ho itlhatswetsa	phaposi ya ho robala	phaposi ya polokelo
ibala	igumbi lokuhlambela	igumbi lokulala	igumbi lokugcina izinto
segotlo	phaposibotlhapelo	phaposiborobalo	phaposi ya bobolokelo
werf	badkamer	slaapkamer	pakkamer
jarata	bohlapelo	borobalelo	phapošibobolokelo

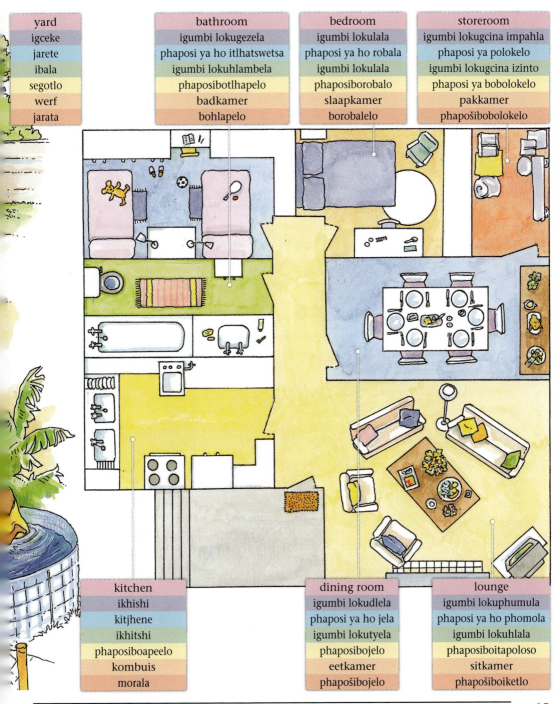

kitchen	dining room	lounge
ikhishi	igumbi lokudlela	igumbi lokuphumula
kitjhene	phaposi ya ho jela	phaposi ya ho phomola
ikhitshi	igumbi lokutyela	igumbi lokuhlala
phaposiboapeelo	phaposibojelo	phaposiboitapoloso
kombuis	eetkamer	sitkamer
morala	phapošibojelo	phapošiboiketlo

sofa
usofa
sofa
isofa
sofa
rusbank
sofa

cushion
ikhushini
mosamo wa setulo
ikhushini
mosamo wa setilo
kussing
mosamelwana

lamp
ilambu
lebone
isibane
lebone
lamp
lelampi

bookshelf
ishalofu lezincwadi
raka ya dibuka
ishelufa yeencwadi
rakana ya dibuka
boekrak
raka ya dipuku

fan
ifeni
fene
isiphephezelisi moya
sefetlhaphefo
waaier
fene

grass mat
icansi
moseme
ukhukho
moseme wa tlhaga
grasmat
mmete wa bjang

side table
itafulana elincane eliseceleni
tafolana
itafilana esecaleni
tafoletlhakore
tafeltjie
tafolana

carpet
ukhaphethi
tapeiti
ikhaphethi
khapete
mat
khapete

Phaposiboitapoloso Sitkamer Phapošiboiketlo

television
umabonakude
thelevishene
umabonakude
thelebišene
televisie
thelebišene

candle
ikhandlela
kerese
ikhandlela
kerese
kers
lekgantlele

fireplace
iziko
leifo
iziko
bogotsetsomolelo
kaggel
sebešo

light
isibani
lebone
isibane
lesedi
lig
seetša

matches
umentshisi
dithutswana tsa mollo
umatshisi
mokgwaro
vuurhoutjies
mantšhese

coal
amalahle
mashala
amalahle
malatlha
steenkool
lelahla

wall unit
ikhabethe lasobondeni
raka ya lebota
ifenitshala yodonga
raka ya lobota
muureenheid
uniti ya lebota

hearth
iziko
leifo
iziko
leiso
vuurherd
sebešo

wall plug
ipulagi esobondeni
sefeqelwana sa lebota
iplagi yodonga
polaka ya lobota
muurprop
pholaka ya lebota

armchair
usofa
sofa
isofa
sofa
armstoel
sofa

firewood
izinkuni
patsi
iinkuni zokubasa
dikgong
vuurmaakhout
dikgong

Dining room	Igumbi lokudlela	Phaposi ya ho jela	Igumbi lokutyela

saucer	cup	teaspoon	teapot
isoso	inkomishi	ithisipuni	itipoti
sosare	komiki	thisipune	ketlele
isosala	ikomityi	itisipuni	itipoti
pirinki	kopi	leswana la tee	ketlele
piering	koppie	teelepel	teepot
sosara	komiki	lehwana la swikiri	pitšana ya teye

vase
ivazi
vase
ivazi
morufašeše
vaas
pitšana ya matšoba

mug
imagi
lebekere
imagi
lebekere
beker
mmaka

sideboard
isayibhodi
saeboto
ikhabhathi emfutshane
saeteboto
buffet
saepoto

stool	table	chair	place mat
isitudlwana	itafula	isitulo	umatana wasetafuleni
setulwana	tafole	setulo	moseme wa tafole
isitulwana	itafile	isitulo	imethi yokubeka izitya etafileni
setulwana	tafole	setilo	moseme wa tafole
stoeltjie	tafel	stoel	plekmatjie
setulo	tafola	setulo	mmetana wa tafola

Phaposibojelo Eetkamer Phapošibojelo

serviette
iseviyethi
fatuku
iseviyeti
sebiete
servet
sebiete

jug
ujeke
jeke
ijagi
jeke
beker
jeke

glass
ingilazi
kgalase
iglasi
galase
glas
galase

knife
ummese
thipa
imela
thipa
mes
thipa

plate
ipuleti
poleiti
ipleyiti
poleite
bord
poleiti

fork
imfologo
fereko
ifolokhwe
foroko
vurk
foroko

spoon
isipuni
kgaba
icephe
leswana
lepel
lelepola

side plate
ipuletana laseceleni
poleiti ya ka thoko
ipleyiti encinci
poleitetlhakore
kleinbordjie
poleiti ya ka thoko

Kitchen Ikhishi Kitjhene Ikhitshi Phaposiboapeelo

container
isitsha sokuphatha
ntho ya ho bolokela
into yokugcina
setshelo
houer
setšhelo

freezer
ifriza
sehwamisi
isikhenkcezisi
setsidifatsi-
kgapetla
vrieskas
segahliši

sink
usinki
sinki
isinki
sinki
opwasbak
sinki

cupboard
ikhabethe
khabote
ikhabhathi
khaboto
kombuiskas
khapoto

fridge
isibandisi
sehatsetsi
ifriji
setsidifatsi
yskas
setšidifatši

plastic wash basin
indishi
basekomo
isitya sokuhlambela
sekotlele
plastiekwasskottel
sekotlelo

stove
isitofu
setofo
isitovu
setofo
stoof
setofo

mop
imophu
mopo
imophu
mmopô
mop
mmopo

counter
ikhawunta
khaontara
ikhawuntari
khaontara
toonbank
khaontara

pail
ibhakede
emere
ithunga
kgamelo
emmer
kgamelo

Kombuis Morala

kettle	toaster	breadboard	sieve	bowl	peeler
iketela	ithosta	ipulangwe lokuqobela	isisefo	ubheseni	okokucwecwa
ketlele	rostere	boroto ya bohobe	sefe	sejana	seebodi
iketile	isigcadi-sonka	ibhodi yokusikela isonka	intluzo	isitya	isixobuli maxolo
ketlele	thousetara	boto ya borotho	sefe	mogopo	seobodi
ketel	rooster	broodbord	sif	bak	skiller
ketlele	sebeši	poroto	sefe	mogopo	seebodi

whisk	ladle	egg flip	wooden spoon	pot	three-legged pot
okokuphehla	iladela	okokuphendula amaqanda	ukhezo	ibhodwe	ibhodwe lesiZulu
lefehlo	kgaba	sepotapotisalehe	mptjhane	pitsa	pitsa e maoto a mararo
isiqhuqhi	umcephe	isiguquli-qanda	iphini	imbiza	imbiza yesiXhosa
wisiki	losô	setsholetsalee	leswana la logong	pitsa	pitsa ya maoto a mararo
klitser	soplepel	eierspaan	houtlepel	pot	driebeenpot
sehuduantši	lelepola la sopo	sephetholalee	lehwana la phata	pitša	pitšana ya maoto a mararo

saucepan	loaf tin	cast-iron pot	calabash	frying pan	grinding stone
isosipani	ipani lesinkwa	ibhodwe lensimbi	igula	ipani lokuthosa	itshe lokugaya
kaseterolo	pane ya bohobe	pitsa ya tshepe	sehwana	pane	lelwala
imbizana enzulu yokupheka	ipani lesonka	ibhakpoti	iselwa	ipani yokuqhotsa	ilitye lokusila
pane	pane ya borotho	pitsa ya tshipi	nkgo	panekgadikelo	tshilo
kastrol	broodpan	ysterpot	kalbas	braaipan	maalklip
sosopane	pane ya borotho	pitša ya Sesotho	mokgopu	pane ya go gadika	tšhilo le lwala

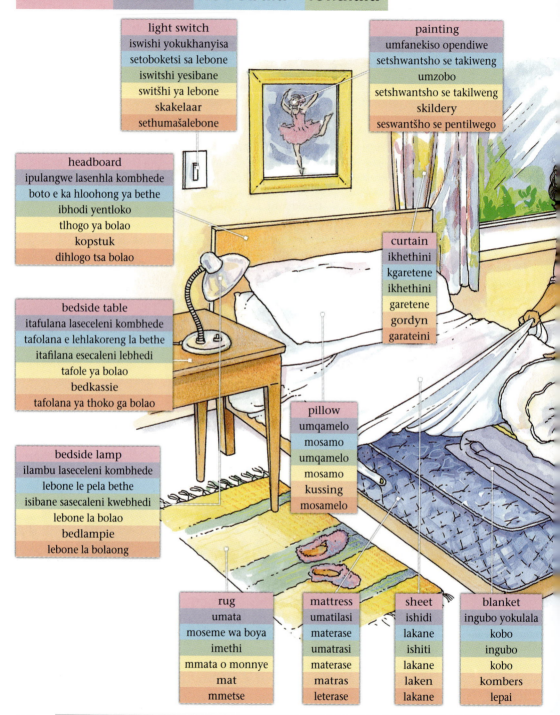

Bedroom	Igumbi lokulala	Phaposi ya ho robala	Igumbi lokulala

light switch
iswishi yokukhanyisa
setoboketsi sa lebone
iswitshi yesibane
switši ya lebone
skakelaar
sethumašalebone

painting
umfanekiso opendiwe
setshwantsho se takiweng
umzobo
setshwantsho se takilweng
skildery
seswantšho se pentilwego

headboard
ipulangwe lasenhla kombhede
boto e ka hloohong ya bethe
ibhodi yentloko
tlhogo ya bolao
kopstuk
dihlogo tsa bolao

curtain
ikhethini
kgaretene
ikhethini
garetene
gordyn
garateini

bedside table
itafulana laseceleni kombhede
tafolana e lehlakoreng la bethe
itafilana esecaleni lebhedi
tafole ya bolao
bedkassie
tafolana ya thoko ga bolao

pillow
umqamelo
mosamo
umqamelo
mosamo
kussing
mosamelo

bedside lamp
ilambu laseceleni kombhede
lebone le pela bethe
isibane sasecaleni kwebhedi
lebone la bolao
bedlampie
lebone la bolaong

rug	**mattress**	**sheet**	**blanket**
umata	umatilasi	ishidi	ingubo yokulala
moseme wa boya	materase	lakane	kobo
imethi	umatrasi	ishiti	ingubo
mmata o monnye	materase	lakane	kobo
mat	matras	laken	kombers
mmetse	leterase	lakane	lepai

Phaposiborobalo Slaapkamer Borobalelo

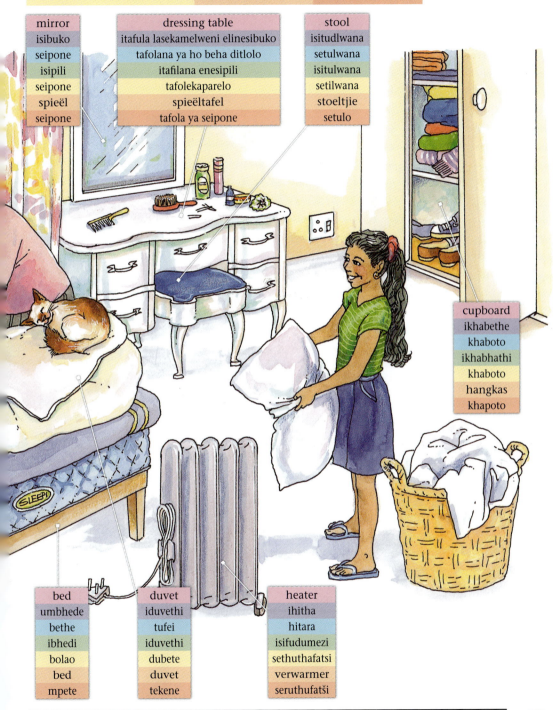

mirror
isibuko
seipone
isipili
seipone
spieël
seipone

dressing table
itafula lasekamelweni elinesibuko
tafolana ya ho beha ditlolo
itafilana enesipili
tafolekaparelo
spieëltafel
tafola ya seipone

stool
isitudlwana
setulwana
isitulwana
setilwana
stoeltjie
setulo

cupboard
ikhabethe
khaboto
ikhabhathi
khaboto
hangkas
khapoto

bed
umbhede
bethe
ibhedi
bolao
bed
mpete

duvet
iduvethi
tufei
iduvethi
dubete
duvet
tekene

heater
ihitha
hitara
isifudumezi
sethuthafatsi
verwarmer
seruthufatši

Bathroom Igumbi lokugezela Phaposi ya ho itlhatswetswa Igumbi lokuhlambela

shower
ishawa
shawara
ishawari
šawara
stort
šawara

shower curtain
ikhethini laseshaweni
kgaretene ya shawara
ikhethini yeshawari
garetene ya šawara
stortgordyn
garateini ya šawara

bathroom mat
umata wasegunjini lokugezela
mmate wa phaposi ya ho itlhatswetsa
imethi yegumbi lokuhlambela
mmata wa phaposibotlhapelo
badkamermat
mmete wa phapošibohlapelo

towel
ithawula
thaole
itawuli
toulo
handdoek
toulo

towel rail
umgibe wokugaxa amathawula
sefole sa thaole
intonga yokuxhoma iitawuli
seanegela-toulo
handdoekreëling
seswaratoulo

soap dish
isitsha sokubeka insipho
sekotlolo sa sesepa
isityana sesepha
sekotlolo sa sesepa
seepbakkie
seswarasesepe

soap
insipho
sesepa
isepha
sesepa
seep
sesepe

bath
ubhavu
bate
ibhafu
bata
bad
pafo

zinc bath
ubhavu owenziwe ngokhethe
bate ya lesenke
ibhafu yezinki
batasenke
sinkbad
pafo ya sinki

tap
umpompi
pompo
itephu
thepe
kraan
pompi

plug
ipulagi
sefeqelwana
iplagi
polaka
prop
pholaka

74

Phaposibotlhapelo Badkamer Bohlapelo

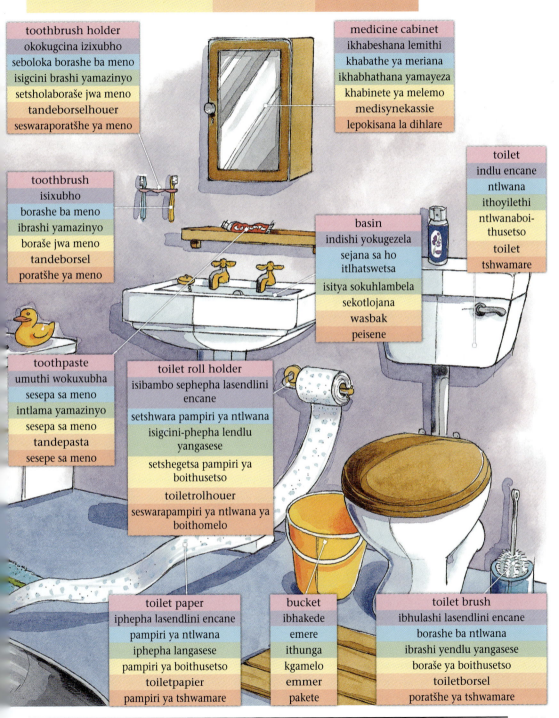

toothbrush holder
okokugcina izixubho
seboloka borashe ba meno
isigcini brashi yamazinyo
setsholaboraše jwa meno
tandeborselhouer
seswaraporatšhe ya meno

medicine cabinet
ikhabeshana lemithi
khabathe ya meriana
ikhabhathana yamayeza
khabinete ya melemo
medisynekassie
lepokisana la dihlare

toilet
indlu encane
ntlwana
ithoyilethi
ntlwanaboi-thusetso
toilet
tshwamare

toothbrush
isixubho
borashe ba meno
ibrashi yamazinyo
boraše jwa meno
tandeborsel
poratšhe ya meno

basin
indishi yokugezela
sejana sa ho itlhatswetsa
isitya sokuhlambela
sekotlojana
wasbak
peisene

toothpaste
umuthi wokuxubha
sesepa sa meno
intlama yamazinyo
sesepa sa meno
tandepasta
sesepe sa meno

toilet roll holder
isibambo sephepha lasendlini encane
setshwara pampiri ya ntlwana
isigcini-phepha lendlu yangasese
setshegetsa pampiri ya boithusetso
toiletrolhouer
seswarapampiri ya ntlwana ya boithomelo

toilet paper
iphepha lasendlini encane
pampiri ya ntlwana
iphepha langasese
pampiri ya boithusetso
toiletpapier
pampiri ya tshwamare

bucket
ibhakede
emere
ithunga
kgamelo
emmer
pakete

toilet brush
ibhulashi lasendlini encane
borashe ba ntlwana
ibrashi yendlu yangasese
boraše ya boithusetso
toiletborsel
poratšhe ya tshwamare

broom
umshanyelo
lefielo
umtshayelo
lefeelo
besem
leswielo

grass handbroom
umshanyelo owenziwe ngotshani
lefielo la jwang
umtshayelo wengca wesandla
lefeelo la matlhokwa
grashandbesem
leswielo la letsogo

brush
ibhulashi
borashe
ibrashi
boraše
borsel
poratšhe

dustpan
isibutho
pane ya dithwele
isiwoli nkunkuma
seolelamatlakala
skoppie
seolelamatlakala

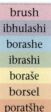

dustbin
umgqomo wezibi
tonkana ya dithwele
umgqomo wenkunkuma
seolelatlakala
vullisblik
motomo wa matlakala

feather duster
izimpaphe zokudasida
masiba a ho phumola lerole
iintsiba zokosula uthuli
setlhotlhoralerole
verestoffer
sefoforalerole

vacuum cleaner
umshini wokushanyela
motjhini wa ho fiela
isixhobo sokumfimfitha inkunkuma
motšhini wa go phepafatsa
stofsuier
motšhenehlwekiša

cloth
indwangu
lesela
ilaphu
lesela
lap
lešela

iron
i-ayina
aene
i-ayini
tshidilo
strykyster
aene

ironing board
ipulangwe loku-ayinela
boroto ya ho aenela
ibhodi yoku-ayinela
sesedilelo
strykplank
tafolana ya aene

pot scourer
ucingo lokukhuhla amabhodwe
sehohlapitsa
isikhuhli-mbiza
segotlhi sa dipitsa
skuurder
sefalo

detergent
umuthi wokuhlanza
sehlwekisi
isihlambululi
sebolayatwatsi
reiniger
sehlwekiši

dishwashing liquid
insipho eluketshezi
mokedikedi wa ho hlatswa dijana
ulwelo lokuhlamba izitya
sesepa sa dijana
opwasmiddel
sesepe sa dibjana

washing powder
insipho eyimpuphu
sesepa sa phofo
isepha engumgubo
sesepa sa lerole
waspoeier
sesepe sa lerole

polish
upholishi
poletjhe
ipolishi
pholitšhi
politoer
pholiši

| Garden tools | Izinto zokusebenza engadini | Disebediswa tsa jareteng | Izixhobo zasegadini | Didiriswa tsa tshingwana |
| Tuingereedskap | Ditlabakelo tša serapana | | | |

spade
ifosholo
kgarafu
umhlakulo
garawe
graaf
garafo

fork
imfologo
fereko
ifolokhwe
foroko
vurk
foroko

hoe
igeja
mohoma
igaba
petlwana
skoffel
letšepe

pick
ipiki
peke
ipeki
peke
pik
peke

hosepipe
ithumbu lokuchelela
lethopo
umbhobho wokunkcenkceshela
lethompo
tuinslang
lethopo

sprinkler
isifafazo
senwesetsi
isifefezi
sekgatshametsi
sproeier
sefafatša

wheelbarrow
ibhala
kiribae
ikiliva
kiribane
kruiwa
kiribane

lawn mower
umshini wokugunda utshani
motjhini wa ho kuta jwang
umatshini wokucheba ingca
motšhini wa tlhaga
grassnyer
sekotabjang

clippers
isiyence
sekere sa difate
iklipa
sekere sa ditlhare
tuinskêr
sekero sa mehlare

Phrases	Amabinzana	Dipolelwana	Amabinzana
Where do you live?	Uhlalaphi?	O dula kae?	Uhlala phi?
I live in a flat in town.	Ngihlala efulethini edolobheni.	Ke dula foleteng toropong.	Ndihlala eflethini edolophini.
How many rooms are there in your home?	Mangaki amagumbi endlu yakini?	Le na le diphaposi tse kae heno?	Mangaphi amagumbi kwikhaya lakho?
My home has four rooms.	Ikhaya lakithi linamagumbi amane.	Diphaposi tsa rona di nne.	Ikhaya lam linamagumbi amane.
We eat in the dining room.	Sidlela egunjini lokudlela.	Re jela ka phaposing ya ho jela.	Sityela kwigumbi lokutyela.
There are two beds in our bedroom.	Kunemibhede emibili ekamelweni lethu.	Ho na le dibethe tse pedi ka phaposing ya rona ya ho robala.	Zimbini iibhedi kwigumbi lethu lokulala.
Are you allowed to come with us to the shops?	Uvunyelwe ukuhamba nathi ukuya ezitolo?	Na le dumelletswe ho ya le rona mabenkeleng?	Uvumelekile ukuhamba nathi siye ezivenkileni?
No, not yet. We must sweep the yard first.	Cha. Hhayi njengamanje. Kufanele sishanyele igceke kuqala.	Tjhe, e seng hona jwale. Re tshwanetse ho fiela pele.	Hayi, okwangoku kufanele sitshayele ibala kuqala.
Do you have a garden?	Ninayo ingadi?	Na le na le serapa/jarete/tshimo ya meroho?	Ninaso isitiya?
Yes we do. We grow vegetables in our garden.	Yebo sinayo. Sitshala imifino engadini yethu.	Ee, re na le sona. Re lema meroho serapeng sa heso.	Ewe sinaso. Silima imifuno kwisitiya sethu.
Do you work in the garden?	Uyasebenza engadini?	Na o sebetsa jareteng?	Ukhe usebenze esitiyeni?
Yes, I help my father pull out weeds. My sister waters the garden.	Yebo. Ngisiza ubaba ukusiphula ukhula. Udadewethu uchelela ingadi.	Ee, ke thusa ntate ho hlaola lehola. Kgaitsedi yena o a nosetsa.	Ewe ndincedisa utata ukutsala ukhula, udade wethu unkcenkceshela isitiya.
What do you use to make sour milk?	Usebenzisani ukuvuba amasi?	Mafi le a etsetsa ho kae?	Usebenzisa ntoni ukwenza amasi?
We make sour milk in a calabash.	Sivubela amasi eguleni.	Re tshela mafi ka sehwaneng.	Senza amasi ngeselwa.
My sister helps me fetch water with a bucket.	Udadewethu ungisiza ukukha amanzi ngebhakede.	Ausi o nthusa ho kga metsi ka emere.	Udade wethu undincedisa ukukha amanzi ngethunga.

Dikapolelo	Frases	Dikafoko
O nna kae?	Waar woon jy?	O dula kae?
Ke nna mo foleteng mo toropong.	Ek woon in 'n woonstel in die stad.	Ke dula foleteng ka toropong.
Go na le diphaposi di le kae kwa legaeng la gago?	Hoeveel kamers is daar in jou huis?	Ntlo ya gago e na le diphapoše tše kae?
Legae la me le na le diphaposi di le nne.	My huis het vier kamers.	Ntlo ya ka e na le diphapoše tše nne.
Re jela mo phaposi-bojelong.	Ons eet in die eetkamer.	Re ja ka phapošing ya bojelo.
Go na le malao a le mabedi mo phaposiborobalong ya rona.	Daar is twee beddens in ons slaapkamer.	Go na le mepete ye mebedi ka borobalelong.
A o letleletswe go ya le rona kwa mabenkeleng?	Mag jy saam met ons winkel toe gaan?	A o dumeletšwe go tla le rena mabenkeleng?
Nnyaa, e seng jaanong. Re tshwanetse go feela segotlo pele.	Nee, nie nou al nie. Ons moet die werf eers vee.	Aowaowa. Re swanetse go swiela jarata pele.
A lo na le tshingwana?	Het julle 'n tuin?	Le na le serapa?
Ee, re na le yona. Re jala merogo mo tshingwaneng ya rona.	Ja, ons het. Ons kweek groente in ons tuin.	Ee, re na le sona. Re bjala merogo ka serapaneng sa rena.
A o tle o dire mo tshingwaneng?	Werk jy in die tuin?	A o šoma ka serapeng?
Ee, ke thusa rre go ntsha mefero. Kgaitsadiake ene o nosetsa tshingwana.	Ja, ek help my pa om die bossies uit te trek. My suster maak die tuin nat.	Ee, ke thuša tate go hlagola. Kgaetšedi o nošetša serapa.
O dirisa eng go dira mašwi a a botlha?	Wat gebruik 'n mens om suurmelk te maak?	O šomiša eng go dira thatha?
Re direla mašwi a botlha mo nkgong.	Ons maak suurmelk in 'n kalbas.	Re dira thatha ka gare ga kgapa.
Kgaitsadiake o nthusa go ga metsi ka kgamelo.	My suster help my om die water in die emmer te gaan haal.	Kgaetšedi o nthuša go kga meetse ka pakete.

Our community

Umphakathi wakithi

Tikoloho ya rona

80

Our community • Umphakathi wakithi • Tikoloho ya rona • Ingingqi esihlala kuyo
Setšhaba sa rona • Ons gemeenskap • Setšhaba sa rena

Ingingqi esihlala kuyo

Setšhaba sa rona

Ons gemeenskap

Setšhaba sa rena

Our community • Umphakathi wakithi • Tikoloho ya rona • Ingingqi esihlala kuyo
Setšhaba sa rona • Ons gemeenskap • Setšhaba sa rena

81

Where we live	Lapho sihlala khona	Moo re dulang teng	Ingingqi esihlala kuyo

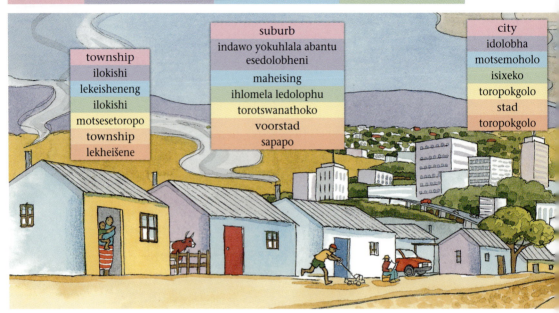

suburb
indawo yokuhlala abantu esedolobheni
maheising
ihlomela ledolophu
torotswanathoko
voorstad
sapapo

township
ilokishi
lekeisheneng
ilokishi
motsesetoropo
township
lekheišene

city
idolobha
motsemoholo
isixeko
toropokgolo
stad
toropokgolo

farm
ipulazi
polasi
ifama
polase
plaas
polasa

Our community • Umphakathi wakithi • Tikoloho ya rona • Ingingqi esihlala kuyo
Setšhaba sa rona • Ons gemeenskap • Setšhaba sa rena

informal settlement
umjondolo
mekhukhu
indawo yamatyotyombe
tulo ya baipei
informele nedersetting
baipei

town
idolobhana
toropo
idolophu
toropo
dorp
toropo

village
ivileji
motse
ilali
motse
dorpie
motse

Our community • Umphakathi wakithi • Tikoloho ya rona • Ingingqi esihlala kuyo
Setšhaba sa rona • Ons gemeenskap • Setšhaba sa rena

83

Our town	Idolobha lethu	Toropo ya rona	Idolophu yethu	Toropo ya rona

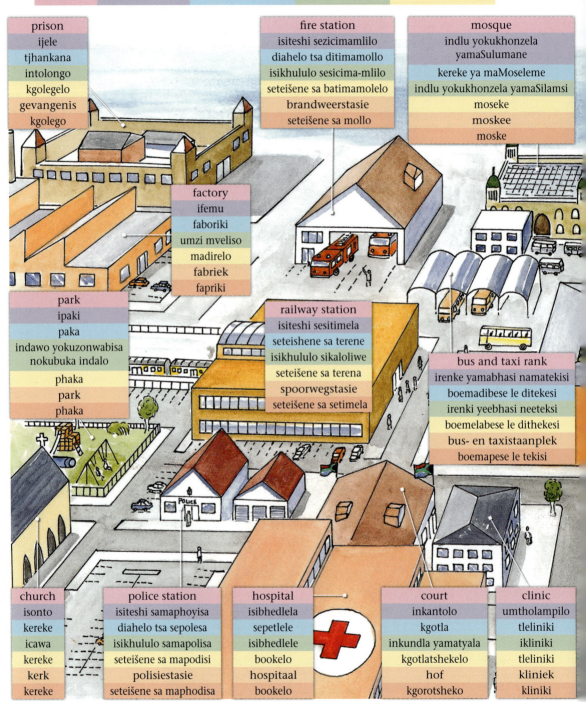

prison
ijele
tjhankana
intolongo
kgolegelo
gevangenis
kgolego

fire station
isiteshi sezicimamlilo
diahelo tsa ditimamollo
isikhululo sesicima-mlilo
seteišene sa batimamolelo
brandweerstasie
seteišene sa mollo

mosque
indlu yokukhonzela yamaSulumane
kereke ya maMoseleme
indlu yokukhonzela yamaSilamsi
moseke
moskee
moske

factory
ifemu
faboriki
umzi mveliso
madirelo
fabriek
fapriki

park
ipaki
paka
indawo yokuzonwabisa nokubuka indalo
phaka
park
phaka

railway station
isiteshi sesitimela
seteishene sa terene
isikhululo sikaloliwe
seteišene sa terena
spoorwegstasie
seteišene sa setimela

bus and taxi rank
irenke yamabhasi namatekisi
boemadibese le ditekesi
irenki yeebhasi neeteksi
boemelabese le dithekesi
bus- en taxistaanplek
boemapese le tekisi

church
isonto
kereke
icawa
kereke
kerk
kereke

police station
isiteshi samaphoyisa
diahelo tsa sepolesa
isikhululo samapolisa
seteišene sa mapodisi
polisiestasie
seteišene sa maphodisa

hospital
isibhedlela
sepetlele
isibhedlele
bookelo
hospitaal
bookelo

court
inkantolo
kgotla
inkundla yamatyala
kgotlatshekelo
hof
kgorotsheko

clinic
umtholampilo
tleliniki
ikliniki
tleliniki
kliniek
kliniki

84

Our community • Umphakathi wakithi • Tikoloho ya rona • Ingingqi esihlala kuyo
Setšhaba sa rona • Ons gemeenskap • Setšhaba sa rena

Ons dorp Toropo ya rena

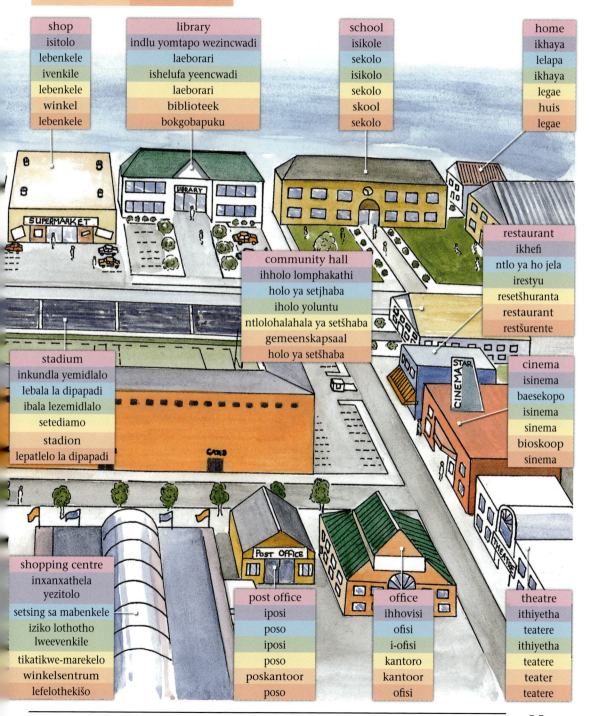

shop	library	school	home
isitolo	indlu yomtapo wezincwadi	isikole	ikhaya
lebenkele	laeborari	sekolo	lelapa
ivenkile	ishelufa yeencwadi	isikolo	ikhaya
lebenkele	laeborari	sekolo	legae
winkel	biblioteek	skool	huis
lebenkele	bokgobapuku	sekolo	legae

community hall
ihholo lomphakathi
holo ya setjhaba
iholo yoluntu
ntlolohalahala ya setšhaba
gemeenskapsaal
holo ya setšhaba

restaurant
ikhefi
ntlo ya ho jela
irestyu
resetšhuranta
restaurant
restšurente

stadium
inkundla yemidlalo
lebala la dipapadi
ibala lezemidlalo
setediamo
stadion
lepatlelo la dipapadi

cinema
isinema
baesekopo
isinema
sinema
bioskoop
sinema

shopping centre
inxanxathela yezitolo
setsing sa mabenkele
iziko lothotho lweevenkile
tikatikwe-marekelo
winkelsentrum
lefelothekišo

post office
iposi
poso
iposi
poso
poskantoor
poso

office
ihhovisi
ofisi
i-ofisi
kantoro
kantoor
ofisi

theatre
ithiyetha
teatere
ithiyetha
teatere
teater
teatere

Our community • Umphakathi wakithi • Tikoloho ya rona • Ingingqi esihlala kuyo
Setšhaba sa rona • Ons gemeenskap • Setšhaba sa rena

85

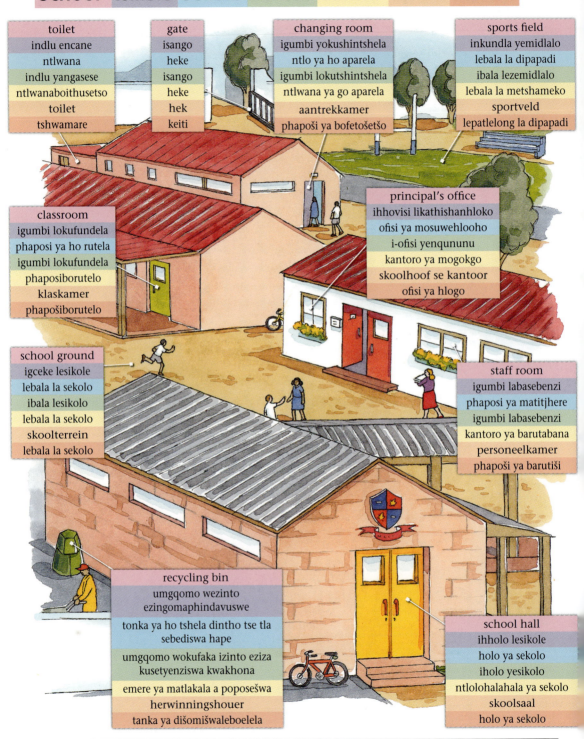

School **Isikole** **Sekolo** **Isikolo** **Sekolo** **Skool** **Sekolo**

toilet
indlu encane
ntlwana
indlu yangasese
ntlwanaboithusetso
toilet
tshwamare

gate
isango
heke
isango
heke
hek
keiti

changing room
igumbi yokushintshela
ntlo ya ho aparela
igumbi lokutshintshela
ntlwana ya go aparela
aantrekkamer
phapoši ya bofetošetšo

sports field
inkundla yemidlalo
lebala la dipapadi
ibala lezemidlalo
lebala la metshameko
sportveld
lepatlelong la dipapadi

principal's office
ihhovisi likathishanhloko
ofisi ya mosuwehlooho
i-ofisi yenqununu
kantoro ya mogokgo
skoolhoof se kantoor
ofisi ya hlogo

classroom
igumbi lokufundela
phaposi ya ho rutela
igumbi lokufundela
phaposiborutelo
klaskamer
phapošiboruteelo

school ground
igceke lesikole
lebala la sekolo
ibala lesikolo
lebala la sekolo
skoolterrein
lebala la sekolo

staff room
igumbi labasebenzi
phaposi ya matitjhere
igumbi labasebenzi
kantoro ya barutabana
personeelkamer
phapoši ya barutiši

recycling bin
umgqomo wezinto
ezingomaphindavuswe
tonka ya ho tshela dintho tse tla
sebediswa hape
umgqomo wokufaka izinto eziza
kusetyenziswa kwakhona
emere ya matlakala a poposešwa
herwinningshouer
tanka ya dišomišwaleboelela

school hall
ihholo lesikole
holo ya sekolo
iholo yesikolo
ntlolohalahala ya sekolo
skoolsaal
holo ya sekolo

Our community • Umphakathi wakithi • Tikoloho ya rona • Ingingqi esihlala kuyo
Setšhaba sa rona • Ons gemeenskap • Setšhaba sa rena

learner	learning area	subject	language	Mathematics	Arts and Culture
umfundi	umkhakha wesifundo	isifundo	ulimi	Izibalo	Ubuciko namasiko
moithuti	thuto	thuto	puo	Dipalo	Bonono le Setso
umfundi	inkalo yesifundo	isifundo	ulwimi	Izibalo	Ubugcisa nenkcubeko
moithuti	karolothuto	serutwa	puo	Mmetshe	Botsweretshi le Setso
leerder	leerarea	vak	taal	Wiskunde	Kuns en Kultuur
moithuti	tikologo ya go ithuta	thuto	polelo	Mathematiki	Bokgabo le Setšo

Social Sciences	History	Geography	Life Orientation
Injula yolwazi lwezempilo	Ezomlando	Ezezwe	Injula yolwazi lokuhlalisana kwabantu
Thuto ya phedisano	Nalane	Jeokerafi	Tsa bophelo
Inzululwazi kwezokuhlala	Ezembali	Ijografi	Izifundo ngezoBomi
Bonetetshi	Hisetori	Thutafatshe	Tebanyo le botshelo
Sosiale Wetenskappe	Geskiedenis	Aardrykskunde	Lewensoriëntering
Saense ya Leago	Histori	Thutafase	Tlwaetšophelo

Economics	Science	Biology	Natural Sciences	Technology
Ezomnotho	Isayensi	Isayensi yokuphilayo	Injula yolwazi lwezemvelo	Ezobuchwepheshe
Thuto ya tsa moruo	Saense	Baoloji		Thekenoloji
Ezoqoqosho	Inzululwazi	Inzululwazi ngezilwanyana nezityalo	Saense ya tlhaho	Ulwazi ngobugcisa
Thuto ya tsa ikonomi	Bonetetshi		Inzululwazi ngendalo	Thekenoloji
Ekonomie	Wetenskap	Thutatshelo	Disaense tsa Tlhago	Tegnologie
Ekonomi	Saense	Biologie	Natuurwetenskappe	Theknolotši
		Thutaphelo	Saense ya Tlhago	

circle	square	rectangle	triangle	cone	cylinder
indilinga	isikwele	unxande	unxantathu	ikhoni	isilinda
sedikadikwe	kgutlonnetsepa	kgutlonne	kgutlotharo	khounu	silinda
isangqa	isikwere	uxande	unxantathu	ibhumbulo	isilinda
sediko	sekwere	khutlonnetsepa	khutlotharo	topo	selennere
sirkel	vierkant	reghoek	driehoek	keël	silinder
sediko	sekwere	khutlonnethwii	khutlotharo	khouni	silintere

sphere	cube	rectangular prism	prism
isiyingi	ikhuyubhu	iphrizimu enama-engela ayisikwele onke	iphrizimu
sefere	tjhupu	porisimo ya kgutlonne	porisimo
ingqukumba	ithyubhu	imilo esicaba eneencam ezifanayo nebuxande	into emacala onke athe tyaba
kgolokwe	popegotaese	khutlonnetsepa ya matlhakoremabapitekano	matlhakoremabapitekano
sfeer	kubus	reghoekige prisma	prisma
nkgokolo	pepegotaese	porisma ya khutlonnethwii	porisma

Our community • Umphakathi wakithi • Tikoloho ya rona • Ingingqi esihlala kuyo
Setšhaba sa rona • Ons gemeenskap • Setšhaba sa rena

87

Classroom	Igumbi lokufundela	Phaposi ya ho rutela	Igumbi lokufundela

wallchart
amashadi asobondeni
dipapetla tsa lebota
iitshati zaseludongeni
tšhate ya lebota
muurkaart
ditšhate tša leboteng

chalkboard
ibhodi lokubhala ngoshoki
letlapa la tjhoko
ibhodi
patitšhoko
skryfbord
letlapa la tšhoko

chalk
ushoki
tjhoko
itshokhwe
tšhoko
bordkryt
tšhoko

display board
ibhodi lemibukiso
letlapa la pepeso
ibhodi yokubonisa
boroto ya dipontsho
uitstalbord
pepetla ya go bontšha

chalkboard duster
idasta yebhodi likashoki
dasetara
isisuli-bhodi
sephimodi
borduitveër
sephumolatšhokoporoto

teacher's desk
ideski likathisha
tafole ya titjhere
idesika katitshala
teseke ya morutabana
onderwyser se lessenaar
teseke ya morutiši

chair
isitulo
setulo
isitulo
setilo
stoel
setulo

bin
umgqomo wezibi
tonkana ya dithwele
umgqomo
seolelamatlakala
snippermandjie
selotatšhila

school bag
isikhwama sesikole
mokotlana wa dibuka
isingxotyana seencwadi
kgetsana ya sekolo
skoolsak
peke ya sekolo

desk
idesiki
teseke
idesika
teseke
lessenaar
teseke

Our community • Umphakathi wakithi • Tikoloho ya rona • Ingingqi esihlala kuyo
Setšhaba sa rona • Ons gemeenskap • Setšhaba sa rena

Phaposiborutelo   Klaskamer   Phapošiborutelo

shelves
amashalofu
diraka
iishelufu
diraka
rakke
diraka

Stationery   Izinsiza-kubhala   Disebediswa tsa ho ngola
Izinto zokubhala namaphepha   Didiriswa tsa kwalelo
Skryfbehoeftes   Ditlabelongwala

pen	pencil	crayon	koki
ipeni	ipensele	ikhilayoni	ikhokhi
pene	pensele	kerayone	khokhi
usiba	ipensile	ikhrayoni	ikoki
pene	phensele	kheraeyone	khoki
pen	potlood	vetkryt	koki
pene	phensele	kherayone	khokhi

nature corner
igumbi lezinto zemvelo
kgutlo ya tlholeho
ikona yendalo
sekhutlhotlholego
natuurhoekie
khutlo ya tlhago

rubber	ruler	sharpener	pencil case
irabha	irula	umshini wokulola ipensele	isikhwama samapeni
raba	rula		lebokose la dipene
irabha	irula	teotsa ya potloloto	isingxobo seepensile
raba	rula	umtshini wokulola	lebokoso la diphensele
uitveër	liniaal	selotsi	potloodhouer
raba	rula	skerpmaker	lepokisana la diphensele
		seloutšo	

mat
umata
mmate
imethi
mmata
mat
mmete

compass	paper	exercise book	textbook
isikhomba-magumbi	iphepha	incwadi yokubhalela	incwadi yokufunda
tshupakgutlo	pampiri	buka ya tlhakiso	buka ya kgakollo
ikhampasi	iphepha	incwadi yokubhalela	incwadi yesikhokelo
tshupantla	pampiri	bukana ya go kwalela	bukakgakololo
passer	papier	oefeningboek	teksboek
tšhupakhutlo	pampiri	puku ya maitekelo	pukukgakallo

Our community • Umphakathi wakithi • Tikoloho ya rona • Ingingqi esihlala kuyo
Setšhaba sa rona • Ons gemeenskap • Setšhaba sa rena

89

Hospital Isibhedlela Sepetlele Isibhedlele

Ward **Igumbi labagulayo** **Phaposi ya bakudi** **Igumbi lezigulana**
Phaposi ya balwetse **Saal** **Kamora ya balwetši**

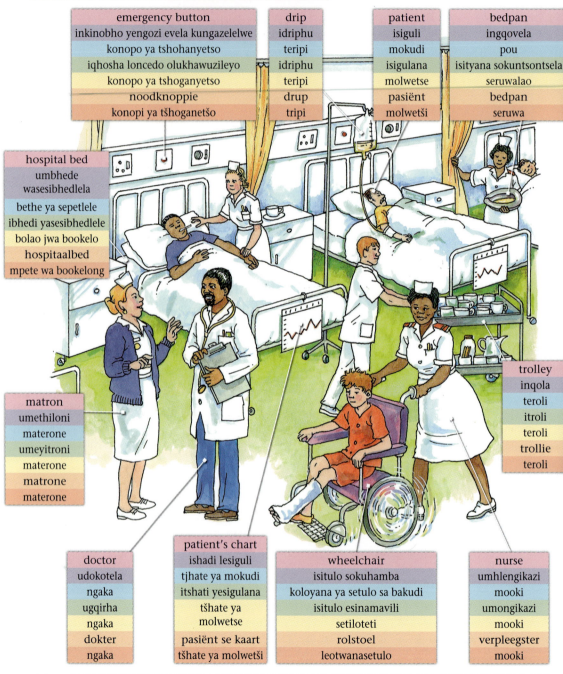

emergency button	drip	patient	bedpan
inkinobho yengozi evela kungazelelwe	idriphu	isiguli	ingqovela
konopo ya tshohanyetso	teripi	mokudi	pou
iqhosha loncedo olukhawuzileyo	idriphu	isigulana	isityana sokuntsontsela
konopo ya tshoganyetso	teripi	molwetse	seruwalao
noodknoppie	drup	pasiënt	bedpan
konopi ya tšhoganetšo	tripi	molwetši	seruwa

hospital bed
umbhede wasesibhedlela
bethe ya sepetlele
ibhedi yasesibhedlele
bolao jwa bookelo
hospitaalbed
mpete wa bookelong

matron
umethiloni
materone
umeyitroni
materone
matrone
materone

trolley
inqola
teroli
itroli
teroli
trollie
teroli

doctor
udokotela
ngaka
ugqirha
ngaka
dokter
ngaka

patient's chart
ishadi lesiguli
tjhate ya mokudi
itshati yesigulana
tšhate ya molwetse
pasiënt se kaart
tšhate ya molwetši

wheelchair
isitulo sokuhamba
koloyana ya setulo sa bakudi
isitulo esinamavili
setiloteti
rolstoel
leotwanasetulo

nurse
umhlengikazi
mooki
umongikazi
mooki
verpleegster
mooki

90

Our community • Umphakathi wakithi • Tikoloho ya rona • Ingingqi esihlala kuyo
Setšhaba sa rona • Ons gemeenskap • Setšhaba sa rena

Bookelo Hospitaal Bookelo

Operating theatre	Igumbi lokuhlinzela	Phaposi ya opereshene	Igumbi lotyando	Phaposikaro	Teater	Teatere ya opareišene

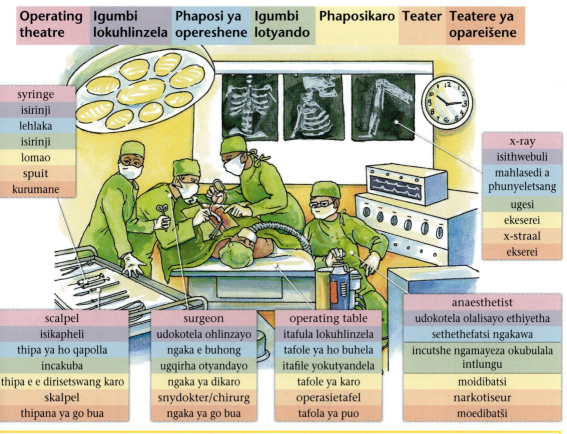

syringe
isirinji
lehlaka
isirinji
lomao
spuit
kurumane

x-ray
isithwebuli
mahlasedi a phunyeletsang
ugesi
ekeserei
x-straal
ekserei

scalpel
isikapheli
thipa ya ho qapolla
incakuba
thipa e e dirisetswang karo
skalpel
thipana ya go bua

surgeon
udokotela ohlinzayo
ngaka e buhong
ugqirha otyandayo
ngaka ya dikaro
snydokter/chirurg
ngaka ya go bua

operating table
itafula lokuhlinzela
tafole ya ho buhela
itafile yokutyandela
tafole ya karo
operasietafel
tafola ya puo

anaesthetist
udokotela olalisayo ethiyetha
sethethefatsi ngakawa
incutshe ngamayeza okubulala intlungu
moidibatsi
narkotiseur
moedibatši

operation
ukuhlinzwa
ho buha
utyando
karo
operasie
puo

emergency
ingozi evela kungazelelwe
tshohanyetso
ingxakeko
tshoganyetso
noodgeval
tšhoganetšo

trauma
ukwethuka
bokudi bo bifileng
ukwenzakala
letshogo
trauma
letšhogo

casualty
inkubele
mahlatsipa
igumbi labonzakeleyo esibhedlela
lefelo la baokelwantle
ongeval
karolo ya baokelwantle

maternity ward
igumbi lokutetela
phaposi ya ho pepela
igumbi lokubelekela
kamotshana ya baimana
kraamsaal
phapoši ya bobelegiši

pregnancy
ukukhulelwa
boimana
ukukhulelwa
boimana
swangerskap
boimana

check-up
ukuhlolwa ngudokotela
tekolo
ukuxilongwa
tlhatlhojo
roetine-ondersoek
tlhahlobo

injection
umjovo
nalete
isitofu
tlhabo
inspuiting
tlhabelo

treatment
ukulashwa
kalafo
unyango
alafiwa
behandeling
kalafo

anaesthetic
umjovo olalisayo noma owenza kube ndikindiki
nalete ya sethethefatsi
isitofu esenza ube ndindisholo
kidibatso
narkose
kedibatšo

Our community • Umphakathi wakithi • Tikoloho ya rona • Ingingqi esihlala kuyo
Setšhaba sa rona • Ons gemeenskap • Setšhaba sa rena

91

Clinic Umtholampilo Tleliniki Ikliniki Tleliniki Kliniek Kliniki

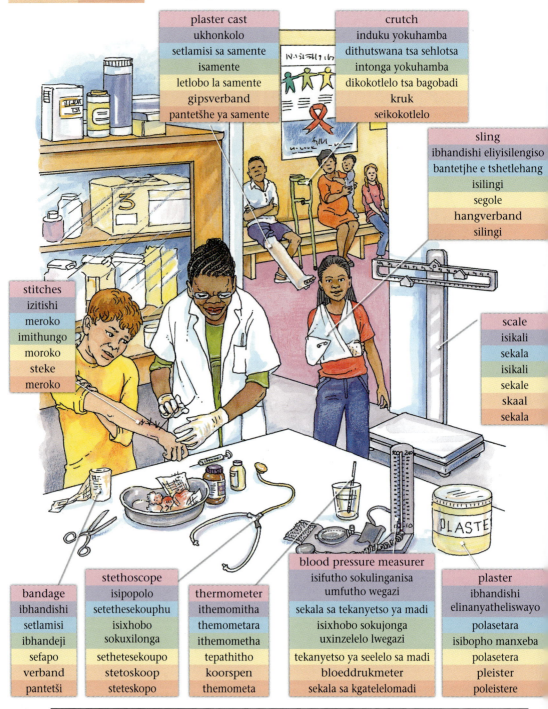

plaster cast
ukhonkolo
setlamisi sa samente
isamente
letlobo la samente
gipsverband
pantetšhe ya samente

crutch
induku yokuhamba
dithutswana tsa sehlotsa
intonga yokuhamba
dikokotlelo tsa bagobadi
kruk
seikokotlelo

sling
ibhandishi eliyisilengiso
bantetjhe e tshetlehang
isilingi
segole
hangverband
silingi

stitches
izitishi
meroko
imithungo
moroko
steke
meroko

scale
isikali
sekala
isikali
sekale
skaal
sekala

bandage
ibhandishi
setlamisi
ibhandeji
sefapo
verband
pantetši

stethoscope
isipopolo
setethesekouphu
isixhobo sokuxilonga
sethetesekoupo
stetoskoop
steteskopo

thermometer
ithemomitha
themometara
ithemometha
tepathitho
koorspen
themometa

blood pressure measurer
isifutho sokulinganisa umfutho wegazi
sekala sa tekanyetso ya madi
isixhobo sokujonga uxinzelelo lwegazi
tekanyetso ya seelelo sa madi
bloeddrukmeter
sekala sa kgatelelomadi

plaster
ibhandishi elinanyatheliswayo
polasetara
isibopho manxeba
polasetera
pleister
poleistere

Our community • Umphakathi wakithi • Tikoloho ya rona • Ingingqi esihlala kuyo
Setšhaba sa rona • Ons gemeenskap • Setšhaba sa rena

Pharmacy/Chemist Ikhemisi Khemese Ikhemesti Khemisi Apteek Khemisi

medicine	antiseptic lotion	tonic	prescription
umuthi	uketshezi oluyisinqanda-kuvunda	umuthi wokuqinisa umzimba	imishanguzo oyibhalelwe ngudokotela
moriana	mokedikedi wa setlolo tshitisi	sematlafatsi	taelo ya meriana
iyeza	amafutha anqanda ukubola	umxube ohlaziyayo	ummiselo
molemo	setlolo sa thibelatwatsi	setiisammele	taelo ya molemo
medisyne	ontsmettingsmiddel	tonikum	voorskrif
sehlare	setlolo sa tšhitišaphero	sematlafatši	taelelo ya sehlare

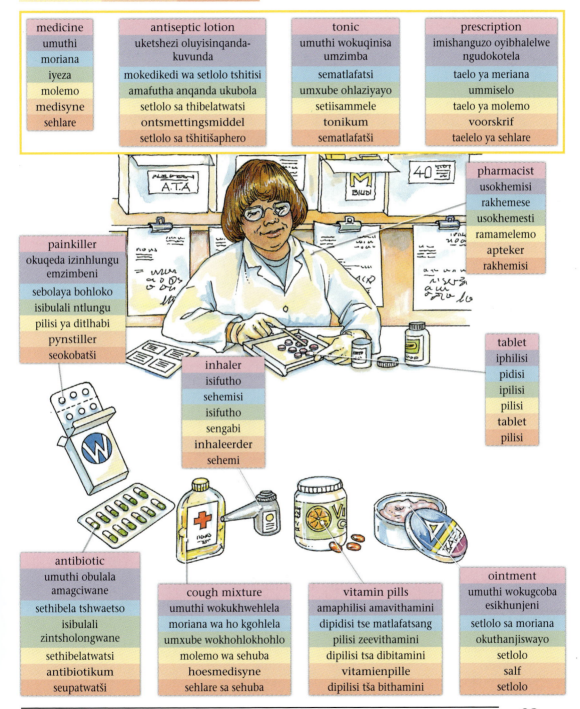

pharmacist
usokhemisi
rakhemese
usokhemesti
ramamelemo
apteker
rakhemisi

painkiller
okuqeda izinhlungu emzimbeni
sebolaya bohloko
isibulali ntlungu
pilisi ya ditlhabi
pynstiller
seokobatši

tablet
iphilisi
pidisi
ipilisi
pilisi
tablet
pilisi

inhaler
isifutho
sehemisi
isifutho
sengabi
inhaleerder
sehemi

antibiotic
umuthi obulala amagciwane
sethibela tshwaetso
isibulali zintsholongwane
sethibelatwatsi
antibiotikum
seupatwatši

cough mixture
umuthi wokukhwehlela
moriana wa ho kgohlela
umxube wokhohlokhohlo
molemo wa sehuba
hoesmedisyne
sehlare sa sehuba

vitamin pills
amaphilisi amavithamini
dipidisi tse matlafatsang
pilisi zeevithamini
dipilisi tsa dibitamini
vitamienpille
dipilisi tša bithamini

ointment
umuthi wokugcoba esikhunjeni
setlolo sa moriana okuthanjiswayo
setlolo
salf
setlolo

Our community • Umphakathi wakithi • Tikoloho ya rona • Ingingqi esihlala kuyo
Setšhaba sa rona • Ons gemeenskap • Setšhaba sa rena

93

Dentist Udokotela wamazinyo Ngaka ya meno
Ugqirha wamazinyo Ngaka ya meno Tandarts
Ngaka ya meno

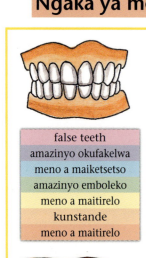

dentist
udokotela wamazinyo
ngaka ya meno
ugqirha wamazinyo
ngaka ya meno
tandarts
rameno

lamp
ilambu
lebone
isibane
lebone
lamp
lebone

false teeth
amazinyo okufakelwa
meno a maiketsetso
amazinyo emboleko
meno a maitirelo
kunstande
meno a maitirelo

drill
ibhola
boro
idrili
boro
boor
boro

braces
izinsimbi zokubopha amazinyo
diterata tsa meno
isixhobo esibotshelelwa emazinyweni ukuwolula
mepako
draadjies
diterata tša meno

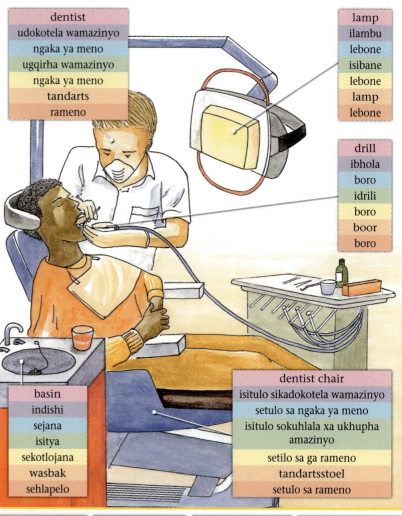

basin
indishi
sejana
isitya
sekotlojana
wasbak
sehlapelo

dentist chair
isitulo sikadokotela wamazinyo
setulo sa ngaka ya meno
isitulo sokuhlala xa ukhupha amazinyo
setilo sa ga rameno
tandartsstoel
setulo sa rameno

filling	extraction	cavity	tooth decay	toothache
usemende wokugcwalisa ezinyweni	ukukhipha izinyo	imbobo ezinyweni	ukubola kwezinyo	izinyo elibuhlungu
sekata masoba a meno	ho ntshwa ha meno	lesoba le bodileng la leino	ho bola ha leino	ho opelwa ke leino
ukuvala umngxunya ezinyweni	ukukhupha izinyo	umngxunya ezinyweni	izinyo elibolileyo	izinyo eliqaqambayo
go tlatsa leino	go ntsha leino	phatlha ya leino	go bola ga leino	setlhabi sa leino
stopsel	tandtrekking	gaatjie	tandbederf	tandpyn
tlaleletšo ya meno	tomolo	sekoti	go bola ga leino	go thunya ga leino

94

Our community • Umphakathi wakithi • Tikoloho ya rona • Ingingqi esihlala kuyo
Setšhaba sa rona • Ons gemeenskap • Setšhaba sa rena

Feeling ill Ukugula Ho kula Ukugula
Go ikutlwa o lwala Olik voel Go lwala

asthma	HIV/AIDS	burn	cancer	broken bone
isifuba somoya	isandulela ngculazi	ukusha	umdlavuza	ithambo elephukile
letshwea	kwatsi ya bosolla hlapi	leqeba la mollo	kankere	lesapo le robehileng
umbefu	uGawulayo nentshologwane	ukutsha	umhlaza	ithambo elaphukileyo
asema	tshitangaka	go ša	kankere	lerapo le le robegileng
asma	MIV/vigs	brand	kanker	beenbreuk
asema	HIV/AIDS	ntho ya mollo	kankere	lerapo la go robega

headache	sore throat	stomach ache	poisoning	snake bite
ikhanda elibuhlungu	umphimbo obuhlungu	isisu esibuhlungu	ubuthi	ukulunywa yinyoka
ho opelwa ke hlooho	mmetso	ho longwa ke mala	mahloko	ho longwa ke noha
intloko ebuhlungu	umqala obuhlungu	isisu esibuhlungu	ityhefu	ukulunywa yinyoka
go opiwa ke tlhogo	mometso o o botlhoko	botlhoko jwa mala	botlhole	molomo wa noga
hoofpyn	seerkeel	maagpyn	vergiftiging	slangbyt
opša ke hlogo	mogolo o bohloko	go longwa ke mala	tšhelela mpholo	go longwa ke noga

fever	meningitis	measles	mumps	cholera
imfiva	isifo solwembu lobuchopho	isimungumungwane	uzagiga	ikholera
feberu	menenjaethisi	mmaselese	manketeya	kholera
umkhuhlane	ukudumba kwenwebu yobuchopho	imasisi	uqwilikane	urhudo
letshoroma	tlhogwana	mmoko	dikodu	kholera
koors	meningitis	masels	pampoentjies	cholera
fišafiša	menenjaethese	mooko	mauwe	kholera

chicken pox	cold	cough	bronchitis	pain
ingxibongo	umkhuhlane	ukukhwehlela	isishiso semithanjana yomoya	izinhlungu
sekgolopane	sefuba	ho kgohlela	mokgokgothwane	bohloko
irhashalala	ingqele	ukhohlokhohlo	unkonkonko	intlungu
sekonkonyanethutwa	mokgotlhwane	kgotlholo	boronkhaithisi	setlhabi
waterpokkies	verkoue	hoes	brongitis	pyn
mabora	mpshikela	sehuba	pronkhaethese	sehlabi

malaria	hay fever	pneumonia	sprain	blister
umalaleveva	imfiva ethimulisayo	amahlaba	isenyelo	ipanyaza
letshollo la madi	sefuba	nyumonia	ho nonyetseha	letswabadi
icesina	imfixane	ukukrala kwemiphunga	ukukruneka	idyungudyungu
letadi	bolwetse jwa ditšhese	nyumonia	tsipoga	pudula
malaria	hooikoors	longontsteking	verstuiting	blaas
letadi	phišokgolo	nyumonia	thinyego	lephone

tonsilitis	appendicitis	influenza (flu)	diarrhoea	tuberculosis (TB)
amathansela	isifo se-aphendiksi	imfuluwenza	ukucubuluza	isifuba sexhwala
ditemetwana	lelana	mokakallane	letshollo	lefuba
isifo samadlala	ukudumba kwethunjana	umkhuhlane	urhudo	isifo sephepha
dikodunnye	lelana	mofikela	letshololo	mafatlha a magolo
mangelontsteking	blindedermontsteking	griep	diarree	turberkulose (TB)
dithaka	bolwetši bja lelana	mokhohlane	letšhologo	bolwetši bja mafahla

---

Our community • Umphakathi wakithi • Tikoloho ya rona • Ingingqi esihlala kuyo   95
Setšhaba sa rona • Ons gemeenskap • Setšhaba sa rena

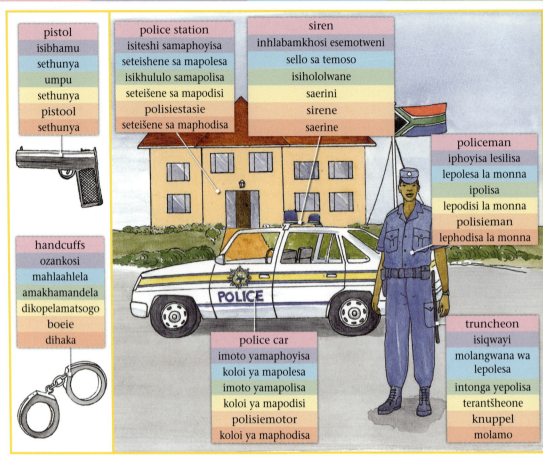

pistol
isibhamu
sethunya
umpu
sethunya
pistool
sethunya

police station
isiteshi samaphoyisa
seteishene sa mapolesa
isikhululo samapolisa
seteišene sa mapodisi
polisiestasie
seteišene sa maphodisa

siren
inhlabamkhosi esemotweni
sello sa temoso
isihololwane
saerini
sirene
saerine

policeman
iphoyisa lesilisa
lepolesa la monna
ipolisa
lepodisi la monna
polisieman
lephodisa la monna

handcuffs
ozankosi
mahlaahlela
amakhamandela
dikopelamatsogo
boeie
dihaka

police car
imoto yamaphoyisa
koloi ya mapolesa
imoto yamapolisa
koloi ya mapodisi
polisiemotor
koloi ya maphodisa

truncheon
isiqwayi
molangwana wa lepolesa
intonga yepolisa
terantšheone
knuppel
molamo

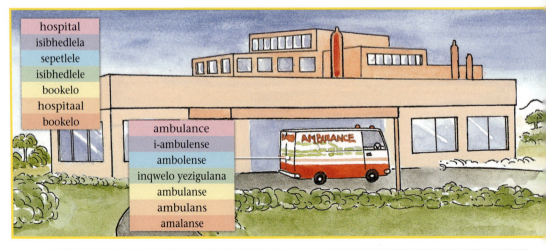

hospital
isibhedlela
sepetlele
isibhedlele
bookelo
hospitaal
bookelo

ambulance
i-ambulense
ambolense
inqwelo yezigulana
ambulanse
ambulans
amalanse

96

Our community • Umphakathi wakithi • Tikoloho ya rona • Ingingqi esihlala kuyo
Setšhaba sa rona • Ons gemeenskap • Setšhaba sa rena

Ditirelo tsa tshoganyetso   Nooddienste   Ditirelotšhoganetšo

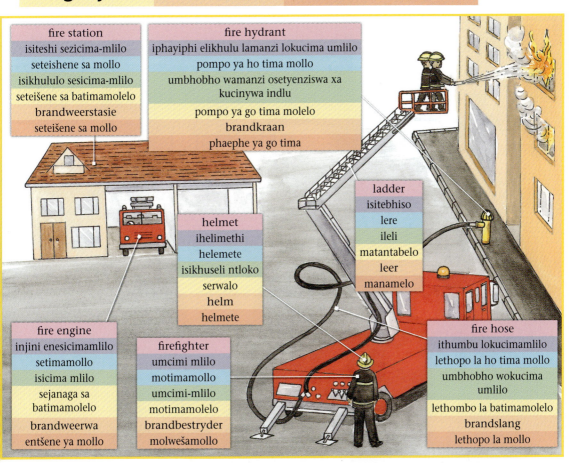

fire station
isiteshi sezicima-mlilo
seteishene sa mollo
isikhululo sesicima-mlilo
seteišene sa batimamolelo
brandweerstasie
seteišene sa mollo

fire hydrant
iphayiphi elikhulu lamanzi lokucima umlilo
pompo ya ho tima mollo
umbhobho wamanzi osetyenziswa xa kucinywa indlu
pompo ya go tima molelo
brandkraan
phaephe ya go tima

ladder
isitebhiso
lere
ileli
matantabelo
leer
manamelo

helmet
ihelimethi
helemete
isikhuseli ntloko
serwalo
helm
helmete

fire hose
ithumbu lokucimamlilo
lethopo la ho tima mollo
umbhobho wokucima umlilo
lethombo la batimamolelo
brandslang
lethopo la mollo

fire engine
injini enesicimamlilo
setimamollo
isicima mlilo
sejanaga sa batimamolelo
brandweerwa
entšene ya mollo

firefighter
umcimi mlilo
motimamollo
umcimi-mlilo
motimamolelo
brandbestryder
molwešamollo

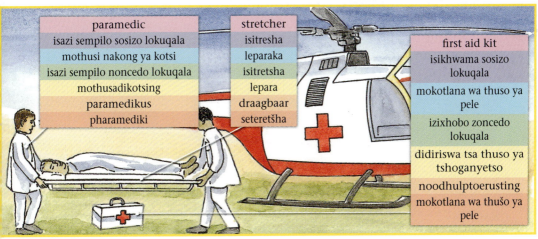

paramedic
isazi sempilo sosizo lokuqala
mothusi nakong ya kotsi
isazi sempilo noncedo lokuqala
mothusadikotsing
paramedikus
pharamediki

stretcher
isitresha
leparaka
isitretsha
lepara
draagbaar
seteretšha

first aid kit
isikhwama sosizo lokuqala
mokotlana wa thuso ya pele
izixhobo zoncedo lokuqala
didiriswa tsa thuso ya tshoganyetso
noodhulptoerusting
mokotlana wa thušo ya pele

Our community • Umphakathi wakithi • Tikoloho ya rona • Ingingqi esihlala kuyo
Setšhaba sa rona • Ons gemeenskap • Setšhaba sa rena

97

Library	Indlu yomtapo wezincwadi	Laeborari	Ithala leencwadi

bookshelf
ishalufu lezincwadi
raka ya dibuka
ishelufa yeencwadi
raka ya dibuka
boekrak
raka ya dipuku

library card
ikhadi lasemtatsheni wezincwadi
karete ya laeborari
ikhadi lethala leencwadi
karata ya laeborari
biblioteekkaart
karata ya bokgobapuku

librarian
umphathi wendawo yomtapo wezincwadi
radibuka
usoncwadi
molaeborari
bibliotekaris
rabokgobapuku

Post office	Iposi	Poso	Iposi

parcel	teller	counter	envelope	registered mail
iphasela	uthela	ikhawunta	imvilophu	incwadi erejistiwe
phasele	thelara	khaontara	omfolopo	lengolo le positsweng ka rejisetara
ipasile	umbali-mali ekhawuntarini	ikhawuntari	imvulophu	incwadi ethunyelwe ngerejista
phasele	mmalamadi	khaontara	enfolopo	lekwalo le le kwadisitsweng
pakkie	teller	toonbank	koevert	geregistreerde pos
phasela	thelara	khaontara	onfolopo	lengwalo la retšistara

Our community • Umphakathi wakithi • Tikoloho ya rona • Ingingqi esihlala kuyo
Setšhaba sa rona • Ons gemeenskap • Setšhaba sa rena

Laeborari Biblioteek Bokgobapuku

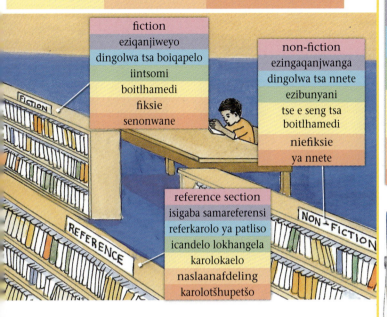

fiction
eziqanjiweyo
dingolwa tsa boiqapelo
iintsomi
boitlhamedi
fiksie
senonwane

non-fiction
ezingaqanjwanga
dingolwa tsa nnete
ezibunyani
tse e seng tsa boitlhamedi
niefiksie
ya nnete

reference section
isigaba samareferensi
referkarolo ya patliso
icandelo lokhangela
karolokaelo
naslaanafdeling
karolotšhupetšo

Poso Poskantoor Poso

postbox
amabhokisi epossi
mabokose a poso
iibhokisi zeeposi
mabokoso a poso
posbus
mapokisi a poso

letter
incwadi
lengolo
incwadi
lekwalo
brief
lengwalo

stamp
isitembu
setempe
isitampu
setempe
seël
setempe

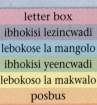

letter box
ibhokisi lezincwadi
lebokose la mangolo
ibhokisi yeencwadi
lebokoso la makwalo
posbus
lepokisi la mangwalo

public telephone
ucingo lomphakathi
mohala wa batho bohle
ifowuni kawonke-wonke
mogala-tlhaeletsano wa botlhe
openbare telefoon
mogala wa pabliki

coin operated phone
lusebenzisa uhlweza lwemali
mohala o kenyang tjhelete
ifoni esebenza nge-engqe-kembe zemali
sediriswa se se dirang ka madi
muntfoon
tšheletetirišo

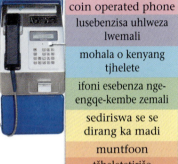

card operated phone
lusebenza ngekhadi
mohala wa karete
ifoni esebenza ngekhadi
founu e e dirisang karata
kaartfoon
karatatirišo

telephone card
ikhadi lokushaya ucingo
karete ya mohala
ikhadi lefowuni
mogalatlhaeletsano wa karata
telefoonkaart
karata ya mogala

Our community • Umphakathi wakithi • Tikoloho ya rona • Ingingqi esihlala kuyo
Setšhaba sa rona • Ons gemeenskap • Setšhaba sa rena

99

Places of worship	Izindawo zokukhonzela	Dibaka tsa ho rapella	Iindawo zokukhonzela

cross
isiphambano
sefapano
umnqamlezo
sefapaano
kruis
sefapano

steeple
umbhoshongo
lenaka le ntjhotjho la moaho wa kereke
uphondo olutsolo kwindlu yecawa
setipele
kerktoring
sehloa

church
isonto
kereke
icawa
kereke
kerk
kereke

bell
insimbi
tshepe
intsimbi
tshipi
klok
tšhipi

church hall
ihholo lesonto
holo ya kereke
iholo lecawa
ntlolohalahala ya kereke
kerksaal
holo ya kereke

Our community • Umphakathi wakithi • Tikoloho ya rona • Ingingqi esihlala kuyo
Setšhaba sa rona • Ons gemeenskap • Setšhaba sa rena

Mafelo a kobamelo   Aanbiddingsplekke   Mafelo a go rapela

minaret
umbhoshongo omude osesontweni lamaSulumane
lenaka le tjhorileng kerekeng ya maMoseleme
uphondo olutsolo lwendlu yamaSilamsi
minarete
minaret
minarete

temple
ithempeli
tempele
itempile
tempele
tempel
tempele

mosque
indlu yokukhonzela yamaSulumane
moaho wa kereke ya maMoseleme
indlu yokukhonzela yamaSilamsi
moseke
moskee
moske

synagogue
isinagogo
senagoge
indlu yesikhungo yamaJuda
senagoge
sinagoge
sinagoge

place of meditation
indawo yokudlinzela
tulo ya ho imamela
indawo yokucamgca
lefelo la boikimololelo
plek vir meditasie
lefelo la maipobolo

Our community • Umphakathi wakithi • Tikoloho ya rona • Ingingqi esihlala kuyo
Setšhaba sa rona • Ons gemeenskap • Setšhaba sa rena

101

Phrases	Amabinzana	Dipolelwana	Amabinzana
Where do you live?	Uhlalaphi?	O dula kae?	Uhla phi?
I live on the farm.	Ngihlala epulazini.	Ke dula polasing.	Ndihlala efama.
We live in the township.	Sihlala elokishini.	Re dula lekeisheneng.	Sihlala elokishini.
Is there a library in your area?	Ikhona indawo yomtapo wezincwadi ngakini?	Na ho na le laeborari moo o dulang teng?	Likhona ithala leencwadi kwingingqi yakho?
No. We have to go to the one close to the school.	Cha. Kumele siye kweseduze nesikole.	Tjhe. Re atisa ho ya ho e pela sekolo.	Hayi alikho, siya kuleya ikufutshane nesikolo.
How often do you go to the community centre?	Uya/Niya kangaki kwisenta yomphakathi?	O ya ha kae setsing sa holo ya setjhaba?	Uya kangaphi kwiziko loluntu?
How do I get to the post office?	Ngingafika kanjani ehhovisi leposi?	Nka fihla jwang posong?	Kuyiwa njani eposini?
The post office is around the corner.	Ihhovisi leposi libude buduze nalapha.	Poso e khoneng mane.	Iposi iphaya ekujikeleni.
I would like to buy some stamps, please.	Ngicela ukuthenga izitembu.	Ke ne nka rata ho reka ditempe.	Ndiqwenela ukuthenga izitampu.
Please may I have some telegram forms.	Ngicela amafomu okushaya ithelegramu.	Na nka fumana diforomo tsa thelekeramo?	Ndicela iifomu zokubhala ucingo?
May I have a R50 telephone card, please?	Ngicela ikhadi lokushaya ucingo lamarandi angama-50?	Na nka fumana dikarete tsa mohala tsa R50?	Ndicela ikhadi lefowuni lama-R50?
Where is the nearest clinic?	Ukuphi umtholampilo oseduze?	Nka e fumana kae tleliniki e haufi?	Iphi ikliniki ekufutshane?
What number must I dial in an emergency?	Ngingashayela kuyiphi inamba uma kuvele ingozi kungazelelwe?	Nka letsetsa nomoro efe ha ke na le mathata?	Kufuneka nditsalele phi xa ndifuna uncedo olungxamisekileyo?
You must dial 107/10111.	Ungashayela kunombolo-107/10111.	O ka letsetsa 107/10111.	Tsalela ku-107/10111.
Help! Call the fire brigade! There is a fire!	Siza bo! Shayela isiteshi sezicima mlilo! Kunomlilo!	Thusa! Letsetsa seteishene sa mollo! Ho a tjha!	Nceda! Biza abacimi-mlilo! Kuyatsha!
There has been an accident. Please call the ambulance and the police.	Kevele ingozi. Ngicela ubize i-ambulense namaphoyisa.	Ho na le kotsi e hlahileng. A ko letsetse koloi ya bakudi le mapolesa.	Kwenzeke ingozi. Nceda biza inqwelo yezigulana namapolisa.

Our community • Umphakathi wakithi • Tikoloho ya rona • Ingingqi esihlala kuyo
Setšhaba sa rona • Ons gemeenskap • Setšhaba sa rena

Dikapolelo	Frases	Dikafoko
O nna/dula kae?	Waar woon jy?	O dula kae?
Ke nna mo polaseng.	Ek bly op die plaas.	Ke dula polaseng.
Re nna mo motsesetoropong.	Ons bly in die township.	Re dula motsesetoropong.
A go na le laeborari mo tulong ya lona?	Is daar 'n biblioteek in jou omgewing?	Go na le bokgobapuku tikologong ya geno?
Nnyaa, re tshwanelwa ke go ya kwa go e e gaufi le sekolo.	Nee. Ons moet na die een naby die skool gaan.	Aowa, re swanelwa ke go ya go ya go yeo e lego kgauswi le sekolo.
O ya ga kae kwa tikwatikweng ya setšhaba?	Hoe gereeld gaan jy na die gemeenskapsentrum?	A o ya gakae bohlakanelong bja setšhaba?
Ke tsamaya jang go ya kwa posong?	Hoe kom 'n mens by die poskantoor uit?	A nka fihla bjang posong?
Poso e fela fa gaufi fano.	Die poskantoor is om die hoek.	Poso e go rarela le sekhutlo.
Ke tla rata go reka ditempe.	Ek wil graag 'n paar seëls koop, asseblief.	Ke nyaka go reka ditempe, hle.
Ke kopa diforomo tsa thelekerama tsweetswee?	Mag ek asseblief 'n paar telegramvorms kry?	Ke kgopela diforomo tša thelekramo?
A nka bona karata ya mogalatlhaeletsano ya R50?	Mag ek asseblief 'n telefoonkaart van R50 kry?	Ke kgopela founokarata ya R50?
Tleliniki e e gaufi e kae?	Waar is die naaste kliniek?	Kliniki ya kgauswi e kae?
Ke dirise nomoro efe fa ke batla go leletsa badiri ba tsa tshoganyetso?	Watter nommer moet ek in geval van 'n noodgeval skakel?	Nka letšetša nomoro efe lebakeng la tšhoganetšo?
O tshwanetse go letsetsa 107 kgotsa 10111.	Jy moet 107/10111 skakel.	O swanetše go letšetša 107/10111.
Thusa! Leletsa seteišene sa batimamolelo! Go a tuka!	Help! Bel die brandweer! Daar is 'n brand!	Thuša! Leletša seteišeneng sa mollo. Go a swa!
Go nnile le kotsi. Ka tsweetswee bitsa ambulanse le mapodisa.	Daar was 'n ongeluk. Skakel asseblief die ambulans en polisie.	Go na le kotsi. Hle, letšetša amalanse le maphodisa.

Our community • Umphakathi wakithi • Tikoloho ya rona • Ingingqi esihlala kuyo
Setšhaba sa rona • Ons gemeenskap • Setšhaba sa rena

103

6

Transport

Izithuthi

Dipalangwang

Izithuthi

Dipalangwa

Vervoer

Dinamelwa

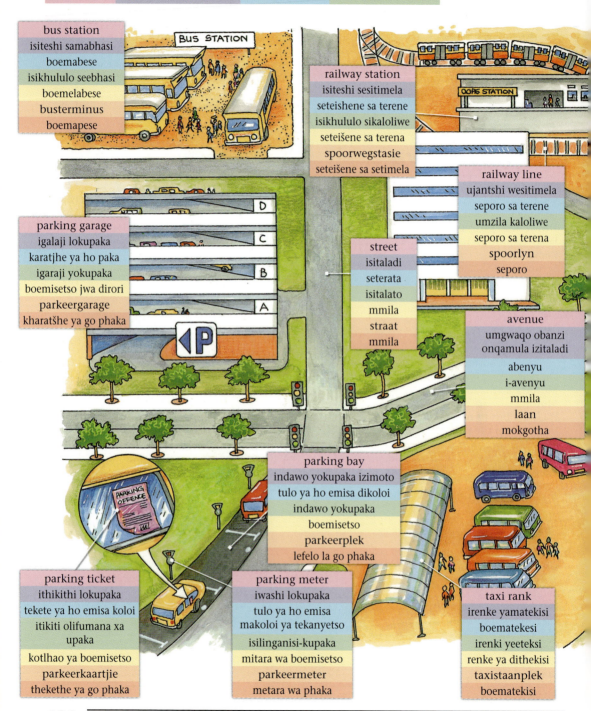

bus station
isiteshi samabhasi
boemabese
isikhululo seebhasi
boemelabese
busterminus
boemapese

railway station
isiteshi sesitimela
seteishene sa terene
isikhululo sikaloliwe
seteišene sa terena
spoorwegstasie
seteišene sa setimela

railway line
ujantshi wesitimela
seporo sa terene
umzila kaloliwe
seporo sa terena
spoorlyn
seporo

parking garage
igalaji lokupaka
karatjhe ya ho paka
igaraji yokupaka
boemisetso jwa dirori
parkeergarage
kharatšhe ya go phaka

street
isitaladi
seterata
isitalato
mmila
straat
mmila

avenue
umgwaqo obanzi
onqamula izitaladi
abenyu
i-avenyu
mmila
laan
mokgotha

parking bay
indawo yokupaka izimoto
tulo ya ho emisa dikoloi
indawo yokupaka
boemisetso
parkeerplek
lefelo la go phaka

parking ticket
ithikithi lokupaka
tekete ya ho emisa koloi
itikiti olifumana xa upaka
kotlhao ya boemisetso
parkeerkaartjie
thekethe ya go phaka

parking meter
iwashi lokupaka
tulo ya ho emisa makoloi ya tekanyetso
isilinganisi-kupaka
mitara wa boemisetso
parkeermeter
metara wa phaka

taxi rank
irenke yamatekisi
boematekesi
irenki yeeteksi
renke ya dithekisi
taxistaanplek
boematekisi

airport
isikhumulo samabhanoyi
boemafofane
isikhululo seenqwelo-moya
boemelafofane
lughawe
boemafofane

road
umgwaqo
mmila
umgaqo
tsela
pad
mmila

freeway road sign
uphawu lomgwaqo onguthela-wayeka
letshwao la tsela ya mmila o potlakileng
uphawu lukahola wendlela
letshwao la tselafefo
snelwegteken
leswao la mmila wa lephefo

freeway
umgwaqo onguthela-wayeka
tsela ya dikoloi tse tsamayang ka potlako
uhola wendlela
tselafefo
snelweg
mmila wa lephefo

bridge
ibhuloho
borokgo
ibhulorho
borogo
brug
leporogo

off-ramp
umgwaqo ochezukayo
mmila o kgelohang
isiphambuka esiphuma kuhola
tsela e e tswang mo go e kgolo
afrit
tselatepogo

on-ramp
umgwaqo ongenayo
mmila o kenang ho o mong
isiphambuka esingena kuhola
tsela e e yang kwa go e kgolo
oprit
tsela e yang go e kgolo

harbour
isikhumulo semikhumbi
boemakepe
izibuko leenqanawa
boemelakepe
hawe
boemakepe

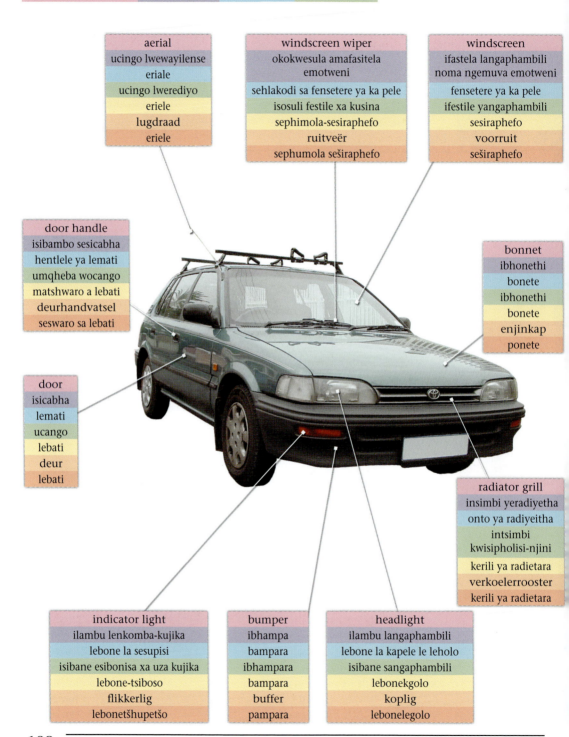

aerial
ucingo lwewayilense
eriale
ucingo lwerediyo
eriele
lugdraad
eriele

windscreen wiper
okokwesula amafasitela emotweni
sehlakodi sa fensetere ya ka pele
isosuli festile xa kusina
sephimola-sesiraphefo
ruitveër
sephumola seširaphefo

windscreen
ifastela langaphambili noma ngemuva emotweni
fensetere ya ka pele
ifestile yangaphambili
sesiraphefo
voorruit
seširaphefo

door handle
isibambo sesicabha
hentlele ya lemati
umqheba wocango
matshwaro a lebati
deurhandvatsel
seswaro sa lebati

bonnet
ibhonethi
bonete
ibhonethi
bonete
enjinkap
ponete

door
isicabha
lemati
ucango
lebati
deur
lebati

radiator grill
insimbi yeradiyetha
onto ya radiyeitha
intsimbi kwisipholisi-njini
kerili ya radietara
verkoelerrooster
kerili ya radietara

indicator light
ilambu lenkomba-kujika
lebone la sesupisi
isibane esibonisa xa uza kujika
lebone-tsiboso
flikkerlig
lebonetšhupetšo

bumper
ibhampa
bampara
ibhampara
bampara
buffer
pampara

headlight
ilambu langaphambili
lebone la kapele le leholo
isibane sangaphambili
lebonekgolo
koplig
lebonelegolo

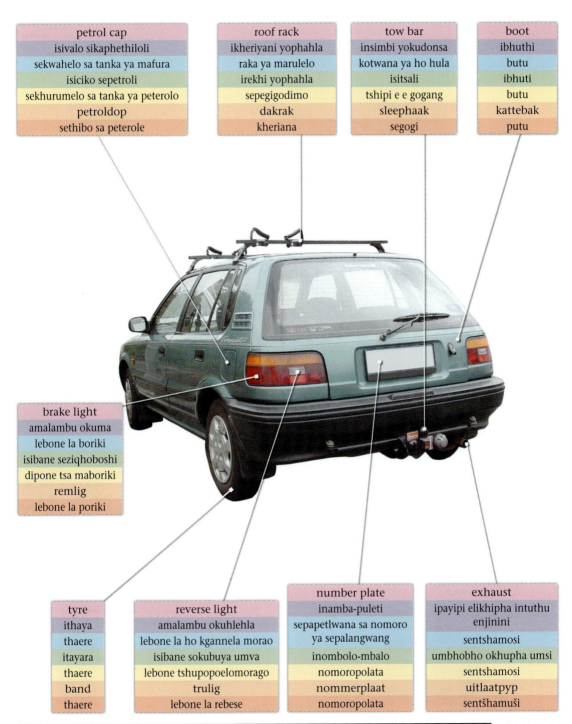

petrol cap
isivalo sikaphethiloli
sekwahelo sa tanka ya mafura
isiciko sepetroli
sekhurumelo sa tanka ya peterolo
petroldop
sethibo sa peterole

roof rack
ikheriyani yophahla
raka ya marulelo
irekhi yophahla
sepegigodimo
dakrak
kheriana

tow bar
insimbi yokudonsa
kotwana ya ho hula
isitsali
tshipi e e gogang
sleephaak
segogi

boot
ibhuthi
butu
ibhuti
butu
kattebak
putu

brake light
amalambu okuma
lebone la boriki
isibane seziqhoboshi
dipone tsa maboriki
remlig
lebone la poriki

tyre
ithaya
thaere
itayara
thaere
band
thaere

reverse light
amalambu okuhlehla
lebone la ho kgannela morao
isibane sokubuya umva
lebone tshupopoelomorago
trulig
lebone la rebese

number plate
inamba-puleti
sepapetlwana sa nomoro
ya sepalangwang
inombolo-mbalo
nomoropolata
nommerplaat
nomoropolata

exhaust
ipayipi elikhipha intuthu
enjinini
sentshamosi
umbhobho okhupha umsi
sentshamosi
uitlaatpyp
sentšhamuši

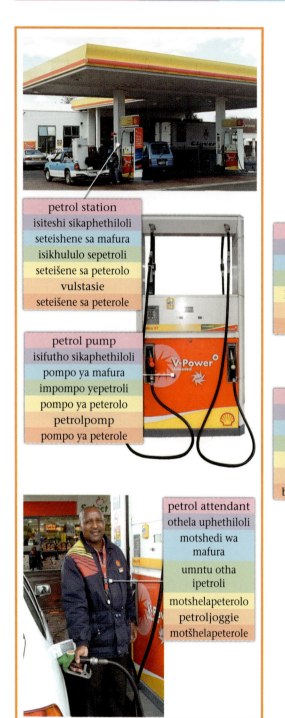

petrol station
isiteshi sikaphethiloli
seteishene sa mafura
isikhululo sepetroli
seteišene sa peterolo
vulstasie
seteišene sa peterole

petrol pump
isifutho sikaphethiloli
pompo ya mafura
impompo yepetroli
pompo ya peterolo
petrolpomp
pompo ya peterole

petrol attendant
othela uphethiloli
motshedi wa mafura
umntu otha ipetroli
motshelapeterolo
petroljoggie
motšhelapeterole

glove compartment
ingosana yamagilavu
phaposana ya ho boloka dintho
ikhompatmenti yezinto
khebule
paneelkassie
kheibole

seat belt
ibhande lesihlalo
lebanta la pholoho
ibhanti lokhuseleko
lebanta la pabalesego
sitplekgordel
lepanta la tšhireletšo

passenger seat
isihlalo somgibeli
setulo sa mopalami
isihlalo somkhweli
setilo sa mopagami
passasiersitplek
bodulo bja monamedi

Sejanaga 2 Motor 2 Sefatanaga 2

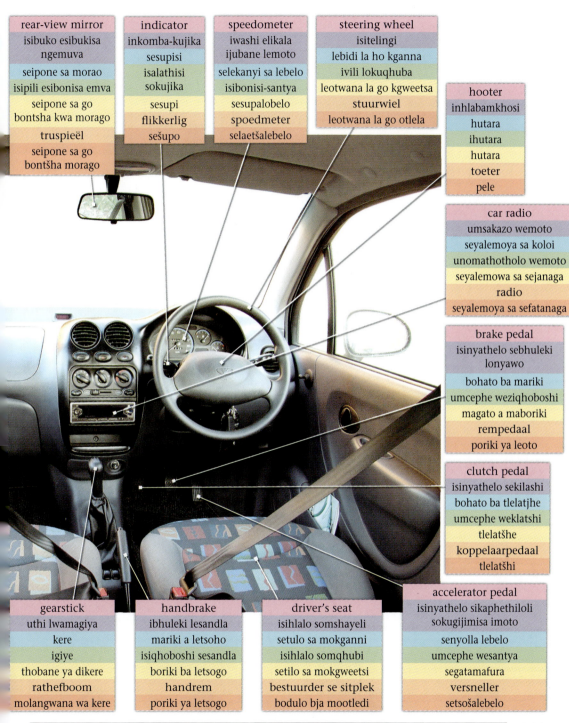

rear-view mirror
isibuko esibukisa ngemuva
seipone sa morao
isipili esibonisa emva
seipone sa go bontsha kwa morago
truspieël
seipone sa go bontšha morago

indicator
inkomba-kujika
sesupisi
isalathisi
sokujika
sesupi
flikkerlig
sešupo

speedometer
iwashi elikala
ijubane lemoto
selekanyi sa lebelo
isibonisi-santya
sesupalobelo
spoedmeter
selaetšalebelo

steering wheel
isitelingi
lebidi la ho kganna
ivili lokuqhuba
leotwana la go kgweetsa
stuurwiel
leotwana la go otlela

hooter
inhlabamkhosi
hutara
ihutara
hutara
toeter
pele

car radio
umsakazo wemoto
seyalemoya sa koloi
unomathotholo wemoto
seyalemowa sa sejanaga
radio
seyalemoya sa sefatanaga

brake pedal
isinyathelo sebhuleki lonyawo
bohato ba mariki
umcephe weziqhoboshi
magato a maboriki
rempedaal
poriki ya leoto

clutch pedal
isinyathelo sekilashi
bohato ba tlelatjhe
umcephe weklatshi
tlelatšhe
koppelaarpedaal
tlelatši

accelerator pedal
isinyathelo sikaphethiloli sokugijimisa imoto
senyolla lebelo
umcephe wesantya
segatamafura
versneller
setsošalebelo

gearstick
uthi lwamagiya
kere
igiye
thobane ya dikere
rathefboom
molangwana wa kere

handbrake
ibhuleki lesandla
mariki a letsoho
isiqhoboshi sesandla
boriki ba letsogo
handrem
poriki ya letsogo

driver's seat
isihlalo somshayeli
setulo sa mokganni
isihlalo somqhubi
setilo sa mokgweetsi
bestuurder se sitplek
bodulo bja mootledi

Take the bus or taxi	Gibela ibhasi noma itekisi	Palama bese kapa tekesi	Thatha ibhasi okanye iteksi

bus driver
umshayeli webhasi
mokganni wa bese
umqhubi kadula-dula
mokgweetsi wa bese
busbestuurder
mootledi wa pese

stop button
inkinobho yokumisa ibhasi
konopo ya ho emisa
iqhosha lokumisa
konopo ya go emisa
stopknoppie
konope ya go emiša

bus stop
isitobhi sebhasi
boemabese
isikhululo sebhasi
boemelabese
bushalte
boemapese

bus seat
isihlalo sebhasi
setulo sa bese
isihlalo sebhasi
setilo sa bese
sitplek
bodulo bja pese

EMERGENCY EXIT

emergency exit
intuba yokuphuma uma kuvela ingozi kungazelelwe
monyako wa tlokotsi
indawo yokuphuma buphuthu-phuthu
kgorwana ya botso jwa tshoganyetso
nooduitgang
botšotšhoganetšo

double-decker bus
ibhasi eyisitezi
bese ya mokolohanyo
ibhasi enemigangatho emibini
bese ya metlhatlagano e mebedi
dubbeldekker
pese ya mahlatlagano

topless bus
ibhasi engenalo uphahla
bese e bulehileng ya bahahlaudi
ibhasi yabakhenkethi engenaluphahla
bese e e senang bogodimo
oopdekbus
pese ya go hloka bogodimo

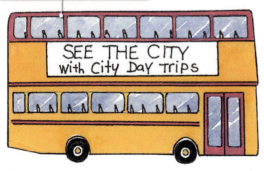

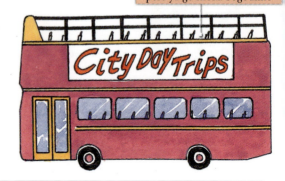

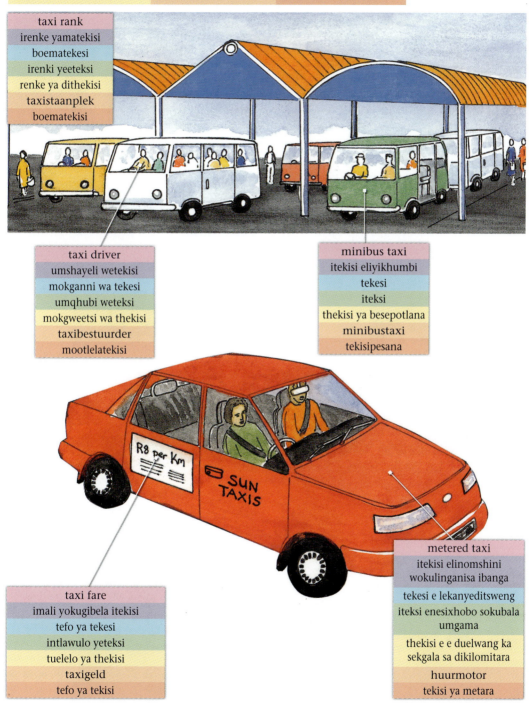

Dirisa bese kgotsa thekisi   **Haal die bus of taxi**   **Namela pese goba tekisi**

taxi rank
irenke yamatekisi
boematekesi
irenki yeeteksi
renke ya dithekisi
taxistaanplek
boematekisi

taxi driver
umshayeli wetekisi
mokganni wa tekesi
umqhubi weteksi
mokgweetsi wa thekisi
taxibestuurder
mootlelatekisi

minibus taxi
itekisi eliyikhumbi
tekesi
iteksi
thekisi ya besepotlana
minibustaxi
tekisipesana

taxi fare
imali yokugibela itekisi
tefo ya tekesi
intlawulo yeteksi
tuelelo ya thekisi
taxigeld
tefo ya tekisi

metered taxi
itekisi elinomshini wokulinganisa ibanga
tekesi e lekanyeditsweng
iteksi enesixhobo sokubala umgama
thekisi e e duelwang ka sekgala sa dikilomitara
huurmotor
tekisi ya metara

Vehicles on the road	Izithuthi emgwaqeni	Dikoloi tsa mmileng	Izithuthi ezindleleni

motorcycle
isithuthuthu
sethuthuthu
isithuthuthu
sethuuthuu
motorfiets
thuthuthu

bicycle
ibhayisikili
baesekele
ibhayisekile
baesekele
fiets
paesekela

scooter
isithuthuthu esincane
sekutara
isikuta
sekutara
bromponie
sekuta

cart
ikalishi
kariki
inqwelo
kariki
kar
kariki

car
imoto
koloi
imoto
koloi
motor
koloi

bakkie
isikeqane
vene
ibhaki
modiro wa bene
bakkie
paki

ambulance
i-ambulense
ambolense
inqwelo yezigulana
ambulanse
ambulans
amalanse

fire engine
injini enesicimamlilo
setimamollo
isicima mlilo
sejanaga sa batimamolelo
brandweerwa
entšene ya mollo

Dijanaga mo tseleng | Voertuie op die pad | Difatanaga mmileng

truck	lorry
ithilakhi	iloli
teraka	lori
inqwelo yempahla	ilori
theraka	lori
trok	vragmotor
theraka	lori

rubbish removal lorry
iloli ethutha udoti
lori ya dithole
inqwelo yokuthutha inkunkuma
seroramatlakala
vulliswa
lori ya go rwala ditshila

forklift
umshini wokufukula
sephahamisi se bofereko
isiphakamisi mpahla
foroko setsholetsi
vurkkraan
foroko ya go sephagamiši

grader
isigugula
kereitara
uganda-ganda
kereitara
skraper
kereitara

earthmover
umshini wokududula inhlabathi
lori e kgathang mobu
isityhala-mhlaba
serorammu
laaigraaf
serwalamabu

concrete mixer
umshini wokuxova usemende
lori e tswakang konkereiti
isixubi-konkriti
setlhakanya konkoreite
betonmenger
sehlakanyakonkorite

tractor
ugandaganda
terekere
itrekta
terekere
trekker
terekere

Bicycle Ibhayisikili Baesekele Ibhayisekile Baesekele Fiets Paesekele

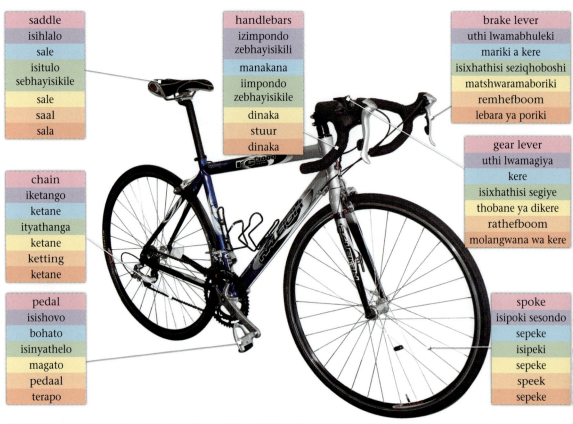

saddle
isihlalo
sale
isitulo sebhayisikile
sale
saal
sala

handlebars
izimpondo zebhayisikili
manakana
iimpondo zebhayisikili
dinaka
stuur
dinaka

brake lever
uthi lwamabhuleki
mariki a kere
isixhathisi seziqhoboshi
matshwaramaboriki
remhefboom
lebara ya poriki

gear lever
uthi lwamagiya
kere
isixhathisi segiye
thobane ya dikere
rathefboom
molangwana wa kere

chain
iketango
ketane
ityathanga
ketane
ketting
ketane

pedal
isishovo
bohato
isinyathelo
magato
pedaal
terapo

spoke
isipoki sesondo
sepeke
isipeki
sepeke
speek
sepeke

tricycle
ibhayisikili elinamasondo amathathu
baesekele e mabidi a mararo
ibhayisekile enamavili amathathu
baesekele ya maoto a mararo
driewiel
paesekele ya maotwana a mararo

mountain bike
ibhayisikili lokucaca intaba
baesekele ya thaba
ibhayisekile yokunyuka intaba
baesekele ya thaba
bergfiets
paesekele ya thaba

racing bike
ibhayisikili lomjaho
baesekele ya mabelo
ibhayisekile yogqatso
baesekele ya lobelo
resiesfiets
paesekele ya go beišana

bicycle pump
isifutho sebhayisikili
pompo ya baesekele
impompo yebhayisekile
pompo ya baesekele
fietspomp
pompo ya paesekele

Motorcycle Isithuthuthu Sethuthuthu Isithuthuthu Sethuuthuu Motorfiets Sethuthuthu

handlebars	brake	accelerator	petrol tank	seat
izimpondo zesithuthuthu	ibhuleki	isinyathelo sikaphethiloli sokukhuphula ijubane	ithangi likaphethiloli	isihlalo
manakana	mariki	senyolla lebelo	tanka ya mafura	setulo
impondo zokuqhuba	isiqhoboshi	umcephe wesantya	itanki lepetroli	isitulo
dinaka	maboriki	seoketsalobelo	tanka ya peterolo	setilo
stuur	rem	versneller	petroltenk	sitplek
manakana	poriki	seoketšamakhura	tanka ya peterole	bodulo

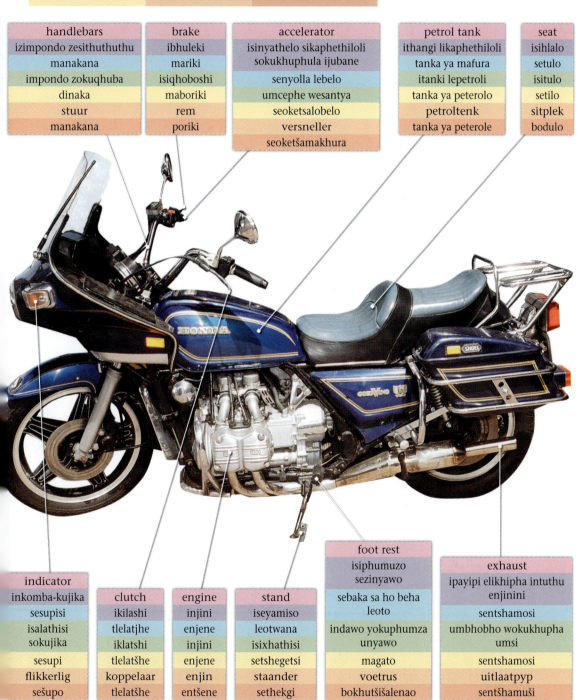

indicator	clutch	engine	stand	foot rest	exhaust
inkomba-kujika				isiphumuzo sezinyawo	ipayipi elikhipha intuthu enjinini
sesupisi	ikilashi	injini	iseyamiso	sebaka sa ho beha leoto	sentshamosi
isalathisi	tlelatjhe	enjene	leotwana	indawo yokuphumza unyawo	umbhobho wokukhupha umsi
sokujika	iklatshi	injini	isixhathisi		
sesupi	tlelatšhe	enjene	setshegetsi	magato	sentshamosi
flikkerlig	koppelaar	enjin	staander	voetrus	uitlaatpyp
sešupo	tlelatšhe	entšene	sethekgi	bokhutšišalenao	sentšhamuši

harvester
umshini wokuvuna
motjhini o kotulang
umatshini wokuvuna
motšhini o o robang
stroper
motšhene wa go buna

trailer
inqola ehudulwayo
sekosekara
inqwelo erhuqwayo
kolotsana
sleepwa
thereilara

horse cart
ikalishi lehhashi
kariki ya dipere
inqwelo yamahashe
kariki ya dipitse
perdekar
kariki ya dipere

Mo polaseng Op die plaas Polaseng

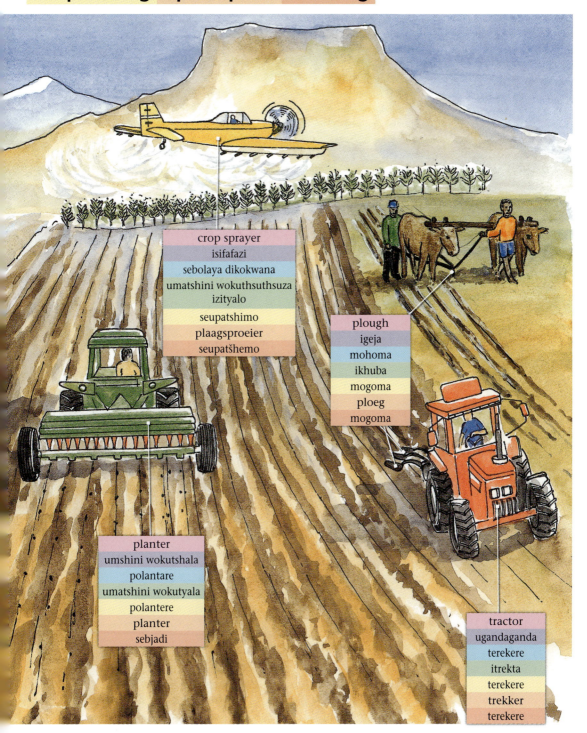

crop sprayer
isifafazi
sebolaya dikokwana
umatshini wokuthsuthsuza izityalo
seupatshimo
plaagsproeier
seupatšhemo

plough
igeja
mohoma
ikhuba
mogoma
ploeg
mogoma

planter
umshini wokutshala
polantare
umatshini wokutyala
polantere
planter
sebjadi

tractor
ugandaganda
terekere
itrekta
terekere
trekker
terekere

On the road Emgwaqweni Mmileng Endleleni

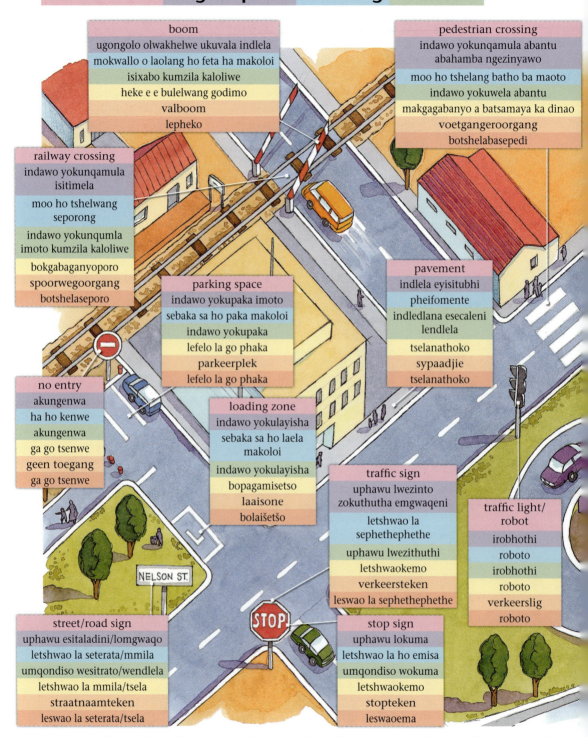

boom
ugongolo olwakhelwe ukuvala indlela
mokwallo o laolang ho feta ha makoloi
isixabo kumzila kaloliwe
heke e e bulelwang godimo
valboom
lepheko

pedestrian crossing
indawo yokunqamula abantu abahamba ngezinyawo
moo ho tshelang batho ba maoto
indawo yokuwela abantu
makgagabanyo a batsamaya ka dinao
voetgangeroorgang
botshelabasepedi

railway crossing
indawo yokunqamula isitimela
moo ho tshelwang seporong
indawo yokunqumla imoto kumzila kaloliwe
bokgabaganyoporo
spoorwegoorgang
botshelaseporo

parking space
indawo yokupaka imoto
sebaka sa ho paka makoloi
indawo yokupaka
lefelo la go phaka
parkeerplek
lefelo la go phaka

pavement
indlela eyisitubhi
pheifomente
indledlana esecaleni lendlela
tselanathoko
sypaadjie
tselanathoko

no entry
akungenwa
ha ho kenwe
akungenwa
ga go tsenwe
geen toegang
ga go tsenwe

loading zone
indawo yokulayisha
sebaka sa ho laela makoloi
indawo yokulayisha
bopagamisetso
laaisone
bolaišetšo

traffic sign
uphawu lwezinto zokuthutha emgwaqeni
letshwao la sephethephethe
uphawu lwezithuthi
letshwaokemo
verkeersteken
leswao la sephethephethe

traffic light/ robot
irobhothi
roboto
irobhothi
roboto
verkeerslig
roboto

NELSON ST.

STOP

street/road sign
uphawu esitaladini/lomgwaqo
letshwao la seterata/mmila
umqondiso wesitrato/wendlela
letshwao la mmila/tsela
straatnaamteken
leswao la seterata/tsela

stop sign
uphawu lokuma
letshwao la ho emisa
umqondiso wokuma
letshwaokemo
stopteken
leswaoema

120

Mo tseleng Op die pad Mmileng

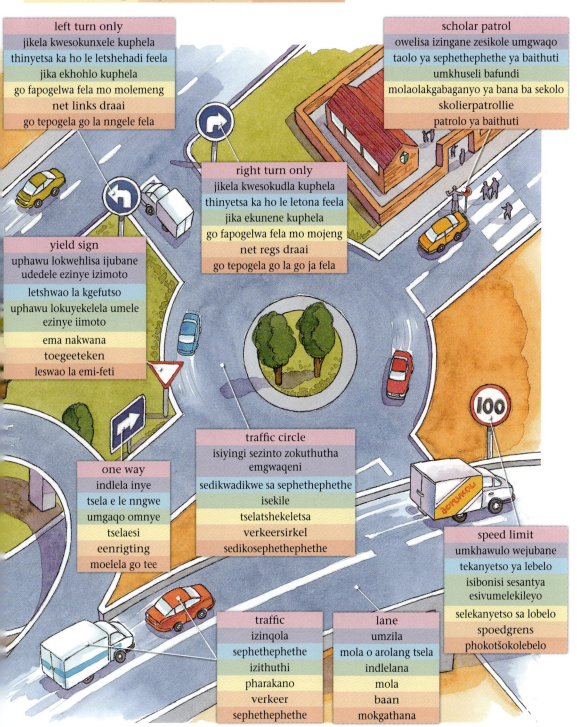

left turn only
jikela kwesokunxele kuphela
thinyetsa ka ho le letshehadi feela
jika ekhohlo kuphela
go fapogelwa fela mo molemeng
net links draai
go tepogela go la nngele fela

scholar patrol
owelisa izingane zesikole umgwaqo
taolo ya sephethephethe ya baithuti
umkhuseli bafundi
molaolakgabaganyo ya bana ba sekolo
skolierpatrollie
patrolo ya baithuti

right turn only
jikela kwesokudla kuphela
thinyetsa ka ho le letona feela
jika ekunene kuphela
go fapogelwa fela mo mojeng
net regs draai
go tepogela go la go ja fela

yield sign
uphawu lokwehlisa ijubane
udedele ezinye izimoto
letshwao la kgefutso
uphawu lokuyekelela umele
ezinye iimoto
ema nakwana
toegeeteken
leswao la emi-feti

one way
indlela inye
tsela e le nngwe
umgaqo omnye
tselaesi
eenrigting
moelela go tee

traffic circle
isiyingi sezinto zokuthutha
emgwaqeni
sedikwadikwe sa sephethephethe
isekile
tselatshekeletsa
verkeersirkel
sedikosephethephethe

speed limit
umkhawulo wejubane
tekanyetso ya lebelo
isibonisi sesantya
esivumelekileyo
selekanyetso sa lobelo
spoedgrens
phokotšokolebelo

traffic
izinqola
sephethephethe
izithuthi
pharakano
verkeer
sephethephethe

lane
umzila
mola o arolang tsela
indlelana
mola
baan
mokgathana

Railway station	Isiteshi sesitimela	Seteishene sa terene	Isikhululo sikaloliwe

electric pylon
isigxobo esikhulu esithwala izintambo zikagesi
lenaka la tshepe la motlakase
uphondo lwenstimbi yombane
lenaka la tshipi la motlakase
elektriese toring
toro ya mohlagase

bridge
ibhuloho
borokgo
ibhulorho
borogo
brug
leporogo

train
isitimela
terene
uloliwe
terena
trein
setimela

signal
inkombisa
letshwao
isalathisi
letshwao
sinjaal
leswao

subway
umgwaqo oguduza ngaphansi
tsela e tswang tlasa seporo
indlela ephuma ngaphantsi
kgogametso
duikweg
bohuhumelo

conductor
unogada
mohlokomedi wa bapalami
umnqomfimatikiti
molaoditereneng
kondukteur
kontae

passenger
umgibeli
mopalami
umkhweli
mopagami
passasier
monamedi

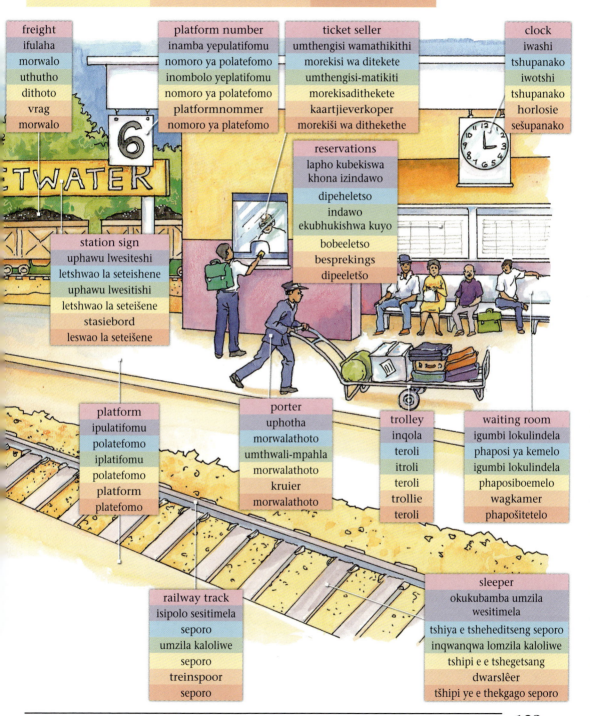

Seteišene sa terena · Spoorwegstasie · Seteišene sa setimela

freight
ifulaha
morwalo
uthutho
dithoto
vrag
morwalo

platform number
inamba yepulatifomu
nomoro ya polatefomo
inombolo yeplatifomu
nomoro ya polatefomo
platformnommer
nomoro ya platefomo

ticket seller
umthengisi wamathikithi
morekisi wa ditekete
umthengisi-matikiti
morekisadithekete
kaartjieverkoper
morekiši wa dithekethe

clock
iwashi
tshupanako
iwotshi
tshupanako
horlosie
sešupanako

reservations
lapho kubekiswa khona izindawo
dipeheletso
indawo ekubhukishwa kuyo
bobeeletso
besprekings
dipeeletšo

station sign
uphawu lwesiteshi
letshwao la seteishene
uphawu lwesitishi
letshwao la seteišene
stasiebord
leswao la seteišene

platform
ipulatifomu
polatefomo
iplatifomu
polatefomo
platform
platefomo

porter
uphotha
morwalathoto
umthwali-mpahla
morwalathoto
kruier
morwalathoto

trolley
inqola
teroli
itroli
teroli
trollie
teroli

waiting room
igumbi lokulindela
phaposi ya kemelo
igumbi lokulindela
phaposiboemelo
wagkamer
phapošitetelo

railway track
isipolo sesitimela
seporo
umzila kaloliwe
seporo
treinspoor
seporo

sleeper
okukubamba umzila wesitimela
tshiya e tsheheditseng seporo
inqwanqwa lomzila kaloliwe
tshipi e e tshegetsang
dwarslêer
tšhipi ye e thekgago seporo

Trains Izitimela Diterene Oololiwe

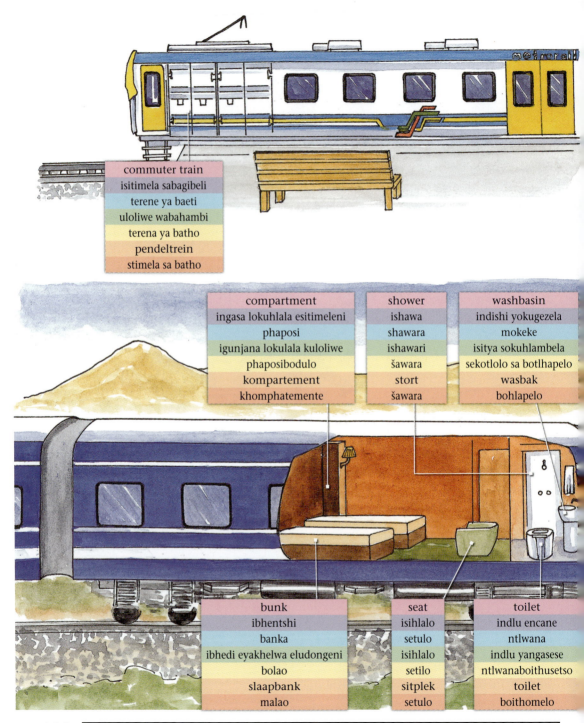

commuter train
isitimela sabagibeli
terene ya baeti
uloliwe wabahambi
terena ya batho
pendeltrein
stimela sa batho

compartment
ingasa lokuhlala esitimeleni
phaposi
igunjana lokulala kuloliwe
phaposibodulo
kompartement
khomphatemente

shower
ishawa
shawara
ishawari
šawara
stort
šawara

washbasin
indishi yokugezela
mokeke
isitya sokuhlambela
sekotlolo sa botlhapelo
wasbak
bohlapelo

bunk
ibhentshi
banka
ibhedi eyakhelwa eludongeni
bolao
slaapbank
malao

seat
isihlalo
setulo
isihlalo
setilo
sitplek
setulo

toilet
indlu encane
ntlwana
indlu yangasese
ntlwanaboithusetso
toilet
boithomelo

Diterena Treine Ditimela

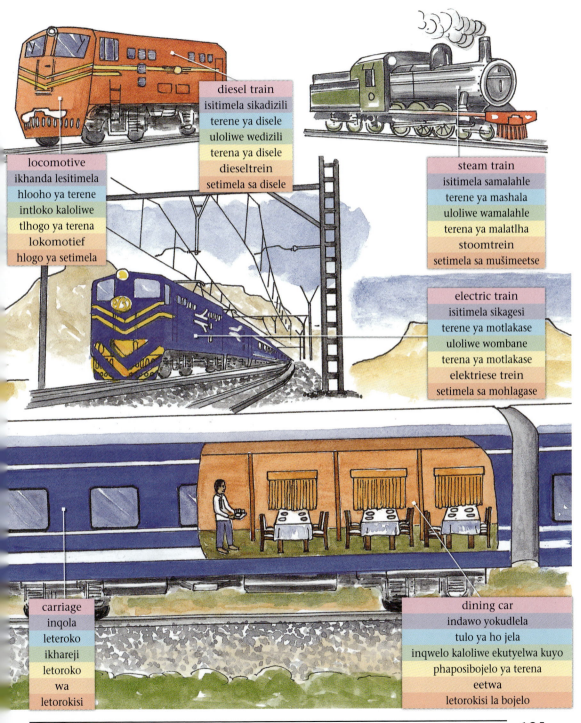

diesel train
isitimela sikadizili
terene ya disele
uloliwe wedizili
terena ya disele
dieseltrein
setimela sa disele

locomotive
ikhanda lesitimela
hlooho ya terene
intloko kaloliwe
tlhogo ya terena
lokomotief
hlogo ya setimela

steam train
isitimela samalahle
terene ya mashala
uloliwe wamalahle
terena ya malatlha
stoomtrein
setimela sa mušimeetse

electric train
isitimela sikagesi
terene ya motlakase
uloliwe wombane
terena ya motlakase
elektriese trein
setimela sa mohlagase

carriage
inqola
leteroko
ikhareji
letoroko
wa
letorokisi

dining car
indawo yokudlela
tulo ya ho jela
inqwelo kaloliwe ekutyelwa kuyo
phaposibojelo ya terena
eetwa
letorokisi la bojelo

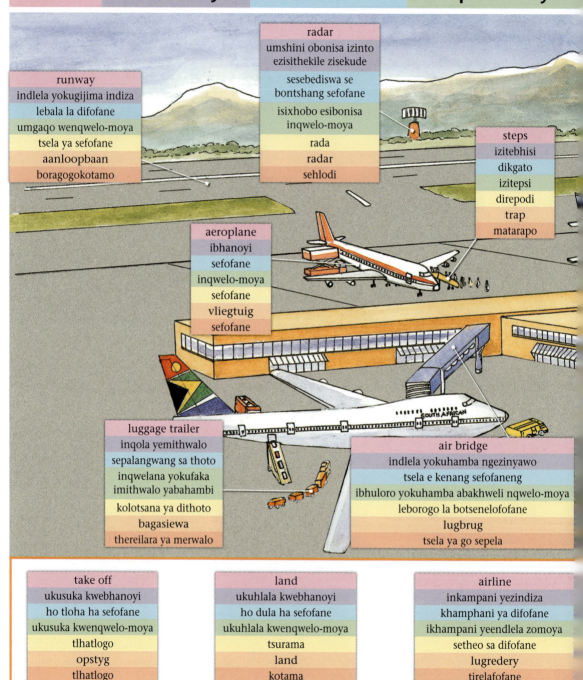

radar
umshini obonisa izinto ezisithekile zisekude
sesebediswa se bontshang sefofane
isixhobo esibonisa inqwelo-moya
rada
radar
sehlodi

runway
indlela yokugijima indiza
lebala la difofane
umgaqo wenqwelo-moya
tsela ya sefofane
aanloopbaan
boragogokotamo

steps
izitebhisi
dikgato
izitepsi
direpodi
trap
matarapo

aeroplane
ibhanoyi
sefofane
inqwelo-moya
sefofane
vliegtuig
sefofane

luggage trailer
inqola yemithwalo
sepalangwang sa thoto
inqwelana yokufaka imithwalo yabahambi
kolotsana ya dithoto
bagasiewa
thereilara ya merwalo

air bridge
indlela yokuhamba ngezinyawo
tsela e kenang sefofaneng
ibhuloro yokuhamba abakhweli nqwelo-moya
leborogo la botsenelofofane
lugbrug
tsela ya go sepela

take off
ukusuka kwebhanoyi
ho tloha ha sefofane
ukusuka kwenqwelo-moya
tlhatlogo
opstyg
tlhatlogo

land
ukuhlala kwebhanoyi
ho dula ha sefofane
ukuhlala kwenqwelo-moya
tsurama
land
kotama

airline
inkampani yezindiza
khamphani ya difofane
ikhampani yeendlela zomoya
setheo sa difofane
lugredery
tirelafofane

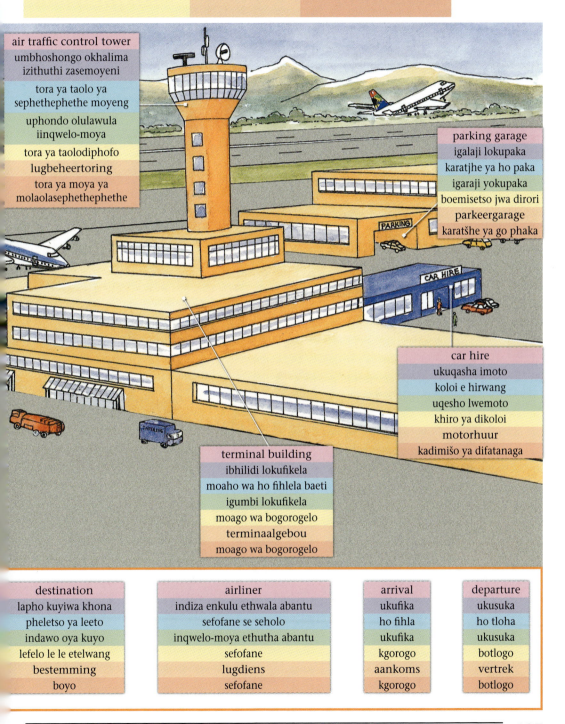

air traffic control tower
umbhoshongo okhalima izithuthi zasemoyeni
tora ya taolo ya sephethephethe moyeng
uphondo olulawula iinqwelo-moya
tora ya taolodiphofo
lugbeheertoring
tora ya moya ya molaolasephethephethe

parking garage
igalaji lokupaka
karatjhe ya ho paka
igaraji yokupaka
boemisetso jwa dirori
parkeergarage
karatšhe ya go phaka

car hire
ukuqasha imoto
koloi e hirwang
uqesho lwemoto
khiro ya dikoloi
motorhuur
kadimišo ya difatanaga

terminal building
ibhilidi lokufikela
moaho wa ho fihlela baeti
igumbi lokufikela
moago wa bogorogelo
terminaalgebou
moago wa bogorogelo

destination	**airliner**	**arrival**	**departure**
lapho kuyiwa khona	indiza enkulu ethwala abantu	ukufika	ukusuka
pheletso ya leeto	sefofane se seholo	ho fihla	ho tloha
indawo oya kuyo	inqwelo-moya ethutha abantu	ukufika	ukusuka
lefelo le le etelwang	sefofane	kgorogo	botlogo
bestemming	lugdiens	aankoms	vertrek
boyo	sefofane	kgorogo	botlogo

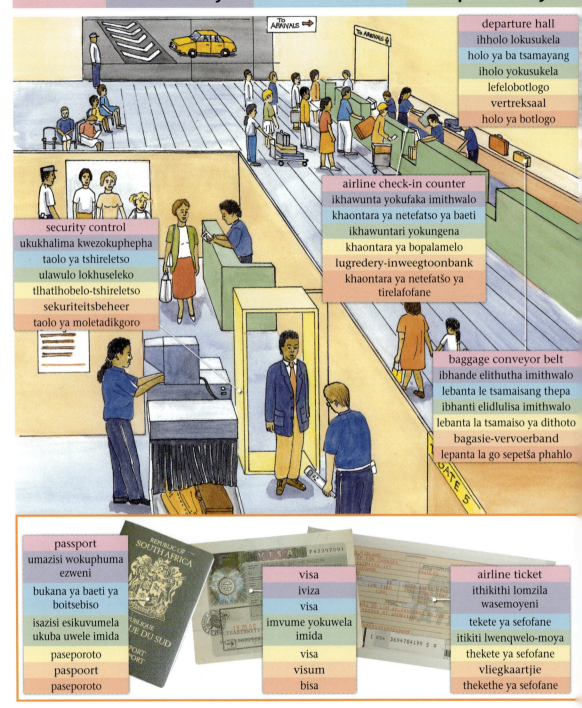

departure hall
ihholo lokusukela
holo ya ba tsamayang
iholo yokusukela
lefelobotlogo
vertreksaal
holo ya botlogo

airline check-in counter
ikhawunta yokufaka imithwalo
khaontara ya netefatso ya baeti
ikhawuntari yokungena
khaontara ya bopalamelo
lugredery-inweegtoonbank
khaontara ya netefatšo ya tirelafofane

security control
ukukhalima kwezokuphepha
taolo ya tshireletso
ulawulo lokhuseleko
tlhatlhobelo-tshireletso
sekuriteitsbeheer
taolo ya moletadikgoro

baggage conveyor belt
ibhande elithutha imithwalo
lebanta le tsamaisang thepa
ibhanti elidlulisa imithwalo
lebanta la tsamaiso ya dithoto
bagasie-vervoerband
lepanta la go sepetša phahlo

passport
umazisi wokuphuma ezweni
bukana ya baeti ya boitsebiso
isazisi esikuvumela ukuba uwele imida
paseporoto
paspoort
paseporoto

visa
iviza
visa
imvume yokuwela imida
visa
visum
bisa

airline ticket
ithikithi lomzila wasemoyeni
tekete ya sefofane
itikiti lwenqwelo-moya
thekete ya sefofane
vliegkaartjie
thekethe ya sefofane

Boemelafofane 2 Lughawe 2 Boemafofane 2

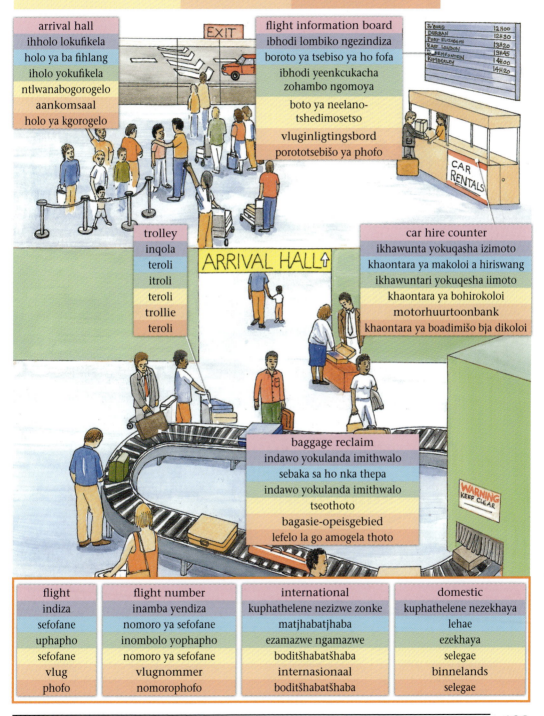

arrival hall
ihholo lokufikela
holo ya ba fihlang
iholo yokufikela
ntlwanabogorogelo
aankomsaal
holo ya kgorogelo

flight information board
ibhodi lombiko ngezindiza
boroto ya tsebiso ya ho fofa
ibhodi yeenkcukacha zohambo ngomoya
boto ya neelano-tshedimosetso
vluginligtingsbord
porototsebišo ya phofo

trolley
inqola
teroli
itroli
teroli
trollie
teroli

car hire counter
ikhawunta yokuqasha izimoto
khaontara ya makoloi a hiriswang
ikhawuntari yokuqesha iimoto
khaontara ya bohirokoloi
motorhuurtoonbank
khaontara ya boadimišo bja dikoloi

baggage reclaim
indawo yokulanda imithwalo
sebaka sa ho nka thepa
indawo yokulanda imithwalo
tseothoto
bagasie-opeisgebied
lefelo la go amogela thoto

flight	**flight number**	**international**	**domestic**
indiza	inamba yendiza	kuphathelene nezizwe zonke	kuphathelene nezekhaya
sefofane	nomoro ya sefofane	matjhabatjhaba	lehae
uphapho	inombolo yophapho	ezamazwe ngamazwe	ezekhaya
sefofane	nomoro ya sefofane	boditšhabatšhaba	selegae
vlug	vlugnommer	internasionaal	binnelands
phofo	nomorophofo	boditšhabatšhaba	selegae

Aeroplane Ibhanoyi Sefofane Inqwelo-moya

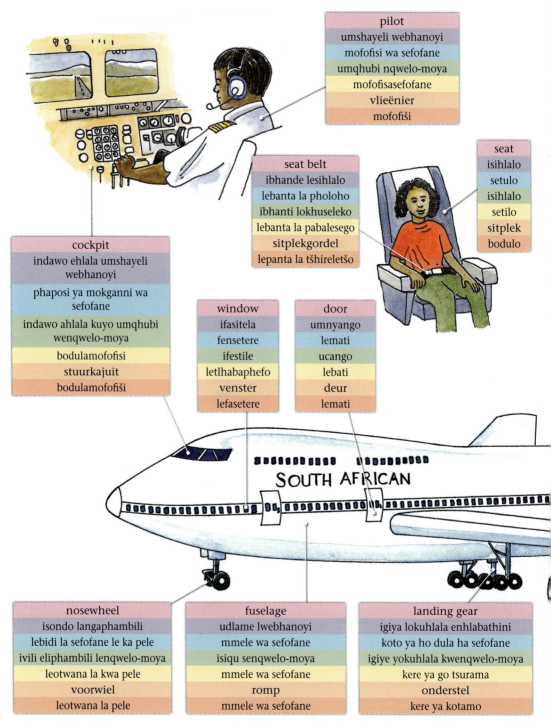

pilot
umshayeli webhanoyi
mofofisi wa sefofane
umqhubi nqwelo-moya
mofofisasefofane
vlieënier
mofofiši

seat
isihlalo
setulo
isihlalo
setilo
sitplek
bodulo

seat belt
ibhande lesihlalo
lebanta la pholoho
ibhanti lokhuseleko
lebanta la pabalesego
sitplekgordel
lepanta la tšhireletšo

cockpit
indawo ehlala umshayeli webhanoyi
phaposi ya mokganni wa sefofane
indawo ahlala kuyo umqhubi wenqwelo-moya
bodulamofofisi
stuurkajuit
bodulamofofiši

window
ifasitela
fensetere
ifestile
letlhabaphefo
venster
lefasetere

door
umnyango
lemati
ucango
lebati
deur
lemati

SOUTH AFRICAN

nosewheel
isondo langaphambili
lebidi la sefofane le ka pele
ivili eliphambili lenqwelo-moya
leotwana la kwa pele
voorwiel
leotwana la pele

fuselage
udlame lwebhanoyi
mmele wa sefofane
isiqu senqwelo-moya
mmele wa sefofane
romp
mmele wa sefofane

landing gear
igiya lokuhlala enhlabathini
koto ya ho dula ha sefofane
igiye yokuhlala kwenqwelo-moya
kere ya go tsurama
onderstel
kere ya kotamo

Sefofane Vliegtuig Sefofane

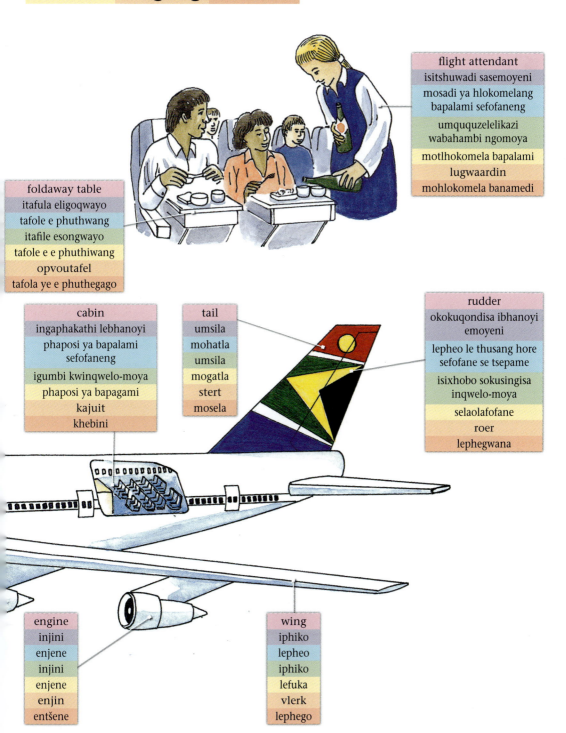

flight attendant
isitshuwadi sasemoyeni
mosadi ya hlokomelang bapalami sefofaneng
umququzelelikazi wabahambi ngomoya
motlhokomela bapalami
lugwaardin
mohlokomela banamedi

foldaway table
itafula eligoqwayo
tafole e phuthwang
itafile esongwayo
tafole e e phuthiwang
opvoutafel
tafola ye e phuthegago

cabin
ingaphakathi lebhanoyi
phaposi ya bapalami sefofaneng
igumbi kwinqwelo-moya
phaposi ya bapagami
kajuit
khebini

tail
umsila
mohatla
umsila
mogatla
stert
mosela

rudder
okokuqondisa ibhanoyi emoyeni
lepheo le thusang hore sefofane se tsepame
isixhobo sokusingisa inqwelo-moya
selaolafofane
roer
lephegwana

engine
injini
enjene
injini
enjene
enjin
entšene

wing
iphiko
lepheo
iphiko
lefuka
vlerk
lephego

Aircraft Ibhanoyi Sefofane Inqwelo-moya

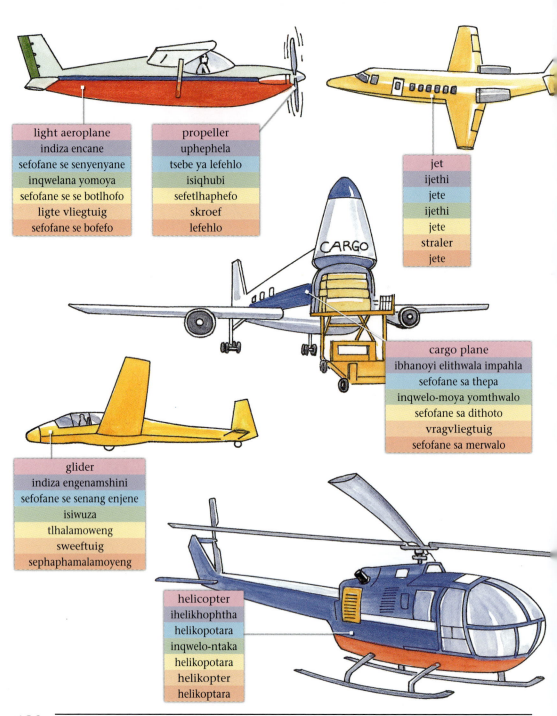

light aeroplane
indiza encane
sefofane se senyenyane
inqwelana yomoya
sefofane se se botlhofo
ligte vliegtuig
sefofane se bofefo

propeller
uphephela
tsebe ya lefehlo
isiqhubi
sefetlhaphefo
skroef
lefehlo

jet
ijethi
jete
ijethi
jete
straler
jete

cargo plane
ibhanoyi elithwala impahla
sefofane sa thepa
inqwelo-moya yomthwalo
sefofane sa dithoto
vragvliegtuig
sefofane sa merwalo

glider
indiza engenamshini
sefofane se senang enjene
isiwuza
tlhalamoweng
sweeftuig
sephaphamalamoyeng

helicopter
ihelikhophtha
helikopotara
inqwelo-ntaka
helikopotara
helikopter
helikoptara

Sefofane Vliegtuie Sefofane

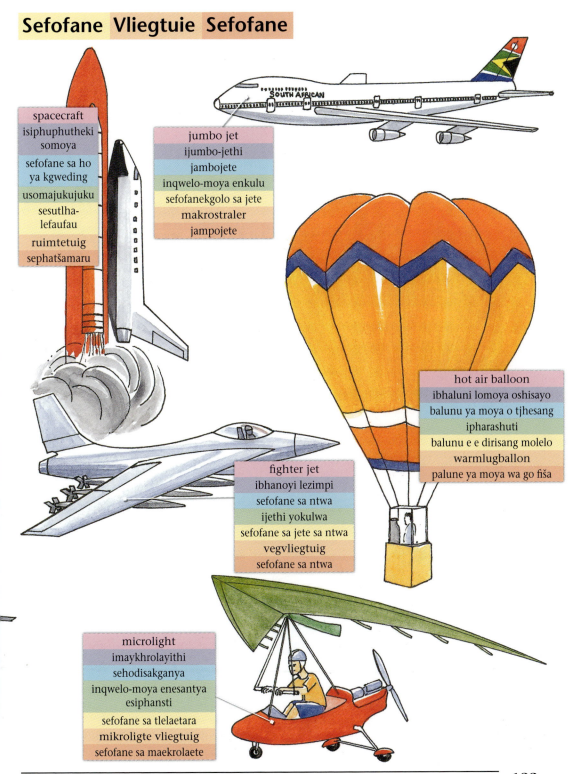

spacecraft
isiphuphutheki somoya
sefofane sa ho ya kgweding
usomajukujuku
sesutlha-lefaufau
ruimtetuig
sephatšamaru

jumbo jet
ijumbo-jethi
jambojete
inqwelo-moya enkulu
sefofanekgolo sa jete
makrostraler
jampojete

hot air balloon
ibhaluni lomoya oshisayo
balunu ya moya o tjhesang
ipharashuti
balunu e e dirisang molelo
warmlugballon
palune ya moya wa go fiša

fighter jet
ibhanoyi lezimpi
sefofane sa ntwa
ijethi yokulwa
sefofane sa jete sa ntwa
vegvliegtuig
sefofane sa ntwa

microlight
imaykhrolayithi
sehodisakganya
inqwelo-moya enesantya esiphansti
sefofane sa tlelaetara
mikroligte vliegtuig
sefofane sa maekrolaete

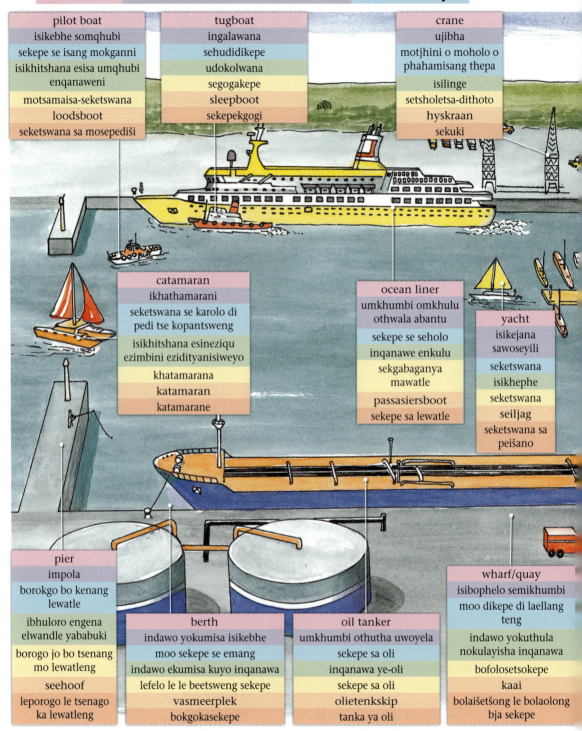

pilot boat
isikebhe somqhubi
sekepe se isang mokganni
isikhitshana esisa umqhubi enqanaweni
motsamaisa-seketswana
loodsboot
seketswana sa mosepediši

tugboat
ingalawana
sehudidikepe
udokolwana
segogakepe
sleepboot
sekepekgogi

crane
ujibha
motjhini o moholo o phahamisang thepa
isilinge
setsholetsa-dithoto
hyskraan
sekuki

catamaran
ikhathamarani
seketswana se karolo di pedi tse kopantsweng
isikhitshana esineziqu ezimbini eziditsyanisiweyo
khatamarana
katamaran
katamarane

ocean liner
umkhumbi omkhulu othwala abantu
sekepe se seholo
inqanawe enkulu
sekgabaganya mawatle
passasiersboot
sekepe sa lewatle

yacht
isikejana sawoseyili
seketswana
isikhephe
seketswana
seiljag
seketswana sa peišano

pier
impola
borokgo bo kenang lewatle
ibhuloro engena elwandle yababuki
borogo jo bo tsenang mo lewatleng
seehoof
leporogo le tsenago ka lewatleng

berth
indawo yokumisa isikebhe
moo sekepe se emang
indawo ekumisa kuyo inqanawa
lefelo le le beetsweng sekepe
vasmeerplek
bokgokasekepe

oil tanker
umkhumbi othutha uwoyela
sekepe sa oli
inqanawa ye-oli
sekepe sa oli
olietenkskip
tanka ya oli

wharf/quay
isibophelo semikhumbi
moo dikepe di laellang teng
indawo yokuthula nokulayisha inqanawa
bofolosetsokepe
kaai
bolaišetšong le bolaolong bja sekepe

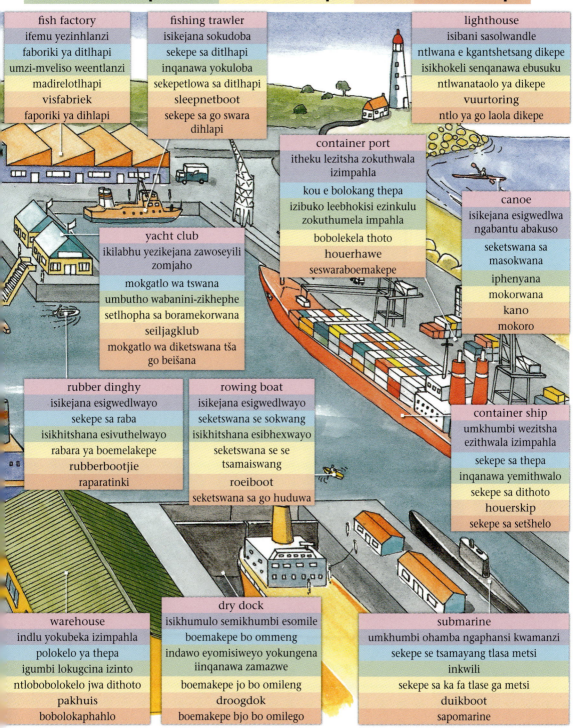

Izibuko leenqanawa Boemelakepe Hawe Boemakepe

fish factory
ifemu yezinhlanzi
faboriki ya ditlhapi
umzi-mveliso weentlanzi
madirelotlhapi
visfabriek
faporiki ya dihlapi

fishing trawler
isikejana sokudoba
sekepe sa ditlhapi
inqanawa yokuloba
sekepetlowa sa ditlhapi
sleepnetboot
sekepe sa go swara
dihlapi

lighthouse
isibani sasolwandle
ntlwana e kgantshetsang dikepe
isikhokeli senqanawa ebusuku
ntlwanataolo ya dikepe
vuurtoring
ntlo ya go laola dikepe

container port
itheku lezitsha zokuthwala
izimpahla
kou e bolokang thepa
izibuko leebhokisi ezinkulu
zokuthumela impahla
bobolekela thoto
houerhawe
seswaraboemakepe

canoe
isikejana esigwedlwa
ngabantu abakuso
seketswana sa
masokwana
iphenyana
mokorwana
kano
mokoro

yacht club
ikilabhu yezikejana zawoseyili
zomjaho
mokgatlo wa tswana
umbutho wabanini-zikhephe
setlhopha sa boramekorwana
seiljagklub
mokgatlo wa diketswana tša
go beišana

rubber dinghy
isikejana esigwedlwayo
sekepe sa raba
isikhitshana esivuthelwayo
rabara ya boemelakepe
rubberbootjie
raparatinki

rowing boat
isikejana esigwedlwayo
seketswana se sokwang
isikhitshana esibhexwayo
seketswana se se
tsamaiswang
roeiboot
seketswana sa go huduwa

container ship
umkhumbi wezitsha
ezithwala izimpahla
sekepe sa thepa
inqanawa yemithwalo
sekepe sa dithoto
houerskip
sekepe sa setšhelo

warehouse
indlu yokubeka izimpahla
polokelo ya thepa
igumbi lokugcina izinto
ntlobobolokelo jwa dithoto
pakhuis
bobolokaphahlo

dry dock
isikhumulo semikhumbi esomile
boemakepe bo ommeng
indawo eyomisiweyo yokungena
iinqanawa zamazwe
boemakepe jo bo omileng
droogdok
boemakepe bjo bo omilego

submarine
umkhumbi ohamba ngaphansi kwamanzi
sekepe se tsamayang tlasa metsi
inkwili
sekepe sa ka fa tlase ga metsi
duikboot
sapomarine

Ship Umkhumbi Sekepe Inqanawa

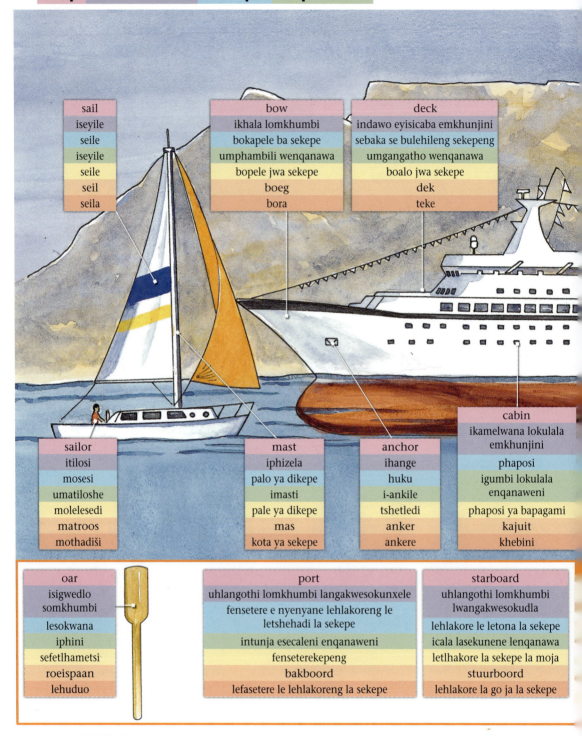

sail
iseyile
seile
iseyile
seile
seil
seila

bow
ikhala lomkhumbi
bokapele ba sekepe
umphambili wenqanawa
bopele jwa sekepe
boeg
bora

deck
indawo eyisicaba emkhunjini
sebaka se bulehileng sekepeng
umgangatho wenqanawa
boalo jwa sekepe
dek
teke

sailor
itilosi
mosesi
umatiloshe
molelesedi
matroos
mothadiši

mast
iphizela
palo ya dikepe
imasti
pale ya dikepe
mas
kota ya sekepe

anchor
ihange
huku
i-ankile
tshetledi
anker
ankere

cabin
ikamelwana lokulala emkhunjini
phaposi
igumbi lokulala enqanaweni
phaposi ya bapagami
kajuit
khebini

oar
isigwedlo somkhumbi
lesokwana
iphini
sefetlhametsi
roeispaan
lehuduo

port
uhlangothi lomkhumbi langakwesokunxele
fensetere e nyenyane lehlakoreng le letshehadi la sekepe
intunja esecaleni enqanaweni
fenseterekepeng
bakboord
lefasetere le lehlakoreng la sekepe

starboard
uhlangothi lomkhumbi lwangakwesokudla
lehlakore le letona la sekepe
icala lasekunene lenqanawa
letlhakore la sekepe la moja
stuurboord
lehlakore la go ja la sekepe

Sekepe Skip Sekepe

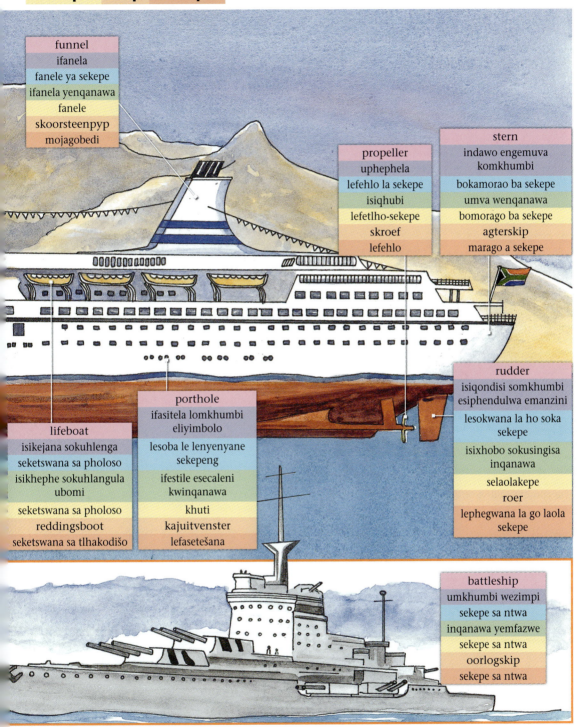

funnel
ifanela
fanele ya sekepe
ifanela yenqanawa
fanele
skoorsteenpyp
mojagobedi

stern
indawo engemuva
komkhumbi
bokamorao ba sekepe
umva wenqanawa
bomorago ba sekepe
agterskip
marago a sekepe

propeller
uphephela
lefehlo la sekepe
isiqhubi
lefetlho-sekepe
skroef
lefehlo

rudder
isiqondisi somkhumbi
esiphendulwa emanzini
lesokwana la ho soka
sekepe
isixhobo sokusingisa
inqanawa
selaolakepe
roer
lephegwana la go laola
sekepe

porthole
ifasitela lomkhumbi
eliyimbolo
lesoba le lenyenyane
sekepeng
ifestile esecaleni
kwinqanawa
khuti
kajuitvenster
lefasetešana

lifeboat
isikejana sokuhlenga
seketswana sa pholoso
isikhephe sokuhlangula
ubomi
seketswana sa pholoso
reddingsboot
seketswana sa tlhakodišo

battleship
umkhumbi wezimpi
sekepe sa ntwa
inqanawa yemfazwe
sekepe sa ntwa
oorlogskip
sekepe sa ntwa

Phrases	Amabinzana	Dipolelwana	Amabinzana
What time does the train leave?	Sisuka ngasikhathi sini isitimela?	Terene e tloha neng?	Uphuma nini uloliwe?
The train leaves at 12 o'clock.	Isitimela sisuka ngehora leshumi nambili ezimpondweni.	Terene e tloha ka hora ya leshome le metso e mmedi.	Uloliwe uphuma ngentsimbi yeshumi elinambini.
Where can I catch the taxi?	Ngingalithola kuphi itekisi?	Nka tshwara tekesi hokae?	Ndingayikhwelela phi iteksi?
The taxi rank is near the station.	Irenke yamatekisi iseduzane nesiteshi.	Boemaditekesi bo haufi le seteishene.	Irenki yeeteksi isecaleni kwesikhululo sikaloliwe.
How much is the bus fare?	Malini ukugibela ibhasi?	Bese ke bokae?	Yimalini uhambo ngebhasi?
It costs R5,00 one way.	Kubiza amarandi amahlanu ukuya.	Ke diranta tse hlano ho ya.	Uhambo olunye ziirandi ezintlanu.
Do you travel by car to get to school?	Uhamba ngemoto yini ukuya esikoleni?	Na o tsamaya ka koloi ho ya sekolong?	Uhamba ngemoto ukuya esikolweni?
Yes, my mother drives my friends and I to school.	Yebo. Umama uyasihambisa nabangane bami esikoleni.	E, mme o isa, nna le metswalle ya ka sekolong.	Ewe umama uyasisa esikolweni nabahlobo bam.
We always wear our seat belts when we travel by car.	Sibopha amabhande ezihlalo njalo uma sihamba ngemoto.	Re tlama mabanta a rona a pholoho kamehla.	Sisoloko sifaka amabhanti esihlalo xa sihamba ngemoto.
Where are you travelling to?	Niyaphi?	Le ya kae?	Niyaphi?
We are sailing to Port Elizabeth.	Siyantweza siqonde eBhayi.	Re ya Port Elizabeth ka sekepe.	Siya eBhayi ngolwandle/ ngenqanawa.
Do you like sailing on the sea?	Uyathanda yini ukuntweza olwandle?	Na o rata ho tsamaya ka sekepe lewatle?	Uyathanda ukuhamba nqanawa emanzini?
No. I get seasick!	Cha. Ngiphathwa yisifo sokuhamba olwandle!	Tjhe! Ke kudiswa ke lewatle!	Hayi. Ndiyaguliswa lulwandle!
We must always cross the road at the pedestrian crossing.	Kufanele sinqamule umgwaqo njalo endaweni yabawela ngezinyawo.	Re lokela ho tshela mmila moo ho tshelwang ka maoto.	Kufuneka sisoloko siwela indlela apho kuwela khona abantu.
Do you have scholar patrol today?	Usebenza ukuqapha izingane zesikole yini namhlanje?	Na le na le baithuti ba laolang sephethephethe kajeno?	Ukhona na umkhuseli wabafundi endleleni namhlanje?
Yes I do.	Yebo, kunjalo.	E, ho jwalo.	Ewe, kunjalo.

Dikapolelo	Frases	Dikafoko
Terena e tloga ka nako mang?	Hoe laat vertrek die trein?	Setimela se tloga nako mang?
Terena e tloga ka ura ya bosomepedi.	Die trein vertrek om twaalfuur.	Setimela se tloga ka iri ya lesomepedi.
Nka tshwara kae thekisi?	Waar kan ek die taxi haal?	Nka hwetša kae tekisi?
Renke e gaufi le seteišene.	Die taxistaanplek is naby die stasie.	Boematekisi bo kgauswi le seteišene.
Madi a go palama bese ke bokae?	Hoeveel kos 'n buskaartjie?	Go lefelwa bokae mo peseng?
Ke diranta di le 5 go ya.	Dit kos R5,00 eenrigting.	Ke R5,00 go ya.
A o tsamaya ka sejanaga go ya kwa sekolong?	Ry jy per motor skool toe?	A o sepela ka sefatanaga go ya sekolong?
Ee, mme o nkisa le ditsala tsa me kwa sekolong.	Ja, my ma neem my en my vriende skool toe.	Ee. Mma o nkiša le bagwera ba ka sekolong.
Re ipofa ka gale ka mabanta a rona a pabalesego fa re tsamaya ka sejanaga.	Ons dra altyd ons sitplekgordels wanneer ons per motor reis.	Re dula re bofile mapanta a tšhireletšo ge re sepela ka sefatanaga.
O ya kae?	Waarheen reis jy?	A o ya kae?
Re lelesela go leba kwa Port Elizabeth.	Ons seil Port Elizabeth toe.	Re thalela Port Elizabeth.
A o rata go lelesela mo lewatleng?	Hou jy daarvan om op see te seil?	A o rata go thala mo lewatleng?
Nnyaa. Ke lwatswa ke lewatle!	Nee. Ek word seesiek!	Aowa. Ke lwatšwa ke go thala!
Re tshwanetse go kgabaga-nya mmila mo lefelong la batsamaya-ka-dinao.	Ons moet die straat altyd by die voetgangeroorgang oorsteek.	Re swanetše go tshela mmila mo go tselago batho ka dinako tšhohle.
A le na le balaolakgabanyo kwa sekolong gompieno?	Het jy vandag skolierpatrollie?	Le na le batshediši ba bana ba sekolo lehono?
Ee go ntse jalo.	Ja, ek het.	Ee, go bjalo.

7

Communication

Ukuxhumana

Kgokahano

Unxibelelwano

Tlhaeletsano

Kommunikasie

Kgokagano

telephone
ucingo
mohala
ifowuni
mogala-tlhaeletsano
telefoon
mogala

receiver
isamukeli
seamohedi
isamkeli
seamogedi
gehoorstuk
seamogedi

answering machine
umshini ophendulayo
motjhini wa melaetsa
umtshini ophendulayo
motšhini wa melaetsa
antwoordmasjien
motšhenekarabo

cord
intambo
kgwele
intambo
mogala
koord
thapo

keypad
inkinobho yocingo
nomorokonopo
iqosha lefowuni
nomorokonopo
toetsbord
khiiphete

fax machine
umshini wokufeksa
motjhini wa fekese
umtshini wokufeksa
motšhini wa fekese
faksmasjien
motšhene wa fekese

document feed
lapho kufakwa khona iphepha
moo ho kengwang pampiri
indawo yokufaka iphepha
seromelapampiri
dokumenttoevoer
seromelapampiri

handset
isibambo socingo
tulo e behwang tsebeng le molomo wa mohlala
umqheba wefoni
sediriswa sa go amogela le go bua
handstel
seswaro

screen
isikrini
sekirini
isikhuseli
sekirini
skerm
sekrini

fax paper
iphepha lokufeksa
pamipri ya ho fekesa
iphepha lefeksi
pampiri ya fekese
fakspapier
lephephe la fekese

Mogala le fekese | Telefoon en faks | Mogala le fekese

cellphone
iselula
mohala wa letheka
unomyayi/
iselfowuni
selula
selfoon
mogalathekeng

screen
isikrini
sekirini
isikhuseli
sekirini
skerm
sekrini

short message system (SMS)
uhlelo lomlayezo omfishane
molaetsa o mokgutshwanyane
inkqubo yokuthumela imiya-lezwana ebhalwayo ngefowuni
tsamaiso ya molaetsakhutshwane
kortboodskapdiens (SMS)
peakanyo ya molaetšakopana

charger
ishaja
motjhini wa ho tlatseletsa mollo
isivuseleli
setlatsa-motlakase
herlaaier
setlatši

telephone directory
incwadi yocingo ephethe amagama namakheli abantu
buka ya dinomoro tsa mohala
incwadi enamagama abantu neefowuni zabo
buka ya dinomoro tsa megala
telefoongids
puku ya motato

ringtone
ukukhala kocingo olungenayo
modumo wa mohala
ithoni yokukhala kwefowuni
modumo wa mogala
luitoon
thouno ya go lla

dialing tone
umsinjwana othi dayela
modumo wa mohala pele o letswa
ithoni yokudayela
modumo wa go ka letsa
skakeltoon
thouno ya go dayela

engaged tone
umsinjwana othi ucingo luyasebenza
modumo wa ha e sebediswa ke motho e mong
ithoni echaza ukuba umnxeba usaxakekile
modumo wa go supa fa e dirisiwa
besettoon
thouno ya go šupa tirišo

telephone number
inamba yocingo
nomoro ya mohala
inombolo yefowuni
nomoro ya mogala-tlhaeletsano
telefoonnommer
nomoro ya mogala

emergency number
inamba yento evela ingazelelwe
nomoro ya mohala ya tshohanyetso
inombolo kaxakeka
nomoro ya tshoganyetso
noodnommer
nomoro ya tšhoganetšo

Computers Amakhompyutha Dikhomputha Iikhompyutha

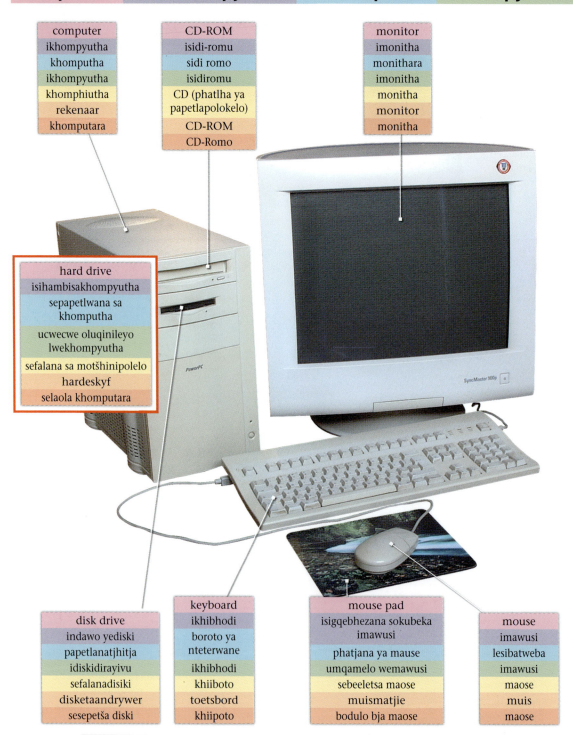

computer
ikhompyutha
khomputha
ikhompyutha
khomphiutha
rekenaar
khomputara

CD-ROM
isidi-romu
sidi romo
isidiromu
CD (phatlha ya papetlapolokelo)
CD-ROM
CD-Romo

monitor
imonitha
monithara
imonitha
monitha
monitor
monitha

hard drive
isihambisakhompyutha
sepapetlwana sa khomputha
ucwecwe oluqinileyo lwekhompyutha
sefalana sa motšhinipolelo
hardeskyf
selaola khomputara

disk drive
indawo yediski
papetlanatjhitja
idiskidirayivu
sefalanadisiki
disketaandrywer
sesepetša diski

keyboard
ikhibhodi
boroto ya nteterwane
ikhibhodi
khiiboto
toetsbord
khiipoto

mouse pad
isigqebhezana sokubeka imawusi
phatjana ya mause
umqamelo wemawusi
sebeeletsa maose
muismatjie
bodulo bja maose

mouse
imawusi
lesibatweba
imawusi
maose
muis
maose

Dikhomphiutha Rekenaars Dikhomputara

paper feed
indawo yokufaka iphepha emshinini
sebaka sa ho fepela pampiri
isihambisi maphepha
sebeelapampiri
papiervoerder
sesepetša dipampiri

printer
iphrinta
sehatisi
isishicileli
segatisi
drukker
phirinthara

CD writer
umshini oqopha ama CD
sengodi sa sidi
umatshini obhala amacwecwe
sekwala-papetlapolokelo
CD-skrywer
sengwadi sa CD

power button
inkinobho yokuvula
konopo ya ho letsa
iqhosha lokuxula
konopo ya motlakase
kragknop
konopi ya mohlagase

paper tray
uqwembe lwephepha
sethebe sa ho kenya pampiri
itreyi ehlala amaphepha
setshola pampiri
papierlaai
therei ya pampiri

laser printer
iphrinta yeleyiza
sehatisi se sebetsang ka mahlasedi
ileyiza printa
segatisi sa leisara
laserdrukker
phirinthara ya leisa

laptop computer
ikhompyutha ephathwayo ongahamba nayo
khomputha ya ho eta
ikhompyutha ephathwayo
lepothopo
skootrekenaar
khomputara ya lapthopo

compact disc (CD)
ikhompekti diski
khompeke disiki
ikhompekthi-diski (iCD)
papetlapolokelo (CD)
kompakte skyf (CD)
diski ya khompekte (CD)

disk
idiski
disiki
idiski
disiki
disket
diski

computer program
uhlelo lwekhompyutha
lenaneo la khomputha
inkqubo yekhompyutha
lenaneo la khomphiutha
rekenaarprogram
lenaneo la khomputara

modem
imodemu
modeme
imodemu
modeme
modem
modemo

| E-mail | I-imeyili | Imeile | I-imeyili | Imeile | E-pos | Imeile |

inbox	outbox	e-mail address
ibhokisana lezincwadi ezingenayo	ibhokisana lezincwadi eziphumayo	ikheli le-imeyili
melaetsa e fihlang	melaetsa e tswang	aterese ya imeile
ibhokisi engaphakathi egcina imiyalezo emitsha	ibhokisi yemiyalezo esele ifundiwe	idilesi ye-imeyili
polokelomelaetsa	polokelomelaetsa e e rometsweng	aterese ya imeile
inmandjie	uitmandjie	e-posadres
lepokisi la melaetša e mefsa	lepokisi la melaetša e tšwago	aterese ya imeile

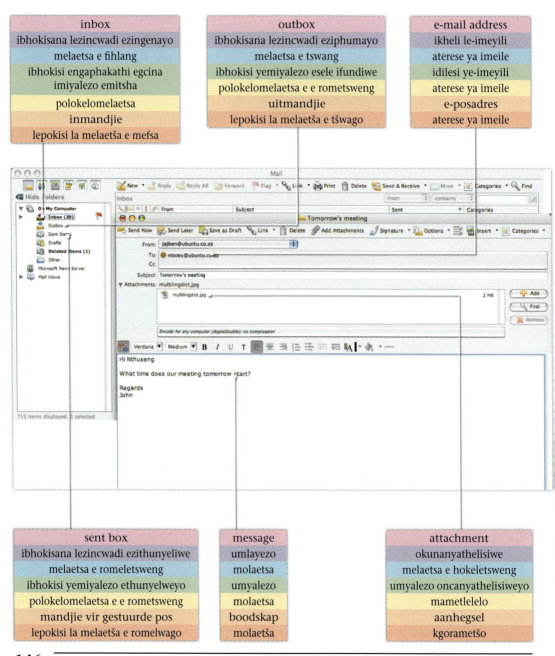

sent box	message	attachment
ibhokisana lezincwadi ezithunyeliwe	umlayezo	okunanyathelisiwe
melaetsa e romeletsweng	molaetsa	melaetsa e hokeletsweng
ibhokisi yemiyalezo ethunyelweyo	umyalezo	umyalezo oncanyathelisiweyo
polokelomelaetsa e e rometsweng	molaetsa	mametlelelo
mandjie vir gestuurde pos	boodskap	aanhegsel
lepokisi la melaetša e romelwago	molaetša	kgorametšo

Imeile le inthanete | E-pos en internet | Imeile le inthanete

Internet | I-inthanethi | Inthanethe | I-intanethi | Inthanete | Internet | Inthanete

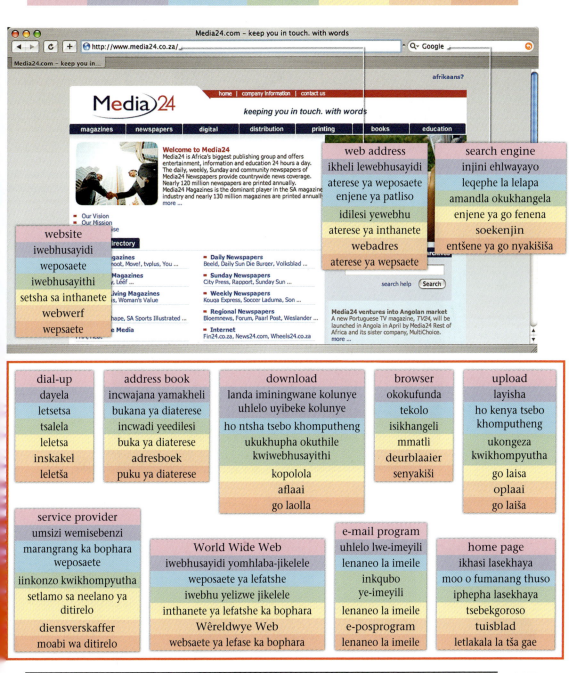

website
iwebhusayidi
weposaete
iwebhusayithi
setsha sa inthanete
webwerf
wepsaete

web address
ikheli lewebhusayidi
aterese ya weposaete
enjene ya patliso
idilesi yewebhu
aterese ya inthanete
webadres
aterese ya wepsaete

search engine
injini ehlwayayo
leqephe la lelapa
amandla okukhangela
enjene ya go fenena
soekenjin
entšene ya go nyakišiša

dial-up
dayela
letsetsa
tsalela
leletsa
inskakel
leletša

address book
incwajana yamakheli
bukana ya diaterese
incwadi yeedilesi
buka ya diaterese
adresboek
puku ya diaterese

download
landa iminingwane kolunye
uhlelo uyibeke kolunye
ho ntsha tsebo khomputheng
ukukhupha okuthile kwiwebhusayithi
kopolola
aflaai
go laolla

browser
okokufunda
tekolo
isikhangeli
mmatli
deurblaaier
senyakiši

upload
layisha
ho kenya tsebo khomputheng
ukongeza kwikhompyutha
go laisa
oplaai
go laiša

service provider
umsizi wemisebenzi
marangrang ka bophara weposaete
iinkonzo kwikhompyutha
setlamo sa neelano ya ditirelo
diensverskaffer
moabi wa ditirelo

World Wide Web
iwebhusayidi yomhlaba-jikelele
weposaete ya lefatshe
iwebhu yelizwe jikelele
inthanete ya lefatshe ka bophara
Wêreldwye Web
websaete ya lefase ka bophara

e-mail program
uhlelo lwe-imeyili
lenaneo la imeile
inkqubo ye-imeyili
lenaneo la imeile
e-posprogram
lenaneo la imeile

home page
ikhasi lasekhaya
moo o fumanang thuso
iphepha lasekhaya
tsebekgoroso
tuisblad
letlakala la tša gae

Television and video | Umabonakude nevidiyo | Thelevishene le vidio | Umabonakude nevidiyo

aerial
i-eriyeli
eriale
ucingo lukamabonakude
lenakaphetisi
lugdraad
eriale

satelite dish aerial
i-eriyeli edonsa emkhathini
eriale ya sathelaete
ucingo lwesitya sesatelayiti
lenakaphetisi la sejana sa sathalaete
satellietskottel
eriale ya sekotlelo sa sathalaete

decoder
idikhoda
dikhouda
idikhowuda
seranodi
dekodeerder
dikhouta

television
umabonakude
thelevishene
umabonakude
thelebišene
televisie
thelebišene

remote control
irimothi
selaodi sa kgokelo
irimowuthi
selaodi sa remouto
afstandbeheer
taolo ya bokgojana

cable
ikhebuli
mohala
intambo
kheibole
kabel
kheipolo

TV guide
incwajana eluleka ngezinhlelo zikamabonakude
sesupisi mananeo sa televishene
isikhokelo sikamabonakude
tshedimosetso ya thelebišene
TV-gids
tlhahlo ya thelebišene

Thelebišene le bidio | Televisie en video | Thelebišene le bideo

video machine	video cassette	rewind	play	stop
umshini wevidiyo	ikhasethi levidiyo	hlehlisa	dlala	misa
motjhini wa vidio	khasete ya vidio	qala qalong	bapala	emisa
umatshini wevidiyo	ikhaseti yevidiyo	phinda udlale	dlalisa	misa
motšhini wa bidio	khasete ya bidio	busetsa-morago	tshameka	emisa
videomasjien	videokasset	terugspeel	speel	stop
motšhene wa bideo	khasete ya bideo	bušeletša	raloka	emiša

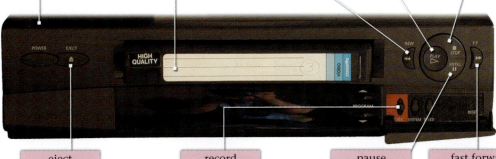

eject	record	pause	fast forward
khipha	qopha	ima isikhawu	qhubekisa
ntsha	rekhota	kgefutsa	isa pele
khupha	rekhoda	nqumama	bhekisa phambili
go ntsha	gatisa	kgaotsa	isa pele ka bonako
uitskop	opneem	pouse	vorentoe speel
ntšha	rekhota	khutša	phetišo ya ka pejana

programme	TV channel	drama	talk show	game show
uhlelo	isiteshi sikamabonakude	umdlalo	umbukiso wengxoxo	umbukiso wezemidlalo
lenaneo	motjha wa thelevishene	tshwantshiso	tshwantshiso	pontsho ya dipapadi
inkqubo	isitishi sikamabonakude	umdlalo	inkqubo-ndaba	ezemidlalo
lenaneo	tšhanele ya thelebišene	terama	thulaganyopuisano	pontsho ya motshameko
program	TV-kanaal	drama	geselsprogram	speletjieprogram
lenaneo	kanale ya thelebišene	papadi	lenaneo la dipolefo	lenaneo la papadi

sitcom	news bulletin	comedy	soap opera	thriller
uhlobo lomdlalo wamahlaya	umbiko wezindaba	umdlalo wamahlaya ya metlae	uchungechunge lomdlalo	indaba evusa usikisiki
metlae	lenaneo la ditaba	pale e tshosang	tshwantshiso ya opera	umdlalo owoyikisayo
ezolonwabo	iindaba	umdlalo oyolisayo	lenaneo la dipuisano	motshameko wa bonokwane
metlae	thulaganyo ya dikgang	motshameko wa metlae	isowuphi ye-ophera	riller
sitcom	nuusbulletin	komedie	kopelo ya ophera	padi goba papadi ya go emiša matswalo
lenaneo la metlae	lenaneo la ditaba	papadi ya metlae	sepie	
			tshwantšhišo ya opera	

Communication • Ukuxhumana • Kgokahano • Unxibelelwano • Tlhaeletsano • Kommunikasie • Kgokagano **149**

Radio **Umsakazo** **Seyalemoya** **Unomathotholo**
Seyalemowa **Radio** **Radio**

radio station
isiteshi somsakazo
seteishene sa seyalemoya
isitishi sikanomathotholo
seteišene sa seyalemowa
radiostasie
seteišene sa radio

tuner dial
idayeli yeziteshi
konopo ya ho batla diteishene
ukufaka isitishi
konopo ya go batla seteišene
instemknoppie
selaolaseteišene

radio
umsakazo
seyalemoya
unomathotholo
seyalemowa
radio
radio

volume dial
idayeli yephimbo
konopo ya modumo
wa seyalemoya
lungisa isandi
konopo ya go laola
modumo
volumeknoppie
selaolabolumo

speaker
amabhokisi akhipha umsindo
sebuelahole
isikhuphi-sandi
sepikara
luidspreker
spikara

CD-player
isidlali masidi
sebapadi sa sidi
isidlali CD
setshameka-CD
CD-speler
sebapala di-CD

walkman
umsakazwana
ophathwayo
seletswa se
bapalwang o tsamaya
unomathotholo
ophathwayo
seyalemowa se se
akgiwang
walkman
radio ya go athiwa

hi-fi
ihayifayi
haefa
igumba-gumba
haefa
hoëtroustel
haefa

DVD-player
isidlali mafilimu
eDVD
sebapala dipolata sa
DVD
umtshini weDVD
setshamika DVD
DVD-speler
sebapala diDVD

headphone
izinto zokulalela
ezifakwa endlebeni
semamedisi sa
ditsebeng
isimameli
esinxitywa entloko
sereetsatsebeng
kopstuk
setšea ka tsebe

tape cassette
isiqophi-mazwi
theipi ya khasete
ikhasethi
khasete ya theipe
kasset
theipikhasete

tape deck
indawo yokufaka
ithephu
sebapala khasete
indawo yekhasethi
setshameka khasete
kassetspeler
theipiteke

Let's read Masifunde Ha re baleng Masifunde
A re baleng Kom ons lees A re baleng

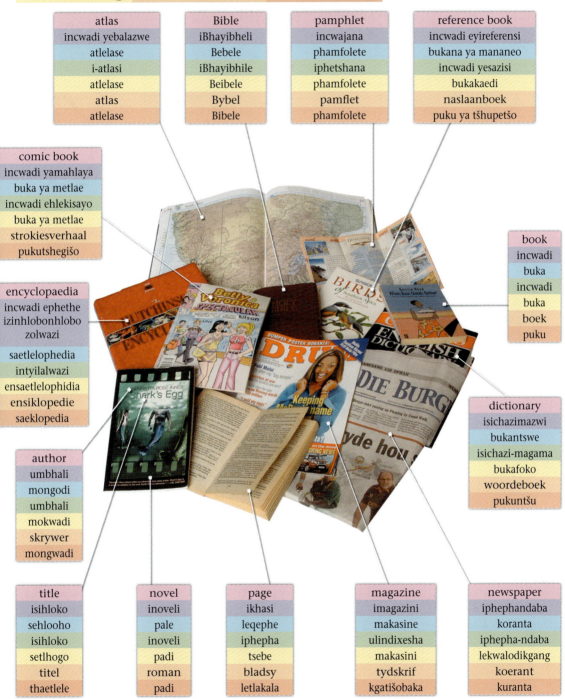

atlas
incwadi yebalazwe
atlelase
i-atlasi
atlelase
atlas
atlelase

Bible
iBhayibheli
Bebele
iBhayibhile
Beibele
Bybel
Bibele

pamphlet
incwajana
phamfolete
iphetshana
phamfolete
pamflet
phamfolete

reference book
incwadi eyireferensi
bukana ya mananeo
incwadi yesazisi
bukakaedi
naslaanboek
puku ya tšhupetšo

comic book
incwadi yamahlaya
buka ya metlae
incwadi ehlekisayo
buka ya metlae
strokiesverhaal
pukutshegišo

book
incwadi
buka
incwadi
buka
boek
puku

encyclopaedia
incwadi ephethe izinhlobonhlobo zolwazi
saetlelophedia
intyilalwazi
ensaetlelophidia
ensiklopedie
saeklopedia

author
umbhali
mongodi
umbhali
mokwadi
skrywer
mongwadi

dictionary
isichazimazwi
bukantswe
isichazi-magama
bukafoko
woordeboek
pukuntšu

title
isihloko
sehlooho
isihloko
setlhogo
titel
thaetlele

novel
inoveli
pale
inoveli
padi
roman
padi

page
ikhasi
leqephe
iphepha
tsebe
bladsy
letlakala

magazine
imagazini
makasine
ulindixesha
makasini
tydskrif
kgatišobaka

newspaper
iphephandaba
koranta
iphepha-ndaba
lekwalodikgang
koerant
kuranta

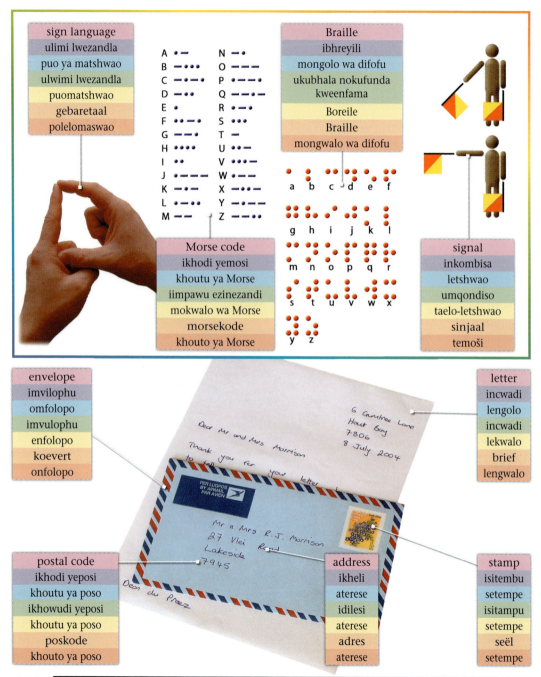

sign language		Braille
ulimi lwezandla		ibhreyili
puo ya matshwao		mongolo wa difofu
ulwimi lwezandla		ukubhala nokufunda kweenfama
puomatshwao		Boreile
gebaretaal		Braille
polelomaswao		mongwalo wa difofu

A •— N —•
B —••• O ———
C —•—• P •——•
D —•• Q ——•—
E • R •—•
F ••—• S •••
G ——• T —
H •••• U ••—
I •• V •••—
J •——— W •——
K —•— X —••—
L •—•• Y —•——
M —— Z ——••

a b c d e f
g h i j k l
m n o p q r
s t u v w x
y z

Morse code
ikhodi yemosi
khoutu ya Morse
iimpawu ezinezandi
mokwalo wa Morse
morsekode
khouto ya Morse

signal
inkombisa
letshwao
umqondiso
taelo-letshwao
sinjaal
temoši

envelope
imvilophu
omfolopo
imvulophu
enfolopo
koevert
onfolopo

letter
incwadi
lengolo
incwadi
lekwalo
brief
lengwalo

6 Gumtree Lane
Hout Bay
7806
8 July 2004

Dear Mr and Mrs Morrison
Thank you for your letter
to tell

Mr a Mrs R.J. Morrison
27 Vlei Road
Lakeside
7945

Deon du Prez

postal code
ikhodi yeposi
khoutu ya poso
ikhowudi yeposi
khoutu ya poso
poskode
khouto ya poso

address
ikheli
aterese
idilesi
aterese
adres
aterese

stamp
isitembu
setempe
isitampu
setempe
seël
setempe

152 Communication • Ukuxhumana • Kgokahano • Unxibelelwano • Tlhaeletsano • Kommunikasie • Kgokagano

Colours Imibala Mebala Imibala Mebala Kleure Mebala

black	white	grey	brown	blue
mnyama	mhlophe	mpunga	nsundu	luhlaza okwesibhakabhaka
ntsho	tshweu	thokwa	sootho	putswa
mnyama	mhlophe	ngwevu	mdaka	zuba
bontsho	bosweu	tuba	bothokwa	botala jwa loapi
swart	wit	grys	bruin	blou
boso	bošweu	modipa	tsothwa	talalerata

purple	pink	red	orange	yellow
bunsomi	bomvana	bomvu	sawolintshi	luphuzi
perese	pinki	kgubedu	mothwebe	tshehla
msobo	pinki	bomvu	orenji	mthubi
phepole	pinki	bohibidu	namune	bosetlha-galaledi
pers	pienk	rooi	oranje	geel
perese	pinki	khubedu	mmala wa namune	serolwane

green	turquoise	gold	silver
luhlaza okotshani	bukhwebezane	sagolide	sasiliva
tala	boperese bo tebileng	kgauta	selevera
luhlaza	buluhlaza	golide	silivere
botala ja ditlhare	serwanatalana	gouta	selefera
groen	turkoois	goud	silwer
tala	thekoise	gauta	silibere

Colour shades Izichasiso Ditlhaloso Izichazi Mothale (mmala) Beskrywings Ditlhalošišo

dark	light	pale	bright	dull	pastel
mnyama	khanyayo	phaphathekile	khanya bha	gqunqile	umbala okhanyayo ngokuphaphathekile
fifetseng	kganyang	retetse	hlakile	thethefetseng	boputswa bo tebileng
ntsundu	khanya	xwebile	qaqamba	mfiliba	qaqamba
bofitshwa	kganya	timpala	phatsimo	letobo	bokganyo jo bo sa tsenelelang
donker	lig	bleek	helder	dof	pastel
mmala o fifetšego	mmala o tagago/ tagilego	mmala o galogilego	mmala o kganyago	mmala o tibilego	pastele

Time Isikhathi Nako Ixesha Nako Tyd Nako

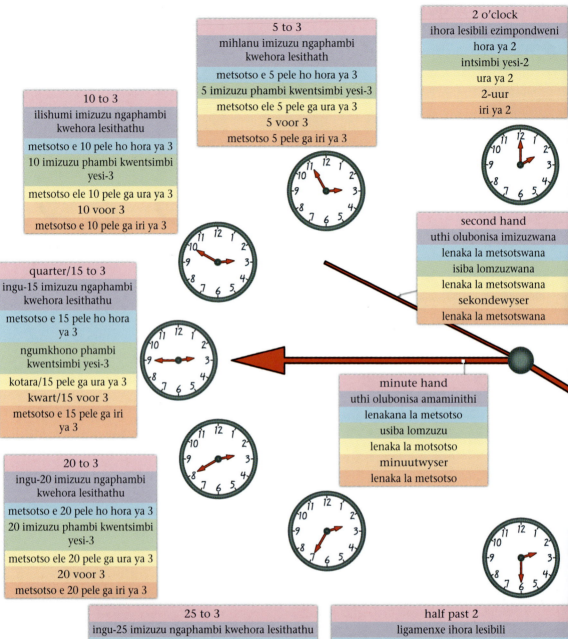

10 to 3
ilishumi imizuzu ngaphambi kwehora lesithathu
metsotso e 10 pele ho hora ya 3
10 imizuzu phambi kwentsimbi yesi-3
metsotso ele 10 pele ga ura ya 3
10 voor 3
metsotso e 10 pele ga iri ya 3

5 to 3
mihlanu imizuzu ngaphambi kwehora lesithath
metsotso e 5 pele ho hora ya 3
5 imizuzu phambi kwentsimbi yesi-3
metsotso ele 5 pele ga ura ya 3
5 voor 3
metsotso 5 pele ga iri ya 3

2 o'clock
ihora lesibili ezimpondweni
hora ya 2
intsimbi yesi-2
ura ya 2
2-uur
iri ya 2

quarter/15 to 3
ingu-15 imizuzu ngaphambi kwehora lesithathu
metsotso e 15 pele ho hora ya 3
ngumkhono phambi kwentsimbi yesi-3
kotara/15 pele ga ura ya 3
kwart/15 voor 3
metsotso e 15 pele ga iri ya 3

second hand
uthi olubonisa imizuzwana
lenaka la metsotswana
isiba lomzuzwana
lenaka la metsotswana
sekondewyser
lenaka la metsotswana

minute hand
uthi olubonisa amaminithi
lenakana la metsotso
usiba lomzuzu
lenaka la motsotso
minuutwyser
lenaka la metsotso

20 to 3
ingu-20 imizuzu ngaphambi kwehora lesithathu
metsotso e 20 pele ho hora ya 3
20 imizuzu phambi kwentsimbi yesi-3
metsotso ele 20 pele ga ura ya 3
20 voor 3
metsotso e 20 pele ga iri ya 3

25 to 3
ingu-25 imizuzu ngaphambi kwehora lesithathu
metsotso e 25 pele ho hora ya 3
25 imizuzu phambi kwentsimbi yesi-3
metsotso ele 25 pele ga ura ya 3
25 voor 3
metsotso e 25 pele ga iri ya 3

half past 2
ligamenxe ihora lesibili
metsotso e mashome a mararo ka mora hora ya 2
icala emva kwentsimbi yesi-2
metsotso e le masomamararo
halfdrie
seripagare go tšwa go iri ya 2

5 past 2
mihlanu imizuzu lishayile ihora lesibili
metsotso e 5 ka mora hora ya 2
5 imizuzu emva kwentsimbi yesi-2
metsotso e le 5 morago ga ura ya 2
5 oor 2
metsotso ye 5 go tšwa go iri ya 2

10 past 2
ilishumi imizuzu lishayile ihora lesibili
metsotso e 10 ka mora hora ya 2
10 imizuzu emva kwentsimbi yesi-2
metsotso e le 10 morago ga ura ya 2
10 oor 2
metsotso ye 10 go tšwa go iri ya 2

hour hand
uthi olubonisa amahora
lenaka la dihora
usiba leyure
lenaka la ura
uurwyser
lenaka la di-iri

quarter/15 past 2
ingu-15 imizuzu lishayile ihora lesibili
metsotso e 15 ka mora hora ya 2
ngumkhono emva kwentsimbi yesi-2
kotara/15 morago ga ura ya 2
kwart/15 oor 2
metsotso ye 15 go tšwa go iri ya 2

20 past 2
ingu-20 imizuzu lishayile ihora lesibili
metsotso e 20 ka mora hora ya 2
20 imzuzu emva kwentsimbi yesi-2
metsotso e le 20 morago ga ura ya 2
20 oor 2
metsotso ye 20 go tšwa go iri ya 2

25 past 2
ingu-25 imizuzu lishayile ihora lesibili
metsotso e 25 ka mora hora ya 2
25 imizuzu emva kwentsimbi yesi-2
metsotso e le 25 morago ga ura ya 2
25 oor 2
metsotso ye 25 go tšwa go iri ya 2

second	minute
umzuzwana	umzuzu
motsotswana	motsotso
umzuzwana	umzuzu
motsotswana	motsotso
sekonde	minuut
motsotswana	motsotso

hour	morning
ihora	ekuseni
hora	hoseng
iyure	intsasa
ura	mosong
uur	oggend
iri	mesong

midday	noon
imini	eminibebade
motsheare	hara mpa ya motsheare
emini emaqanda	emini emaqanda
motshegare	sethoboloko
teen middag	twaalfuur
mosegare wa sekgalela	mosegare

afternoon	evening
ntambama	kusihlwa
thapama	mantsiboya
emva kwemini	matshona
tshokologo	maitseboa
middag	aand
ka merithi	mantšiboa

night	midnight
ebusuku	ebusuku kwamabili
bosiu	kgitla
ubusuku	ezinzulwimi zobusuku
bosigo	bosigogare
nag	middernag
bošego	bošegogare

daytime	nighttime
isikhathi sasemini	isikhathi sasebusuku
motsheare	bosiu
ixesha lasemini	ixesha lasebusuku
nako ya motshegare	nako ya bosigo
in die dag	in die nag
nako ya mosegare	nako ya bošego

Calendar Ikhalenda Alemanaka Ikhalenda

Days Izinsuku Matsatsi Iintsuku Malatsi Dae Matšatši

Sunday	Monday	Tuesday	Wednesday	Thursday	Friday	Saturday
iSonto	uMsombuluko	uLwesibili	uLwesithathu	uLwesine	uLwesihlanu	uMgqibelo
Sontaha	Mantaha	Labobedi	Laboraro	Labone	Labohlano	Moqebelo
Cawa	Mvulo	LwesiBini	LwesiThathu	LweSine	LwesiHlanu	Mgqibelo
Latshipi	Mosupologo	Labobedi	Laboraro	Labone	Labotlhano	Lamatlhatso
Sondag	Maandag	Dinsdag	Woensdag	Donderdag	Vrydag	Saterdag
Lamorena	Mošupologo	Labobedi	Laboraro	Labone	Labohlano	Mokibelo

Time periods Izikhathi Nako Amaxesha Dipaka Tydperke Tšhupanako

century	decade	year	month	week
iminyaka eyikhulu	iminyaka eyishumi	unyaka	inyanga	isonto
ngwaholakola	dilemo tse leshome	selemo	kgwedi	beke
ikhulu leminyaka	ishumi leminyaka	unyaka	inyanga	iveki
ngwagakgolo	ngwagasome	ngwaga	kgwedi	beke
eeu	dekade	jaar	maand	week
ngwagakgolo	ngwagasome	ngwaga	kgwedi	beke

weekend	day	today	tomorrow	yesterday	next week
impelasonto	usuku	namhlanje	kusasa	izolo	ngesonto elizayo
mafelo a beke	letsatsi	kajeno	hosane	maobane	beke e tlang
impela veki	usuku	namhlanje	ngomso	izolo	kwiveki ezayo
bokhutlo jwa beke	letsatsi	gompieno	ka moso	maabane	beke e e tlang
naweek	dag	vandag	môre	gister	volgende week
mafelelo a beke	letsatsi	lehono	gosasa	maabane	beke ye etlago

next month	next year	last week	last month
ngenyanga ezayo	ngonyaka ozayo	ngesonto eledlule	ngenyanga eyedlule
kgwedi e tlang	selemo se tlang	beke e fedileng	kgwedi e fedileng
kwinyanga ezayo	unyaka ozayo	kwiveki ephelileyo	kwinyanga ephelileyo
kgwedi e e tlang	ngwaga e e tlang	beke e e fetileng	kgwedi e e fetileng
volgende maand	volgende jaar	verlede week	verlede maand
kgwedi ye etlago	išago	beke ya go feta	kgwedi ya go feta

last year	date	public holiday
ngonyaka owedlule	usuku	iholide likawonkewonke
selemo se fetileng	letsatsi kgweding	letsatsi la phomolo
unyaka ophelileyo	umhla	usuku lweholide kawonke-wonke
ngwaga e e fetileng	letlha	malatsi a boikhutso a botlhe
verlede jaar	datum	openbare vakansiedag
ngwagola	letšatšikgwedi	letšatši la maikhutšo

Khalentara Kalender Khalentara

Months **Izinyanga** **Dikgwedi** **Iinyanga** **Dikgwedi** **Maande** **Dikgwedi**

1	2	3	4	5	6	7

January
uJanuwari/uMasingana
Pherekgong
Janyuwari/EyoMqungu
Ferikgong
Januarie
Janaware/Pherekgong

8, 14, 15, 21, 22, 28, 29, 30, 31

1	2	3	4

February
uFebuwari/uNhlolanja
Hlakola
Febuwari/EyoMdumba
Tlhakole
Februarie
Fepereware/Dibokwane

5, 11, 12, 18, 19, 25, 26, 27, 28

1	2	3	4

March
uMashi/uNdasa
Hlakubele
Matshi/EyoKwindla
Mopitlwe
Maart
Matšhe/Hlakola

5, 10, 11, 12, 17, 18, 19, 24, 25, 26, 27, 28, 29, 30, 31

April
u-Ephreli/uMbasa
Mmesa
Epreli/EkaTshazimpunzi
Moranang
April
Aporele/Moranang

30, 1, 2, 8, 9, 15, 16, 22, 23, 24, 25, 26, 27, 28, 29

May
uMeyi/uNhlaba
Motsheanong
Meyi/EkaCanzibe
Motsheganong
Mei
Mei/Mopitlo

1, 2, 3, 4, 5, 6, 7, 13, 14, 20, 21, 27, 28, 29, 30, 31

June
uJuni/uNhlangulana
Phupjane
Juni/EyeSilimela
Seetebosigo
Junie
June/Ngwatobošego

1, 2, 3, 4, 10, 11, 17, 18, 24, 25, 26, 27, 28, 29, 30

July
uJulayi/uNtulikazi
Phupu
Julayi/EyeKhala
Phukwi
Julie
Julae/Mosegamanye

30, 31, 1, 2, 8, 9, 15, 16, 22, 23, 24, 25, 26, 27, 28, 29

August
u-Agasti/uNcwaba
Phato
Agasti/EyeThupha
Phatwe
Augustus
Agostose/Phato

1, 2, 3, 4, 5, 6, 12, 13, 19, 20, 26, 27, 28, 29, 30, 31

September
uSephthemba/uMandulo
Loetse
Septemba/EyoMsintsi
Lwetse
September
Setemere/Lewedi

1, 2, 3, 9, 10, 16, 17, 23, 24, 25, 26, 27, 28, 29, 30

October
u-Okthoba/uMfumfu
Mphalane
Oktobha/EyaDwarha
Diphalane
Oktober
Oktoboro/Diphalana

1, 2, 3, 4, 5, 6, 7, 8, 14, 15, 21, 22, 28, 29, 30, 31

November
uNovemba/uLwezi
Pudungwana
Novemba/EyeNkanga
Ngwanatsele
November
Nofemere/Dibatsela

1, 2, 3, 4, 5, 11, 12, 18, 19, 25, 26, 27, 28, 29, 30

December
uDisemba/uZibandlela
Tshitwe
Disemba/EyoMnga
Sedimonthole
Desember
Desemere/Manthole

31, 1, 2, 3, 9, 10, 16, 17, 23, 24, 25, 26, 27, 28, 29, 30

Numbers Izinombolo Dinomoro Amanani

0
zero
iqanda
lefeela
iqanda
lefela
nul
lefeela

1
one
kunye
nngwe
nye
nngwe
een
tee

2
two
kubili
pedi
mbini
pedi
twee
pedi

3
three
kuthathu
tharo
ntathu
tharo
drie
tharo

4
four
kune
nne
ne
nne
vier
nne

5
five
kuhlanu
hlano
ntlanu
tlhano
vyf
hlano

6
six
isithupha
tshelela
ntandathu
thataro
ses
tshela

7
seven
isikhombisa
supa
sixhenxe
supa
sewe
šupa

8
eight
isishiyagalombili
robedi
sibhozo
robedi
agt
seswai

9
nine
isishiyagalolunye
robong
sithoba
robonngwe
nege
senyane

10
ten
ishumi
leshome
lishumi
some
tien
lesome

11
eleven
ishumi nanye
leshome le motso o mong
ishumi elinanye
somenngwe
elf
lesometee

12
twelve
ishumi nambili
leshome le metso e mmedi
ishumi elinambini
somepedi
twaalf
lesomepedi

13
thirteen
ishumi nantathu
leshome le metso e meraro
ishumi elinesithathu
sometharo
dertien
lesometharo

14
fourteen
ishumi nane
leshome le metso e mene
ishumi elinesine
somenne
veertien
lesomenne

15
fifteen
ishumi nanhlanu
leshome le metso e mehlano
ishumi elinesihlanu
sometlhano
vyftien
lesomehlano

16
sixteen
ishumi nesithupha
leshome le metso e tsheletseng
ishumi elinesithandathu
somethataro
sestien
lesometshela

17
seventeen
ishumi nesikhombisa
leshome le metso e supileng
ishumi elinesixhenxe
somesupa
sewentien
lesomešupa

18
eighteen
ishumi nesishiyagalombili
leshome le metso e robedi
ishumi elinesibhozo
somerobedi
agtien
lesomeseswai

19
nineteen
ishumi nesishiyagalolunye
leshome le metso e robong
ishumi elinesithoba
somerobonngwe
negentien
lesomesenyane

20
twenty
amashumi amabili
mashome a mabedi
amashumi amabini
somamabedi
twintig
masomepedi

21
twenty-one
amashumi amabili nanye
mashome a mabedi a motso o mong
amashumi amabini ananye
somamabedinngwe
een-en-twintig
masomepeditee

Dipalo Getalle Dinomoro

22
twenty-two
amashumi amabili nambili
mashome a mabedi a metso e mmedi
amashumi amabini anambini
somamabedipedi
twee-en-twintig
masomepedipedi

30
thirty
amashumi amathathu
mashome a mararo
amashumi amathathu
somamararo
dertig
masometharo

40
forty
amashumi amane
mashome a mane
amashumi amane
somamane
veertig
masomenne

50
fifty
amashumi amahlanu
mashome a mahlano
amashumi amahlanu
somamatlhano
vyftig
masomehlano

60
sixty
amashumi ayisithupha
mashome a tsheletseng
amashumi amathandathu
somamarataro
sestig
masometshela

70
seventy
amashumi ayisikhombisa
mashome a supileng
amashumi asixhenxe
somasupa
sewentig
masomešupa

80
eighty
amashumi ayisishiyagalombili
mashome a robedi
amashumi asibhozo
somarobedi
tagtig
masomeseswai

90
ninety
amashumi ayisishiyagalolunye
mashome a robong
amashumi alithoba
somarobonngwe
negentig
masomesenyane

100
one hundred
ikhulu
lekgolo
ikhulu
lekgolo
een honderd
lekgolo

500
five hundred
amakhulu amahlanu
makgolo a mahlano
amakhulu amahlanu
kgolamatlhano
vyf honderd
makgolohlano

1 000
one thousand
inkulungwane
sekete
iwaka
sekete
een duisend
sekete

1 000 000
one million
isigidi
milione
isigidi
milione
een miljoen
milione

1 000 000 000

one billion
izigidi eziyisigidi
bilione
isigidi sezigidi
bilione
een miljard
bilione

first (1st)	second (2nd)	third (3rd)	fourth (4th)	fifth (5th)	sixth (6th)
kuqala	isibili	isithathu	isine	isihlanu	isithupha
pele	bobedi	boraro	bone	bohlano	botshelela
eyokuqala	eyesibini	eyesithathu	eyesine	eyesihlanu	eyesithandathu
bonngwe	bobedi	boraro	bone	botlhano	borataro
eerste (1ste)	tweede (2de)	derde (3de)	vierde (4de)	vyfde (5de)	sesde (6de)
pele	bobedi	boraro	bone	bohlano	botshelela

Phrases	Amabinzana	Dipolelwana	Amabinzana
What time is it?	Ubani isikhathi?	Nako ke mang?	Ngubani ixesha?
It is half past two.	Ligamenxe ihora lesibili.	Ke mashome a mararo ka mora hora ya bobedi.	Licala emva kwentsimbi yesibini.
When is your birthday?	Lunini usuku lwakho lokuzalwa?	O tswetswe neng?	Unini umhla wokuzalwa kwakho?
My birthday in on the 5th of August.	Usuku lwami lokuzalwa lungamhla zihlanu ku-Agasti/Ncwaba.	Ke tswetswe ka la 5 Phato.	Ngumhla wesi-5 nekweyeThupha/kuAgasti.
What is the date today?	Ngumhla kabani namhlanje?	Ke la dikae?/Ke dikae?	Uthini umhla wanamhlanje?
It is the 3rd of December.	Zintathu kuDisemba.	Ke letsatsi la boraro kgweding ya Tshitwe.	Ngumhla wesi-3 kuDisemba.
May I use your phone card please? I want to phone my …	Ngicela ukusebenzisa ikhadi lakho lokushaya ucingo? Ngifuna ukushayela u …	Ke kopa ho sebedisa karete ya hao ya mohala, ke batla ho letsetsa … .	Ndicela ukusebenzisa ikhadi lakho lokufowuna? Ndifuna ukufowunela … wam.
Here, use my cellphone instead.	Mina. Sebenzisa iselula yami okungcono.	Nka, sebedisa selefounu ya ka.	Hayi. Sebenzisa iselfowuni yam.
Hello. May I speak to … please?	Sawubona. Ngicela ukukhuluma no … ?	Dumela. Na nka bua le … ?	Molo. Ndingathetha no … ?
Yes, please hold. I will put you through.	Yebo kulungile, ngicela ubambe. Ngizokufaka kuye.	Tshwara hanyenyane, ke tla o fetisetsa ho yena.	Ewe, nceda ubambe. Ndiza kukhuphela kuye.
She is not available. May I take a message?	Akekho. Ngicela ukuthatha umlayezo.	Ha a fumanehe, na nka nka molaetsa?	Akafumaneki. Ndinga-wuthatha umyalezo?
Yes, please. Ask her to phone me back. My name is … and my number is (011) 665-0964.	Yebo, kulungile. Umcele ukuba angishayele ucingo. Igama lami ngingu … kanti inombolo yami ithi (011) 665-0964.	E, a ko mo kope hore a ntetsetse nomorong ena (011) 665-0964.	Ewe, nceda umcele anditsalele umnxeba. Igama lam ngu … inombolo yam ithi (011) 665-0964.
Thank you. Good bye.	Ngiyabonga. Sala kahle.	Ke a leboha. Sala hantle.	Enkosi.Sala kakuhle.
Do you have e-mail?	Unayo i-imeyili?	Na o na le imeile?	Unayo i-imeyile?
Yes. What is your e-mail address?	Yebo. Lithini ikheli lakho le-imeyili?	E, aterese ya imeile ya hao ke mang?	Ewe. Ithini idilesi yakho ye i-meyile?

Dikapolelo	Frases	Dikafoko
Ke nako mang?	Hoe laat is dit?	Ke nako mang?
Ke somamararo morago ga ura ya bobedi.	Dit is halfdrie.	Ke seripagare go tšwa iring ya bobedi.
Letsatsi la gago la matsalo le leng?	Wanneer verjaar jy?	Na o belegwe neng?
Letsatsi la me la matsalo ke kgwedi ya Phatwe a tlhola malatsi a le matlhano.	My verjaarsdag is op 5 Augustus.	Ka la 5 Agostose.
Go dikae gompieno?	Wat is vandag se datum?	Ke di kae lehono?
Ke la boraro la Sedimonthole.	Dit is vandag die 3de Desember.	Ke letšatši la boraro la Desemere.
A nka dirisa karata ya gago ya mogala ka tsweetswee? Ke batla go leletsa …	Mag ek asseblief jou foonkaart gebruik? Ek wil my … bel.	A nka šomiša karata ya gago ya mogala? Ke nyaka go leletša …
Tsaya, dirisa selula ya me bogolo.	Hierso, gebruik gerus my selfoon.	Tšea. Šomiša sellathekeng sa ka.
Dumela, tsweetswee, a nka bua le …	Hallo, mag ek asseblief met … praat?	Thobela. A nka bolela le …?
Ee, tshwara jalo ka tsweetswee. Ke go fetisetsa kwa go ene.	Ja, wag net 'n oomblik, asseblief. Ek skakel u deur.	Ee, swara bjalo, ke tla go iša go yena.
Ga a teng. A nka tsaya molaetsa?	Sy is nie beskikbaar nie. Kan ek 'n boodskap neem?	Ga a gona. A nka tšea molaetša?
Ee, tsweetswee. Mo kope gore a buse mogala wa me. Leina la me ke … mme nomoro ya me ya mogala ke (011) 665-0964.	Ja, asseblief. Vra haar om my terug te skakel. My naam is … en my nommer is (011) 665-0964.	Ee, hle, mo kgopele a nteletše. Nomoro ya ka ke (011) 665-0964.
Ke a leboga. Sala sentle.	Dankie. Totsiens.	Ke lebogile. O šale gabotse.
A o na le imeile?	Het jy e-pos?	A o na le imeile?
Ee. Aterese ya gago ya imeile ke mang?	Ja, wat is jou e-posadres?	Ee. Aterese ya gago ya imeile ke efe?

Economy

Umnotho

Moruo

Uqoqosho

Ikonomi

Ekonomie

Ikonomi

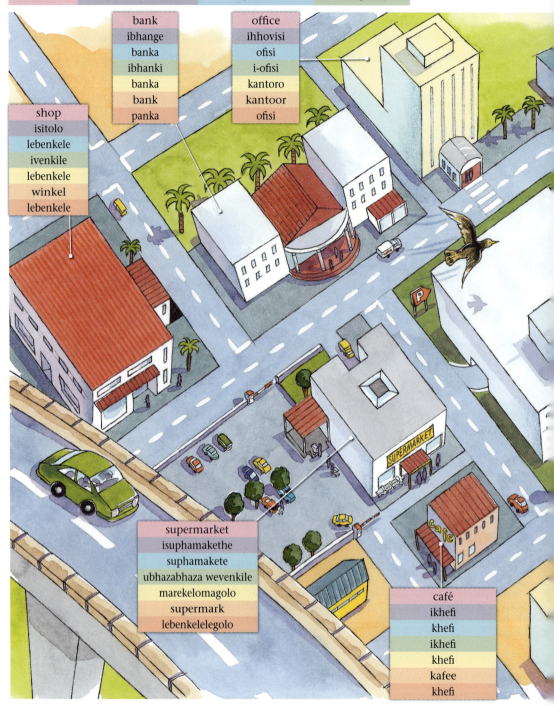

Town centre	Maphakathi nedolobha	Setsing sa toropo	Umbindi-dolophu

bank
ibhange
banka
ibhanki
banka
bank
panka

office
ihhovisi
ofisi
i-ofisi
kantoro
kantoor
ofisi

shop
isitolo
lebenkele
ivenkile
lebenkele
winkel
lebenkele

supermarket
isuphamakethe
suphamakete
ubhazabhaza wevenkile
marekelomagolo
supermark
lebenkelelegolo

café
ikhefi
khefi
ikhefi
khefi
kafee
khefi

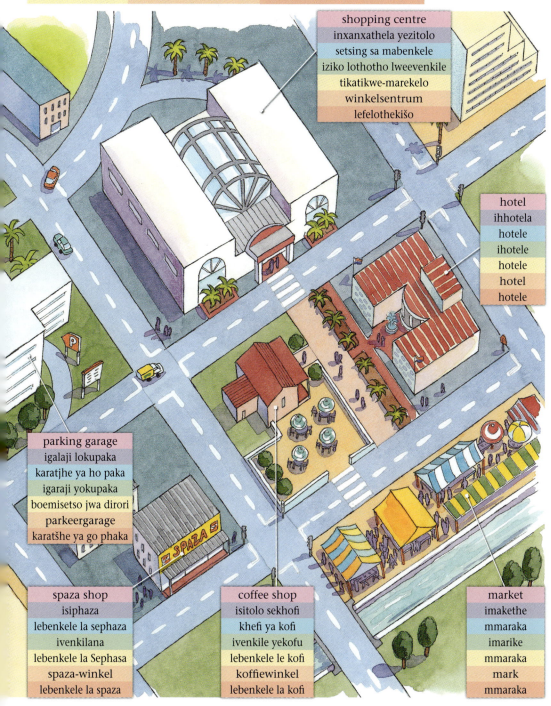

shopping centre
inxanxathela yezitolo
setsing sa mabenkele
iziko lothotho lweevenkile
tikatikwe-marekelo
winkelsentrum
lefelothekišo

hotel
ihhotela
hotele
ihotele
hotele
hotel
hotele

parking garage
igalaji lokupaka
karatjhe ya ho paka
igaraji yokupaka
boemisetso jwa dirori
parkeergarage
karatšhe ya go phaka

spaza shop
isiphaza
lebenkele la sephaza
ivenkilana
lebenkele la Sephasa
spaza-winkel
lebenkele la spaza

coffee shop
isitolo sekhofi
khefi ya kofi
ivenkile yekofu
lebenkele le kofi
koffiewinkel
lebenkele la kofi

market
imakethe
mmaraka
imarike
mmaraka
mark
mmaraka

Market Imakethe Mmaraka Imarike

curios
amaqabuqabu
dimpho tse rekwang ke baeti
imijingo
lebenkele la dilwana tse di botlhokwa
kuriositeite
ditlabelo tše e sego tša mehleng

flea market
imakethe elivulekile
mmaraka o rekisang tsohle
ulwatsaka lwemarike
mmaraka mo phatlhalatseng
vlooimark
mmaraka wa mmileng

vegetable seller
umthengisi wemifino
morekisi wa meroho
umthengisi wemifuno
morekisa-merogo
groenteverkoper
morekiši wa merogo

fruit seller
umthengisi wezithelo
morekisi wa ditholwana
umthengisi weziqhamo
morekisa-maungo
vrugteverkoper
morekiši wa dienywa

arts and crafts
imisebenzi yobuciko eyenziwe ngezandla
bonono le tse betlilweng
umsebenzi wobugcisa bezandla
botsweretshi le didirwa ka diatla
kuns en kunsvlyt
bokgabo le bobetli

boerewors stand
itafula lamavosi
tafolana e rekisang boroso
itafile ethengisa ibhure vorsi
lefelothekisetso la boroso
boereworsstalletjie
borekišetšo bja boroso

Mmaraka Mark Mmaraka

hamburger stand
itafula lamabhega
tafolana e rekisang hambeka
itafile ethengisa iibhega
lefelothekisetso la hambeka
hamburgerstalletjie
borekišetšo bja hampeka

candyfloss
uswidi owenziwe
ngoshukela obilisiwe
pompong e kang boya
ilekese efana nomqhaphu
dimonamone
spookasem
khentifoloso

second-hand clothes seller
umthengisi wezingubo ezingamasekeni
morekisi wa diphahlo tse kileng tsa sebediswa
umthengisi weempahla ezisetyenzisiweyo
morekisa dikapolelwa
gebruikteklere-verkoper
morekiši wa dikapolelo

cooldrink vendor
umthengisi weziphuzo ezibandayo
morekisi wa senomaphodi
umthengisi wesiselo esibandayo
morekisadinotsididi
koeldrankverkoper
morekiši wa dinotšididi

hot dog seller
umthengisi wamahodogi
morekisi wa hotedoko
umthengisi weroli eneviyena
morekisa-hotedoko
worsbroodjie-verkoper
morekišahotdoko

cooldrink	tea	rice
isiphuzo esibandayo	itiye	ilayisi
senomaphodi	tee	raese
isiselo esibandayo	iti	irayisi
senotsididi	tee	reisi
koeldrank	tee	rys
senotšididi	teye	raese

coffee
ikhofi
kofi
ikofu
kofi
koffie
kofi

bread
isinkwa
bohobe
isonka
borotho
brood
borotho

milk	vegetables	biscuits	cooking oil	beans
ubisi	imifino	amabhisikidi	uwoyela wokupheka	ubhontshisi
lebese	meroho	dibisikiti	oli e phehang	dinawa
ubisi	imifuno	iibhiskiti	i-oli yokupheka	iimbotyi
mašwi	merogo	dibisikiti	oli e e apayang	dinawa
melk	groente	koekies	kookolie	boontjies
maswi	merogo	dipiskiti	oli ya go apea	dinawa

Lebenkele la Sephasa Spaza-winkel Lebenkele la spaza

sugar
ushukela
tswekere
iswekile
sukiri
suiker
swikiri

mealie meal
impuphu
phofo
umgubo
bupi
mieliemeel
bupi

samp
isitambu
setampo
umngqusho
setampa
stampmielies
setampa

flour
ufulawa
folouru
umgubo wesonka
folouru
meel
flouro

shopkeeper
umphathi wesitolo
ralebenkele
umnini venkile
ralebenkele
winkelier
mong wa lebenkele

sweets
amaswidi
dipompong
iilekese
dimonamone
lekkers
malekere

counter
ikhawunta
khaontara
ikhawuntari
khaontara
toonbank
khaontara

soap
insipho
sesepa
isepha
sesepa
seep
sesepe

paraffin
uphalafini
parafene
iparafini
parafene
paraffien
parafene

jelly
ujeli
jeli
ijeli
jeli
jellie
jeli

yeast
imvubelo
tomoso
igwele
tlhabego
suurdeeg
komelo

matches
umentshisi
dithutswana tsa mollo
umatshisi
mokgwaro
vuurhoutjies
mentšhese

candles
amakhandlela
dikerese
amakhandlela
dikerese
kerse
dikerese

Shopping centre | Inxanxathela yezitolo | Setsing sa mabenkele | Iziko lothotho lweevenkile

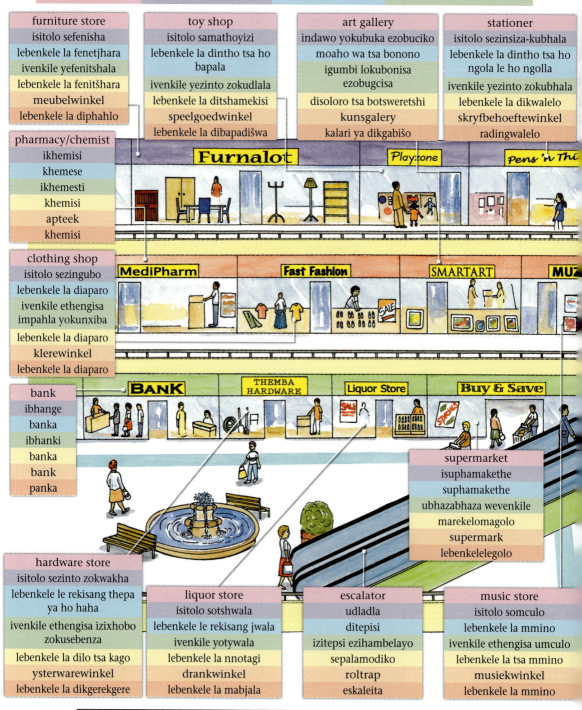

furniture store
isitolo sefenisha
lebenkele la fenetjhara
ivenkile yefenitshala
lebenkele la fenitšhara
meubelwinkel
lebenkele la diphahlo

pharmacy/chemist
ikhemisi
khemese
ikhemesti
khemisi
apteek
khemisi

clothing shop
isitolo sezingubo
lebenkele la diaparo
ivenkile ethengisa impahla yokunxiba
lebenkele la diaparo
klerewinkel
lebenkele la diaparo

bank
ibhange
banka
ibhanki
banka
bank
panka

hardware store
isitolo sezinto zokwakha
lebenkele le rekisang thepa ya ho haha
ivenkile ethengisa izixhobo zokusebenza
lebenkele la dilo tsa kago
ysterwarewinkel
lebenkele la dikgerekgere

toy shop
isitolo samathoyizi
lebenkele la dintho tsa ho bapala
ivenkile yezinto zokudlala
lebenkele la ditshamekisi
speelgoedwinkel
lebenkele la dibapadišwa

art gallery
indawo yokubuka ezobuciko
moaho wa tsa bonono
igumbi lokubonisa ezobugcisa
disoloro tsa botsweretshi
kunsgalery
kalari ya dikgabišo

stationer
isitolo sezinsiza-kubhala
lebenkele la dintho tsa ho ngola le ho ngolla
ivenkile yezinto zokubhala
lebenkele la dikwalelo
skryfbehoeftewinkel
radingwalelo

supermarket
isuphamakethe
suphamakethe
ubhazabhaza wevenkile
marekelomagolo
supermark
lebenkelelegolo

liquor store
isitolo sotshwala
lebenkele le rekisang jwala
ivenkile yotywala
lebenkele la nnotagi
drankwinkel
lebenkele la mabjala

escalator
udladla
ditepisi
izitepsi ezihambelayo
sepalamodiko
roltrap
eskaleita

music store
isitolo somculo
lebenkele la mmino
ivenkile ethengisa umculo
lebenkele la tsa mmino
musiekwinkel
lebenkele la mmino

Signs in illustration: Furnalot, Play:zone, Pens 'n Thi, MediPharm, Fast Fashion, SMARTART, MUZ, BANK, THEMBA HARDWARE, Liquor Store, Buy & Save

Tikatikwe-marekelo Winkelsentrum Lefelothekišo

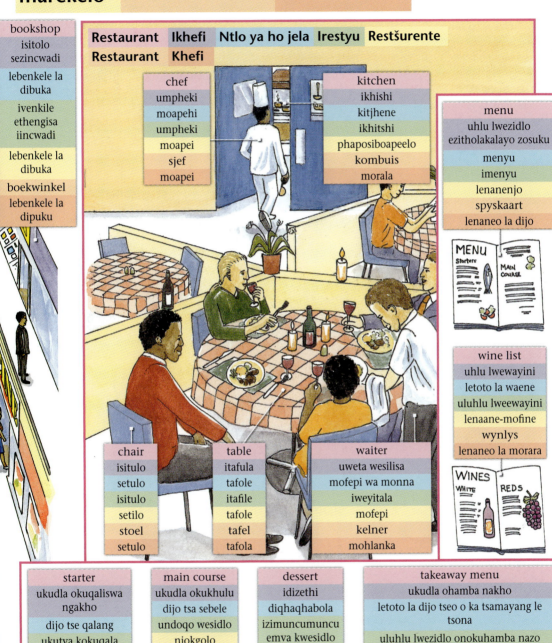

Restaurant	Ikhefi	Ntlo ya ho jela	Irestyu	Restšurente
Restaurant	Khefi			

bookshop
isitolo sezincwadi
lebenkele la dibuka
ivenkile ethengisa iincwadi
lebenkele la dibuka
boekwinkel
lebenkele la dipuku

chef
umpheki
moapehi
umpheki
moapei
sjef
moapei

kitchen
ikhishi
kitjhene
ikhitshi
phaposiboapeelo
kombuis
morala

menu
uhlu lwezidlo ezitholakalayo zosuku
menyu
imenyu
lenanenjo
spyskaart
lenaneo la dijo

wine list
uhlu lwewayini
letoto la waene
uluhlu lweewayini
lenaane-mofine
wynlys
lenaneo la morara

chair
isitulo
setulo
isitulo
setilo
stoel
setulo

table
itafula
tafole
itafile
tafole
tafel
tafola

waiter
uweta wesilisa
mofepi wa monna
iweyitala
mofepi
kelner
mohlanka

starter
ukudla okuqaliswa ngakho
dijo tse qalang
ukutya kokuqala
njokaletso
voorgereg
sethomi

main course
ukudla okukhulu
dijo tsa sebele
undoqo wesidlo
njokgolo
hoofgereg
dijo tše kgolo

dessert
idizethi
diqhaqhabola
izimuncumuncu emva kwesidlo
sedigela
nagereg
tlhatswapelo

takeaway menu
ukudla ohamba nakho
letoto la dijo tseo o ka tsamayang le tsona
uluhlu lwezidlo onokuhamba nazo
lenaane la dijo tse o tsamayang ka tsona
wegneemspyskaart
dijo tše o sepelago natšo

parcel counter
ikhawunta yamaphasela
khaontara ya ho boloka diphahlo tsa bareki
ikhawuntari yeepasile
khaontara ya dithoto
pakkiestoonbank
khaontara ya diphasela

customer
umthengi
moreki
umthengi
moreki
klant
moreki

fruit and vegetables
izithelo nemifino
ditholwana le meroho
iziqhamo nemifuno
maungo le merogo
vrugte en groente
dikenywa le merogo

trolley
inqola
teroli
itroli
teroli
trollie
teroli

basket
ubhasikidi
basekete
ibhaskithi
basekete
mandjie
mmanki

product
umkhiqizo
sehlahiswa
imveliso
kungo
produk
setšweletšwa

packer
umpakishi wezimpahla
mopaki
umpakishi
mopaki
pakker
mopaki

cleaning supplies
izimpahla zokuhlanza indlu
disebediswa tsa ho hlwekisa
izinto zokucoca
didiriswa tse di phepafatsang
skoonmaakmiddels
dihlwekiša

plastic bags
izikhwama zepulasitiki
mekotlana ya polasetiki
iingxowa zeplastiki
dikgetsana tsa polasetiki
plastieksakke
mekotlana ya polastiki

cashier
umphathi wemali
molefisi
umtshintshi-mali
mmalamadi
kassier
mmalatšhelete

till
isisefo
thili
umatshini wemali
thili
kasregister
thili

change
ushintshi
tjhentjhe
itshintshi
tšhentšhi
kleingeld
tšhentšhi

Marekelomagolo Supermark Lebenkelelegolo

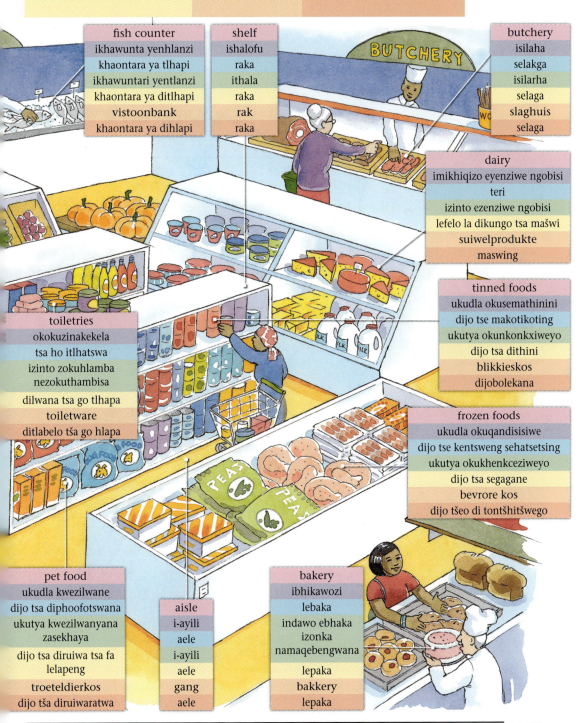

fish counter
ikhawunta yenhlanzi
khaontara ya tlhapi
ikhawuntari yentlanzi
khaontara ya ditlhapi
vistoonbank
khaontara ya dihlapi

shelf
ishalofu
raka
ithala
raka
rak
raka

butchery
isilaha
selakga
isilarha
selaga
slaghuis
selaga

dairy
imikhiqizo eyenziwe ngobisi
teri
izinto ezenziwe ngobisi
lefelo la dikungo tsa mašwi
suiwelprodukte
maswing

tinned foods
ukudla okusemathinini
dijo tse makotikoting
ukutya okunkonkxiweyo
dijo tsa dithini
blikkieskos
dijobolekana

toiletries
okokuzinakekela
tsa ho itlhatswa
izinto zokuhlamba nezokuthambisa
dilwana tsa go tlhapa
toiletware
ditlabelo tša go hlapa

frozen foods
ukudla okuqandisisiwe
dijo tse kentsweng sehatsetsing
ukutya okukhenkceziweyo
dijo tsa segagane
bevrore kos
dijo tšeo di tontšhitšwego

pet food
ukudla kwezilwane
dijo tsa diphoofotswana
ukutya kwezilwanyana zasekhaya
dijo tsa diruiwa tsa fa lelapeng
troeteldierkos
dijo tša diruiwaratwa

aisle
i-ayili
aele
i-ayili
aele
gang
aele

bakery
ibhikawozi
lebaka
indawo ebhaka
izonka namaqebengwana
lepaka
bakkery
lepaka

Bank Ibhange Banka Ibhanki Banka Bank Panka

bank manager	enquiries counter	teller	counter
imenenja yebhange	ikhawunta yemibuzo	umamukeli nombali wezimali	ikhawunta
mookamedi wa banka	khaontara ya dipatlisiso	mothusi ya khaontareng	khaontara
umphathi webhanki	ikhawuntari yemibuzo	umntu othatha imali ebhankini	ikhawuntari
motsamaisi wa banka	khaontara ya go botsa dipotso	mmalamadi	khaontara
bankbestuurder	navraagtoonbank	teller	toonbank
menetšere wa panka	khaontareng ya dinyakišišo	thelara	khaontara

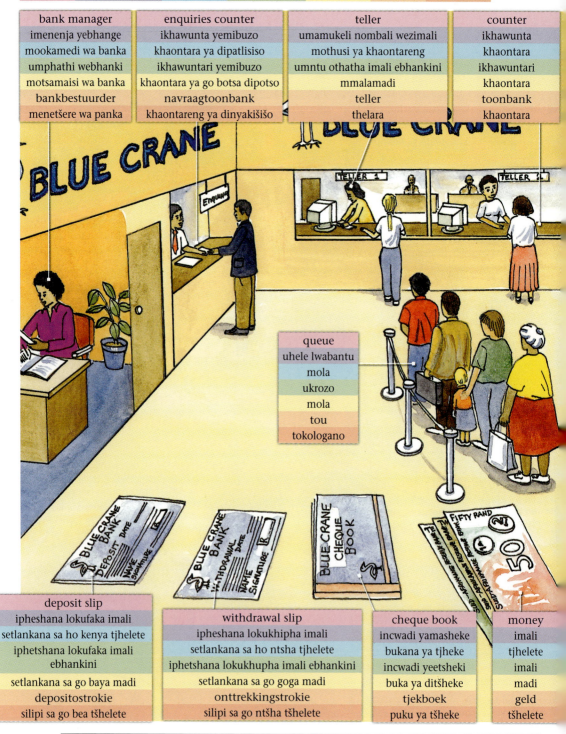

queue
uhele lwabantu
mola
ukrozo
mola
tou
tokologano

deposit slip	withdrawal slip	cheque book	money
iphesana lokufaka imali	iphesana lokukhipha imali	incwadi yamasheke	imali
setlankana sa ho kenya tjhelete	setlankana sa ho ntsha tjhelete	bukana ya tjheke	tjhelete
iphetshana lokufaka imali ebhankini	iphetshana lokukhupha imali ebhankini	incwadi yeetsheki	imali
setlankana sa go baya madi	setlankana sa go goga madi	buka ya ditšheke	madi
depositostrokie	onttrekkingstrokie	tjekboek	geld
silipi sa go bea tšhelete	silipi sa go ntšha tšhelete	puku ya tšheke	tšhelete

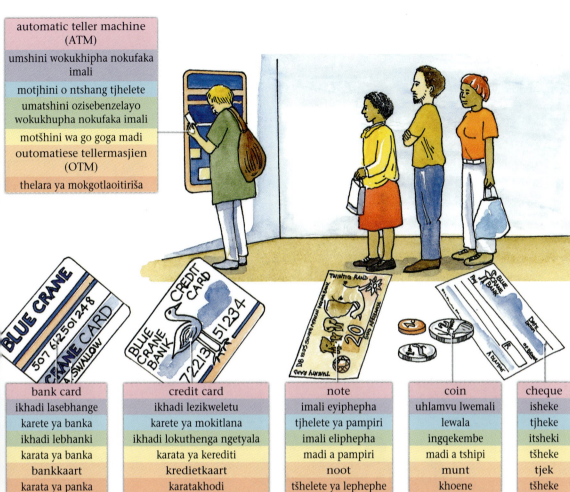

automatic teller machine (ATM)
umshini wokukhipha nokufaka imali
motjhini o ntshang tjhelete
umatshini ozisebenzelayo wokukhupha nokufaka imali
motšhini wa go goga madi
outomatiese tellermasjien (OTM)
thelara ya mokgotlaoitiriša

bank card	credit card	note	coin	cheque
ikhadi lasebhange	ikhadi lezikweletu	imali eyiphepha	uhlamvu lwemali	isheke
karete ya banka	karete ya mokitlana	tjhelete ya pampiri	lewala	tjheke
ikhadi lebhanki	ikhadi lokuthenga ngetyala	imali eliphepha	ingqekembe	itsheki
karata ya banka	karata ya kerediti	madi a pampiri	madi a tshipi	tšheke
bankkaart	kredietkaart	noot	munt	tjek
karata ya panka	karatakhodi	tšhelete ya lephephe	khoene	tšheke

bank account	savings account	interest	cash
i-akhawunti yasebhange	i-akhawunti yokulondoloza imali	inzalo	ukheshe
akhaonte ya bankeng	akhaonte ya pokello	phaello	tjhelete e matsohong
i-akhawunti yebhanki	imali egcinwe ebhankini enenzala	inzala	imali ezinkozo
akhaonto ya banka	akhaonto ya polokelo	morokotso	madi a a seatleng
bankrekening	spaarrekening	rente	kontant
akhaonto ya panka	akhaonto ya poloko	tswalo	tšhelete

investment	credit	debit	PIN number
imali ebekwe isikhathi eside ukuze izale	isikweletu	-zuzisa	inamba yakho eyimfihlo
poloko ya tjhelete e tswalang	molato	molato	nomoro ya sephiri
ukuzalisa imali	ityala	ityala	inani lakho eliyimfihlelo
peeletso	molato	tebiti	nomoro ya sephiri
belegging	krediet	debiet	PIN-nommer
peeletšo	mokitlana	sekoloto	nomorosephiri

foyer
umhubhe
moo ho fihlelang baeti
igumbi lokulinda
boletelo
voorportaal
botsenelobogolo

receptionist
umamukeli wezihambi
moamohedi
umamkeli-zindwendwe
moamogedi
ontvangspersoon
moamogedi

meeting room
igumbi lokuhlanganela
phaposi ya kopano
igumbi lentlanganiso
phaposi ya dikopano
vergaderlokaal
phapošikopanelo

employee
umqashwa
mosebetsi
umqeshwa
mothapiwa
werknemer
modiredi

filing cabinet
ikhabethe lokufaka amafayili
khabathe ya ho boloka difaele
ikhabhinethi yeefayile
khaboto ya difaele
liasseerkas
khabinete ya difaele

desk
ideski
teseke
idesika
teseke
lessenaar
teseke

Mo kantorong By die kantoor Ofising

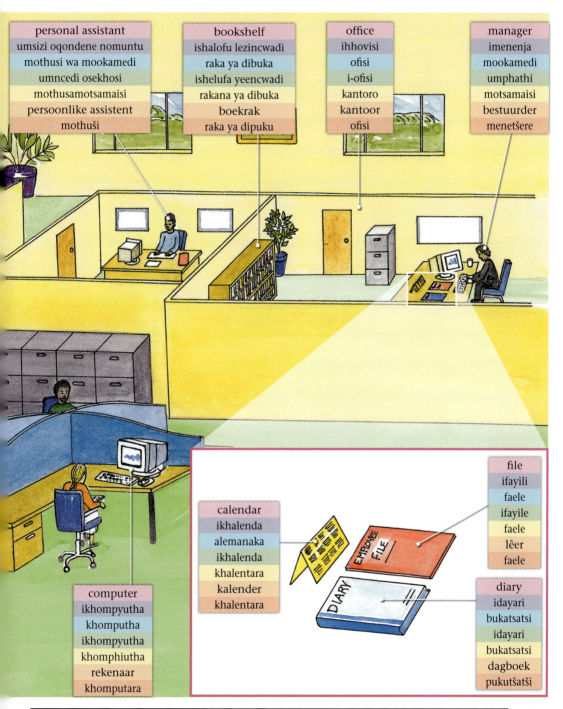

personal assistant
umsizi oqondene nomuntu
mothusi wa mookamedi
umncedi osekhosi
mothusamotsamaisi
persoonlike assistent
mothuši

bookshelf
ishalofu lezincwadi
raka ya dibuka
ishelufa yeencwadi
rakana ya dibuka
boekrak
raka ya dipuku

office
ihhovisi
ofisi
i-ofisi
kantoro
kantoor
ofisi

manager
imenenja
mookamedi
umphathi
motsamaisi
bestuurder
menetšere

calendar
ikhalenda
alemanaka
ikhalenda
khalentara
kalender
khalentara

file
ifayili
faele
ifayile
faele
lêer
faele

computer
ikhompyutha
khomputha
ikhompyutha
khomphiutha
rekenaar
khomputara

diary
idayari
bukatsatsi
idayari
bukatsatsi
dagboek
pukutšatši

hotel room
igumbi lasehhotela
phaposi ya hotele
igumbi lehotele
phaposi ya hotele
hotelkamer
phapoši ya hotela

hotel manager
imenenja yasehhotela
mookamedi wa hotele
umphathi hotele
motsamaisi wa hotele
hotelbestuurder
menetšere wa hotela

lounge
igumbi lokuphumula
phaposi ya ho phomola
igumbi lokuhlala
phaposiboitapoloso
sitkamer
phapošiboiketlo

lift
isikhwelisi
khetjhe
isinyusi
khetše
hysbak
sekuki

hotel room *(see above)*

kitchen
ikhishi
kitjhene
ikhitshi
phaposiboapeelo
kombuis
morala

chef
umpheki
moapehi
umpheki
moapei
sjef
moapei

reception
lapho kwamukelwa khona izihambi
kamohelong
indawo yokwamkela iindwendwe
kamogelo
ontvangs
boamogelo

duty manager
imenenja esebenzayo
mookamedi wa letsatsi leo
umanejala womsebenzi
motsamaisitiro
diensbestuurder
menetšere wa mediro

doorman
umqaphi wasemnyango
molebedi wa monyako
umgcini-sango
motlhokomedi wa kgoro
deurwag
moleti wa mojako

porter
uphotha
motho ya thothang diphahlo tsa baeti
umthwali weempahla
morwalathoto
portier
morwalathoto

foyer
umhubhe
moo ho fihlelang baeti
igumbi lokulinda
boletelo
voorportaal
botsenelobogolo

suite	double room	single room
igumbi lokulala elihlangene negumbi lokugezela	igumbi elingumbaxambili	igumbi elingumbaxanye
phaposi e kgolohadi ya borobalo	phaposipedi	phaposinngwe
amagumbi ahambelanayo	igumbi lababini	igumbi lomnye
phaposiborobalo	phaposi e e tsayang bobedi	phaposi e tsayang a le mongwe
suite	dubbelkamer	enkelkamer
phapošiboiketlo	phapošipedi	phapoši ya bodulanoši

conference room	terrace
igumbi lezimbizo	ithala
phaposi ya seboka	moo ho phomolwang kantle
igumbi lokubambela iintlanganiso	indawo yokuhlala esecaleni kwendlu
phaposi ya dikhonferense	therese
konferensiesaal	terras
phapoši ya khonferense	therese

dining room	bar	restaurant	swimming pool
igumbi lokudlela	inkantini	ikhefi	ichibi lokubhukuda
phaposi ya ho jela	bara	ntlo ya ho jela	letamo la ho sesa
igumbi lokutyela	ibhari	irestyu	idama lokuqubha
phaposibojelo	lefelo la nnotagi	resetšhuranta	letangwana la go thumela
eetkamer	kroeg	restaurant	swembad
phapošibojelo	para	restšurente	bodibaruthelo

Occupation Imisebenzi Mosebetsi Umsebenzi

accountant
umgcini nomcwaningi
wamabhuku emali
mmadi wa ditjhelete
umbali-zimali
mmalatlotlo
rekenmeester
moakhaonthente

architect
umklami wokwakhiwa
kwezindlu
ya tlwebang meaho
umyili wezakhiwo
ramaanokago
argitek
moagi

banker
umphathi webhange
ramatlotlo wa banka
umntu ogcina imali
ebhankini
rabanka
bankier
rapanka

actor
umdlali wasesiteji wesilisa
setshwantshisi
umdlali weqonga
modiragatsi
akteur
moraloki

artist
umdwebi
motaki
igcisa
motaki
kunstenaar
rabokgabo

barber
umgundi wezinwele
mokuti
umchebi
mmeolamoriri
haarkapper
mokotameriri

actress
umdlali wasesiteji wesifazane
setshwantshisi
umdlalikazi weqonga
modiragatsi (mosadi)
aktrise
moralokigadi

attorney
ummeli
mmuelli
igqwetha
mmueledi
prokureur
ramolao

barman
umsebenzi wasenkantini
morekisi wa jwala
umncedi ebharini
morekisannotagi
kroegman
rapara

air traffic controller
umphathi wezithuthi
zasemoyeni
molaola sephethephethe
moyeng
igosa lolawulo
lweenqwelo-moya
molaodi wa pharakano
ya difofane
lugvaartkontroleur
molaolasephethephethe
sa lefaufau

author
umbhali
mongodi
umbhali
mokwadi
skrywer
mongwadi

bishop
umbhishobhi
mobishopo
ubhishophu
bišopo
biskop
morutimogolo

archaeologist
usosayensi ophenya
ngendulo
mofuputsi ya tsetollang
dintho tsa kgale
incutshe ngezakudala
moitseanape wa thutamarope
argeoloog
moakhiolotši

ballet dancer
umdansi webhaleyi
motantshi wa balei
umdanisi webhaleyi
motantshi wa balei
balletdanser
sebinapalei

builder
umakhi
moahi
umakhi
moagi
bouer
moagi

Economy • Umnotho • Moruo • Uqoqosho • Ikonomi • Ekonomie • Ikonomi

Maemo a tiro Beroep Mešomo

carpenter
umbazi
mmetli
umchweli
mmetli
skrynwerker
mmetli

designer
umsunguli nomdwebi wezinto ngobuciko
moqapi
umyili
moakanyetsi
ontwerper
moakanyi

driver
umshayeli
mokganni
umqhubi
mokgweetsi
bestuurder
mootledi

chef
umpheki
moapehi
umpheki
moapei
sjef
moapei

detective
umseshi
lefokisi
umcuphi
letseka
speurder
letseka

electrician
umsebenzi kagesi
ramotlakase
ichule lombane
ramotlakase
elektrisiën
ramohlagase

cleaner
umsebenzi ohlanza izindawo
mohlwekisi
umcoci
mophepafatsi
skoonmaker
mohlwekiša

director
umqondisi
molaodi
umkhokheli
mokaedi
regisseur
mookamedi

engineer
unjiniyela
moenjenere
injineli
moenjeniri
ingenieur
moentšinere

dancer
umdansi
motantshi
umdanisi
motantshi
danser
sebini

doctor
udokotela
ngaka
ugqirha
ngaka
dokter
ngaka

farm worker
umsebenzi wasepulazini
mosebeletsi wa polasi
umsebenzi wasefama
modiri wa mo polaseng
plaaswerker
mošomedi wa polase

data capturer
umlondolozi wemininingwane
mongodi ya bokellang tsebo
umqokeleli wolwazi
mmolokatshedimosetso
dataverwerker
moswaratsebo

domestic worker
umsebenzi wasezindlini
mosebeletsi wa lelapa
umsebenzi wasekhaya
modiri wa mo gae
huiswerker
mošomi wa ka gae

farmer
umnini-pulazi
rapolasi
umfama
molemirui
boer
rapolasa

fashion designer
umsunguli nomdwebi wengqephu
moqapi wa feshene
ichule ekuthungeni ifeshini
moitseanape wa fešene
modeontwerper
mmeakanyi wa difešene

geologist
isazi kwisayensi yomumo womhlaba
mofuputsi wa tsa boemo ba lefatshe
ichule kwinzululwazi yokwakhiwa komhlaba
moitseanape wa majwe
geoloog
setsebi sa maswika

journalist
intatheli
moqolotsi wa ditaba
umcholacholi-ndaba
mmegadikgang
joernalis
raditaba

firefighter
umcimi mlilo
motimamollo
umcimi-mlilo
motimamolelo
brandbestryder
molwešamollo

guard
unogada
molebedi
unogada
motlhokomedi
wag
moleti

judge
ijaji
moahlodi
ijaji
moatlhodi
regter
moahlodi

fisherman
umdobi wezinhlanzi
motshwasi wa ditlhapi
umlobi
motshwara ditlhapi
visserman
mothei wa dihlapi

hairdresser
umcwali-zinwele ya lokisang moriri
umlungisi-zinwele
modira ka meriri
haarkapper
rameriri

lawyer
ummeli
akgente
igqwetha
mmueledi
regspraktisyn
ramolao

game warden
umlimi wezinyamazane
mohlokomedi wa serapa sa diphoofolo
igosa kwithanga lezilwanyana
molepaserapa
wildbewaarder
mohlapetšadiphoofolo

interior decorator
umhlobisi wangaphakathi lendlu ya kgabisang bokahare ba ntlo
umhombisi ngaphakathi
mokgabisi wa mo gare ga ntlo
binneversierder
mokgabišagare

lecturer
umfundisi wasesikhungweni semfundo ephakeme
morupelli
umhlohli ngaphaya kwematriki
motlhatlheledi
dosent
mofahloši

gardener
umsebenzi wasengadini
mosebeletsi wa jareteng
umsebenzi wasegadini
modiri wa tshingwana
tuinier
raserapana

jockey
ujokhi
sepalami sa dipere
umkhweli-mahashe
mopalami wa dipitse
jokkie
mokatišapere

mechanic
umakheniki
motehi
umkhandi weematshini
mosiamisadikoloi
meganikus
mekhaniki

miner
umsebenzi wasemayini
mosebeletsi wa morafong
umsebenzi-mgodini
modiramoepong
mynwerker
ramoepo

paramedic
isazi sempilo sosizo lokuqala
mothusi nakong ya kotsi
isazi sempilo noncedo lokuqala
mothusadikotsing
paramedikus
pharamediki

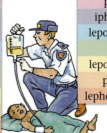

policeman
iphoyisa lesilisa
lepolesa la monna
ipolisa
lepodisi la monna
polisieman
lephodisa la monna

musician
umculi
sebini
umculi
seopedi
musikant
rammino

personal assistant
umsizi oqondene nemenja
mothusi wa mookamedi
umncedi womphathi
motshusamotsamaisi
persoonlike assistent
mothuši wa menentšere

policewoman
iphoyisa lesifazane
lepolesa la mosadi
ipolisakazi
lepodisi la mosadi
polisievrou
lephodisa la mosadi

news reader
umfundi wezindaba
mmadi wa ditaba
umfundi weendaba
mmaladikgang
nuusleser
mmadi wa ditaba

pharmacist
usokhemisi
rakhemese
usokhemesti
ramamelemo
apteker
rakhemisi

politician
usopolitiki
radipolotiki
umpolitiki
mmadipolotiki
politikus
radipolotiki

nurse
umhlengikazi
mooki
umongikazi
mooki
verpleegster
mooki

pilot
umshayeli webhanoyi
mofofisi wa sefofane
umqhubi nqwelo-moya
mofofisasefofane
vlieënier
mofofiši

president
umongameli
moporesitente
umongameli
moporesidente
president
mopresitente

opera singer
umculi we-ophera
sebini sa opera
umculi we-ophera
moopedi wa ophera
operasanger
moopedi wa opera

plumber
upulamba
polamara
umlungisi wemibhobho yamanzi
polamara
loodgieter
radipompi

priest
umfundisi
moruti
umfundisi
moruti
priester
moruti

printer
umshicileli
mohatisi
umshicileli
mogatisi
drukker
mogatiši

referee
unompempe
moletsaphala
usompempe
moletsaphala
skeidsregter
malokwane

secretary
unobhala
mongodi
unobhala
mokwaledi
sekretaresse
mongwaledi

prison guard
umlindi wejele
molebedi wa tjhankana
unogada entolongweni
motlhokomedi wa dikgolegelo
tronkbewaarder
moletakgolego

restaurateur
umphathi wasekhefi
monnga ntlo ya ho jela
umphathi yo werestyu
monngwa-lebenkele la dijo
restourateur
mongwa restšurente

shop assistant
umsizi wasesitolo
mothusi lebenkeleng
umncedisi evenkileni
mothusi wa mo lebenkeleng
winkelassistent
mothušaralebenkele

professor
usolwazi
moporofesara
unjingalwazi
moporofesara
professor
moprofesa

sailor
itilosi
mosesi
umatiloshe
molelesedi
matroos
mothadiši

shopkeeper
umphathi wesitolo
ralebenkele
umnini venkile
ralebenkele
winkelier
ralebenkele

prosecutor
umshushisi
motjhotjhisi
umtshutshisi
motšhotšhisi
aanklaer
motšhotšhisi

sales representative
umthengisi
moemedi wa dithekiso
umthengisi
moemedi wa dithekiso
verkoops-verteenwoordiger
moemedithekišo

singer
umculi
sebini
umculi
seopedi
sanger
moopedi

radio disc jockey
umsakazi ophathelene nezomculo
sebohodi
umdlali mculo kunomathotholo
mogasi wa mananeo a seyalemowa
platejoggie
molaolammino

seamstress
umthungikazi
serokihadi
umthungikazi
moroki
klerewerkster
moroki

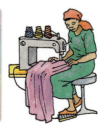

social worker
usonhlalakahle
mosebeletsi wa setjhaba
unontlalontle
modirediloago
sosiale werker
modirelaleago

184

sportsman
umdlali wesilisa
radipapadi
umdlali
rametshameko
sportman
radipapadi

supervisor
umphathi
motshwari
umphathi
motlhokomedi
opsigter
mohlahlobedi

travel agent
umsebenzi ophathelene
nezokuhamba
mothusi wa baeti
umququzeli wabahambi
motlhankedi wa tsa
bojanala
reisagent
mohlankelabaeti

sportswoman
umdlali wesifazane
mmadipapadi
umdlali wasetyhini
mmametshameko
sportvrou
mmadipapadi

surgeon
udokotela ohlinzayo
ngaka e buhang
ugqirha otyandayo
ngaka ya dikaro
snydokter/chirurg
ngaka ya go bua

trainer
umqeqeshi
mokwetlisi
umqeqeshi
mokatisi
afrigter
mokatiši

steward
umsizi wabagibeli
wesilisa
leqosa
umququzeleli
molebeledi mo
sefofaneng
vlugkelner
mohlokomedi wa
baeti ka phepo

teacher
umfundisi
titjhere
umfundisi-ntsapho
morutabana
onderwyser
morutiši

veterinarian
udokotela wezilwane
ngaka ya diphoofolo
uqgirha wezilwanyana
ngaka ya diphologolo
veearts
ngaka ya diphoofolo

flight attendant
umsizi wabagibeli
wesifazane
leqosa la mosadi
umququzelikazi
motlhokomela
bapalami
lugwaardin
mofepabaeti ba
sefofane

tour guide
umkhaphi wezivakashi
mosupatsela wa
bahahlaudi
umkhokeli
wabakhenkethi
mokaelatsela
toergids
tlhahlabaeti

waitress
uweta wesifazane
mofepi wa mosadi
iweyitresi
mofepi (mosadi)
kelnerin
mohlankagadi

stock broker
umthengisi wamashezi
moemedi wa
khamphani kgwebong
umthengi
morekisi wa matlole
aandelemakelaar
morekela-a-rekišetša

traffic officer
iphoyisa lomgwaqo
molaola sephethephethe
igosa lezendlela
motlhankedi wa
pharakano
verkeersbeampte
molaolasehethephethe

waiter
uweta wesilisa
mofepi wa monna
iweyitala
mofepi (monna)
kelner
mohlanka

Economy • Umnotho • Moruo • Uqoqosho • Ikonomi • Ekonomie • Ikonomi

185

Tools of the trade	Amathuluzi emisebenzi	Disebediswa	Izixhobo zokusebenza

saw
isaha
sakga
isarha
saga
saag
saga

chainsaw
isaha lezinsimbi
sakga ya ketane
umatshini wesarha
saga ya diketane
kettingsaag
saga ya ketane

hammer
isando
hamore
ihamile
hamore
hamer
noto

nail
isipikili
sepekere
isikhonkwana
sepekere
spyker
sepikiri

screwdriver
isikuludrayiva
sekuruteraefara
isijiji sikrufu
sesokakurufu
skroewedraaier
setšhophakurufu

screw
isikulufo
sekorufu
isikrufu
sekurufu
skroef
sekurufu

pliers
udlawu
kinipitang
iplayasi
kinipitang
tang
kinipitane

wire cutter
isizece socingo
ntho e kgaolang terata
isixhobo sokuqhawula iingcingo
sekgaola-diterata
draadknipper
seripathale

plane
isiphalo
phalo
isichwelo
sekafo
skaaf
sekhafo

sandpaper
usaniphepha
sehohlathupa
isigudisi mthi
pampiri e e gotlhang
skuurpapier
pampirisegohlo

spanner
isipanela
sepannere
isipanela
sepanere
moersleutel
sepanere

chisel
ishizolo
tjhesele
isitshwezi
tšhesele
beitel
tšhisele

wrench
ubhobhoshane
bobojane
isixhobo sokujija
bobojane
stelbare sleutel
popojane

tape measure
ithephu yokukala
tekanyo ya bonamo ba theipi
iteyiphi yokulinganisa
selekanyi sa theipi
maatband
lentitekanyo

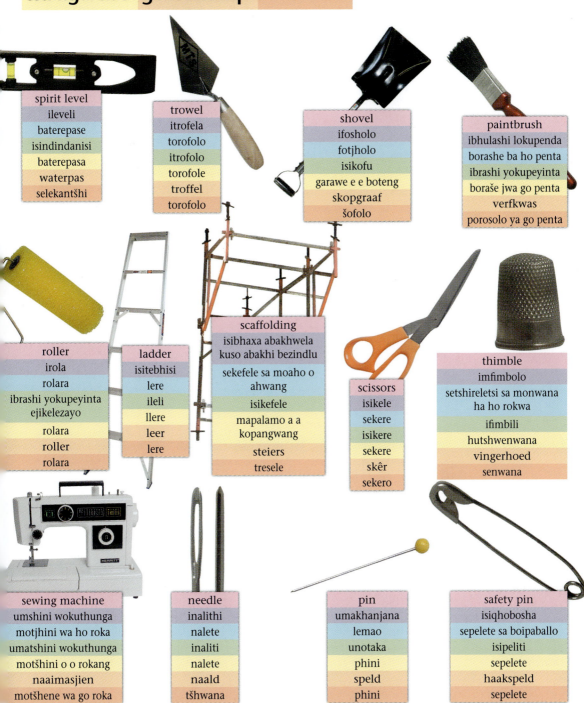

spirit level
ileveli
baterepase
isindindanisi
baterepasa
waterpas
selekantši

trowel
itrofela
torofolo
itrofolo
torofole
troffel
torofolo

shovel
ifosholo
fotjholo
isikofu
garawe e e boteng
skopgraaf
šofolo

paintbrush
ibhulashi lokupenda
borashe ba ho penta
ibrashi yokupeyinta
boraše jwa go penta
verfkwas
porosolo ya go penta

roller
irola
rolara
ibrashi yokupeyinta ejikelezayo
rolara
roller
rolara

ladder
isitebhisi
lere
ileli
llere
leer
lere

scaffolding
isibhaxa abakhwela kuso abakhi bezindlu
sekefele sa moaho o ahwang
isikefele
mapalamo a a kopangwang
steiers
tresele

scissors
isikele
sekere
isikere
sekere
skêr
sekero

thimble
imfimbolo
setshireletsi sa monwana ha ho rokwa
ifimbili
hutshwenwana
vingerhoed
senwana

sewing machine
umshini wokuthunga
motjhini wa ho roka
umatshini wokuthunga
motšhini o o rokang
naaimasjien
motšhene wa go roka

needle
inalithi
nalete
inaliti
nalete
naald
tšhwana

pin
umakhanjana
lemao
unotaka
phini
speld
phini

safety pin
isiqhobosha
sepelete sa boipaballo
isipeliti
sepelete
haakspeld
sepelete

Phrases	Amabinzana	Dipolelwana	Amabinzana
I would like to deposit R100 into my savings account.	Ngithanda ukubeka imali engamarandi ayikhulu ku-akhawunti yami yokulondoloza imali.	Ke batla ho kenya R100 polokelong ya ka ya tjhelete.	Ndinqwenela ukufaka imali eli-R100 kwi-akhawunti yam.
I expect to get a good interest rate on my investment.	Ngilindele ukuthola inzalo enhle emalini engiyibekile.	Ke lebeletse ho fumana phaello e ntle polokelong ya ka.	Ndilindele ukufumana inzala entle kule mali ndiyibekileyo.
May I help you?	Ngingakusiza?	Nka o thusa?	Ndingakunceda na?
Yes please. I would like a packet of candles, a bag of mealie meal and a bunch of carrots please.	Yebo. Ngicela iphakethe lamakhandlela, nesaka lempuphu nesixha sezanqante.	Ee, ke tla kopa pakethe e le nngwe ya dikerese, phofo ya poone le dihwete.	Ndincede ngepakethi yamakhandlela, ingxowa yomgubo wombona, nesihlahla seminqathe.
How much will that cost?	Kuzobiza malini lokho?	E tla ba bokae?	Ziza kuba yimalini?
That will be R20, please.	Kubiza amarandi angamashumi amabili.	E tla ba R20.	Ziza kuba ngama- R20.
Here is R50.	Nanka amarandi angamashumi amahlanu.	R50 ke ena.	Nanga ama-R50.
Thank you. Here's your R30 change.	Ngiyabonga. Nanku ushintshi wamarandi angamashumi amathathu.	Ke a leboha. Tjhentjhe ya hao ya R30 ke ena.	Enkosi. Nanga ama-R30 ayitshintshi yakho.
Where did you cut your hair?	Uzigundephi izinwele zakho?	O kutile moriri wa hao hokae?	Uyichebe phi intloko yakho?
The barber down the road cut my hair.	Umgundi wezinwele osezansi nomgwaqo ongigundile.	Mokuti ya dulang tlasenyana seterateng sena ke yena ya nkutileng moriri.	Kumchebi, phaya emazantsi endlela.
Where is the ice-cream section?	Ngingayitholaphi ingxenye ethengisa ngo-ayisikhilimu?	Nka fumana hokae ayesekhirimi?	Ndingayifumana phi indawo yocwambu olukhenkceziweyo?
It is down the third aisle.	Isezansi esikhaleni sesithathu esiphakathi kwezinhla.	E tlasenyana moleng wa boraro.	Ikule ayile yesithathu xa usihla.
Do you need any plastic bags?	Uyasidinga yini isikhwama sepulasitiki?	Na o hloka mekotlana ya dipolasetiki?	Ingaba ufuna iingxowa zeplastiki.
No, I have my own bag, thank you.	Cha. Nginaso isikhwama sami. Ngiyabonga.	Tjhe, ke na le mokotlana wa ka, ke a leboha.	Hayi, ndinayo eyam. Enkosi.

Dikapolelo	Frases	Dikafoko
Ke batla go banka R100 mo tshupapolokelong ya me.	Ek wil graag R100 in my spaarrekening deponeer.	Ke nyaka go bea R100 akhaonteng ya ka ya polokelo.
Ke solofela go bona kelomorokotso e ntle mo peeletsong ya me.	Ek verwag om 'n goeie rentekoers op my belegging te kry.	Ke hutša go humana mašokotšo a mabotse go dipeeletšo tša ka.
A nka go thusa?	Kan ek help?	A nka go thuša?
Ee, tsweetswee. Ke batla/lopa sephuthelwana sa dikerese, kgetse ya bupi gammogo le digwete tsweetswee.	Ja, asseblief. Ek wil graag 'n pakkie kerse, 'n sak mieliemeel en 'n bos wortels hê, asseblief.	Ee, hle, ke nyaka pakana ya dikerese, mokotla wa bupi le ngatana ya dikherote, hle.
Di tlile go ja bokae?	Hoeveel sal dit kos?	A di tla bitša bokae?
Di tla ja R20.	Dit sal R20 wees, asseblief.	E tla ba R20.
Diranta di le R50 ke tseno.	Hier is R50.	R50 ke ye.
Ke lebogile. Tšhentšhi ya gago ya R30 ke e.	Dankie. Hier is jou kleingeld van R30.	Ke lebogile.Tšhentšhi ya gago ya R30 ke yeo.
O beotse kae moriri wa gago?	Waar het jy jou hare laat sny?	O kotile kae meriri ya gago?
Mmeodi yo o kwa tlase kwa mo mmileng o mpeotse.	Die haarkapper hier onder in die straat het my hare gesny.	Go mokuti yo a lego tlasenyana mo mmileng.
Nka bona kae karolo e e nang le bebetsididi?	Waar is die roomysafdeling?	Nka humana kae lefelo la lebebetšididi?
Mo mogogorong wa boraro go ya kwa tlase.	Dit is in die derde gang.	Tlase phasetšeng ya boraro.
A o batla dikgetsana tsa polasetiki?	Het u plastieksakke nodig?	O nyaka mokotla wa polastiki?
Nnyaa, ke na le kgetsana ya me. Ke a leboga.	Nee, ek het my eie sak, dankie.	Ke lebogile, ke na le wa ka.

9

Nature and us

Imvelo nathi

Tlholeho le rona

Nature and us • Imvelo nathi • Tlholeho le rona • Indalo kunye nathi
Tlhago le rona • Ons en die natuur • Tlhago le rena

Indalo kunye nathi

Tlhago le rona

Ons en die natuur

Tlhago le rena

Nature and us • Imvelo nathi • Tlholeho le rona • Indalo kunye nathi
Tlhago le rona • Ons en die natuur • Tlhago le rena

191

Milky Way
umthala
Molala
uMnyele Wezulu
Tlhatlaganonaledi
Melkweg
Molala

star
inkanyezi
naledi
inkwenkwezi
naledi
ster
naledi

Uranus
uYurenasi
Yuranese
uYurenasi
Yuranase
Uranus
Yurenase

Neptune
uNephthuni
Nepetjhunu
iNephthuni
Nepetšhunu
Neptunus
Neputhuni

Pluto
uPlutho
Puluto
uPluto
Pholuto
Pluto
Pluto

planet
unozungezilanga
polanete
iplanethi
polanete
planeet
polanete

192

Nature and us • Imvelo nathi • Tlholeho le rona • Indalo kunye nathi
Tlhago le rona • Ons en die natuur • Tlhago le rena

Jupiter
iNdonsakusa
Jupita
uJupita
Selemela
Jupiter
Jupita

Mercury
uMekhyuri
Mekhuri
uMetyhuri
Mekhuri
Mercurius
Mekhuri

Sun
iLanga
Letsatsi
iLanga
Letsatsi
Son
Letšatši

moon
inyanga
kgwedi
inyanga
ngwedi
maan
ngwedi

Mars
uMarzi
Mase
uMarsi
Mase
Mars
Mmase

Earth
uMhlaba
Lefatshe
uMhlaba
Lefatshe
Aarde
lefase

Venus
uVinasi
Vinase
uVenasi
Benase
Venus
Mphatlalatšane

Saturn
uSarthana
Satene
iSateni
Sathene
Saturnus
Satuni

galaxy
umthala
molala
ingqumba yeenkwenkwezi
motšhotšhonono
sterrestelsel
motšhotšhonono

Nature and us • Imvelo nathi • Tlholeho le rona • Indalo kunye nathi
Tlhago le rona • Ons en die natuur • Tlhago le rena

193

Earth Umhlaba Lefatshe Ilizwe

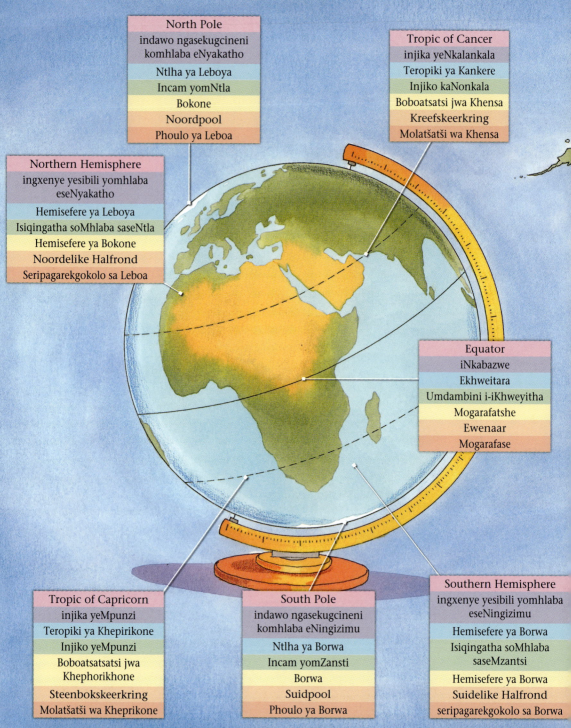

North Pole
indawo ngasekugcineni komhlaba eNyakatho
Ntlha ya Leboya
Incam yomNtla
Bokone
Noordpool
Phoulo ya Leboa

Tropic of Cancer
injika yeNkalankala
Teropiki ya Kankere
Injiko kaNonkala
Boboatsatsi jwa Khensa
Kreefskeerkring
Molatšatši wa Khensa

Northern Hemisphere
ingxenye yesibili yomhlaba eseNyakatho
Hemisefere ya Leboya
Isiqingatha soMhlaba saseNtla
Hemisefere ya Bokone
Noordelike Halfrond
Seripagarekgokolo sa Leboa

Equator
iNkabazwe
Ekhweitara
Umdambini i-iKhweyitha
Mogarafatshe
Ewenaar
Mogarafase

Tropic of Capricorn
injika yeMpunzi
Teropiki ya Khepirikone
Injiko yeMpunzi
Boboatsatsatsi jwa Khephorikhone
Steenbokskeerkring
Molatšatši wa Kheprikone

South Pole
indawo ngasekugcineni komhlaba eNingizimu
Ntlha ya Borwa
Incam yomZansti
Borwa
Suidpool
Phoulo ya Borwa

Southern Hemisphere
ingxenye yesibili yomhlaba eseNingizimu
Hemisefere ya Borwa
Isiqingatha soMhlaba saseMzantsi
Hemisefere ya Borwa
Suidelike Halfrond
seripagarekgokolo sa Borwa

194

Lefatshe Aarde Lefase

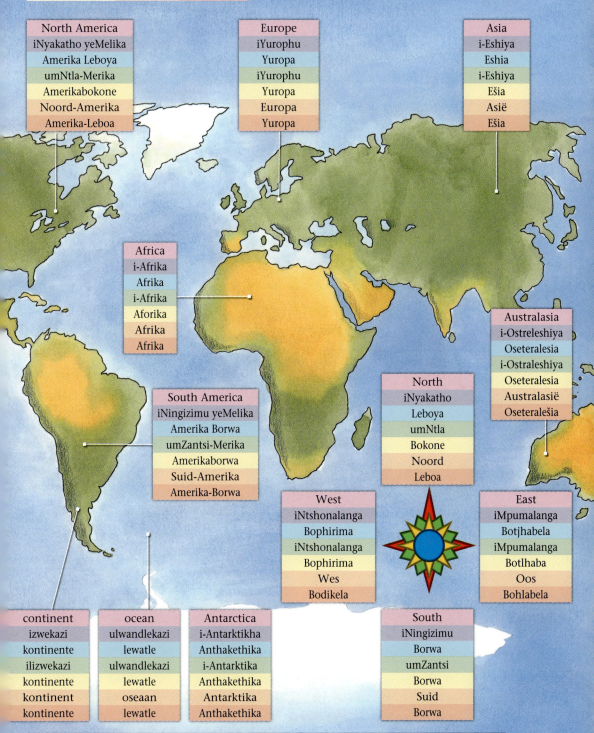

North America
iNyakatho yeMelika
Amerika Leboya
umNtla-Merika
Amerikabokone
Noord-Amerika
Amerika-Leboa

Europe
iYurophu
Yuropa
iYurophu
Yuropa
Europa
Yuropa

Asia
i-Eshiya
Eshia
i-Eshiya
Ešia
Asië
Ešia

Africa
i-Afrika
Afrika
i-Afrika
Aforika
Afrika
Afrika

Australasia
i-Ostreleshiya
Oseteralesia
i-Ostraleshiya
Oseteralesia
Australasië
Oseteralešia

South America
iNingizimu yeMelika
Amerika Borwa
umZantsi-Merika
Amerikaborwa
Suid-Amerika
Amerika-Borwa

North
iNyakatho
Leboya
umNtla
Bokone
Noord
Leboa

West
iNtshonalanga
Bophirima
iNtshonalanga
Bophirima
Wes
Bodikela

East
iMpumalanga
Botjhabela
iMpumalanga
Botlhaba
Oos
Bohlabela

continent
izwekazi
kontinente
ilizwekazi
kontinente
kontinent
kontinente

ocean
ulwandlekazi
lewatle
ulwandlekazi
lewatle
oseaan
lewatle

Antarctica
i-Antarktikha
Anthakethika
i-Antarktika
Anthakethika
Antarktika
Anthakethika

South
iNingizimu
Borwa
umZantsi
Borwa
Suid
Borwa

Nature and us • Imvelo nathi • Tlholeho le rona • Indalo kunye nathi
Tlhago le rona • Ons en die natuur • Tlhago le rena

195

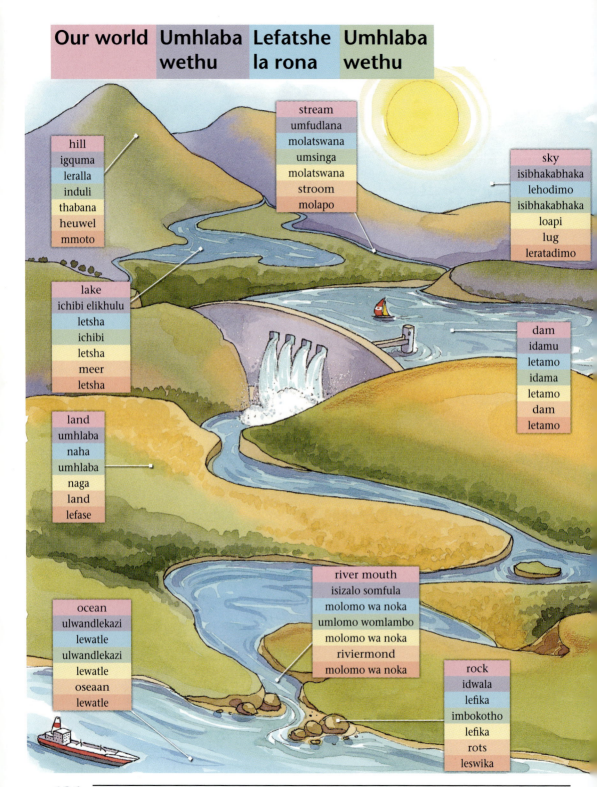

hill
igquma
leralla
induli
thabana
heuwel
mmoto

stream
umfudlana
molatswana
umsinga
molatswana
stroom
molapo

sky
isibhakabhaka
lehodimo
isibhakabhaka
loapi
lug
leratadimo

lake
ichibi elikhulu
letsha
ichibi
letsha
meer
letsha

dam
idamu
letamo
idama
letamo
dam
letamo

land
umhlaba
naha
umhlaba
naga
land
lefase

river mouth
isizalo somfula
molomo wa noka
umlomo womlambo
molomo wa noka
riviermond
molomo wa noka

ocean
ulwandlekazi
lewatle
ulwandlekazi
lewatle
oseaan
lewatle

rock
idwala
lefika
imbokotho
lefika
rots
leswika

196

Nature and us • Imvelo nathi • Tlholeho le rona • Indalo kunye nathi
Tlhago le rona • Ons en die natuur • Tlhago le rena

Lefatshe la rona   Ons wêreld   Lefase la rena

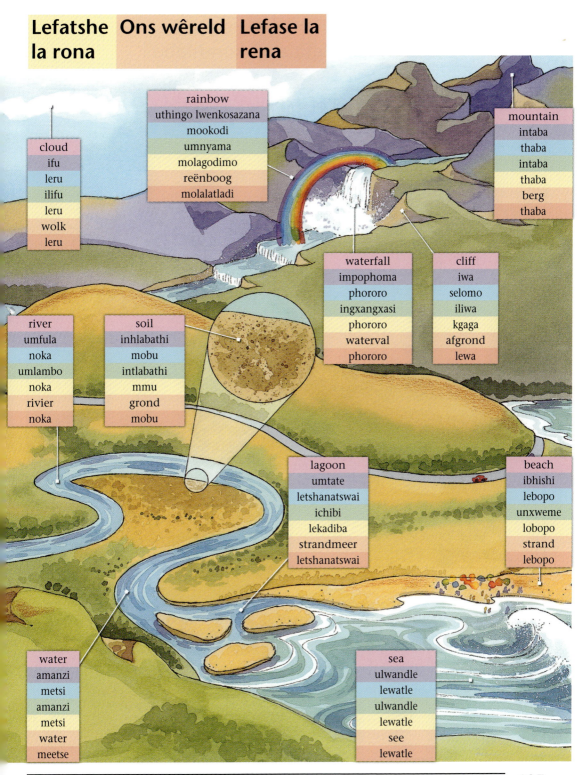

cloud
ifu
leru
ilifu
leru
wolk
leru

rainbow
uthingo lwenkosazana
mookodi
umnyama
molagodimo
reënboog
molalatladi

mountain
intaba
thaba
intaba
thaba
berg
thaba

waterfall
impophoma
phororo
ingxangxasi
phororo
waterval
phororo

cliff
iwa
selomo
iliwa
kgaga
afgrond
lewa

river
umfula
noka
umlambo
noka
rivier
noka

soil
inhlabathi
mobu
intlabathi
mmu
grond
mobu

lagoon
umtate
letshanatswai
ichibi
lekadiba
strandmeer
letshanatswai

beach
ibhishi
lebopo
unxweme
lobopo
strand
lebopo

water
amanzi
metsi
amanzi
metsi
water
meetse

sea
ulwandle
lewatle
ulwandle
lewatle
see
lewatle

Nature and us • Imvelo nathi • Tlholeho le rona • Indalo kunye nathi
Tlhago le rona • Ons en die natuur • Tlhago le rena

197

Under the surface	Ngaphansi komhlaba	Ka tlasa lefatshe	Phantsi komhlaba

Minerals and metals	Okusansimbi okumbiwa phansi	Dirashwa le dimethale	liminerali neemethali
Ditswammung le dimetale	Minerale and metale	Diminerale le dimetale	

gold	silver	platinum	iron	coal
igolide	isiliva	iplathinamu	insimbi	ilahle
kgauta	silevera	polatinamo	tshepe	mashala
igolide	isilevere	iplatinami	intsimbi	ilahle
gauta	selefera	polatinamo	tshipi	malatlha
goud	silwer	platinum	yster	steenkool
gauta	silibere	polatinamo	tšhipi	lelahla

copper	tin	zinc	aluminium	brass
ikhopha	ithini	uzinki	insimbi emhlophe elula	ithusi
koporo	thini	zinki	aleminiamo	boraso
ikopolo	itoti	izinki	i-aluminiyami	ixina
kopore	thini	senke	aluminiamo	borase
koper	tin	sink	aluminium	geelkoper
koporo	thini	sinki	aliminiamo	porase

bronze	steel	stainless steel
insimbi eyinhlanganisela yezinsimbi	isitili	isitili esihlanzekile
boronse	tshepe	tshepe e sa ruseng
ubhedu	isinyithi	isinyithi esicocekileyo
boronse	tshipi	tshipi e e sa ruseng
brons	staal	vlekvrye staal
poronse	setala	setala sa go se ruse

Fuel	Izibaso	Dibeso	Amafutha	Dibeso	Brandstof	Makhura

oil	gas	petrol	diesel	paraffin
uwoyela	okusamoya	uphethiloli	udizili	uphalafini
oli	kgase	peterole	disele	parafene
i-oli	irhasi	ipetroli	idizili	iparafini
oli	gase	peterolo	disele	parafene
olie	gas	petrol	diesel	paraffien
oli	gase	peterole	disele	parafene

Gemstones and stones	Amatshana namatshe ayigugu	Mahakwe le majwe	Amatye anqabileyo namatye
Dibenya le matlapana	Edelgesteentes en klippe	Mabje	

diamond
idayimane
taemane
idayimani
taemane
diamant
taemane

ruby
irubi
rubi
irubhi
rubi
robyn
legakadima

opal
i-ophali
opale
i-ophali
ophale
opaal
opale

emerald
igwadle eliluhlaza
emerale
i-imeraldi
emerale
smarag
emerale

sapphire
umsafaya
safaya
ilitye elizuba
safire
saffier
safaya

amethyst
amethisi
ametisete
amethisi
ametisiti
ametis
ametisi

granite
igwadle
kgeranata
inyengane
gerenaete
graniet
krenate

sandstone
ichoba
lesehlwa
ilitye lentlabathi
letlapamotlhaba
sandsteen
mogohlo

quartz
igcaki
kwaretse
ikhristali
ntswanatshipi
kwarts
kwatshe

marble
imabuli
mabole
ibhastile
mmabole
marmer
mmabole

Nature and us • Imvelo nathi • Tlholeho le rona • Indalo kunye nathi
Tlhago le rona • Ons en die natuur • Tlhago le rena

199

Seasons Izikhathi zonyaka Dinako tsa selemo

spring
intwasahlobo
selemo
intwasahlobo
dikgakologo
lente
seruthwana

summer
ihlobo
hlabula
ihlobo
selemo
somer
selemo

Weather Isimo sezulu Tsa boemo ba lehodimo

lightning	hail	snow	wind	mist	fog
umbani	isichotho	iqhwa	umoya	inkungu	umlalamvubu
lehadima	sefako	lehlwa	moya	mohodi	mohodi
umbane	isichotho	iliqhwa	umoya	inkungu	inkungu
legadima	sefako	segagane	phefo	mouwane	semathane
weerlig	hael	sneeu	wind	mis	mis
legadima	sefako	lehlwa	phefo	mouwane	kgodi

storm	cyclone	tornado	cold front
Imvula enesiphepho	isishingishane	isiphepho esikhulu	umoya obandayo
sefefo	setsokotsane	kganyapa	moya o batang
isiphango	inkanyamba	inkanyamba	umsinga womoya obandayo
setsuatsue	kgwanyape	kgwanyape	phefo e e tsididi ya borwa
storm	sikloon	tornado	koue front
ledimo	saeklone	mamogašwa	moya o tonyago tonyi

heat wave	dust storm	dew	frost
isivuvu	umoya oyisiphepho	amazolo	isithwathwa
moya o tjhesang	lerole	phoka	serame
umsinga womoya oshushu	isaqhwithi	umbethe	iqabaka
mogote o o tseremang	dithunthung	monyo	semathane
hittegolf	stofstorm	dou	ryp
moya wo o fišago tšhiritšhiri	lerole la ledimo	phoka	tšhwaane

Nature and us • Imvelo nathi • Tlholeho le rona • Indalo kunye nathi
Tlhago le rona • Ons en die natuur • Tlhago le rena

Amaxesha onyaka Ditlha tsa ngwaga Seisoene Dikga

autumn
ikwindla
hwetla
ukwindla
letlhabula
herfs
lehlabula

winter
ubusika
mariha
ubusika
mariga
winter
marega

Imozulu Bosa Weer Boso

sun	cloud	drizzle	rain	showers	thunderstorm
ilanga	ifu	umkhemezelo	imvula	izihlambi zemvula	ukuduma kwezulu
letsatsi	leru	matheaditsintsi	pula	mafafatsane	sekgohola
ilanga	ilifu	umkhumezelo	imvula	umtshizo	isiphango
letsatsi	leru	koma-koma	pula	mokomakomane	matlakadibe
son	wolk	motreën	reën	reënbuie	donderstorm
letšatši	leru	mohuhwane	pula	mosarasarane	matlakadibe

temperature	pressure	wind speed	ice	freezing
izinga lokushisa	isisindo somoya	ijubane lomoya	iqhwa	iiqeqeba lamakhaza
themperetjhara	kgatello	lebelo la moya	leqhwa	mohatsela
iqondo lobushushu	uxinzelelo	isantya somoya	umkhenkce	chachatheka
thempereitšha	kgatelelo	lebelo la phefo	dikgapetla	gatsetsa
temperatuur	lugdruk	windspoed	ys	ysig
themperetšha	kgatelelo	lebelo la phefo	lehlwa	kgatselo

cold	hot	wet	dry	flood	drought	climate
kuyabanda	kuyashisa	-manzi	-omile	isikhukhula	isomiso	ubunjalo bezulu
bata	tjhesa	mongobo	omme	sekgohola	komello	boemo
ingqele	kushushu	ubumanzi	ukoma	isikhukula	imbalela	imozulu
tsididi	bolelo	kolobileng	omeletse	morwalela	komelelo	maemo a bosa
koud	warm	nat	droog	vloed	droogte	klimaat
phefo	fiša	koloba	oma	morwalela	komelelo	tlelaemete

Nature and us • Imvelo nathi • Tlholeho le rona • Indalo kunye nathi
Tlhago le rona • Ons en die natuur • Tlhago le rena

201

tail	paw	parrot
umsila	isidladla	upholi
mohatla	leoto la phoofolo	papakgaye
umsila	imphuphu	isikhwenene
mogatla	leroo	papagae
stert	poot	papegaai
mosela	borofa	papagai

canary
umzwilili
tswere
umlonji
khanari
kanarie
kanari

cat
ikati
katse
ikati
katse
kat
katse

dog
inja
ntja
inja
ntšwa
hond
mpša

hamster
uhemusta
lebodi
isikrekrethi esifana nebuzi
hamosetere
hamster
legotlwana

horse
ihhashi
pere
ihashe
pitse
perd
pere

hoof
inselo
tlhako
uphuphu
tlhako
hoef
tlhako

rabbit
unogwaja
mmutlanyana
umvundla
mmutla
konyn
mmutla

chicken
inkukhu
kgoho
inkukhu
kgogo
hoender
kgogo

cow
inkomazi
kgomo
inkomo
kgomo
koei
kgomotshadi

pig	sheep	goat
ingulube	isiklabhu/imvu	imbuzi
fariki	nku	podi
ihagu	igusha	ibhokhwe
kolobe	nku	podi
vark	skaap	bok
kolobe	nku	pudi

202

Nature and us • Imvelo nathi • Tlholeho le rona • Indalo kunye nathi
Tlhago le rona • Ons en die natuur • Tlhago le rena

Baby animals	Abantwana bezilwane	Bana ba diphoofolo	Abantwana bezilwanyana
Bana ba diphologolo	Klein diertjies	Bana ba diphoofolo	

Male and female	Enduna nensikazi
Botona le botshehadi	Iduna nokhomokazi
Bongtona le Bongtshadi	Manlik en vroulik
Botona le botshadi	

kitten
umthiyane
ledinyane la katse
intshontsho lekati
katsana
katjie
katsana

puppy
umwundlwane
mootlwana
umbudlwana
ntšwanyana
hondjie
mpšanyana

foal
inkonyane yehhashi
petsana
inkonyana yehashe
petsana
vulletjie
pešara

piglet
ichwane
lengulube
fakatshana
intshontsho lehagu
kolojane
varkie
kolobjana

lamb
izinyane
konyana
itakane
konyana
lammetjie
kwana

chick
ichwane
tsuonyana
intshontsho lenkukhu
tsuanyane
kuiken
lefotwana

calf
inkonyane
namane
ithole
namane
kalfie
namane

kid
izinyane
potsanyane
itakane lebhokhwe
potsane
boklam
putšana

cow
inkomazi
kgomo
imazi yenkomo
kgomo
koei
kgomotshadi

bull
inkunzi
poho
inkunzi yenkomo
poo
bul
pholo

mare
ihhashi lensikazi
pere e tshehadi
imazi yehashe
tshegadi
merrie
peregadi

stallion
inkunzi yehhashi
pere e tona
inkunzi yehashe
tonanyana
hings
peretona

ewe
imvukazi
pere e tshehadi
imazi yegusha
namagadi
ooi
tshelau

ram
inqama
pheleu
inkunzi yegusha
phelehu
ram
kgapa

hen
isikhukhukazi
sethole
isikhukhukazi
sethole
hen
kgogotshadi

cockerel
iqhude
mokokwana
umqhagi osemncinane
mokoko
haan
mokokwana

Nature and us • Imvelo nathi • Tlholeho le rona • Indalo kunye nathi
Tlhago le rona • Ons en die natuur • Tlhago le rena

203

lion
ibhubesi
tau
ingonyama
tau
leeu
tau

cheetah
ingulule
lengau
ingwenkala
lengau
jagluiperd
lepogo

eland
impofu
phofu
impofu
tholo
eland
phofu

leopard
ihlosi
lengau
ihlosi
nkwe
luiperd
lepogo

mane
umhlwenga
moetse
isingci
moetse
maanhare
mariri

kudu
bheka
tholo
iqhude
tholo
koedoe
tholo

gemsbok
ijemsbhoki
kgama
ijemsbhokhwe
kgama
gemsbok
kgama

wild cat
imbodla
setsetse
ingada
phage
wildekat
phaga

waterbuck
iphiva
pabala
imbabala
phuti ya metsi
waterbok
kwele

warthog
indlovudawana
kolobemoru
ihodi
kolobe ya naga
vlakvark
kolobe ya naga

rhinoceros (rhino)
ubhejane
tshukudu
umkhombe
tshukudu
renoster
tšhukudu

Nature and us • Imvelo nathi • Tlholeho le rona • Indalo kunye nathi
Tlhago le rona • Ons en die natuur • Tlhago le rena

giraffe	buffalo	elephant
indlulamithi	inyathi	indlovu
thuhlo	nare	tlou
indlulamthi	inyathi	indlovu
thutlwa	nare	tlou
kameelperd	buffel	olifant
thutlwa	nare	tlou

tusk
izinyo lendlovu
lenaka la tlou
ibamba
lenaka
olifanttand
lenaka la tlou

nyala
inyala
nyala
inyala
nyala
njala
nyala

bushbuck
imbabala
phuthi
imbabala
phuti
bosbok
phuti

springbuck
insephe
tshepe
ibhadi
tshepe
springbok
tshepe

impala	horn	zebra	hippopotamus
impala	uphondo	idube	imvubu
phala	lenaka	qwaha	kubu
i-impala	uphondo	iqwarhashe	imvubu
phala	lonaka	pitse ya naga	kubu
impala	horing	sebra	seekoei
phala	lenaka	pitsi	kubu

Nature and us • Imvelo nathi • Tlholeho le rona • Indalo kunye nathi
Tlhago le rona • Ons en die natuur • Tlhago le rena

205

chimpanzee
uhlobo lwemfene enkulu
tjhempantse
itshimpanzi
tšhimpanse
sjimpansee
tšhimpase

gorilla
gorila
korela
igorila
korela
gorilla
korila

monkey
inkawu
kgabo
inkawu
kgabo
aap
kgabo

baboon
imfene
tshwene
imfene
tshwene
bobbejaan
tšhwene

bushpig
ingulube yehlathi
kolobemoru
ingulube
kolobe ya naga
bosvark
kolobe ya naga

jackal
ujakalase
phokojwe
udyakalashe
phokojwe
jakkals
phukubje

aardvark/
ant bear
isambane
thakadi
ibhenxa
isimbamgodi
thakadu
erdvark
thakadu

hyena
impisi
lefiritshwana
ingcuka
phiri
hiëna
phiri

Nature and us • Imvelo nathi • Tlholeho le rona • Indalo kunye nathi
Tlhago le rona • Ons en die natuur • Tlhago le rena

squirrel
ingwejeje
modube
unomatse
setlhora
eekhorinkie
sehlora

bushbaby
isinkwe
api ya bosiu
inkawana yasebusuku
api ya bosigo
nagapie
kgabo ya bošego

dassie
imbili
pela
imbila
pela
dassie
pela

meerkat
ububhibhi
mosha
igala
mošwe
meerkat
kgano

wild dog
inja yehlathi
lekanyane
inja yasendle
lekanyane
wildehond
lehlalerwa

porcupine
ingungumbane
noko
incanda
noko
ystervark
noko

hare
unogwaja
mmutla
umvundla
mmutla
haas
mmutla

mouse
igundwane
tweba
impuku
legotlo
muis
peba

rat
ibuzi
kgoto
ibuzi
legotlo
rot
legotlo

Nature and us • Imvelo nathi • Tlholeho le rona • Indalo kunye nathi
Tlhago le rona • Ons en die natuur • Tlhago le rena

207

fox
impungushe
mopheme
impungutye
thukgwe
vos
phukubje

reindeer
inyamazana ehlala kwindawo ebandayo
kgama
ixhama
kgama
rendier
kgamakgolo

bear
ibhele
bere
ibhere
bera
beer
bere

panda
uhlobo lwebhele
bere
uhlobo oluthile lwebhere
bera
panda
phantabera

deer
inyamazana enezimpondo egingamagatsha
kgama
ixhama
kgama
hert
kgama

koala bear
uhlobo lwebhele
bera ya koala
uhlobo oluthile lwebhere
bera ya koala
koalabeer
koalabere

tiger
ingwe
nkwe
ingwe
nkwe
tier
nkwe

kangaroo
umlalaphansi
tshipho
ikhangaru
khankaru
kangaroe
kome

Nature and us • Imvelo nathi • Tlholeho le rona • Indalo kunye nathi
Tlhago le rona • Ons en die natuur • Tlhago le rena

Diphologolo tse dingwe | Ander diere | Diphoofolo tše dingwe

platypus
isilwane saseOstreliya
polatipase
iplatipasi
polatipase
eendbekdier
poletipasa

panther
uhlobo lwengwe lengau
ingwe
nkwe
panter
pantere

orang-utan
imfene enkulu yasemahlathini
tshwene e kgolo ya morung
i-orangitangi
ora-utang
orangoetang
orangutang

jaguar
uhlobo lwengwe enkulu
jakwa
ingwe
jakhwa
jaguar
jakwa

lynx
ilinksi
thwane
ingqawa
linkise
rooikat
linkise

llama
ilama
lama
ilama
llama
llama
lama

camel
ikameli
kamele
inkamela
kamela
kameel
kamela

alligator
ingwenya
kwena
ingwenya
kwena
alligator
kwena

Nature and us • Imvelo nathi • Tlholeho le rona • Indalo kunye nathi
Tlhago le rona • Ons en die natuur • Tlhago le rena

209

Birds 1 Izinyoni 1 Dinonyana 1 Iintaka 1

beak
uqhwaku
molomo wa nonyana
umlomo wentaka
molomo wa nonyane
snawel
molomo

wing
iphiko
lepheo
iphiko
lefuka
vlerk
lephego

ostrich
intshe
mpshe
inciniba
ntšhwe
volstruis
mpšhe

hornbill
insingizi
honbili
umkhwane
korwe
neushoringvoël
honobili

eagle
ukhozi
ntsu
ukhozi
ntsu
arend
ntšhu

flamingo
umakholwane
mokotatsie
ikholwane
folaminko
flamink
kokolohuto

hoopoe
uziningweni
popopo
ihupu
lehututu
hoep-hoep
hupu

pelican
ivuba
pelikene
ingcwangube
phelekene
pelikaan
phelikene

egret
ilanda
leholosiane
ilanda
mogolodi
witreier
kgogobadimo

weaver
ihlokohloko
letholoptje
iwiva
thaga
vink
thaga

Nature and us • Imvelo nathi • Tlholeho le rona • Indalo kunye nathi
Tlhago le rona • Ons en die natuur • Tlhago le rena

Dinonyane 1 Voëls 1 Dinonyana 1

kite
inyoni yephepha
kgodi
umdlampuku
khaete
wou/valk
khaete

stork
unogolantethe
mokotatsie
unocofu
mmamoleyane
ooievaar
leakabosane

hawk
uklebe
phakwe
ukhetshe
nkgodi
valk
pekwa

owl
isikhova
sephooko
isikhova
morubisi
uil
leribiši

claw
uzipho
lenala la nonyana
amaqoqo
monoto
klou
monotlo

vulture
inqe
lenong
ixhalanga
lenong
aasvoël
lenong

secretary bird
intinginono
mmamolangwane
ingxangxosi
mmamolangwana
sekretarisvoël
tlhame

blue crane
uhlobo lwendwandwe
moholodi
indwe
mogolodi
bloukraanvoël
mogolodi

heron
indwandwe
kokolofitwe
ukhwalimanzi
kokolohute
reier
kokoluhute

crow
igwababa
lekgwaba
unomyayi
legakabe
kraai
legokobu

swallow
inkonjane
lefokotsane
inkonjane
peolwane
swael
peolane

Nature and us • Imvelo nathi • Tlholeho le rona • Indalo kunye nathi
Tlhago le rona • Ons en die natuur • Tlhago le rena

211

seagull
inyoni yasogwini
lolwandle
sikale
ingabangaba
lenongwatle
seemeeu
lenongwatle

pigeon
ijuba
leeba
ihobe
leeba
duif
leeba

dove
ihobhe
leebanakgorwana
ivukuthu
leebarope
duifie
leeba

penguin
iphengwini
phenkwene
unombombiya
phenkwine
pikkewyn
phenkhwini

starling
igwinsi
sekgodi
inyakrini
legodi
spreeu
legodi

cormorant
izinhlobo zezinyoni zasolwandle
khomorante/seenodi
ugwidi
timeletsane
duiker
komorente

kingfisher
unongozolo
majatlhapi
uxomoyi
nonyane e e tshelang
ka tlhapi
visvanger
majahlapi

sunbird
uhlobo
lwencuncu
taletale
intaka yelanga
senwaboropi
suikerbekkie
senwamanopi

Dinonyane 2 Voëls 2 Dinonyana 2

bee-eater
inyoni edla izinambuzane
sejakgekge
isidlanyosi
sejadinotshe
byevreter
sejanose

sparrow
umathebethebane
serobele
unondlwane
serobele
mossie
phorokgohlo

lourie
igwalagwala
lori
iluri
mokowe
loerie
lori

peacock
impigogo
pikoko
ipikoko
phikoko
pou
phikoko

goose
ihansi
letata
irhanisi
ganse
gans
legantshe

duck
idada
lekau
idada
pidipidi
eend
lepelepele

white-eye
umehlwana
thaha
umehlwana
lephoi le le nang le matlho a masweu
glasogie
madišadikgomo

woodpecker
isiqophamithi
mohetle
isinqolamthi
kopaopa
houtkapper
sephaphadikota

swan
ikewu
kgantshi
untamonde wedada
pidipidi
swaan
mamašianoka

Nature and us • Imvelo nathi • Tlholeho le rona • Indalo kunye nathi
Tlhago le rona • Ons en die natuur • Tlhago le rena

213

Reptiles Izilwane ezihuquzelayo Dihahabi

crocodile
ingwenya
kwena
ingwenya
kwena
krokodil
kwena

leguan
isigcikilisha
lakabane
uxam
gopane
likkewaan
lehopane

frog
ixoxo
senqanqana
isele
segwagwa
padda
segwagwa

gecko
iqhimilili
tjhetjheiki
unomfulwana
mmamagwatagwatane
geitjie
kodutala

chameleon
unwabu
lempetje
ilovane
leobu
verkleurmannetjie
leobu

lizard
isibankwa
mokgodutswane
icikilishe
mokgatitswane
akkedis
mokgaditswane

Nature and us • Imvelo nathi • Tlholeho le rona • Indalo kunye nathi
Tlhago le rona • Ons en die natuur • Tlhago le rena

Izilwanyana ezirhubuluzayo Digagabi Reptiele Digagabi

Snakes Izinyoka Dinoha Iinyoka Dinoga Slange Dinoga

python
inhlwathi
tlhware
intlwathi
tlhware
luislang
hlware

boomslang
ifulwa
noha ya difate
inyoka yomthi
moselenyane
boomslang
mosenene

mamba
imamba
mamba
inyushu
mokwepa
mamba
mokopa

cobra
imfezi
masumu
iphimpi
kake
kobra
peetla

viper
indlondlo
marabe
irhamba
baephara
adder
marabe

ringhals
iphimpi
lehwere
iphimpi
rankalese
rinkhals
renkalse

puff adder
ibululu
marabe
irhamba
lebolobolo
pofadder
letsolobolo

snake
inyoka
noha
inyoka
noga
slang
noga

tortoise
ufudu
kgudu
ufudo
khudu
skilpad
khudu

Nature and us • Imvelo nathi • Tlholeho le rona • Indalo kunye nathi
Tlhago le rona • Ons en die natuur • Tlhago le rena

215

Life in water | Impilo yasemanzini | Bophelo ka metsing | Ubomi basemanzini

Freshwater Amanzi amtoti Metsi a matjha Izidalwa zamanzi
Metsi a a phepa Vars water Meetsemahlweki

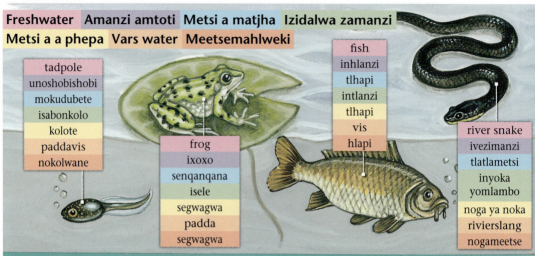

tadpole	fish
unoshobishobi	inhlanzi
mokudubete	tlhapi
isabonkolo	intlanzi
kolote	tlhapi
paddavis	vis
nokolwane	hlapi

frog	river snake
ixoxo	ivezimanzi
senqanqana	tlatlametsi
isele	inyoka yomlambo
segwagwa	noga ya noka
padda	rivierslang
segwagwa	nogameetse

Seawater Amanzi olwandle Metsi a lewatle Amanzi olwandle
Metsi a lewatle Seewater Meetsewatle

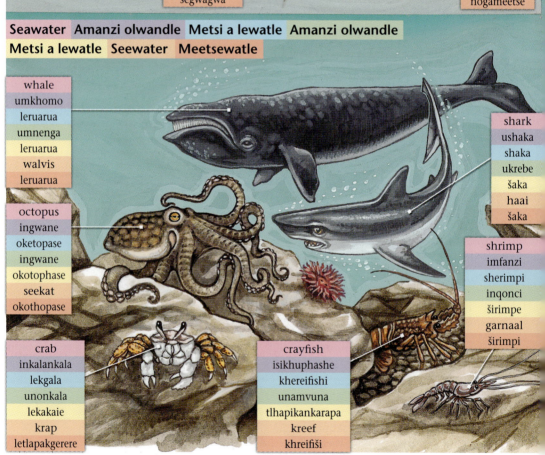

whale	shark
umkhomo	ushaka
leruarua	shaka
umnenga	ukrebe
leruarua	šaka
walvis	haai
leruarua	šaka

octopus	shrimp
ingwane	imfanzi
oketopase	sherimpi
ingwane	inqonci
okotophase	širimpe
seekat	garnaal
okothopase	širimpi

crab	crayfish
inkalankala	isikhuphashe
lekgala	khereifishi
unonkala	unamvuna
lekakaie	tlhapikankarapa
krap	kreef
letlapakgerere	khreifiši

216

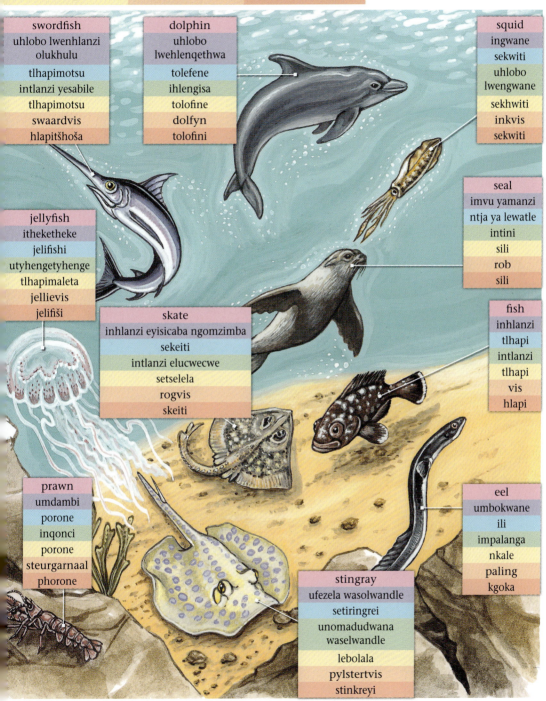

swordfish
uhlobo lwenhlanzi olukhulu
tlhapimotsu
intlanzi yesabile
tlhapimotsu
swaardvis
hlapitšhoša

dolphin
uhlobo lwehlenqethwa
tolefene
ihlengisa
tolofine
dolfyn
tolofini

squid
ingwane
sekwiti
uhlobo lwengwane
sekhwiti
inkvis
sekwiti

jellyfish
itheketheke
jelifishi
utyhengetyhenge
tlhapimaleta
jellievis
jelifiši

seal
imvu yamanzi
ntja ya lewatle
intini
sili
rob
sili

skate
inhlanzi eyisicaba ngomzimba
sekeiti
intlanzi elucwecwe
setselela
rogvis
skeiti

fish
inhlanzi
tlhapi
intlanzi
tlhapi
vis
hlapi

prawn
umdambi
porone
inqonci
porone
steurgarnaal
phorone

stingray
ufezela wasolwandle
setiringrei
unomadudwana waselwandle
lebolala
pylstertvis
stinkreyi

eel
umbokwane
ili
impalanga
nkale
paling
kgoka

Nature and us • Imvelo nathi • Tlholeho le rona • Indalo kunye nathi
Tlhago le rona • Ons en die natuur • Tlhago le rena

217

Creepy crawlies	Izinambuzane nezilwane ezinwabuzelayo	Dikokonyana

ant
intuthwane
kokonyana
imbovane
tshoswane
mier
tšhošane

locust
iqhwagi
lerutle
inkumbi
tsie
sprinkaan
tšie

praying mantis
isithwalambiza
serwalankgwana
umnt'anezulu
tsiakgopi
mantis
mmaseletswane

grasshopper
intethe
kgupi
umqhadi
tsie
grassprinkaan
ngwana wa tšie

termite
umuhlwa
lesetlaoko
intubi
motlhwa
termiet
mohlwa

fly
impukane
ntsintsi
impukane
ntsi
vlieg
ntši

spider
isicabucabu
sekgo
isigcawu
segokgo
spinnekop
segokgo

flea
izeze
letsetse
intakumba
letsetse
vlooi
letsetse

dragonfly
uzekamanzi
lefehlo
uhlub'amanzi
ntshikgolo
naaldekoker
leponono

scorpion
ufezela
phepheng
unomadukudwane
phepheng
skerpioen
phepheng

snail
umnenke
kgofu
usinyeke
kgopa
slak
kgopa

centipede
inkuma
mosikaphalla
inkuma
mositaphala
honderdpoot
mosetaphala

millipede
ishongololo
lefokolodi
isongololo
sebokolodi
duisendpoot
mogokolodi

218

Izinambuzane Ditshenekegi Goggas Dikhunkhwane

butterfly
uvemvane
serurubele
ibhabhathane
serurubele
skoenlapper
serurubele

caterpillar
isibungu
leqepe
umbungu
seboko
ruspe
seboko

bee
inyosi
notshi
inyosi
notshe
by
nose

beetle
ibhungane
kgolabolokwe
uqongqothwane
khukhwane
tor
sekgobaboloko

moth
ibhu
mmoto
ivivingane
mmoto
mot
mmoto

horsefly
isibawu samabashi
seboba
isibawu
seboba
perdevlieg
poba

cockroach
ikokoloshe
lephele
iphela
lefele
kakkerlak
lefele

fishmoth
inyundu
tshwele
inundu
tlhapimmoto
vismot
hlapimmoto

wasp
umnyovu
bobi
unomeva
lerwane
perdeby
mobu

dung beetle
inkumabulongwe
kgolabolokwe
inkababulongwe
pitiki
miskruier
sekgobaboloko

earthworm
umsundu
nyonyobetsane
umsundululu
monopi
erdwurm
nogametsana

mosquito
umiyane
monwang
ingcongconi
monang
muskiet
monang

gnat
insensane
tsie
imbuzane
nete
muggie
nete

Nature and us • Imvelo nathi • Tlholeho le rona • Indalo kunye nathi
Tlhago le rona • Ons en die natuur • Tlhago le rena

219

Plants Izitshalo Dimela Izityalo

petal
igcebe lembali
petale
igqabi lentyatyambo
phetale
blomblaar
letlakalatšoba

flower
imbali
palesa
intyatyambo
sethunya
blom
letšoba

grass
utshani
jwang
ingca
tlhaga
gras
bjang

stem
isiqu
kutu
isiqu
kutu
stingel
thito

weed
ukhula
lehola
ukhula
mofero
onkruid
sekoro

seed
imbewu
peo
imbewu
peo
saad
peu

leaf
icembe
lehlaku
igqabi
letlhare
blaar
letlakala

fern
uhlinzafuku
fene
ifeni
fene
varing
mmalewaneng

root
impande
motso
ingcambu
modi
wortel
modu

shrub
isihlahlana
sehlahla
ityholo
setlhatsana
struik
mohlašana

bush
ihlathi
mofero
ityholo
setlhatlha
bos
sethokgwa

forest
ihlathi
moru
ihlathi
sekgwa
woud
sekgwa

Nature and us • Imvelo nathi • Tlholeho le rona • Indalo kunye nathi
Tlhago le rona • Ons en die natuur • Tlhago le rena

Dijalo Plante Mehlare

tree
isihlahla
sefate
umthi
setlhare
boom
mohlare

twig
igatshana
lekalana
isetyana
kalana
takkie
lekalana

branch
igatsha
lekala
isebe
kala
tak
lekala

blossom
qhakaza
thungthung
ukudubula kwentyantyambo
thunya
bloeisel
kutu

creeper
izitshalo ezenabayo
leraka
isityalo esirhubuluzayo
moithari
rankplant/klimop
motatane

pine cone
isithelo sephayini
khounu ya phaene
umbhumbhulu wepayina
leungo la setlhare sa phaene
dennebol
phaenekhouni

pod
umdumba
nawa
umdumba
sephotlwa
peul
sephotlwa

trunk
isiqu
kutu
isiqu
kutu
boomstam
thito

bark
igxolo lomuthi
letlalo la kutu ya sefate
ixolo lomthi
lekwati
bas
lekwamati

Nature and us • Imvelo nathi • Tlholeho le rona • Indalo kunye nathi
Tlhago le rona • Ons en die natuur • Tlhago le rena

221

Flowers Izimbali Dipalesa Iintyantyambo

sunflower
ubhekilanga
sonobolomo
ujongilanga
sonobolomo
sonneblom
sonopolomo

aloe
inhlaba
lekgala
ikhala
kgopane
aalwyn
kgopa

strelitzia
isigude
seterelitsia
ikhamanzi
steterelezia
strelitzia
seterelesia

rose
irozi
rosa
irozi
rouse
roos
rosa

protea
iprothiya
porotia
isiqwane
phorothia
protea
poroteye

hydrangea
ihayidrenjiya
haedranjea
ihandrinjiya
haeterakia
krismisroos
haeterentšea

geranium
uhlobo lwembali
jeraniamo
ijereniyami
jereniamo
malva
tšeraneamo

fynbos
ifinibhosi
feinbose
ifeyinbhosi
feineboso
fynbos
feinposo

pansy
iphenzi
phensi
ipentsi
phensi
gesiggie
phensei

sweat pea
isithiphi
switipi
i-ertyisi eswiti
tšhese e e nang le tatso e e botshe
pronkertjie
switiphi

erica
i-erikha
erika
i-erika
erika
erika
erika

arum lily
imbali yentebe
mohaladitwe
i-aram lili
aramo lili
aronskelk
aramolili

iris
i-ayirisi
aerisi
i-ayirisi
aerise
iris
aerisi

orchid
i-oshidi
otjhiti
i-otshidi
otšhete
orgidee
otšhiti

daisy
imbali efana nodlutshana
teisi
ideyizi
teise
madeliefie
teisi

222

Dithunya Blomme Matšoba

hibiscus
ihayibhisikhasi
haebisikase
ihibisikasi
hibesekase
hibiskus
letšobahipiskose

poppy
iphophi
popi
ipopi
popi
papawer
letšobapopi

water lily
izibu
lili ya metsi
intyatyambo yamanzi
tswii
waterlelie
lili ya meetse

lavender
ilavenda
lavenda
ilavenda
labenta
laventel
lafentere

jasmine
ijasimini
jasemaene
ijasmini
jasemine
jasmyn
jasemine

Trees Izihlahla Difate imithi Ditlhare Bome Mehlare

yellowwood
umsonti
sefate se se sehla
umkhoba
logong lo lo setlha
geelhoutboom
moserolwane

pine tree
isihlala sephayini
sefate sa phaene
umthi wepayina
setlhare sa phaene
denneboom
mophaene

palm tree
isundu
palema
isundu
mokolane
palmboom
mopalema

stinkwood
isitingawothi
setinkiwute
umsimbithi
logong lo lo nkgang
stinkhoutboom
modupe

baobab
ubhawobhabhu
baobabo
ibhowabhi
mowana
kremetartboom
moboi

jacaranda
ijakharanda
jakaranda
ijakaranda
jakaranda
jakaranda
mojakaranta

thorn tree
umdolofiya
leoka
umthi onameva
mooka
doringboom
mošwana

willow
umnyezane
moduwane
umngcunube
moduwane
wilgerboom
motswapitswapi

oak
i-okhi
ouku
um-okhi
ouku
eikeboom
moeike

silver tree
umuthi wesiliva
sefate sa silivera
umthi wesilivere
setlhareselefere
silwerblaarboom
mosilibere

Nature and us • Imvelo nathi • Tlholeho le rona • Indalo kunye nathi
Tlhago le rona • Ons en die natuur • Tlhago le rena

223

Crops Izilimo Dijalo Izityalo ezivelisa iziqhambo

barley
ubhali
harese
irhasi
bali
gort
garase

sorghum
amabele
mabele
amazimba
mabele
sorghum
mabele

oats
izinhlamvu zefijoli
habore
i-habile
outshe
hawer
outse

maize
ummbila
poone
umbona
mmopo
mielie
lehea

wheat
ukolo
koro
ingqolowa
korong
koring
korong

tobacco
ugwayi
kwae
icuba
motsoko
tabak
motšoko

cotton
ugampokwe
kgareng
umqhaphu
tlhale
katoen
leokodi

millet
unyawothi
ntshwe
amazimba
lebelebele
trosgras
leotša

lucerne
ulusene
lesere
ilusini
losereng
lusern
lesereng

canola
ikhanola
khanola
ikhala
khanola
kanola
kanola

soya
isoya
soya
isoya
soya
soja
soya

sunflower
ubhekilanga
sonobolomo
ujongilanaga
sonobolomo
sonneblom
sonopolomo

224

Nature and us • Imvelo nathi • Tlholeho le rona • Indalo kunye nathi
Tlhago le rona • Ons en die natuur • Tlhago le rena

Dijalo Oeste Dibjalo

citrus
amasithrasi
molamunu
isitrasi
monamune
sitrus
monamune

sugar cane
umoba
mmoba
umphurhu
nyoba
suikerriet
nyoba

fruit
izithelo
ditholwana
iziqhamo
leungo
vrugte
kenywa

vegetables
imifino
meroho
imifuno
merogo
groente
merogo

flowers
izimbali
dipalesa
iintyatyambo
dithunya
blomme
matšoba

vineyard
isivini
masimo a morara
umyezo weediliya
segotlo sa morara
wingerd
serapa sa meterebe

plantation
ihlathi lokutshalwa
serapa sa difate
ihlathi elityaliweyo
polantasi
plantasie
plantasi

orchard
insimu yezihlahla zezithelo
masimo a ditholwana
umyezo
tshimo ya maungo
boord
serapa sa dikenywa

field
insimu
tshimo
intsimi
tshimo
veld
tšhemo

Nature and us • Imvelo nathi • Tlholeho le rona • Indalo kunye nathi
Tlhago le rona • Ons en die natuur • Tlhago le rena

225

Phrases	Amabinzana	Dipolelwana	Amabinzana
How is the weather today?	Linjani izulu namhlanje?	Maemo a lehodimo a jwang kajeno?	Injani imozulu namhlanje?
It is cold and rainy.	Limakhaza futhi liyana.	Ho a bata e bile pula e a na.	Kuyabanda kwaye kuyana.
It is hot today. The temperature is 30 degrees.	Kuyashisa namhlanje. Izinga lokushisa lingamadigri angamashumi amathathu.	Ho a tjhesa kajeno. Themperetjhara ke dikgarata tse 30.	Kushushu namhlanje. Amaqondo obushushu ame kuma 30.
There will be a thunderstorm this afternoon.	Lizoduma ntambama.	Sefefo se a tla motsheare wa mantsiboya.	Kuza kubakho isiphango ngale mvakwemini.
What will the weather be like tomorrow?	Lizoba njani izulu kusasa?	Maemo a lehodimo a tla ba jwang hosane?	Imozulu iza kuba njani ngomso?
It may snow on the mountains.	Lingase likhithike ezintabeni.	Le ka kgetheha dithabeng.	Kungalala ikhephu ezintabeni.
There may be hail.	Lingase line isiqhotho.	Ho ka nna ha eba le sefako.	Kungakho isichotho.
It will be very windy.	Kuzoba nomoya omkhulu.	Ho tla ba le moya o matla.	Kuza kubakho umoya ovuthuza ngamandla.
Do you think it will rain today?	Ucabanga ukuthi lizona namhlanje?	Na o nahana hore pula e ka na kajeno?	Ucinga ukuba imvula ingana namhlanje?
Yes, but it will only drizzle.	Yebo, kodwa lizokhemezela.	Ee, empa e tla ba matheadintsintsi feela.	Ewe, kodwa iza kokhumezela/iza kuchaphaza.
What is your favourite flower?	Iyiphi imbali oyithandayo?	O rata palesa efe haholo?	Yeyiphi eyona ntyantyambo oyithandayo?
I like the aloes that grow in the Eastern Cape.	Ngithanda inhlaba emila eMpumalanga yeKapa.	Ke rata lekgala le melang Kapa Botjhabela.	Ndiyawathanda amakhala akhula eMpuma-Koloni.
What is your favourite season of the year?	Yisiphi isikhathi sonyaka osithandayo?	Nako ya hao ya selemo eo o e ratang ke efe?	Leliphi elona xesha ulithandayo enyakeni?
I like summer, because one can go swimming.	Ngithanda ihlobo ngoba umuntu uyakwazi ukuyobhukuda.	Ke rata lehlabula hobane motho a ka sesa.	Ndithanda ihlobo kuba ubani angaqubha.
Do you have any pets?	Sikhona isilwane osifuyile?	Na o ruile diphoofolo tsa hae?	Unaso isilwanyana sasekhaya?
Yes, I have a dog and a cat.	Yebo, ngifuye inja nekati.	Ee, ke na le ntja le katse.	Ewe, ndinenja nekati.

226

Nature and us • Imvelo nathi • Tlholeho le rona • Indalo kunye nathi
Tlhago le rona • Ons en die natuur • Tlhago le rena

Dikapolelo	Frases	Dikafoko
Bosa bo eme/ntse jang gompieno?	Hoe is die weer vandag?	Boso bja lehono bo bjang?
Go tsididi le pula e a na.	Dit is koud en dit reën.	Go a tonya, ebile e a na.
Go mogote gompieno. Thempereitšha ke digerata di le 30.	Dit is warm vandag. Die temperatuur is 30 grade.	Go a fiša lehono. Thempereitšha ke digrata tše 30.
Go tlile go nna le ditsuatsue mo tshokologong ya gompieno.	Daar gaan vanmiddag 'n donderstorm wees.	Go tla ba le matlakadibe thapama.
Maemo a bosa a tlile go nna jang ka moso?	Hoe sal die weer môre wees?	Boso bo ka ba bjang gosasa?
Go ka nna ga wa semathane mo dithabeng.	Dit sal miskien op die berge sneeu.	Go ka ba le lehlwa kua dithabeng.
Go ka nna ga wa sefako.	Dit kan dalk hael.	Go ka ba le sefako.
Go tlile go nna diphefo thata.	Dit sal baie winderig wees.	Go tla ba le phefo.
A o bona gore pula e ka na gompieno?	Dink jy dit gaan vandag reën?	O nagana gore e ka na lehono?
Ee, fela e tlile go koma-koma fela.	Ja, maar dit sal net motreën wees.	Ee, go tla no ba le mohuhwane.
Ke sethunya sefe se o se ratang?	Wat is jou gunsteling-blom?	O rata letšoba lefe gagolo?
Ke rata kgopane e e tlhogang/melang kwa Kapa Botlhaba.	Ek hou van die aalwyne wat in die Oos-Kaap groei.	Ke rata dikgopa tšeo di melago Kapa-Bohlabela.
Ke setlha sefe se o se ratang mo ngwageng?	Wat is jou gunsteling-seisoen?	O rata sehla sefe sa ngwaga?
Ke rata selemo, ka motho a ka ya go thuma.	Ek hou van die somer, omdat 'n mens kan gaan swem.	Ke rata selemo gagolo ka gore nka rutha.
A o na le diphologolo tsa legae/lelapeng?	Het jy enige troeteldiere?	A o na le seruiwaratwa?
Ee, ke na le ntšwa le katse.	Ja, ek het 'n hond en 'n kat.	Ee, ke na le mpša le katse.

Nature and us • Imvelo nathi • Tlholeho le rona • Indalo kunye nathi
Tlhago le rona • Ons en die natuur • Tlhago le rena

227

10

Food and drink

Ukudla neziphuzo

Dijo le dino

Ukutya neziselo

Dijo le dino

Kos en drinkgoed

Dijo le dino

Fruit Izithelo Ditholwana Iziqhamo

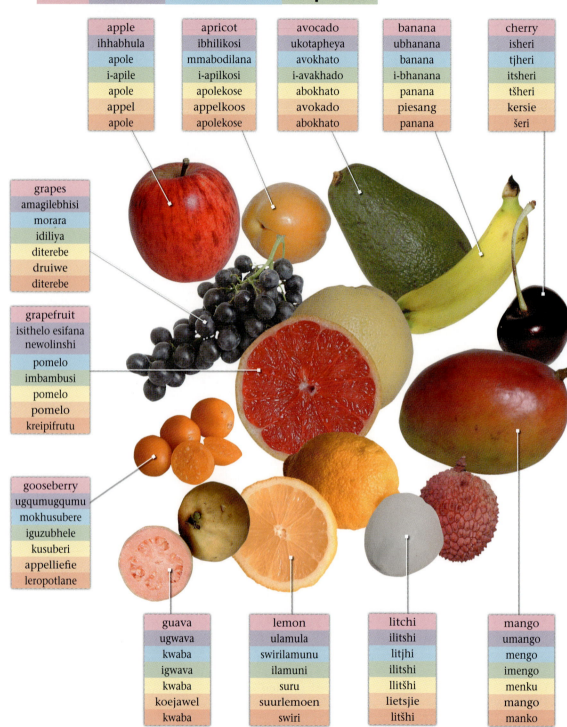

apple	apricot	avocado	banana	cherry
ihhabhula	ibhilikosi	ukotapheya	ubhanana	isheri
apole	mmabodilana	avokhato	banana	tjheri
i-apile	i-apilkosi	i-avakhado	i-bhanana	itsheri
apole	apolekose	abokhato	panana	tšheri
appel	appelkoos	avokado	piesang	kersie
apole	apolekose	abokhato	panana	šeri

grapes
amagilebhisi
morara
idiliya
diterebe
druiwe
diterebe

grapefruit
isithelo esifana newolinshi
pomelo
imbambusi
pomelo
pomelo
kreipifrutu

gooseberry
ugqumugqumu
mokhusubere
iguzubhele
kusuberi
appelliefie
leropotlane

guava	lemon	litchi	mango
ugwava	ulamula	ilitshi	umango
kwaba	swirilamunu	litjhi	mengo
igwava	ilamuni	ilitshi	imengo
kwaba	suru	llitšhi	menku
koejawel	suurlemoen	lietsjie	mango
kwaba	swiri	litšhi	manko

Maungo Vrugte Dienywa

melon	nectarine	papaya	peach	orange
ibhece	uhlobo lwepentshisi	uphopho	ipentshisi	iwolintshi
sepansepeke	neterine	phoopho	perekisi	lamunu
imelon	ipesika	ipopo	ipesika	i-orenji
legapu	perekisi	phopho	perekisi	namune
spanspek	nektarien	papaja	perske	lemoen
sepansepeke	nektarine	papaya	perekisi	namune

pear
ipheya
pere
ipere
pere
peer
pere

plum
ipulamu
poreimi
iplam
poreimi
pruim
poreime

strawberry	watermelon	tangerine	raspberry
isitrobheli	ikhabe	uhlobo lwenantshi	ijingijokolo
monokotshwai	lehapu	thangerine	monokotshwai wa basadi
iqunube	ivatala	inarityisi	iqunube
setoroberi	legapu	nnariki	mmurubele
aarbei	waatlemoen	nartjie	framboos
setoroperi	legapu	nariki	raseperi

Vegetables 1 Imifino 1 Meroho 1 Imifuno 1

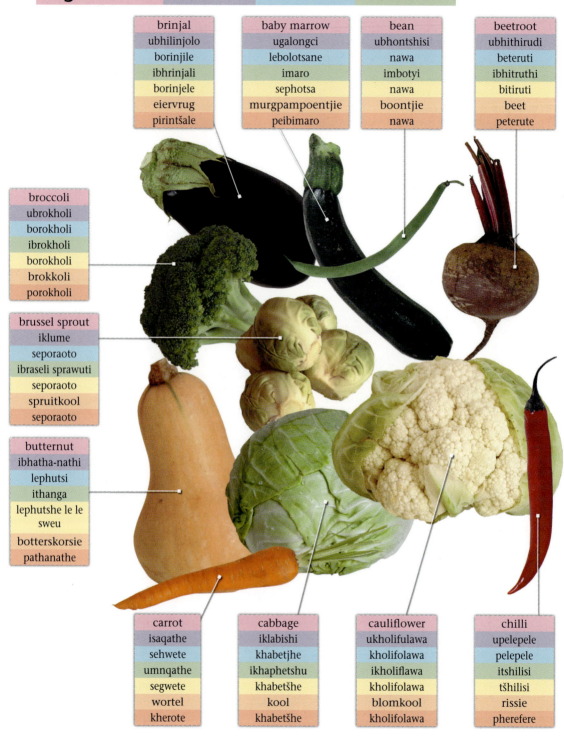

brinjal	baby marrow	bean	beetroot
ubhilinjolo	ugalongci	ubhontshisi	ubhithirudi
borinjile	lebolotsane	nawa	beteruti
ibhrinjali	imaro	imbotyi	ibhitruthi
borinjele	sephotsa	nawa	bitiruti
eiervrug	murgpampoentjie	boontjie	beet
pirintšale	peibimaro	nawa	peterute

broccoli
ubrokholi
borokholi
ibrokholi
borokholi
brokkoli
porokholi

brussel sprout
iklume
seporaoto
ibraseli sprawuti
seporaoto
spruitkool
seporaoto

butternut
ibhatha-nathi
lephutsi
ithanga
lephutshe le le sweu
botterskorsie
pathanathe

carrot	cabbage	cauliflower	chilli
isaqathe	iklabishi	ukholifulawa	upelepele
sehwete	khabetjhe	kholifolawa	pelepele
umnqathe	ikhaphetshu	ikholiflawa	itshilisi
segwete	khabetšhe	kholifolawa	tšhilisi
wortel	kool	blomkool	rissie
kherote	khabetšhe	kholifolawa	pherefere

Food and drink • Ukudla neziphuzo • Dijo le dino • Ukutya neziselo
Dijo le dino • Kos en drinkgoed • Dijo le dino

Merogo 1 Groente 1 Merogo 1

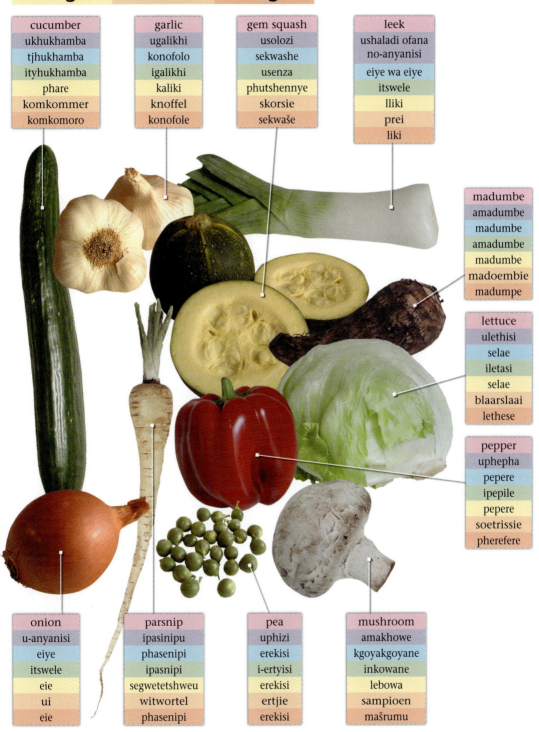

cucumber
ukhukhamba
tjhukhamba
ityhukhamba
phare
komkommer
komkomoro

garlic
ugalikhi
konofolo
igalikhi
kaliki
knoffel
konofole

gem squash
usolozi
sekwashe
usenza
phutshennye
skorsie
sekwaše

leek
ushaladi ofana no-anyanisi
eiye wa eiye
itswele
lliki
prei
liki

madumbe
amadumbe
madumbe
amadumbe
madumbe
madoembie
madumpe

lettuce
ulethisi
selae
iletasi
selae
blaarslaai
lethese

pepper
uphepha
pepere
ipepile
pepere
soetrissie
pherefere

onion
u-anyanisi
eiye
itswele
eie
ui
eie

parsnip
ipasinipu
phasenipi
ipasnipi
segwetetshweu
witwortel
phasenipi

pea
uphizi
erekisi
i-ertyisi
erekisi
ertjie
erekisi

mushroom
amakhowe
kgoyakgoyane
inkowane
lebowa
sampioen
mašrumu

Vegetables 2 Imifino 2 Meroho 2 Imifuno 2

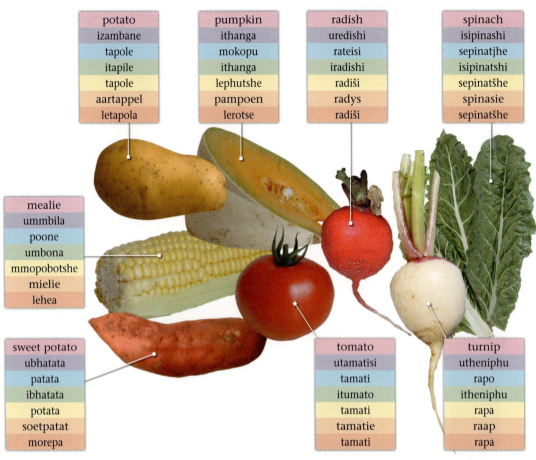

potato
izambane
tapole
itapile
tapole
aartappel
letapola

pumpkin
ithanga
mokopu
ithanga
lephutshe
pampoen
lerotse

radish
uredishi
rateisi
iradishi
radiši
radys
radiši

spinach
isipinashi
sepinatjhe
isipinatshi
sepinatšhe
spinasie
sepinatšhe

mealie
ummbila
poone
umbona
mmopobotshe
mielie
lehea

sweet potato
ubhatata
patata
ibhatata
potata
soetpatat
morepa

tomato
utamatisi
tamati
itumato
tamati
tamatie
tamati

turnip
utheniphu
rapo
itheniphu
rapa
raap
rapa

Dried food Ukudla okomisiwe Dijo tse omisitsweng Ukutya okomisiweyo

lentil
ilentili
lentili
ilentile
lentile
lensie
tlhodi

rice
ilayisi
raese
irayisi
reisi
rys
raese

split pea
udali
erekisi
i-ertyisi
nawaphatlo
split-ertjie
photla

Food and drink • Ukudla neziphuzo • Dijo le dino • Ukutya neziselo
Dijo le dino • Kos en drinkgoed • Dijo le dino

Merogo 2 Groente 2 Merogo 2

Herbs Amakhambi okunonga ukudla Ditlamatlama Amachiza
Ditlama Kruie Digwere

parsley	basil	rosemary
iphasli	ubhezili	irozimeri
phasili	basele	rousemeri
ipasli	ibhasili	irosmeri
phaseli	basile	rosemeri
pietersielie	basiliekruid	roosmaryn
phaseli	peisele	rosemeri

origanum	thyme	mint
i-origanumi	itayimi	iminti
origanumu	thaeme	minti
i-oringanam	iteme	iminti
orikanamo	thaeme	minti
origanum	tiemie	ment
orikanamo	thaeme	minti

Dijo tse di omisitsweng Droë kosse Dijo tše di omilego

bean	soya bean
ubhontshisi	ubhontshisi isoya
nawa	soya
imbotyi	imbotyi zesoya
nawa	dinawa tsa soya
boontjie	sojaboon
nawa	nawa ya soya

sorghum
amabele
mabele
amazimba
mabele
sorghum
mabele

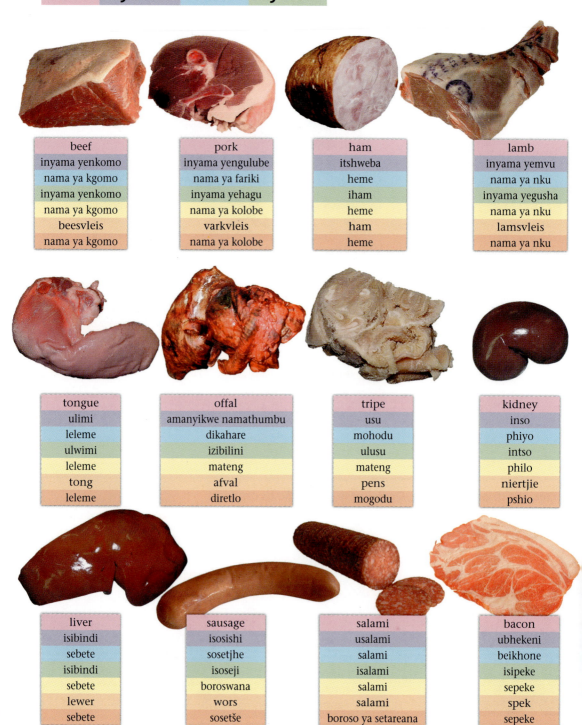

beef	pork	ham	lamb
inyama yenkomo	inyama yengulube	itshweba	inyama yemvu
nama ya kgomo	nama ya fariki	heme	nama ya nku
inyama yenkomo	inyama yehagu	iham	inyama yegusha
nama ya kgomo	nama ya kolobe	heme	nama ya nku
beesvleis	varkvleis	ham	lamsvleis
nama ya kgomo	nama ya kolobe	heme	nama ya nku

tongue	offal	tripe	kidney
ulimi	amanyikwe namathumbu	usu	inso
leleme	dikahare	mohodu	phiyo
ulwimi	izibilini	ulusu	intso
leleme	mateng	mateng	philo
tong	afval	pens	niertjie
leleme	diretlo	mogodu	pshio

liver	sausage	salami	bacon
isibindi	isosishi	usalami	ubhekeni
sebete	sosetjhe	salami	beikhone
isibindi	isoseji	isalami	isipeke
sebete	boroswana	salami	sepeke
lewer	wors	salami	spek
sebete	sosetše	boroso ya setareana	sepeke

Nama Vleis Nama

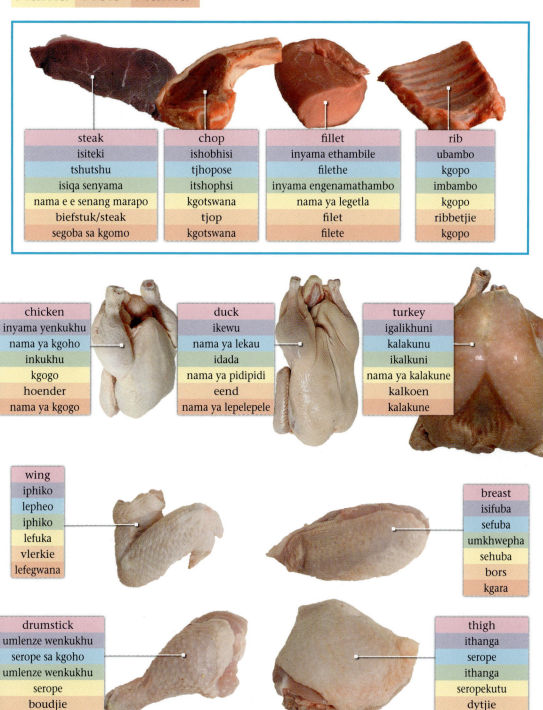

steak	chop	fillet	rib
isiteki	ishobhisi	inyama ethambile	ubambo
tshutshu	tjhopose	filethe	kgopo
isiqa senyama	itshophsi	inyama engenamathambo	imbambo
nama e e senang marapo	kgotswana	nama ya legetla	kgopo
biefstuk/steak	tjop	filet	ribbetjie
segoba sa kgomo	kgotswana	filete	kgopo

chicken	duck	turkey
inyama yenkukhu	ikewu	igalikhuni
nama ya kgoho	nama ya lekau	kalakunu
inkukhu	idada	ikalkuni
kgogo	nama ya pidipidi	nama ya kalakune
hoender	eend	kalkoen
nama ya kgogo	nama ya lepelepele	kalakune

wing
iphiko
lepheo
iphiko
lefuka
vlerkie
lefegwana

breast
isifuba
sefuba
umkhwepha
sehuba
bors
kgara

drumstick
umlenze wenkukhu
serope sa kgoho
umlenze wenkukhu
serope
boudjie
serope sa kgogo

thigh
ithanga
serope
ithanga
seropekutu
dytjie
serope

Food and drink • Ukudla neziphuzo • Dijo le dino • Ukutya neziselo
Dijo le dino • Kos en drinkgoed • Dijo le dino

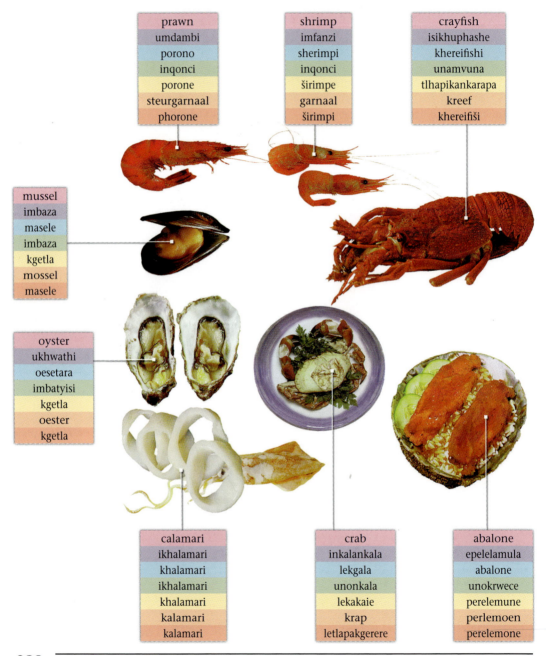

prawn
umdambi
porono
inqonci
porone
steurgarnaal
phorone

shrimp
imfanzi
sherimpi
inqonci
širimpe
garnaal
širimpi

crayfish
isikhuphashe
khereifishi
unamvuna
tlhapikankarapa
kreef
khereifiši

mussel
imbaza
masele
imbaza
kgetla
mossel
masele

oyster
ukhwathi
oesetara
imbatyisi
kgetla
oester
kgetla

calamari
ikhalamari
khalamari
ikhalamari
khalamari
kalamari
kalamari

crab
inkalankala
lekgala
unonkala
lekakaie
krap
letlapakgerere

abalone
epelelamula
abalone
unokrwece
perelemune
perlemoen
perelemone

Fish | Inhlanzi | Tlhapi | Intlanzi | Tlhapi | Vis | Hlapi

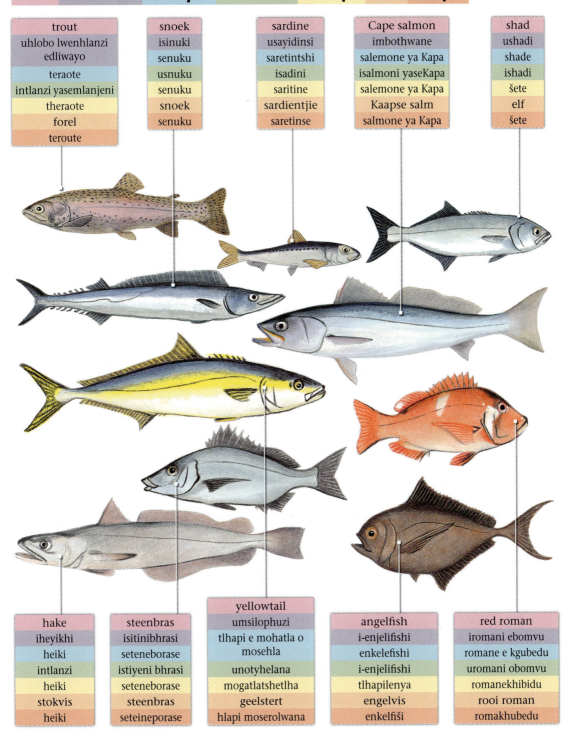

trout
uhlobo lwenhlanzi edliwayo
teraote
intlanzi yasemlanjeni
theraote
forel
teroute

snoek
isinuki
senuku
usnuku
senuku
snoek
senuku

sardine
usayidinsi
saretintshi
isadini
saritine
sardientjie
saretinse

Cape salmon
imbothwane
salemone ya Kapa
isalmoni yaseKapa
salemone ya Kapa
Kaapse salm
salmone ya Kapa

shad
ushadi
shade
ishadi
šete
elf
šete

hake
iheyikhi
heiki
intlanzi
heiki
stokvis
heiki

steenbras
isitinibhrasi
seteneborase
istiyeni bhrasi
seteneborase
steenbras
seteineporase

yellowtail
umsilophuzi
tlhapi e mohatla o mosehla
unotyhelana
mogatlatshetlha
geelstert
hlapi moserolwana

angelfish
i-enjelifishi
enkelefishi
i-enjelifishi
tlhapilenya
engelvis
enkelfiši

red roman
iromani ebomvu
romane e kgubedu
uromani obomvu
romanekhibidu
rooi roman
romakhubedu

Dairy Imikhiqizo yobisi Teri Imveliso yobisi
Dikungo tsa mašwi Suiwel Teri

milk
ubisi
lebese
ubisi
mašwi
melk
maswi

longlife milk
ubisi oluhlala isikhathi eside
lebese le sa beng bodila kapele
ubisi olunocwambu
mašwi a a tsayang lobaka lo
leele go senyega
rakmelk
maswiphelotelele

milk powder
ubisi oluyimpuphu
lebese la phofo
ubisi lomgubo
mašwi a bupi
melkpoeier
maswilerole

skimmed milk
umbhobe
motsara
umjijwa
motalala
afgeroomde melk
motsaro

butter
ibhotela
botoro
ibhotolo
botoro
botter
potoro

margarine
imajarini
majarine
imajarina
mejerine
margarien
matšarine

cream
ukhilimu
lebejana
ucwambu
lobebe
room
lebebe

yoghurt
iyogathi
yokate
iyogathi
yokate
jogurt
yokate

cheese
ushizi
sereledi
isonka samasi
tšhisi
kaas
tšhese

cottage cheese
ushizi omhlophe
sereledi sa mafi
isonka samasi
tšhisintshwamafura
maaskaas
tšhese ya khothetše

240

Egg Iqanda Lehe Iqanda Lee Eier Lee

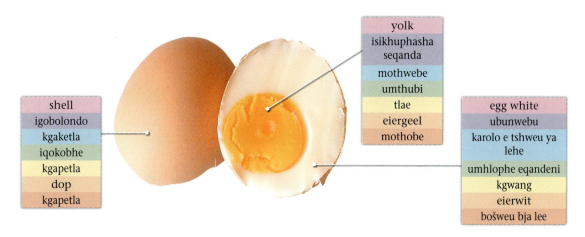

shell
igobolondo
kgaketla
iqokobhe
kgapetla
dop
kgapetla

yolk
isikhuphasha seqanda
mothwebe
umthubi
tlae
eiergeel
mothobe

egg white
ubunwebu
karolo e tshweu ya lehe
umhlophe eqandeni
kgwang
eierwit
bošweu bja lee

Nuts Amantongomane Matokomane Amantongomane Kgeru Neute Dikgeru

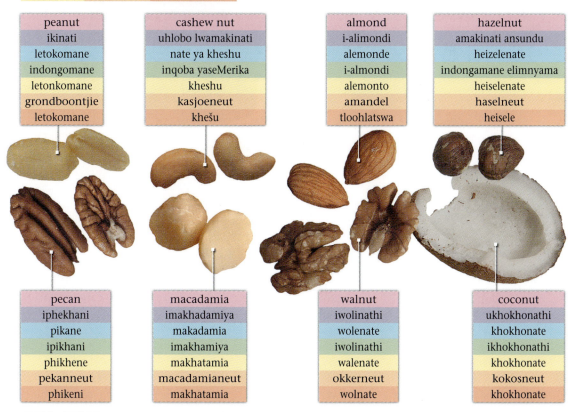

peanut	cashew nut	almond	hazelnut
ikinati	uhlobo lwamakinati	i-alimondi	amakinati ansundu
letokomane	nate ya kheshu	alemonde	heizelenate
indongomane	inqoba yaseMerika	i-almondi	indongamane elimnyama
letonkomane	kheshu	alemonto	heiselenate
grondboontjie	kasjoeneut	amandel	haselneut
letokomane	khešu	tloohlatswa	heisele

pecan	macadamia	walnut	coconut
iphekhani	imakhadamiya	iwolinathi	ukhokhonathi
pikane	makadamia	wolenate	khokhonate
ipikhani	imakhamiya	iwolinathi	ikhokhonathi
phikhene	makhatamia	walenate	khokhonate
pekanneut	macadamianeut	okkerneut	kokosneut
phikeni	makhatamia	wolnate	khokhonate

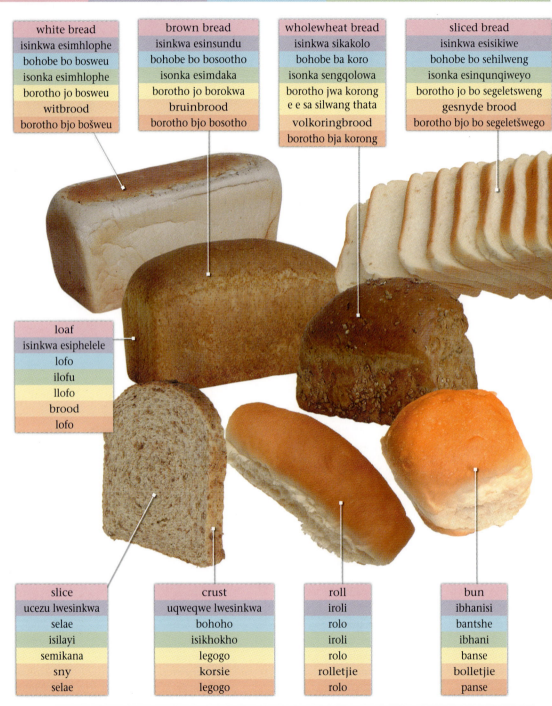

white bread	brown bread	wholewheat bread	sliced bread
isinkwa esimhlophe	isinkwa esinsundu	isinkwa sikakolo	isinkwa esisikiwe
bohobe bo bosweu	bohobe bo bosootho	bohobe ba koro	bohobe bo sehilweng
isonka esimhlophe	isonka esimdaka	isonka sengqolowa	isonka esinqunqiweyo
borotho jo bosweu	borotho jo borokwa	borotho jwa korong e e sa silwang thata	borotho jo bo segeletsweng
witbrood	bruinbrood	volkoringbrood	gesnyde brood
borotho bjo bošweu	borotho bjo bosotho	borotho bja korong	borotho bjo bo segeletšwego

loaf
isinkwa esiphelele
lofo
ilofu
llofo
brood
lofo

slice	crust	roll	bun
ucezu lwesinkwa	uqweqwe lwesinkwa	iroli	ibhanisi
selae	bohoho	rolo	bantshe
isilayi	isikhokho	iroli	ibhani
semikana	legogo	rolo	banse
sny	korsie	rolletjie	bolletjie
selae	legogo	rolo	panse

cake
ikhekhe
kuku
ikeyiki
kuku
koek
khekhe

muffin
imafini
mafine
imafini
mafene
muffin
mafene

scone
isikoni
leqebekwane
isikonsi
sekonse
skon
sekontshe

tart
ithathi
thate
ithathi
thate
tert
terete

doughnut
idonadi
donate
idonathi
tounate
oliebol
tonate

pie
uphaya
pae
ipayi
phae
pastei
phae

pastry
iphastri
hlama
ipastri
pasetiri
pasteideeg
hlama

biscuit
ibhisikidi
bisikiti
iqebengwana
bisekite
koekie
pesikiti

dough
inhlama
hlama
intlama
tlhama
deeg
hlama

Food 1 Ukudla 1 Dijo 1 Ukutya 1

| Meals | Ukudla | Dijo | Izityo | Dijo | Maaltye | Dijo |

breakfast	lunch	supper	dinner	tea break	snack
ibhulakufesi	ukudla kwasemini	ukudla kwakusihlwa	idina	isikhathi setiye	ukudla okuncane okulula
dijo tsa hoseng	dijo tsa motsheare	dijo tsa mantsiboya	dijo tsa mantsiboya	nako ya tee	setshwaramoya
isidlo sakusasa	isidlo sasemini	isidlo sasebusuku	isidlo sasemini	ixesha leti	amashwamshwam
sefitlholo	dijotshegare	dilalelo	dijo tsa mantsiboa	nakokgaotso ya go nwa tee	seneke
ontbyt	middagete	aandete	aandete	teetyd	peuselhappie
sefihlolo	letena	selalelo	selalelo	nakokgaotša ya go nwa teye	sesolana

egg	bacon	toast	jam
iqanda	ubhekeni	ithosi	ujamu
lehe	beikhone	bohobe bo tjhisitsweng	jeme
iqanda	isipeke	isonka esigcadiweyo	ijem
lee	sepeke	borotho jo bo besitsweng	jeme
eier	spek	roosterbrood	konfyt
lee	peikhone	senkgwabešwa	kgatlaomone

scrambled eggs	bread
amaqanda abondiwe	isinkwa
mahe a fehlilweng	bohobe
amaqanda aqhuqhiweyo	isonka
mae a a fuduilweng	borotho
roereier	brood
mae a huduilwego	borotho

omelette	poached egg	boiled egg
u-omeleti	iqanda eliphekwa ngamanzi	iqanda elibilisiwe
omelete	mahe a thuhetsweng metsing a belang	lehe le bedisitsweng
i-omeleti	iqanda eliqhekezelwe emanzini	iqanda elibilisiweyo
omelete	lee le le gadikwang le sa tlhakatlhangwa	lee le le bidisitsweng
omelet	geposjeerde eier	gekookte eier
omelete	lee le le gadikilwego le sa hlakantšhwa	leebedišwa

Dijo 1 Kos 1 Dijo 1

yoghurt	**soup**	**cereal**	**fruit**
iyogathi	isobho	isiriyali	isithelo
yokate	sopo	dihleferetsi	ditholwana
iyogathi	isuphu	isiriyeli	isiqhamo
yokate	sopo	lethoro	leungo
jogurt	sop	ontbytgraan	vrugte
yokate	sopo	sirele	kenywa

muesli
umuwesili
musile
imusli
mmuseli
muesli
musli

porridge
iphalishi
lesheleshele
isidudu
motogo
pap
motogo

salad	**sandwich**	**stew**	**meat and vegetables**
usaladi	isemeshi	isitshulu	inyama nemifino
salate	samentjhese	setjhu	nama le meroho
isaladi	iqebengwana	isityu	inyama nemifuno
salate	borothopate	setšhuu	nama le merogo
slaai	toebroodjie	bredie	vleis en groente
salate	sangwetše	setšhu	nama le merogo

Dessert Idizethi Diqhaqhabola

ice-cream
u-ayisikhilimu
ayesikhirimi
ucwambu olukhenkceziweyo
sereledi
roomys
lebebetšididi

trifle
ithrayfuli
teraefole
itrayifile
theraefole
koekstruif
teraefole

fish
inhlanzi
tlhapi
intlanzi
tlhapi
vis
hlapi

chicken
inkukhu
nama ya kgoho
inkukhu
nama ya kgogo
hoender
nama ya kgogo

pancake
qebelengwana
panekuku
ipankeyiki
panekuku
pannekoek
panekuku

chocolate éclair
ikhekhe lashokoledi
tjhokolethe
itshokolethi
tšhokolete
sjokolade éclair
tšhokolete-ikla

stir-fried vegetables
imifino ethosiwe
meroho e hadikilweng
imifuno eqhotsiweyo
merogo e e gadikilweng
roerbraaigroente
merogo ye e gadikilwego

custard
ukhastadi
khasetate
ikhastadi
khasetete
vla
khastete

fruit cake
ikhekhe lezithelo
kuku ya ditholwana
ikeyiki yeziqhamo
kukumaungo
vrugtekoek
khekhekenywa

Izimuncumuncu emva kwesidlo Sedigela Nagereg Tlhatswapelo

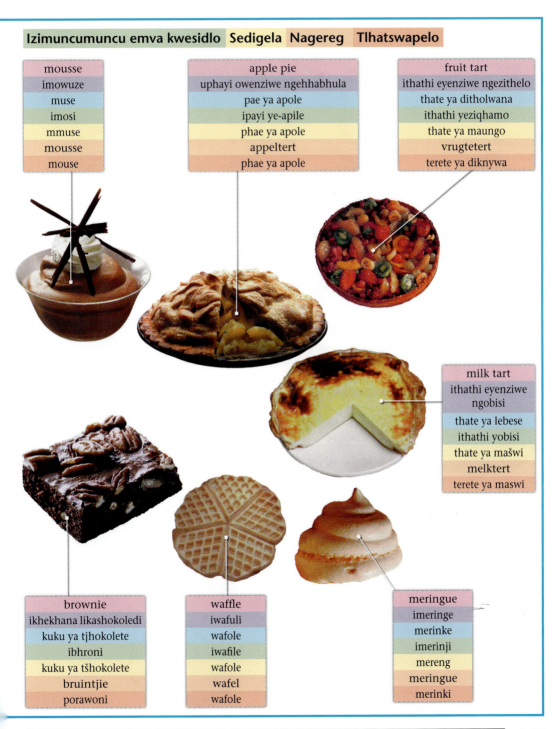

| mousse |
| imowuze |
| muse |
| imosi |
| mmuse |
| mousse |
| mouse |

| apple pie |
| uphayi owenziwe ngehhabhula |
| pae ya apole |
| ipayi ye-apile |
| phae ya apole |
| appeltert |
| phae ya apole |

| fruit tart |
| ithathi eyenziwe ngezithelo |
| thate ya ditholwana |
| ithathi yeziqhamo |
| thate ya maungo |
| vrugtetert |
| terete ya diknywa |

| milk tart |
| ithathi eyenziwe ngobisi |
| thate ya lebese |
| ithathi yobisi |
| thate ya mašwi |
| melktert |
| terete ya maswi |

| brownie |
| ikhekhana likashokoledi |
| kuku ya tjhokolete |
| ibhroni |
| kuku ya tšhokolete |
| bruintjie |
| porawoni |

| waffle |
| iwafuli |
| wafole |
| iwafile |
| wafole |
| wafel |
| wafole |

| meringue |
| imeringe |
| merinke |
| imerinji |
| mereng |
| meringue |
| merinki |

prickly pear
isihlehle
torofeie
itolofiya
motoroko
turksvy
toro

sour fig
ikhiwane elimuncu
feiya e bodila
ifiya elimuncu
feie e e botlha
suurvy
feie ye bodila

milk tart
ithathi eyenziwe ngobisi
thate ya lebese
ithathi yobisi
thate ya mašwi
melktert
terete ya maswi

rusk
iraski
raseke
iraski
komeletsane
beskuit
raske

boerewors
ivosi
boroso
ivosi
boroso
boerewors
boroso

mealie meal porridge
uphuthu
papa
umqa papa
bogobe jwa bupi jo bosweu
mieliepap
bogobe bja lehea

morogo
imifino
moroho
utyuthu
morogo
marog
morogo

bobotie
ibhabhuti
boboti
ibhabhuti
boboti
bobotie
popoti

bunny chow
ibhanitshawe
bantjhawa
isonka esifakwe inyama
banitšhau
kerriebrood
panitšhoo

roti
uroti
roti
iroti
roti
roti
roti

waterblommetjie bredie
isitshalo samanzi esinezimbali ezidliwayo
palesa ya metsing e jewang
intyatyanbo yamanzi etyiwayo
namamorogo ya llili
waterblommetjiebredie
setšhu sa letšobameetse

Dijo tsa mo Aforika Borwa	Suid-Afrikaanse kos	Dijo tša Afrika Borwa

samoosa
usamusa
samusa
isamusa
samusa
samoesa
samusa

sorghum and beans
izindlubu nobhontshisi
monyakapola
idubhayi
dikgobe
sorghum-en-boontjies
mabele le dinawa

finely-chopped offal
iqobelo
diretlo
unqweme
diretlo
fyngekookte afval
malamogodu

steamed bread
ujeqe
bohobe ba metsi
idombolo
borotho bo metsi
stoombrood
letompolo

biryani
ubhriyani
boriyane
ibhiriyani
boriyane
birjani
piriane

samp
isitambu
setampo
umngqusho
setampa
stampmielies
setampa

mopane worms
amacimbi
maqephe
amaqonya
mopane
mopaniewurms
mašotša

cooked dried mealies
izinkobe
qhubu
iinkobe
kabu
kaboemielies
lekokoro

mashed meat
inyama egayiwe
lekgotlwane
inyama ecoliweyo
tšhotlo
fynvleis
nama ye e thumeletšwego

pumpkin and mealies
ithanga nommbila
nyekwe
umxhaxha
legodu
pampoen-en-mielies
lefodi le lehea

Other foods Okunye ukudla Dijo tse ding Okunye ukutya

**Fast food Ukudla okusheshayo Dijo tse potlakileng Ukutya okukhawulezileyo
Dijo tsa ka bonako Kitskos Dijo tša ka pejana**

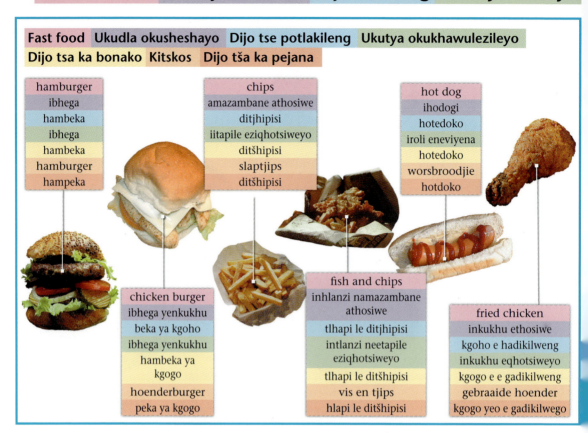

hamburger	chips	hot dog
ibhega	amazambane athosiwe	ihodogi
hambeka	ditjhipisi	hotedoko
ibhega	iitapile eziqhotsiweyo	iroli eneviyena
hambeka	ditšhipisi	hotedoko
hamburger	slaptjips	worsbroodjie
hampeka	ditšhipisi	hotdoko

chicken burger	fish and chips	fried chicken
ibhega yenkukhu	inhlanzi namazambane athosiwe	inkukhu ethosiwe
beka ya kgoho	tlhapi le ditjhipisi	kgoho e hadikilweng
ibhega yenkukhu	intlanzi neetapile eziqhotsiweyo	inkukhu eqhotsiweyo
hambeka ya kgogo	tlhapi le ditšhipisi	kgogo e e gadikilweng
hoenderburger	vis en tjips	gebraaide hoender
peka ya kgogo	hlapi le ditšhipisi	kgogo yeo e gadikilwego

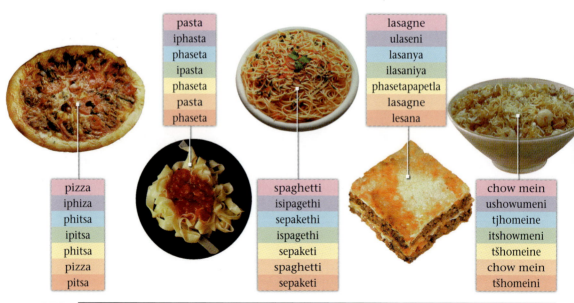

pasta	lasagne
iphasta	ulaseni
phaseta	lasanya
ipasta	ilasaniya
phaseta	phasetapapetla
pasta	lasagne
phaseta	lesana

pizza	spaghetti	chow mein
iphiza	isipagethi	ushowumeni
phitsa	sepakethi	tjhomeine
ipitsa	ispagethi	itshowmeni
phitsa	sepaketi	tšhomeine
pizza	spaghetti	chow mein
pitsa	sepaketi	tšhomeini

Dijo tse dingwe Ander kosse Dijo tše dingwe

sweet and sour pork
inyama yengulube eswidi nobumuncu
nama ya fariki e nang le tswekere e bodila
ihagu eyenziwe yabumuncu nabuswiti
nama ya kolobe e e botshe-botlhanyana
soet-en-suur varkvleis
nama ya kolobe ya basana le bodilana

sushi
isushi
sushi
isushi
suši
soesji
suši

spring roll
iroli eneshaladi
rolo
ispringroli
roloporeng
Sjinese rolletjie
sepringrolo

sauerkraut
iklabishi elibabayo
khabetjhe e bodila
isokrati
khabetšhe e bodila
suurkool
sekeraoti

pita bread
isinkwa iphitha
bohobe ba pita
isonka sepita
borotho jwa ditlhaletlhale
pita-brood
borotho bja pita

meze
umizi
meze
imeze
mese
meze
mese

quiche
ukhwishi
khishe
ikhwintshi
khiše
quiche
khwiše

curry and rice
ukhari nerayisi
kheri le raese
irayisi enekheri
kheri le reisi
kerrie-en-rys
kheri le raese

peri-peri chicken
inkukhu ebabayo
kgoho e tshetsweng periperi
inkukhu eneperi-peri
kgogo ya peri-peri
peri-perihoender
nama ya kgogo ya pherefere

sweets
amaswidi
dipompong
iilekese
dimonamone
lekkers
malekere

toffee
uthofi
thofi
ithofi
thofi
toffie
thofi

chewing gum
intshungama
tjhungama
itshungama
tšhunkama
kougom
tšhinkamo

chocolate
ushokoledi
tjhokolethe
itshokolethi
tšhokolete
sjokolade
tšhokolete

marshmallow
amaswidi imashimalo
dipompong tse bonolo
intam-ntam
monamone e e sepontšhe
malvalekker
mašamalo

liquorice
ilikhorishi
dipompong tse mebalabala
ilikhorayisi
likhwaraese
drop
likhwirisi

Seasoning Ukuyolisa Dinoko Iziqholo zokutya Diloki Geurmiddels Dinoki

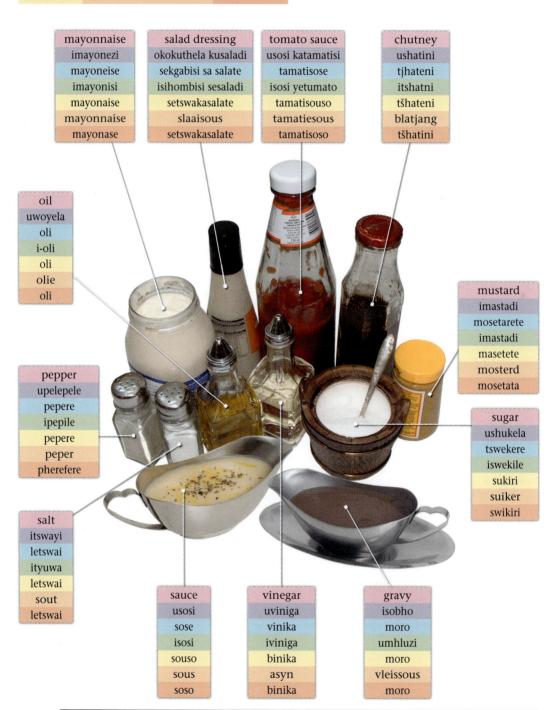

mayonnaise	salad dressing	tomato sauce	chutney
imayonezi	okokuthela kusaladi	usosi katamatisi	ushatini
mayoneise	sekgabisi sa salate	tamatisose	tjhateni
imayonisi	isihombisi sesaladi	isosi yetumato	itshatni
mayonaise	setswakasalate	tamatisouso	tšhateni
mayonnaise	slaaisous	tamatiesous	blatjang
mayonase	setswakasalate	tamatisoso	tšhatini

oil
uwoyela
oli
i-oli
oli
olie
oli

mustard
imastadi
mosetarete
imastadi
masetete
mosterd
mosetata

pepper
upelepele
pepere
ipepile
pepere
peper
pherefere

sugar
ushukela
tswekere
iswekile
sukiri
suiker
swikiri

salt
itswayi
letswai
ityuwa
letswai
sout
letswai

sauce	vinegar	gravy
usosi	uviniga	isobho
sose	vinika	moro
isosi	iviniga	umhluzi
souso	binika	moro
sous	asyn	vleissous
soso	binika	moro

roast
-chochobalisa
hadika
gcada
besa
braai
rousta

bake
-bhaka
baka
bhaka
baka
bak
paka

grill
-chochobalisa
besa
yosa
lesimelo
rooster
šimela

fry
-thosa
hadika
qhotsa
gadika
diepbraai
gadika

boil
-bilisa
bedisa
bilisa
apaya ka metsi fela
kook
bediša

stewed
-pheka
setjhu
-phekwe emhluzini
setšhuu
gestoofde
khušitšwego

peeled
-cwecwiwe
ebotswe
-xotyuliwe
obotsweng
geskil
ebotšwego

chopped
-qotshiwe
kgabetswe
-nqunqiwe
kgabetleletsweng
gekap
phaphilwego

strain
cwengiwe
motlhotlo
hluziwe
tlhotlha
filtreer
sefa

cooked
-phekiwe
phehilweng
-ophekiwe
apeilweng
gekook/gaar
apeilwego

raw
-luhlaza
tala
-luhlaza
tala
rou
tala

burnt
-shisiwe
tjhele
-tshile
fisitse
verbrand
tšhumilwe

flavour
-nonga
tatso
incasa
tatso
geur
natefiša

salty
-nongiwe ngosawoti
letswai
-butyuwara
letswaana
sout
letswai

sweet
-swidi
tswekere
-switi
botshe
soet
bose

sour
-muncu
bodila
-muncu
bodila
suur
galaka

bitter
-yababa
baba
-yakrakra
botlhoko kgotsa bogalaka
bitter
baba

savoury
-klabusile
hlaboseha
inencasa
balolang
geurig
latswegago

spicy
-kunezinongonongo
dinoko tse monate
iyanambitheka
-tswaiso
pikant
nokilwego

carbohydrate
ikhabhohayidirethi
khabohaetereiti
ikhabohayidrethi
khabohaetereiti
stysel
khapohaitreiti

protein
amaphrotheni
dihaha mmele
iprotheni
poroteine
proteïen
poroteini

fat
amafutha
mafura
amafutha
mafura
vet
makhura

vitamin
ivithamini
vitamine
ivithamini
bitamini
vitamien
bithamini

mineral
osawoti bomzimba
minerale
ityuwa yomhlaba
minerale
mineraal
minerale

nutrient
umsoco
sematlafatsi
inesondlo
dikotla
voedingstof
sefepi

water	tea	tea bag	rooibos tea	coffee
amanzi	itiye	isikhwanyana setiye	uzintana	ikhofi
metsi	tee	tee e mokotlaneng	tee ya sehlahlana se sefubedu	kofi
amanzi	iti	isingxotyana seti	iti ebomvu	ikofu
metsi	tee	kgetsanatee	tee ya maditlhokwana	kofi
water	tee	teesakkie	rooibostee	koffie
meetse	teye	mokotlanateye	roiboso	kofi

hot chocolate	fruit juice	cooldrink	lemonade	milkshake
ushokoledi oshisayo	isiphuzo sezithelo	isiphuzo esibandayo	ulemonedi	isiphuzo sobisi
tjhokolethe e tjhesang	lero la ditholwana	senomaphodi	namoneiti	namoneite ya lebese
itshokoleti ephungwayo	isiselo seziqhamo	isiselo esibandayo	ilemonadi	ubisi okuhlukuhliweyo
khoukhou	matute a maungo	senotsididi	lemoneite	senomašwi
warm sjokolade	vrugtesap	koeldrank	limonade	melkskommel
tšhokolete ye e fišago	matute	senotšididi	namoneiti	šeiki ya maswi

drinking yoghurt	milk	sour mealie porridge	sour milk
iyogathi ephuzwayo	ubisi	amahewu	amasi
yokate e nowang	lebese	mahleu	mafi
iyogathi eselwayo	ubisi	amarhewu	amasi
yokatemetsi	mašwi	mageu	madila
drinkjogurt	melk	suurmelkpap	suurmelk
yokate ya go nwa	maswi	mageu	hloa

beer	sorghum beer	cider	sherry	wine
ubhiya	umqombothi	isayida	isheri	iwayini
biri	jwala ba setho	saeta	sheri	veini
ibhiya	umqombothi	isayida	isheri	iwayini
biri	bojalwa jwa mabele	saeta	šeri	mofine
bier	sorghumbier	sider	sjerrie	wyn
piri	bjala bja mabele	beine ya saeta	šeri	beine

sparkling wine	brandy	port	liqueur
iwayini elizoyizayo	ibhrendi	iphothi	utshwala
veine e hlwahlwaselang	boranti	pote	jwala
iwayini ehlwahlwazayo	igrangqa	iwayini ebomvu	utywala
mofinepodula	boranti	mofinebotshe	senotagi-tlhoswana
vonkelwyn	brandewyn	port	likeur
beinekganya	poranti	poto	likere

whisky	gin	rum	vodka
iwiskhi	ijini	iramu	ivodga
whisiki	jini	ramo	voteka
iwiski	ijini	iram	ivodga
wisikhi	jini	ramo	boteka
whisky	jenewer	rum	wodka
wisiki	jini	ramo	boteka

Phrases	Amabinzana	Dipolelwana	Amabinzana
I am very thirsty.	Ngomile kakhulu.	Ke nyorilwe haholo.	Ndixanwe kakhulu/ ndomile.
What would you like to drink?	Uzothanda ukuphuzani?	O lakatsa ho nwa eng?	Ungathanda ukusela ntoni?
May I have some juice please?	Ngicela isiphuzo sezithelo?	Ke kopa juse hle?	Ndingafumana isiselo seziqhamo?
Yes you may. What flavour would you like?	Yebo kulungile. Uthanda nhloboni?	Ee, o ka e fumana, o rata e jwang?	Ewe.Ungathanda esiphi?
Apple or guava please.	Ngicela owehhabhula noma ugwava.	Ya apole kapa ya kwaba.	Ese-apile okanye esegwava.
Are you hungry?	Ulambile?	O lapile/Na o lapile?	Ulambile na?
I am starving! I hope there is lots of food!	Ngifile yindlala! Ngiyethemba kuningi ukudla.	Ke shwele ke tlala! Ke tshepa hore o na le dijo tse ngata.	Ndilambe kakhulu ingathi ndingatya ukutya okuninzi.
Do you serve vegetarian food?	Ninakho ukudla okungenanyama?	Na o rekisa dijo tse entsweng ka meroho?	Ninako na ukutya kwabadla imifuno kuphela?
Yes, we have samp and beans.	Yebo, sinesitambu nobhontshisi.	Ee, re na le setampo se nang le dinawa.	Ewe sinawo umngqusho oneembotyi.
What would you like to eat?	Uzothanda ukudlani?	O lakatsa ho ja eng?	Ungathanda ukutya ntoni?
I would like roast chicken and roast potatoes.	Ngithanda inkukhu kanye namazambane athosiwe.	Nka thabela nama ya kgoho le ditapole tse hadikilweng.	Ndingathanda inkukhu neetapile eziqhotsiweyo.
People drank a lot of sorghum beer at the wedding.	Abantu baphuza umqombothi omningi emshadweni.	Batho ba nwele jwala ba mabele bo bongata lenyalong.	Abantu basela umqombothi omninzi emtshatweni.
Did you enjoy the food at the wedding?	Kwakunjani ukudla emshadweni?	Dijo di ne di le jwang lenyalong?	Ingaba wakonwabela ukutya emtshatweni?
Yes, it was very tasty and the desserts were delicious!	Kwakumnandi kwehla esiphundu!	Di ne di le monate di hlabosa. Diqhaqhabola di ne dihlaboseha haholo!	Ewe kwakunencasa kakhulu, nezimuncumuncu zazinambitheka!

Dikapolelo	Frases	Dikafoko
e tshwerwe ke lenyora ota.	Ek is baie dors.	Ke nyorilwe kudu.
tla rata go nwa eng?	Wat sal jy drink?	O nyaka go nwa eng?
e kopa matute weetswee?	Mag ek 'n bietjie sap kry, asseblief?	A nka humana matute?
e, go a kgonega. O batla a atso efe?	Ja, natuurlik. Watter geur verkies jy?	O ka e hwetša. O nyaka e bjang?
pole kgotsa kwaba weetswee.	Appel of koejawel, asseblief.	Apolo goba kwaba, hle.
o tshwerwe ke tlala?	Is jy honger?	A o swerwe ke tlala?
e tshwerwe ke tlala tota! e solofela fa go na le dijo se dintsi!	Ek sterf van die honger! Ek hoop daar is baie kos.	Ke swerwe ke tlala! Ke holofela gore go na le dijo tše ntši.
lo tshola/rekisa le dijo tse i nang le merogo fela?	Bedien julle vegetariese kos?	A o na le dijo tša yo phelago ka merogo fela?
e, re na le setampa le inawa.	Ja, ons het stampmielies en boontjies.	Ee, re na le setampa le dinawa.
tla rata go ja eng?	Waarvoor is jy lus?	O tla rata go ja eng?
e batla go ja kgogo e e adikilweng le ditapole tse li gadikilweng.	Ek is lus vir gebraaide hoender en aartappels.	Ke nyaka kgogo ye e roustilwego le matapola a roustilwego.
atho ba nole bojalwa jo ontsi jwa mabele kwa enyalong.	Die mense het baie sorghumbier by die bruilof gedrink.	Batho ba nwele bjala bja mabele kudu monyanyeng.
o itumeletse dijo kwa enyalong?	Hoe was die kos by die bruilof?	A o ipshinne ka dijo lenyalong?
e, di ne di le monate tota, e ditleketleke di ne di lhabosa!	Dit was baie smaaklik en die nagereg was uit die boonste rakke!	Ee, di be di latswega kudu gape difetišakateng di be di tsefa!

11

Our spare time

Sichitha isikhathi sethu

Nako ya rona ya boikgutso

258

Our spare time • Sichitha isikhathi sethu • Nako ya rona ya boikgutso
Ixesha lokuzonwabisa • Nako ya rona ya boiketlo • Ons vrye tyd • Nako ya boikhutšo

Ixesha lokuzonwabisa

Nako ya rona ya boiketlo

Ons vrye tyd

Nako ya boikhutšo

Our spare time • Sichitha isikhathi sethu • Nako ya rona ya boikgutso
Ixesha lokuzonwabisa • Nako ya rona ya boiketlo • Ons vrye tyd • Nako ya boikhutšo

259

Sports Imidlalo Tsa dipapadi Imidlalo

soccer	rugby	netball	hockey	cricket
ibhola likanobhutshuzwayo	irabhi	ibhola lomnqakiswano	ihokhi	ikhilikithi
bolo ya maoto	rakebi	bolo ya matsoho	hoki	kherikete
ibhola ekhatywayo	umbhoxo	ibhola yomnyazi	ihoki	iqakamba
kgwele ya dinao	rakibii	bolotlowa	hoki	kherikete
sokker	rugby	netbal	hokkie	krieket
kgwele ya maoto	rakbi	kgwele ya diatla	hoki	kherikete

basketball	baseball	cycling	badminton	athletics
ibhola lomnqakiswano	ibhesibholi	ukugibela ibhayisikili	ibhedimintoni	imidlalo yabasubathi
baseketebolo	bolo ya botlatsa	papadi ya baesekele	beteminthone	tsa mabelo
ibhola yomnyazi	umdlalo webhola wephini	ugqatso lweebhayisekile	intenetya	ezeembaleki
bolotlowa	bolo ya tlase	motabogo wa dibaesekele	beteminthone	atleletiki
korfbal	bofbal	fietsry	pluimbal	atletiek
kgwele ya diatla	peisepolo	papadi ya dipaesekele	petmintone	diatleletiki

swimming	judo	karate	tennis	table tennis
ukubhukuda	ijudo	umkhalambazo	ibhola lomphebezo	ibhola lomphebezo wasetafuleni
ho sesa	juto	karate	tenese	tenese ya tafole
ukudada	ijudo	ikarati	intenetya	intenetya yetafile
go thuma	juto	karate	thenese	thenese ya tafole
swem	judo	karate	tennis	tafeltennis
go rutha	juto	karate	thenese	thenese ya tafola

260

Our spare time • Sichitha isikhathi sethu • Nako ya rona ya boikgutso
Ixesha lokuzonwabisa • Nako ya rona ya boiketlo • Ons vrye tyd • Nako ya boikhutšo

Metshameko Sport Meraloko

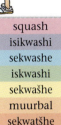

golf	horse racing	squash	motor racing	boxing
igalofu	umjaho wamahhashi	isikwashi	umjaho wezimoto	amankomane
kolofo	mojaho wa dipere	sekwashe	mojaho wa dikoloi	ditebele
igalufa	ugqatso lwamahashe	iskwashi	umdyarho weemoto	amanqindi
kolofo	lobelo lwa dipitse	sekwašhe	lobelo lwa dijanaga	motshameko wa mabole
gholf	perderesies	muurbal	motorresies	boks
kolofo	mokato wa dipere	sekwatšhe	peišano ya dikoloi	tša matswele

wrestling	marathon	volleyball	surfing	sailing
umdlalo wokubambana ngamandla	imarathoni	ibhola levoli	umdlalo emadlambini	ukuntweza
petano	lebelo la mokoka	volibolo	ho thellisa maqhubung	ho sesisa sekepe
ukungqula	ugqatso olude	ivolibholi	ukutyibilika ngeplangana elwandle	ukuhamba ngesikhephe
motshameko wa go kampana	marathone	bolokitlwa	go lelesela ka boto mo lewatleng	go tsamaya ka sekepe
stoei	marathon	vlugbal	branderry	seil
mokatano	marathoni	bolipolo	safing	go thala ka sekepe

windsurfing	waterpolo	gymnastics	canoeing
ukuntweza emadlambini omoya	umdlalo webhola emanzini	ukuvocavoca umzimba	ukugwedla isikebhe
ho sesa ka matla a moya	papadi ya bolo ya metsing	ho thapa ha mmele	ho tsamaisa seketswana
ukungcakaza ngomoya elwandle	ibhola yasemanzini	ezomthambo	ugqatso lwamaphenyane
tsamaiswa ke phefo	kgwele ya mo metsing	ikotlololo	motshameko wa mekorwana
seilplankry	waterpolo	gimnastiek	kanovaart
go thala ka maatla a moya	papadi ya kgwele ka meetseng	dithobollo	kanoing

Our spare time • Sichitha isikhathi sethu • Nako ya rona ya boikgutso
Ixesha lokuzonwabisa • Nako ya rona ya boiketlo • Ons vrye tyd • Nako ya boikhutšo

261

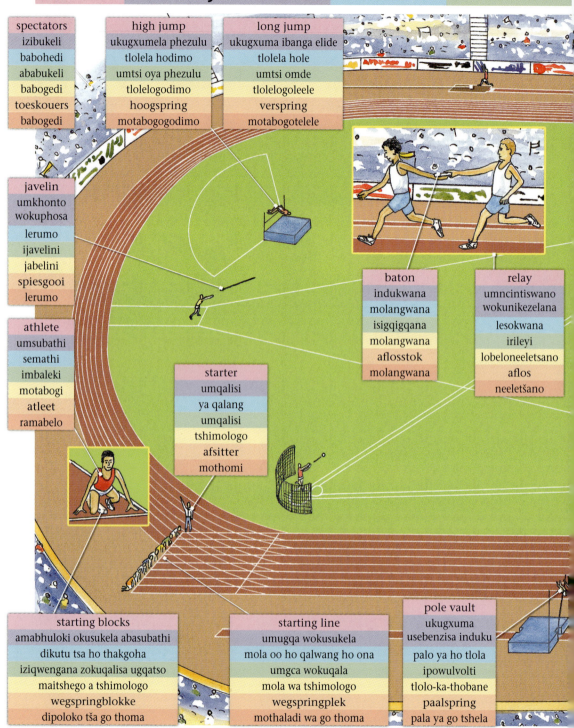

spectators
izibukeli
babohedi
ababukeli
babogedi
toeskouers
babogedi

high jump
ukugxumela phezulu
tlolela hodimo
umtsi oya phezulu
tlolelogodimo
hoogspring
motabogogodimo

long jump
ukugxuma ibanga elide
tlolela hole
umtsi omde
tlolelogoleele
verspring
motabogotelele

javelin
umkhonto
wokuphosa
lerumo
ijavelini
jabelini
spiesgooi
lerumo

athlete
umsubathi
semathi
imbaleki
motabogi
atleet
ramabelo

starter
umqalisi
ya qalang
umqalisi
tshimologo
afsitter
mothomi

baton
indukwana
molangwana
isigqigqana
molangwana
aflosstok
molangwana

relay
umncintiswano
wokunikezelana
lesokwana
irileyi
lobeloneeletsano
aflos
neeletšano

starting blocks
amabhuloki okusukela abasubathi
dikutu tsa ho thakgoha
iziqwengana zokuqalisa ugqatso
maitshego a tshimologo
wegspringblokke
dipoloko tša go thoma

starting line
umugqa wokusukela
mola oo ho qalwang ho ona
umgca wokuqala
mola wa tshimologo
wegspringplek
mothaladi wa go thoma

pole vault
ukugxuma
usebenzisa induku
palo ya ho tlola
ipowulvolti
tlolo-ka-thobane
paalspring
pala ya go tshela

Our spare time • Sichitha isikhathi sethu • Nako ya rona ya boikgutso
Ixesha lokuzonwabisa • Nako ya rona ya boiketlo • Ons vrye tyd • Nako ya boikhutšo

Atleletiki Atletiek Diatleletiki

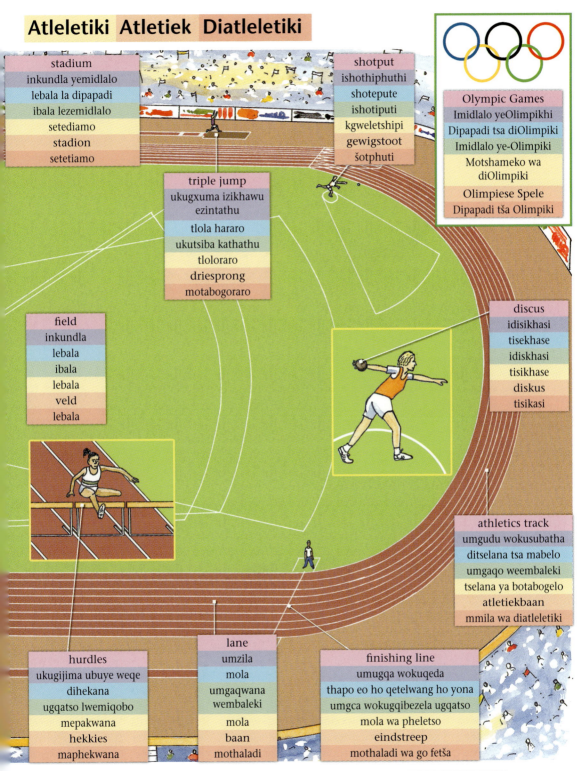

stadium
inkundla yemidlalo
lebala la dipapadi
ibala lezemidlalo
setediamo
stadion
setetiamo

shotput
ishothiphuthi
shotepute
ishotiputi
kgweletshipi
gewigstoot
šotphuti

Olympic Games
Imidlalo yeOlimpikhi
Dipapadi tsa diOlimpiki
Imidlalo ye-Olimpiki
Motshameko wa diOlimpiki
Olimpiese Spele
Dipapadi tša Olimpiki

triple jump
ukugxuma izikhawu ezintathu
tlola hararo
ukutsiba kathathu
tloloraro
driesprong
motabogoraro

discus
idisikhasi
tisekhase
idiskhasi
tisikhase
diskus
tisikasi

field
inkundla
lebala
ibala
lebala
veld
lebala

athletics track
umgudu wokusubatha
ditselana tsa mabelo
umgaqo weembaleki
tselana ya botabogelo
atletiekbaan
mmila wa diatleletiki

hurdles
ukugijima ubuye weqe
dihekana
ugqatso lwemiqobo
mepakwana
hekkies
maphekwana

lane
umzila
mola
umgaqwana wembaleki
mola
baan
mothaladi

finishing line
umugqa wokuqeda
thapo eo ho qetelwang ho yona
umgca wokugqibezela ugqatso
mola wa pheletso
eindstreep
mothaladi wa go fetša

Our spare time • Sichitha isikhathi sethu • Nako ya rona ya boikgutso
Ixesha lokuzonwabisa • Nako ya rona ya boiketlo • Ons vrye tyd • Nako ya boikhutšo

263

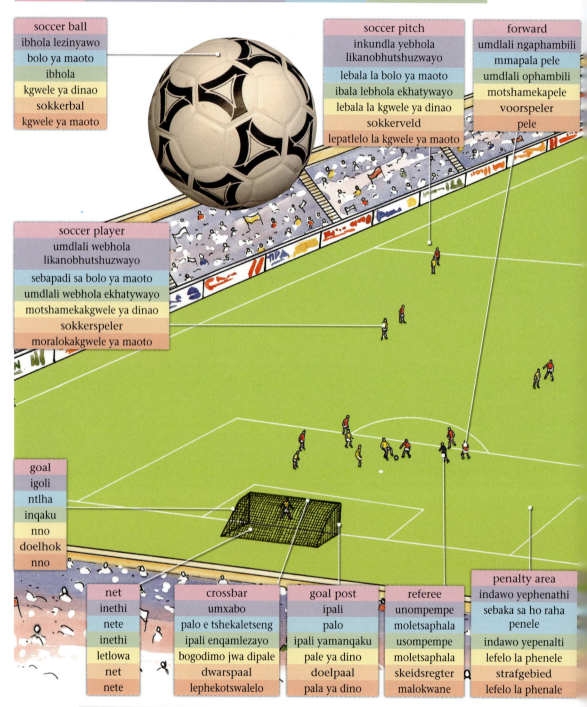

Soccer Ibhola likanobhutshuzwayo — Bolo ya maoto Ibhola ekhatywayo

soccer ball
ibhola lezinyawo
bolo ya maoto
ibhola
kgwele ya dinao
sokkerbal
kgwele ya maoto

soccer pitch
inkundla yebhola likanobhutshuzwayo
lebala la bolo ya maoto
ibala lebhola ekhatywayo
lebala la kgwele ya dinao
sokkerveld
lepatlelo la kgwele ya maoto

forward
umdlali ngaphambili
mmapala pele
umdlali ophambili
motshamekapele
voorspeler
pele

soccer player
umdlali webhola likanobhutshuzwayo
sebapadi sa bolo ya maoto
umdlali webhola ekhatywayo
motshamekakgwele ya dinao
sokkerspeler
moralokakgwele ya maoto

goal
igoli
ntlha
inqaku
nno
doelhok
nno

net
inethi
nete
inethi
letlowa
net
nete

crossbar
umxabo
palo e tshekaletseng
ipali enqamlezayo
bogodimo jwa dipale
dwarspaal
lephekotswalelo

goal post
ipali
palo
ipali yamanqaku
pale ya dino
doelpaal
pala ya dino

referee
unompempe
moletsaphala
usompempe
moletsaphala
skeidsregter
malokwane

penalty area
indawo yephenathi
sebaka sa ho raha penele
indawo yepenalti
lefelo la phenele
strafgebied
lefelo la phenale

Our spare time • Sichitha isikhathi sethu • Nako ya rona ya boikgutso
Ixesha lokuzonwabisa • Nako ya rona ya boiketlo • Ons vrye tyd • Nako ya boikhutšo

Kgwele ya dinao | **Sokker** | **Kgwele ya maoto**

centre circle
isiyingi esiphakathi nenkundla
sedikadikwe sa bohare ba lebala
isangqa esisesazulwini
sediko sa bogare ba lebala
middelsirkel
sedikogare

defender
umdlali wasemuva
mmapala morao
umdlali wasemva
mosireletsi
verdediger
mošireletši

goalkeeper
unozinti
sethibathibane
unozinti
motshwaradino
doelwagter
mothibadino

coach
umqeqeshi
mokwetlisi
umqeqeshi
mokatisi
afrigter
mohlahli

corner
ikhona
huku
ikona
sekhutlo
hoek
khutlo

linesman
usomugqa
ramola
usomgca
ramolantle
lynregter
molaolamothaladi

substitute
umbambeli
ya kenelang ya tswang
ibambela
motsenedi
plaasvervanger
moemedi

pass
-nikeza
fetisa
gqithisa
fetisetsa
aangee
fetiša

shoot
-gadla
hlaba ntlha
khabela ezimpodweni
go raga
skiet
raga

half-time
isikhathi sekhefu
nako ya kgefutso
ixesha lekhefu
nako ya go ikhutsa
halftyd
boikhutšo

penalty
iphenathi
penele
ipenalti
phenele
strafskop
kotlo

off-side
i-ofusayidi
ho etella ba kgahlanong le wena pele
i-ofusayidi
kekgwelepele
onkant
lehlakore leo le sa tsenwego

score
igoli
ntlha
inqaku
ntlha
verdoel
sekoro

extra time
isikhathi esengeziwe
nako e ekeditsweng
ixesha elongezelelweyo
nako e e okeditsweng
beseringstyd
nakokoketšo

corner
ikhona
huku
ikona
sekhutlo
hoek
khutlo

throw-in
ukuphosa ibhola
akgela ka lebaleng
faka ibhola ebaleni
go latlhela
ingooi
lahlela ka gare

foul
ifawuli
phoso
dlala kakubi
phoso
vuil spel
thalokomakgwakgwa

tackle
linga ukuthatha ibhola komunye
hlasela
wisa
kgopakgopetsa
doodvat
hlasela

save
-vikela
thiba
nqanda inqaku
lingangeni
go sireletsa
red
phemiša

Our spare time • Sichitha isikhathi sethu • Nako ya rona ya boikgutso
Ixesha lokuzonwabisa • Nako ya rona ya boiketlo • Ons vrye tyd • Nako ya boikhutšo

265

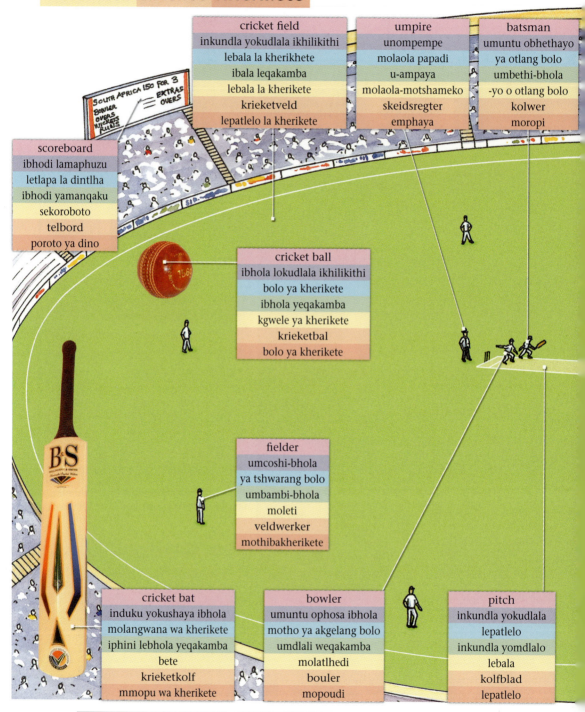

Cricket Ikhilikithi Kherikete Iqakamba
Kherikete Krieket Kherikete

cricket field
inkundla yokudlala ikhilikithi
lebala la kherikhete
ibala leqakamba
lebala la kherikete
krieketveld
lepatlelo la kherikete

umpire
unompempe
molaola papadi
u-ampaya
molaola-motshameko
skeidsregter
emphaya

batsman
umuntu obhethayo
ya otlang bolo
umbethi-bhola
-yo o otlang bolo
kolwer
moropi

scoreboard
ibhodi lamaphuzu
letlapa la dintlha
ibhodi yamanqaku
sekoroboto
telbord
poroto ya dino

SOUTH AFRICA 150 FOR 3
BOWLER — EXTRAS
OVERS — OVERS
WICKETS
RUNS

cricket ball
ibhola lokudlala ikhilikithi
bolo ya kherikete
ibhola yeqakamba
kgwele ya kherikete
krieketbal
bolo ya kherikete

fielder
umcoshi-bhola
ya tshwarang bolo
umbambi-bhola
moleti
veldwerker
mothibakherikete

cricket bat
induku yokushaya ibhola
molangwana wa kherikete
iphini lebhola yeqakamba
bete
krieketkolf
mmopu wa kherikete

bowler
umuntu ophosa ibhola
motho ya akgelang bolo
umdlali weqakamba
molatlhedi
bouler
mopoudi

pitch
inkundla yokudlala
lepatlelo
inkundla yomdlalo
lebala
kolfblad
lepatlelo

Our spare time • Sichitha isikhathi sethu • Nako ya rona ya boikgutso
Ixesha lokuzonwabisa • Nako ya rona ya boiketlo • Ons vrye tyd • Nako ya boikhutšo

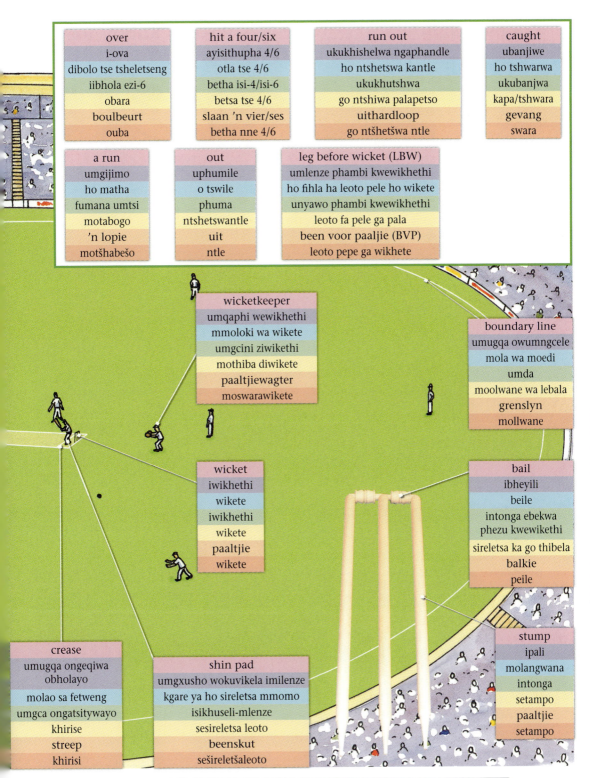

over
- i-ova
- dibolo tse tsheletseng
- iibhola ezi-6
- obara
- boulbeurt
- ouba

hit a four/six
- ayisithupha 4/6
- otla tse 4/6
- betha isi-4/isi-6
- betsa tse 4/6
- slaan 'n vier/ses
- betha nne 4/6

run out
- ukukhishelwa ngaphandle
- ho ntshetswa kantle
- ukukhutshwa
- go ntshiwa palapetso
- uithardloop
- go ntšhetšwa ntle

caught
- ubanjiwe
- ho tshwarwa
- ukubanjwa
- kapa/tshwara
- gevang
- swara

a run
- umgijimo
- ho matha
- fumana umtsi
- motabogo
- 'n lopie
- motšhabešo

out
- uphumile
- o tswile
- phuma
- ntshetswantle
- uit
- ntle

leg before wicket (LBW)
- umlenze phambi kwewikhethi
- ho fihla ha leoto pele ho wikete
- unyawo phambi kwewikhethi
- leoto fa pele ga pala
- been voor paaljie (BVP)
- leoto pepe ga wikhete

wicketkeeper
- umqaphi wewikhethi
- mmoloki wa wikete
- umgcini ziwikethi
- mothiba diwikete
- paaltjiewagter
- moswarawikete

boundary line
- umugqa owumngcele
- mola wa moedi
- umda
- moolwane wa lebala
- grenslyn
- mollwane

wicket
- iwikhethi
- wikete
- iwikhethi
- wikete
- paaltjie
- wikete

bail
- ibheyili
- beile
- intonga ebekwa phezu kwewikethi
- sireletsa ka go thibela
- balkie
- peile

crease
- umugqa ongeqiwa obholayo
- molao sa fetweng
- umgca ongatsitywayo
- khirise
- streep
- khirisi

shin pad
- umgxusho wokuvikela imilenze
- kgare ya ho sireletsa mmomo
- isikhuseli-mlenze
- sesireletsa leoto
- beenskut
- sešireletšaleoto

stump
- ipali
- molangwana
- intonga
- setampo
- paaltjie
- setampo

Our spare time • Sichitha isikhathi sethu • Nako ya rona ya boikgutso
Ixesha lokuzonwabisa • Nako ya rona ya boiketlo • Ons vrye tyd • Nako ya boikhutšo

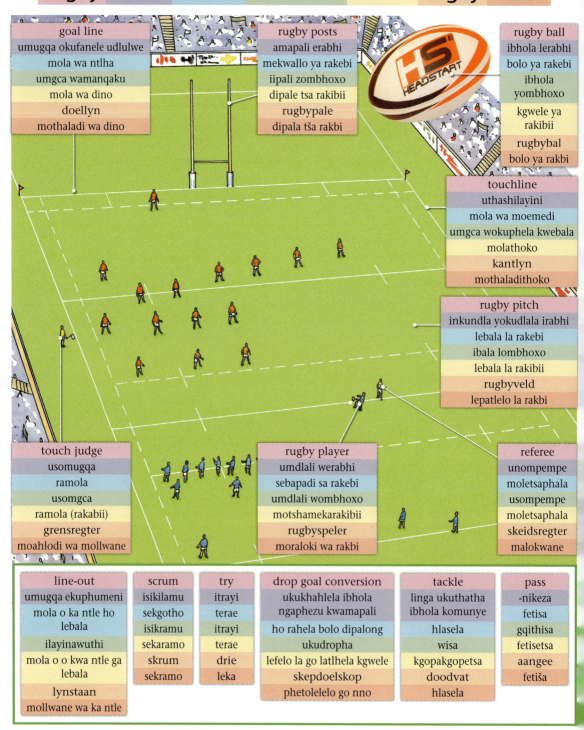

Rugby Irabhi Rakebi Umbhoxo Rakibii Rugby Rakbi

goal line
umugqa okufanele udlulwe
mola wa ntlha
umgca wamanqaku
mola wa dino
doellyn
mothaladi wa dino

rugby posts
amapali erabhi
mekwallo ya rakebi
iipali zombhoxo
dipale tsa rakibii
rugbypale
dipala tša rakbi

rugby ball
ibhola lerabhi
bolo ya rakebi
ibhola yombhoxo
kgwele ya rakibii
rugbybal
bolo ya rakbi

touchline
uthashilayini
mola wa moemedi
umgca wokuphela kwebala
molathoko
kantlyn
mothaladithoko

rugby pitch
inkundla yokudlala irabhi
lebala la rakebi
ibala lombhoxo
lebala la rakibii
rugbyveld
lepatlelo la rakbi

touch judge
usomugqa
ramola
usomgca
ramola (rakabii)
grensregter
moahlodi wa mollwane

rugby player
umdlali werabhi
sebapadi sa rakebi
umdlali wombhoxo
motshamekarakibii
rugbyspeler
moraloki wa rakbi

referee
unompempe
moletsaphala
usompempe
moletsaphala
skeidsregter
malokwane

line-out
umugqa ekuphumeni
mola o ka ntle ho lebala
ilayinawuthi
mola o o kwa ntle ga lebala
lynstaan
mollwane wa ka ntle

scrum
isikilamu
sekgotho
isikramu
sekaramo
skrum
sekramo

try
itrayi
terae
itrayi
terae
drie
leka

drop goal conversion
ukukhahlela ibhola ngaphezu kwamapali
ho rahela bolo dipalong
ukudropha
lefelo la go latlhela kgwele
skepdoelskop
phetolelelo go nno

tackle
linga ukuthatha ibhola komunye
hlasela
wisa
kgopakgopetsa
doodvat
hlasela

pass
-nikeza
fetisa
gqithisa
fetisetsa
aangee
fetiša

Our spare time • Sichitha isikhathi sethu • Nako ya rona ya boikgutso
Ixesha lokuzonwabisa • Nako ya rona ya boiketlo • Ons vrye tyd • Nako ya boikhutšo

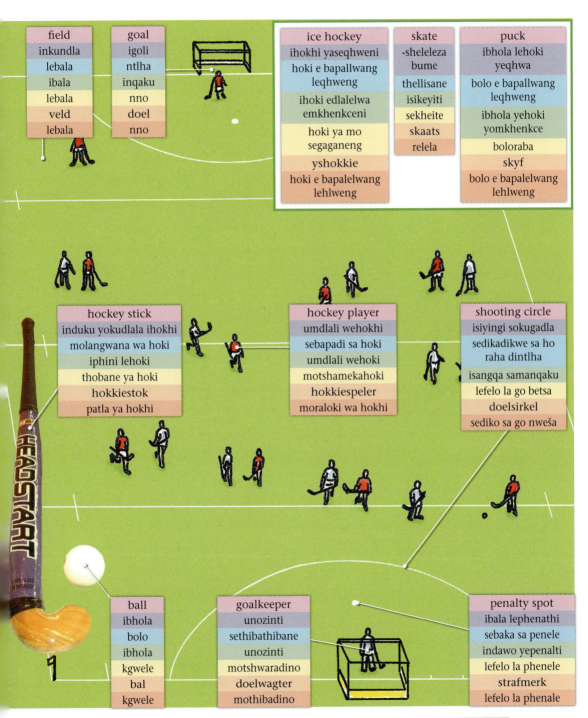

field
inkundla
lebala
ibala
lebala
veld
lebala

goal
igoli
ntlha
inqaku
nno
doel
nno

ice hockey
ihokhi yaseqhweni
hoki e bapallwang leqhweng
ihoki edlalelwa emkhenkceni
hoki ya mo segaganeng
yshokkie
hoki e bapalelwang lehlweng

skate
-sheleleza bume
thellisane
isikeyiti
sekheite
skaats
relela

puck
ibhola lehoki yeqhwa
bolo e bapallwang leqhweng
ibhola yehoki yomkhenkce
boloraba
skyf
bolo e bapalelwang lehlweng

hockey stick
induku yokudlala ihokhi
molangwana wa hoki
iphini lehoki
thobane ya hoki
hokkiestok
patla ya hokhi

hockey player
umdlali wehokhi
sebapadi sa hoki
umdlali wehoki
motshamekahoki
hokkiespeler
moraloki wa hokhi

shooting circle
isiyingi sokugadla
sedikadikwe sa ho raha dintlha
isangqa samanqaku
lefelo la go betsa
doelsirkel
sediko sa go nweša

ball
ibhola
bolo
ibhola
kgwele
bal
kgwele

goalkeeper
unozinti
sethibathibane
unozinti
motshwaradino
doelwagter
mothibadino

penalty spot
ibala lephenathi
sebaka sa penele
indawo yepenalti
lefelo la phenele
strafmerk
lefelo la phenale

Our spare time • Sichitha isikhathi sethu • Nako ya rona ya boikgutso
Ixesha lokuzonwabisa • Nako ya rona ya boiketlo • Ons vrye tyd • Nako ya boikhutšo

269

Netball Ibhola lomnqakiswano Bolo ya matsoho
Ibhola yomnyazi Bolotlowa Netbal Kgwele ya diatla

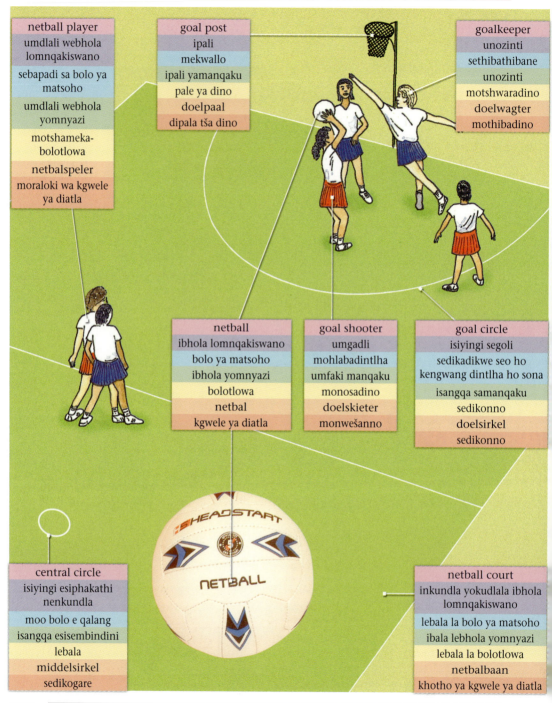

netball player
umdlali webhola lomnqakiswano
sebapadi sa bolo ya matsoho
umdlali webhola yomnyazi
motshameka-bolotlowa
netbalspeler
moraloki wa kgwele ya diatla

goal post
ipali
mekwallo
ipali yamanqaku
pale ya dino
doelpaal
dipala tša dino

goalkeeper
unozinti
sethibathibane
unozinti
motshwaradino
doelwagter
mothibadino

netball
ibhola lomnqakiswano
bolo ya matsoho
ibhola yomnyazi
bolotlowa
netbal
kgwele ya diatla

goal shooter
umgadli
mohlabadintlha
umfaki manqaku
monosadino
doelskieter
monwešanno

goal circle
isiyingi segoli
sedikadikwe seo ho kengwang dintlha ho sona
isangqa samanqaku
sedikonno
doelsirkel
sedikonno

central circle
isiyingi esiphakathi nenkundla
moo bolo e qalang
isangqa esisembindini
lebala
middelsirkel
sedikogare

netball court
inkundla yokudlala ibhola lomnqakiswano
lebala la bolo ya matsoho
ibala lebhola yomnyazi
lebala la bolotlowa
netbalbaan
khotho ya kgwele ya diatla

270

Our spare time • Sichitha isikhathi sethu • Nako ya rona ya boikgutso
Ixesha lokuzonwabisa • Nako ya rona ya boiketlo • Ons vrye tyd • Nako ya boikhutšo

Tennis Ibhola lomphebezo Tenese Intenetya Thenese Tennis Thenese

baseline
umugqa ongaphansi
mola o kantle
ibheyisilayini
molantle
agterlyn
mothalotheo

service line
umuda wokuseva
mola wa ho fepela
umgca wokuseva
molatatlhelo
afslaanlyn
mothalo wa go ropa

umpire
unompempe
molaola papadi
u-amphaya
molaola-motshameko
skeidsregter
emphaya

tennis racket
irekhethi yebhola lomphebezo
rakete ya ho otla bolo
irekhethi yentenetya
rekhete
tennisraket
rakhete ya thenese

tennis player
umdlali webhola lomphebezo
sebapadi sa tenese
umdlali wentenetya
motshamekathenese
tennisspeler
moraloki wa thenese

tennis court
inkundla yebhola lomphebezo
lebala la tenese
ibala lakudlalela intenetya
lebala la thenese
tennisbaan
khoto ya thenese

net
inethi
nete
umnatha
letlowa
net
nete

tennis ball
ibhola lomphebezo
bolo ya tenese
ibhola yentenetya
bolo ya thenese
tennisbal
kgwele ya thenese

serve
ukuqala ukushaya ibhola
fepela
seva
tatlhelo
afslaan
ropa

set
isethi
sete
iseti
nakotshameko
stel
sete

singles
abadlali abadlala ngabodwana
ba bapalang ka bonngwe
abadlali abadlala ngabanye
tshameka ka bongwe
enkelspel
papadi ya ka o tee, ka o tee

doubles
abadlali abadlala ngababili
ba bapalang ka bobedi
abadlali abadlala ngababini
bobedi matlhakore otlhe
dubbelspel
papadi ya bobedi ka bobedi

fault
iphutha
phoso
isiphene
phoso
fout
phošo

love
iguncu
lehe
iqanda
lefela
stroop
go swiela dintlha ka moka pele go sete

deuce
ijusi
maleka
amanqaku alinganayo
maleka
gelyk
maleka

advantage
inzuzo
monyetla
inzuzo
ntlha morago ga maleka
voordeel
monyetla

match
umdlalo womqhudelwano
qothisano
ukhuphiswano
kgaisano
wedstryd
phadišano

game
umdlalo
papadi
umdlalo
motshameko
spel
papadi

Our spare time • Sichitha isikhathi sethu • Nako ya rona ya boikgutso
Ixesha lokuzonwabisa • Nako ya rona ya boiketlo • Ons vrye tyd • Nako ya boikhutšo

271

Water sports	Imidlalo yasemanzini	Dipapadi tsa metsing	Imidlalo yasemanzini

Metshameko ya mo metsing	Watersport	Meraloko ya ka meetseng

diving board
ibhodi lokugxumela emanzini
boroto ya ho sesa
ibhodi yokudayiva
boto ya go itatlhela
duikplank
poroto ya mosobeledi

diver
umuntu ogxumela emanzini
seqwedi
umntywili
mothumi
duiker
mosobeledi

swimming pool
ichibi lokubhukuda
letamo la ho sesa
idama lokuqubha
letangwana la go thumela
swembad
bodibaruthelo

swimmer
umbhukudi
sesesi
indadi
mothumi
swemmer
moruthi

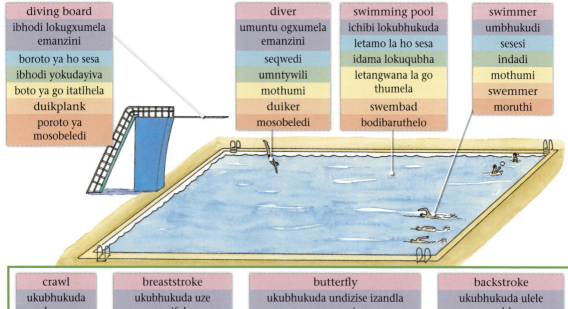

crawl
ukubhukuda sakugaqa
kgasa
ukugaqa
gagaba
kruipslag
abula

breaststroke
ukubhukuda uze ngesifuba
ya sesang ka sefuba
ukuqubha ngesifuba
go itaya sememi
borsslag
go rutha ka sefega

butterfly
ukubhukuda undizise izandla emoyeni
ya sesang jwalo ka serurubele
ukuqubha uxelisa ibhabhathane
go thuma joaka serurubele
vlinderslag
serurubele

backstroke
ukubhukuda ulele ngomhlane
ya sesang ka mokokotlo
ukuqubha ngomqolo
molelesedi ka mokokotlo
rugslag
go rutha ka mokokotla

surfer
umuntu ohlamba emadlambini olwandle
sebapadi sa metsing
umtyibilizi wamaza
molelesedi
branderryer
mothadi wa maphotho

wet suit
isudi lokubhukuda
sutu ya metsing
isuthi yasemanzini
sutu ya mo metsing
duikpak
sutu ya meetseng

surfboard
ibhodi lokuhlamba emadlambini olwandle
boroto ya ho sesa
iplanga lokutyibilika
seaparo sa go thuma se se metsi
branderplank
porotothadi

squash court
inkundla yokudlala isikwashi
lebala la sekwashe
ibala lesikwashi
lebala la sekwaše
muurbalbaan
lepatlelo la sekwatše

gym
ijimi
boikwetliso
ijimu
lefeloitshidilo
gimnasium
bothobollong

boxing ring
iringi yamankomane
lesakana la ditebele
iqonga lomdlalo wamanqindi
mosako wa mabole
bokskryt
mosako wa matswele

boxer
umshayi-sibhakela
raditebele
umdlali manqindi
ramabole
bokser
ramatshwele

boxing glove
igilavu lokushaya isibhakela
ditlelafo tsa raditebele
igilavu yamanqindi
tlelafo ya mabole
bokshandskoen
tlelafo ya ramatswele

golf club
induku yokushaya ibhola legalofu
molangwana wa kolofo
intonga yegalufa
molangwanakolofo
gholfklub
thobane ya kolofo

golf ball
ibhola legalofu
bolo ya kolofo
ibhola yegalufa
bolo ya kolofo
gholfbal
bolo ya kolofo

golf course
inkundla yokudlala igalofu
lebala la kolofo
ibala legalufa
lebala la kolofo
gholfbaan
lepatleokolofo

putting green
ukushaya ufike ohlazeni olunomgodi
ho otla o fihlelle botaleng
ibalana elinomngxuma wegalufa
tlhagamoseme
setperk
go otlela malebišong

bunker
isikhisi
santa lebaleng la kolofo
isigingqi esinentlabathi
karolwana ya motlhaba mo lebaleng la kolofo
sandkuil
santa rebaleng la kolofo

motor racing track
umzila wezimoto zomjaho
motjha wa dikoloi
umgaqo womdyarho weemoto
tselana ya lebelo la dijanaga
motorrenbaan
tsejana ya mokato wa dikoloi

racing car
imoto yomjaho
koloi ya mabelo
imoto yomdyarho
sejanaga sa kgaisano ya mabelo
renmotor
koloi ya peišano

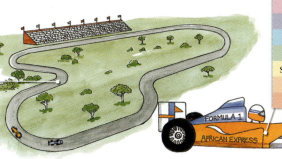

Our spare time • Sichitha isikhathi sethu • Nako ya rona ya boikgutso
Ixesha lokuzonwabisa • Nako ya rona ya boiketlo • Ons vrye tyd • Nako ya boikhutšo

273

Games Imidlalo Dipapadi Imidlalo

hopscotch	skipping	skateboarding	doll	board games
ugxa	ingqathu	ibhodi lokusheleleza	unodoli	imidlalo eba semabhodini
tjhekwana	kgati	sekeitiboroto	popi	
unochwela	ugqaphu	ibhodi yokuchebeleza	unodoli	dipapadi tse bapallwang letlapeng
patlaka	go tlola	botoleleselo	mpopi	
eenbeentjie	touspring	skaatsplankry	pop	imidlalo edlalelwa ebhodini
oposekhotši	kgati	theledi	popi	
				metshameko ya boto
				bordspeletjies
				poroto ya dipapadi

chess	listening to music	reading	computer games
ishesi	ukulalela umculo	ukufunda	imidlalo yekhompyutha
tjhese	ho mamela mmino	ho bala	dipapadi tsa khomputha
itshesi	ukumamela umculo	ukufunda	imidlalo yekhompyutha
tšhese	utlweletse mmino	go bala	metshameko ya khomphiutha
skaak	na musiek luister	lees	rekenaarspeletjies
tšhese	go theeletša mmino	go bala	dipapadi tša khomputha

card games	dominoes	marbles	camping	hiking
amakhadi	amadayisi	izimabuli	ukukhempa	ukuhamba ngezinyawo
dipapadi tsa karete	ditomino	dimabole	ho kampa	ho hlwa thaba
imidlalo yamakhasi	iidomino	amapetyu	ukukhempa	ukuhayika
metshameko ya dikarata	ditomino	dimabole	go kampa	go palama dithaba
kaartspel	domino's	albaster	kampeer	stap
dipapadi tša dikarata	ditomino	memabolo	go kampa	go haeka

Our spare time • Sichitha isikhathi sethu • Nako ya rona ya boikgutso
Ixesha lokuzonwabisa • Nako ya rona ya boiketlo • Ons vrye tyd • Nako ya boikhutšo

Metshameko Speletjies Dipapadi

painting
ukupenda
ho penta
ukupeyinta
botaki
skilder
go penta

drawing
ukudweba
ho taka
ukuzoba
go tshwatsho
teken
thala

making things
ukwenza izinto
ho etsa dintho
ukwenza izinto
go dira dilo
dinge maak
go dira dilo

horseriding
ukugibela amahhashi
ho palama dipere
ukukhwela amahashe
go palama dipitse
perdry
go katiša dipere

draughts
amadrawuthi
morabaraba
umrabaraba
morabaraba
dambord
terafo

hide-and-seek
umacashelana
boleki ba ipatile
undize
mmampatile
wegkruipertjie
mmampatile

toy
ithoyizi
thoye
into yokudlala
setshamekisi
speelgoed
sebapadišwa

cycling
ukugibela ibhayisikili
papadi ya baesekele
ugqatso lweebhayisekile
motabogo ka
dibaesekele
fietsry
papadi ya dipaesekele

**Collecting ... Ukuqoqa ... Ho bokella ... Ukuqokelela ...
Kokoanya ... Versameling ... Kgoboketša ...**

stamps	cards	coins	insects	shells
izitembu	amakhadi	izinhlamvu zemali	izinambuzane	amagobolondo
ditempe	dikarete	lewala	dikokonyana	dikgaketlana
izitampu	amakhadi	iingqekembe zemali	izinambuzane	oonokrwece
ditempe	dikarata	madi a tshipi	ditshenekegi	dikgapa
seëls	kaartjies	munte	insekte	skulpe
ditempe	dikarata	tšhelete ya tšhipi	khunkhwane	dikgapetla

Our spare time • Sichitha isikhathi sethu • Nako ya rona ya boikgutso
Ixesha lokuzonwabisa • Nako ya rona ya boiketlo • Ons vrye tyd • Nako ya boikhutšo

275

Cinema Isinema Baesekopo Isinema Sinema Fliek Sinema

box office
lapho kuthengwa khona amathikithi
ofisi ya ditekete
i-ofisi yamatikiti
kantoro ya dithekete
loket
kantoro ya dithekethe

ticket
ithikithi
tekete
itikiti
thekete
kaartjie
thekethe

usher
umngenisi
mothusi
impelesi
maomogela-baeng
plekaanwyser
molaetšabodulo

emergency exit
intuba yokuphuma uma kuvela ingozi kungazelelwe
monyako wa tlokotsi
umnyango wokuphuma
lebati kgotsa kgoro ya tshoganyetso
nooduitgang
monyako wa tšhoganetšo

film
isithombe
filimi
ifilimu
filimi
film
filimi

screen
isenqo
sebhayisi-kobho
sekirini
isikhuseli
sekirini
skerm/doek
sekrini

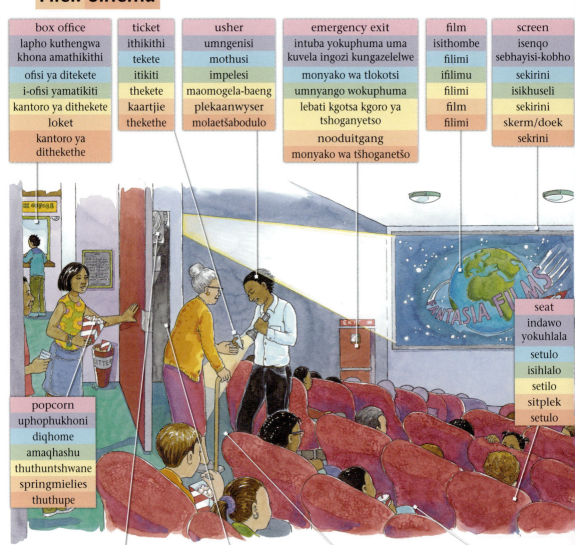

popcorn
uphophukhoni
diqhome
amaqhashu
thuthuntshwane
springmielies
thuthupe

seat
indawo yokuhlala
setulo
isihlalo
setilo
sitplek
setulo

film projector
iphrojektha yefilimu
sebapaladitshwantsho
umatshini wokubonisa ifilimu
porojeketara ya filimi
filmprojektor
protšektara ya filimi

projector room
igumbi lephrojektha
phaposi ya porojeketara
igumbi lomatshini wokubonisa ifilimu
phaposi ya porojeketara
projektorkamer
phapoši ya protšektara

aisle
i-ayili
aele
i-ayili
aele
gang
aele

row
uhlu lwezindawo zokuhlala
mola
uluhlu lweendawo zokuhlala
mola
ry
molokoloko

276

Theatre Ithiyetha Teatere Ithiyetha Teatere Teater Teatere

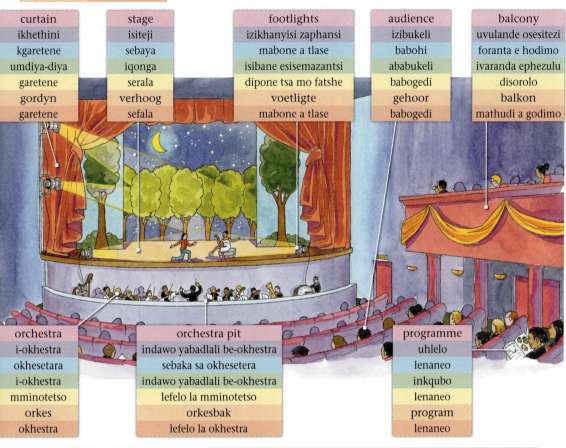

curtain
ikhethini
kgaretene
umdiya-diya
garetene
gordyn
garetene

stage
isiteji
sebaya
iqonga
serala
verhoog
sefala

footlights
izikhanyisi zaphansi
mabone a tlase
isibane esisemazantsi
dipone tsa mo fatshe
voetligte
mabone a tlase

audience
izibukeli
babohi
ababukeli
babogedi
gehoor
babogedi

balcony
uvulande osesitezi
foranta e hodimo
ivaranda ephezulu
disorolo
balkon
mathudi a godimo

orchestra
i-okhestra
okhesetara
i-okhestra
mminotetso
orkes
okhestra

orchestra pit
indawo yabadlali be-okhestra
sebaka sa okhesetera
indawo yabadlali be-okhestra
lefelo la mminotetso
orkesbak
lefelo la okhestra

programme
uhlelo
lenaneo
inkqubo
lenaneo
program
lenaneo

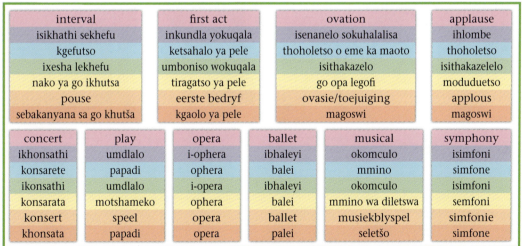

interval
isikhathi sekhefu
kgefutso
ixesha lekhefu
nako ya go ikhutsa
pouse
sebakanyana sa go khutša

first act
inkundla yokuqala
ketsahalo ya pele
umboniso wokuqala
tiragatso ya pele
eerste bedryf
kgaolo ya pele

ovation
isenanelo sokuhalalisa
thoholetso o eme ka maoto
isithakazelo
go opa legofi
ovasie/toejuiging
magoswi

applause
ihlombe
thoholetso
isithakazelelo
moduduetso
applous
magoswi

concert
ikhonsathi
konsarete
ikonsathi
konsarata
konsert
khonsata

play
umdlalo
papadi
umdlalo
motshameko
speel
papadi

opera
i-ophera
ophera
i-opera
ophera
opera
opera

ballet
ibhaleyi
balei
ibhaleyi
balei
ballet
palei

musical
okomculo
mmino
okomculo
mmino wa diletswa
musiekblyspel
seletšo

symphony
isimfoni
simfone
isimfoni
semfoni
simfonie
simfone

Our spare time • Sichitha isikhathi sethu • Nako ya rona ya boikgutso
Ixesha lokuzonwabisa • Nako ya rona ya boiketlo • Ons vrye tyd • Nako ya boikhutšo

277

Music Umculo Mmino Umculo

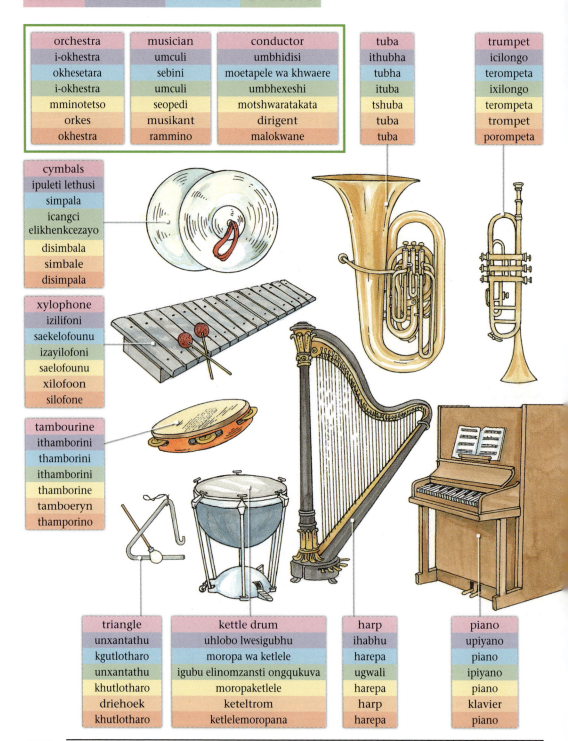

orchestra	musician	conductor
i-okhestra	umculi	umbhidisi
okhesetara	sebini	moetapele wa khwaere
i-okhestra	umculi	umbhexeshi
mminotetso	seopedi	motshwaratakata
orkes	musikant	dirigent
okhestra	rammino	malokwane

tuba
ithubha
tubha
ituba
tshuba
tuba
tuba

trumpet
icilongo
terompeta
ixilongo
terompeta
trompet
porompeta

cymbals
ipuleti lethusi
simpala
icangci elikhenkcezayo
disimbala
simbale
disimpala

xylophone
izilifoni
saekelofounu
izayilofoni
saelofounu
xilofoon
silofone

tambourine
ithamborini
thamborini
ithamborini
thamborine
tamboeryn
thamporino

triangle
unxantathu
kgutlotharo
unxantathu
khutlotharo
driehoek
khutlotharo

kettle drum
uhlobo lwesigubhu
moropa wa ketlele
igubu elinomzantsi ongqukuva
moropaketlele
keteltrom
ketlelemoropana

harp
ihabhu
harepa
ugwali
harepa
harp
harepa

piano
upiyano
piano
ipiyano
piano
klavier
piano

Our spare time • Sichitha isikhathi sethu • Nako ya rona ya boikgutso
Ixesha lokuzonwabisa • Nako ya rona ya boiketlo • Ons vrye tyd • Nako ya boikhutšo

Mmino Musiek Mmino

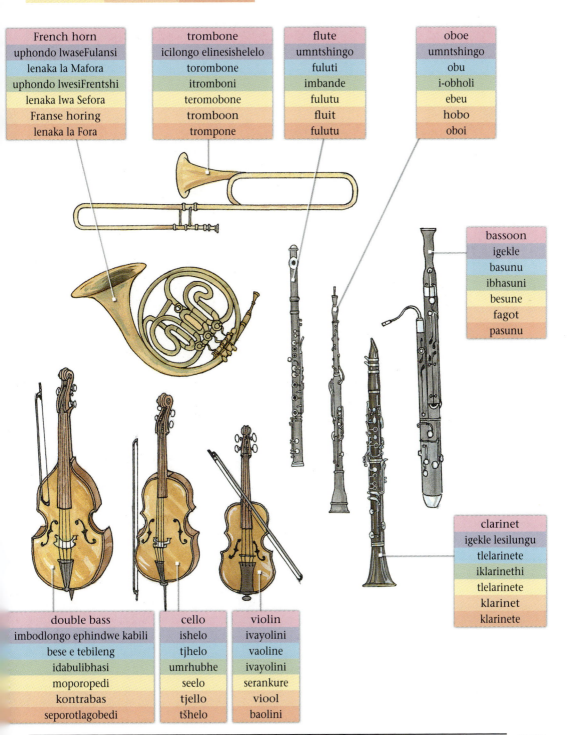

French horn
uphondo lwaseFulansi
lenaka la Mafora
uphondo lwesiFrentshi
lenaka lwa Sefora
Franse horing
lenaka la Fora

trombone
icilongo elinesishelelo
torombone
itromboni
teromobone
tromboon
trompone

flute
umntshingo
fuluti
imbande
fulutu
fluit
fulutu

oboe
umntshingo
obu
i-obholi
ebeu
hobo
oboi

bassoon
igekle
basunu
ibhasuni
besune
fagot
pasunu

clarinet
igekle lesilungu
tlelarinete
iklarinethi
tlelarinete
klarinet
klarinete

double bass
imbodlongo ephindwe kabili
bese e tebileng
idabulibhasi
moporopedi
kontrabas
seporotlagobedi

cello
ishelo
tjhelo
umrhubhe
seelo
tjello
tšhelo

violin
ivayolini
vaoline
ivayolini
serankure
viool
baolini

Our spare time • Sichitha isikhathi sethu • Nako ya rona ya boikgutso
Ixesha lokuzonwabisa • Nako ya rona ya boiketlo • Ons vrye tyd • Nako ya boikhutšo

279

drum	keyboard	hand piano	musical instrument
isigubhu	ikhibhodi	upiyano lwesandla	imfijoli
moropa	khiboroto	piano ya letsoho	seletswa sa mmino
igubu	ikhibhodi	ipiyano yesandla	isixhobo somculo
moropa	khiiboto	piano ya letsogo	seletswa sa mmino
trom	sleutelbord	handklavier	musiekinstrument
moropa	khiipoto	piano ya seatla	seletšo sa mmino

base guitar	shaker	saxophone	guitar
isigingci esikhipha ibhesi	ukhehlekhehle	isekzofoni	isigingci
katara ya beise	morutlhwana	saksfounu	katara
isiginci esingqokolayo	isishukumisi	isaksofoni	isiginci
katara ya kodu	setšhakgatšhakga	sakesofounu	katara
baskitaar	skudder	saksofoon	kitaar
katara ya go porotla	sešikinyi	sekisofoune	katara

Music style	Izinhlobo zomculo	Mofuta wa mmino	Uhlobo lomculo		
rock	pop	jazz	rhythm and blues	rap	kwaito
irokhi	iphophu	ijezi	isigqi somcabango	irephu	ikwayito
rokho	phopo	jese	morethetho wa menahano	repe	kwaito
irokhu	ipopu	ijezi	onesingqi nocingisayo	irephu	ikwayito
roko	phopo	jese	moribo le mmino wa maikutlo	repe	kwaito
rock	popmusiek	jazz	rhythm en blues	rap	kwaito
rokho	mmino wa phopo	jese	morethetho le ditlhologelo	go repha	kwaeto

Our spare time • Sichitha isikhathi sethu • Nako ya rona ya boikgutso
Ixesha lokuzonwabisa • Nako ya rona ya boiketlo • Ons vrye tyd • Nako ya boikhutšo

Rock concert **Ikhonsathi yomculo werokhi** **Konsarete ya mmino wa rokho**
Ikonsathi yerokhu **Konsarata ya mmino wa roko** **Rock-konsert** **Khonsate ya roko**

drummer	guitarist
umshayi wogubhu	umshayi wesigingci
rameropa	rakatara
umdlali magubu	umdlali wesiginci
moletsi wa moropa	moletsi wa katara
tromspeler	kitaarspeler
moletšamoropa	rakatara

soloist
umuntu ocula yedwa
ya tsanyaolang a le mong
umculi ocula yedwa
moopelanosi
solosanger
moopelanoši

pop group
iqembu lomculo wephophu
sehlopha sa phopo
iqela lepophu
setlhopha sa phopo
popgroep
sehlopa sa phopo

rock band	fans	lead singer
ibhendi yerokhi	abalandeli	umculi oholayo
sehlopha sa dibini tsa rokho	batshehetsi	sephokodi
ibhendi yerokhu	abalandeli	umculi okhokelayo
setlhopha sa mmino wa roko	balatedi	motlhabeletsi
rock-groep	aanhangers	hoofsanger
pente ya roko	balatedi	mohlabeledi

Setaelemmino **Musiekstyl** **Setaelemmino**

heavy metal	classical	dance	gospel	reggae	disco
insimbi enesingqi esikhulu	unqambothi	ukudansa	umculo wokholo	iregeyi	idiskho
tshepe e boima	tlelasiki	tantshi	mmino wa sedumedi	rekei	disiko
onesandi esikhulu	ezodidi	danisa	umculo wokholo	iregeyi	umngqungqo
ditshipintsi	tlelasiki	motantsho	mmino wa sedumedi	rekei	tisiko
heavy metal	klassiek	dans	gospel	reggae	disko
tšhipi ye boima	setlelasiki	tansa	mmino wa sedumedi	rikae	diskho

Our spare time • Sichitha isikhathi sethu • Nako ya rona ya boikgutso
Ixesha lokuzonwabisa • Nako ya rona ya boiketlo • Ons vrye tyd • Nako ya boikhutšo

281

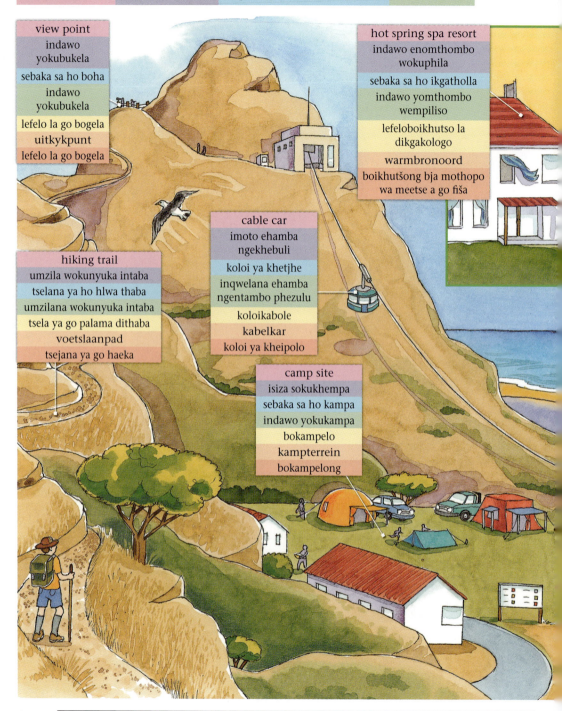

Going on holiday | Ukuchitha iholide | Ho ya matsatsing a phomolo | Ukuya ekhefini

view point
indawo yokubukela
sebaka sa ho boha
indawo yokubukela
lefelo la go bogela
uitkykpunt
lefelo la go bogela

hot spring spa resort
indawo enomthombo wokuphila
sebaka sa ho ikgatholla
indawo yomthombo wempiliso
lefeloboikhutso la dikgakologo
warmbronoord
boikhutšong bja mothopo wa meetse a go fiša

cable car
imoto ehamba ngekhebuli
koloi ya khetjhe
inqwelana ehamba ngentambo phezulu
koloikabole
kabelkar
koloi ya kheipolo

hiking trail
umzila wokunyuka intaba
tselana ya ho hlwa thaba
umzilana wokunyuka intaba
tsela ya go palama dithaba
voetslaanpad
tsejana ya go haeka

camp site
isiza sokukhempa
sebaka sa ho kampa
indawo yokukampa
bokampelo
kampterrein
bokampelong

282

Our spare time • Sichitha isikhathi sethu • Nako ya rona ya boikgutso
Ixesha lokuzonwabisa • Nako ya rona ya boiketlo • Ons vrye tyd • Nako ya boikhutšo

wine route
indlela yasezivandeni zewayini
tsela e lekolang dibaka tsa veini
indlela kwiifama zomdiliya
lefelo la ditlhare tsa mofine
wynroete
tsela ya beine

nature reserve
imvelo ebekiweyo
serapa sa tlhaho
iziko lezendalo
serapa sa tlhago
natuurreservaat
bobolokatlhago

game reserve
isiqiwu sezinyamazane
serapa sa polokelo ya diphoofolo
iziko lezilwanyana zasendle
serapa sa diphologolo
wildreservaat
lešoka la diphoofolo

beach
ibhishi
lebopo
unxweme
lobopo
strand
lebopo

mountain resort
izindlu zabavakashi ezisentabeni
sebaka sa ho phomola thabeng
izindlwana zokuhlala entabeni
ntloborobalo kwa thabeng
bergoord
boikhutšong bja thaba

curio shop
indawo ethengisa amaqabuqabu
lebenkele la bonono
ivenkilana yezinto ezinqabileyo
lebenkele la dikgabisa tsa botlhokwa
aandenkingswinkel
lebenkele la tšeo di sa tlwaelegago

tour bus
ibhasi lezivakashi
bese ya bahahlaudi
ibhasi yabakhenkethi
bese ya baeti
toerbus
pese ya leeto

tour guide
umkhaphi wezivakashi
mosupatsela wa bahahlaudi
umkhokeli wabakhenkethi
mokaelatsela
toergids
tlhahlabaeti

tourist
isivakashi
mohahlaudi
umkhenkethi
mojanala
toeris
moeti

Our spare time • Sichitha isikhathi sethu • Nako ya rona ya boikgutso
Ixesha lokuzonwabisa • Nako ya rona ya boiketlo • Ons vrye tyd • Nako ya boikhutšo

283

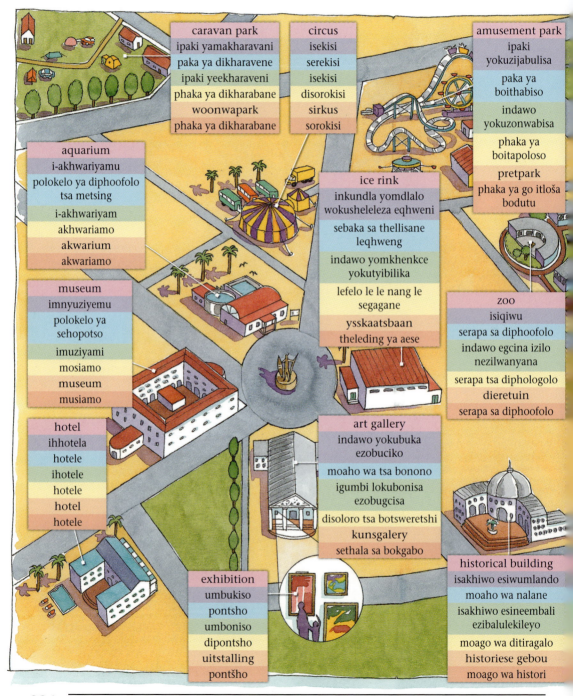

caravan park
ipaki yamakharavani
paka ya dikharavene
ipaki yeekharaveni
phaka ya dikharabane
woonwapark
phaka ya dikharabane

circus
isekisi
serekisi
isekisi
disorokisi
sirkus
sorokisi

amusement park
ipaki yokuzijabulisa
paka ya boithabiso
indawo yokuzonwabisa
phaka ya boitapoloso
pretpark
phaka ya go itloša bodutu

aquarium
i-akhwariyamu
polokelo ya diphoofolo tsa metsing
i-akhwariyam
akhwariamo
akwarium
akwariamo

ice rink
inkundla yomdlalo wokusheleleza eqhweni
sebaka sa thellisane leqhweng
indawo yomkhenkce yokutyibilika
lefelo le le nang le segagane
ysskaatsbaan
theleding ya aese

museum
imnyuziyemu
polokelo ya sehopotso
imuziyami
mosiamo
museum
musiamo

zoo
isiqiwu
serapa sa diphoofolo
indawo egcina izilo nezilwanyana
serapa tsa diphologolo
dieretuin
serapa sa diphoofolo

hotel
ihhotela
hotele
ihotele
hotele
hotel
hotele

art gallery
indawo yokubuka ezobuciko
moaho wa tsa bonono
igumbi lokubonisa ezobugcisa
disoloro tsa botsweretshi
kunsgalery
sethala sa bokgabo

historical building
isakhiwo esiwumlando
moaho wa nalane
isakhiwo esineembali ezibalulekileyo
moago wa ditiragalo
historiese gebou
moago wa histori

exhibition
umbukiso
pontsho
umboniso
dipontsho
uitstalling
pontšho

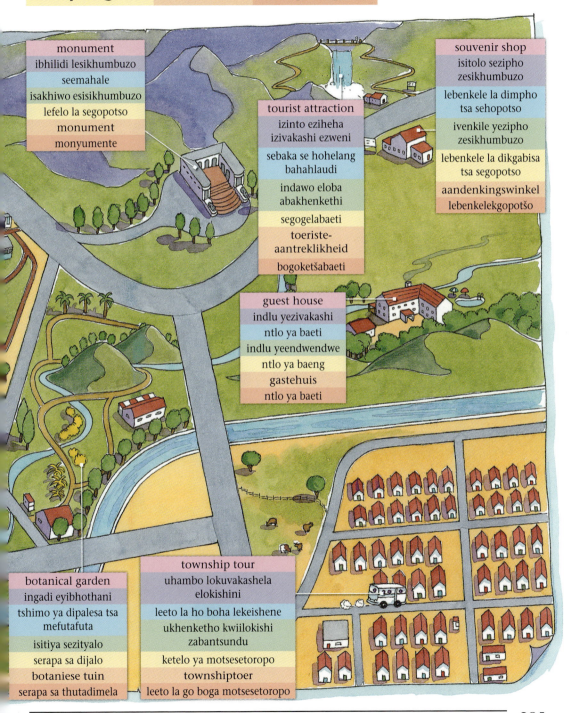

monument
ibhilidi lesikhumbuzo
seemahale
isakhiwo esisikhumbuzo
lefelo la segopotso
monument
monyumente

tourist attraction
izinto eziheha izivakashi ezweni
sebaka se hohelang bahahlaudi
indawo eloba abakhenkethi
segogelabaeti
toeriste-aantreklikheid
bogoketšabaeti

souvenir shop
isitolo sezipho zesikhumbuzo
lebenkele la dimpho tsa sehopotso
ivenkile yezipho zesikhumbuzo
lebenkele la dikgabisa tsa segopotso
aandenkingswinkel
lebenkelekgopotšo

guest house
indlu yezivakashi
ntlo ya baeti
indlu yeendwendwe
ntlo ya baeng
gastehuis
ntlo ya baeti

botanical garden
ingadi eyibhothani
tshimo ya dipalesa tsa mefutafuta
isitiya sezityalo
serapa sa dijalo
botaniese tuin
serapa sa thutadimela

township tour
uhambo lokuvakashela elokishini
leeto la ho boha lekeishene
ukhenketho kwiilokishi zabantsundu
ketelo ya motsesetoropo
townshiptoer
leeto la go boga motsesetoropo

Our spare time • Sichitha isikhathi sethu • Nako ya rona ya boikgutso
Ixesha lokuzonwabisa • Nako ya rona ya boiketlo • Ons vrye tyd • Nako ya boikhutšo

285

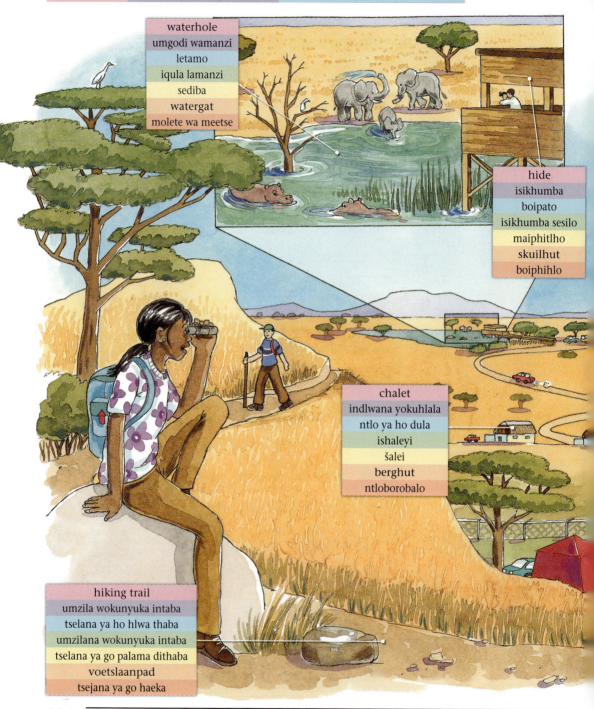

Game reserve	Isiqiwu sezinyamazane	Serapa sa polokelo ya diphoofolo

waterhole
umgodi wamanzi
letamo
iqula lamanzi
sediba
watergat
molete wa meetse

hide
isikhumba
boipato
isikhumba sesilo
maiphitlho
skuilhut
boiphihlo

chalet
indlwana yokuhlala
ntlo ya ho dula
ishaleyi
šalei
berghut
ntloborobalo

hiking trail
umzila wokunyuka intaba
tselana ya ho hlwa thaba
umzilana wokunyuka intaba
tselana ya go palama dithaba
voetslaanpad
tsejana ya go haeka

Our spare time • Sichitha isikhathi sethu • Nako ya rona ya boikgutso
Ixesha lokuzonwabisa • Nako ya rona ya boiketlo • Ons vrye tyd • Nako ya boikhutšo

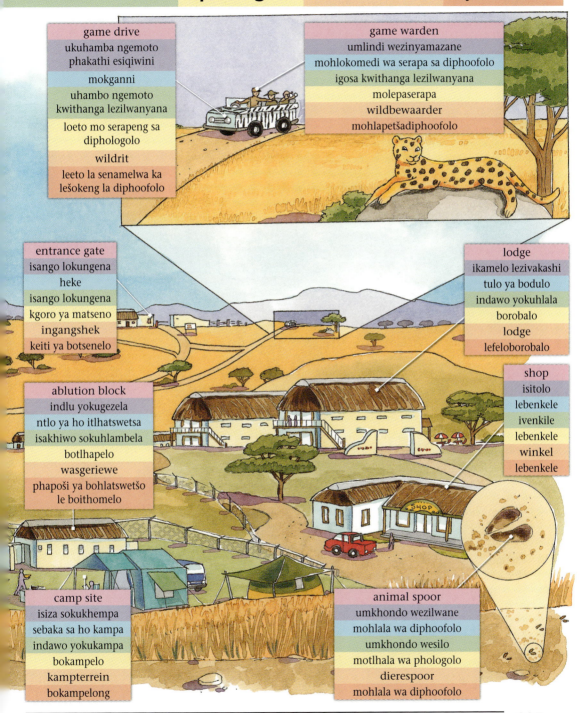

game drive
ukuhamba ngemoto phakathi esiqiwini
mokganni
uhambo ngemoto kwithanga lezilwanyana
loeto mo serapeng sa diphologolo
wildrit
leeto la senamelwa ka lešokeng la diphoofolo

game warden
umlindi wezinyamazane
mohlokomedi wa serapa sa diphoofolo
igosa kwithanga lezilwanyana
molepaserapa
wildbewaarder
mohlapetšadiphoofolo

entrance gate
isango lokungena
heke
isango lokungena
kgoro ya matseno
ingangshek
keiti ya botsenelo

ablution block
indlu yokugezela
ntlo ya ho itlhatswetsa
isakhiwo sokuhlambela
botlhapelo
wasgeriewe
phapoši ya bohlatswetšo le boithomelo

lodge
ikamelo lezivakashi
tulo ya bodulo
indawo yokuhlala
borobalo
lodge
lefeloborobalo

shop
isitolo
lebenkele
ivenkile
lebenkele
winkel
lebenkele

camp site
isiza sokukhempa
sebaka sa ho kampa
indawo yokukampa
bokampelo
kampterrein
bokampelong

animal spoor
umkhondo wezilwane
mohlala wa diphoofolo
umkhondo wesilo
motlhala wa phologolo
dierespoor
mohlala wa diphoofolo

Our spare time • Sichitha isikhathi sethu • Nako ya rona ya boikgutso
Ixesha lokuzonwabisa • Nako ya rona ya boiketlo • Ons vrye tyd • Nako ya boikhutšo

287

The beach Ibhishi Lebopo Unxweme

sea
ulwandle
lewatle
ulwandle
lewatle
see
lewatle

wave
igagasi
leqhubu
iliza
lekhubu
brander
lephotho

lighthouse
isibani sasolwandle
ntlwana e kgantshetsang dikepe
isikhokeli senqanawa ebusuku
ntlwanataolo ya dikepe
vuurtoring
ntloseetša

umbrella
isambulela
sekgele
isambrela
sekhukhu
sambreel
samporele

rock
idwala
lefika
ilitye
lefika
rots
leswika

seaweed
ulele lwasolwandle
lehola la lewatle
ingca yolwandle
mefero ya lewatle
seewier
mabjang a lewatle

picnic hamper
ubhasikidi wephikiniki
basekete ya dijo
ingobozi yepikiniki
manki wa pikiniki
piekniekmandjie
mmanki wa pikiniki

shell
igobolondo
kgaketla
unokrwece
kgopana
skulp
kgapetlana

288

Lobopo Die strand Lebopo

lifeguard
umlindi wababhukudi
mopholosi
umlindi wabaqubhi
motlhokomela-bathumi
lewensredder
mohlakodiši

promenade
indawo yokuchanasa
peivemente
lebopong la lewatle
indawo yokuhamba-
hamba
tselanatantabelo
promenade
mokgothalewatle

beachfront hotel
ihhotela elingasebhishi
hotele e lebopong la
lewatle
ihotele eselunxwemeni
lolwandle
hotelekokamawatle
strandfronthotel
hotele ya lebopong

shower
ishawa
shawara
ishawari
šawara
stort
šawara

beach volleyball
ibhola lombhoxo lasebhishi
volibolo e bapallwang lewatle
ivolibholi yaselunxwemeni
bolokitlwa ya mo lobopong
strandvlugbal
bolipolo ya lebopong

cooler box
ibhokisi eliyisibandisi
sehatsetsi sa dijo le dinomaphodi
ibhokisi egcina ukutya kubanda
lebokoso le le tsidifatsang
koelhouer
lepokisitšidifatši

sand
isihlabathi
lehlabathe
intlabathi
motlhaba
sand
santa

bin
umgqomo
tonkana ya
matlakala
umgqomo
seolelamatlakala
vullisblik
motoma wa
matlakala

towel
ithawula
thaole
itawuli
toulo
handdoek
toulo

suntan lotion
iloshini yokuvikela
isikhumba elangeni
mafura a ho itshereletsa
letsatsing
isithambisi sokuzikhusela
kwiimitha yelanga
setlolo sa karameloletsatsi
sonbrandmiddel
setlolo sa go šireletša
letšatši

driftwood
ibibi
mahohodi
isiqobo esidudulwa
lulwandle
magogodi
dryfhout
legong la go phaphamala

Our spare time • Sichitha isikhathi sethu • Nako ya rona ya boikgutso
Ixesha lokuzonwabisa • Nako ya rona ya boiketlo • Ons vrye tyd • Nako ya boikhutšo

Amusement park | Ipaki yokuzijabulisa | Paka ya boithabiso | Indawo yokuzonwabisa

clown
umhlekisi
seswasi
umonwabisi
modirametlae
hanswors
mosegiši

mime artist
ingcweti yokulingisa buthule
sebini sa setshwantshisi
igcisa lokulinganisa
moetsisi wa botsweretshi
mimiekkunstenaar
rabokgabomankekišane

magic show
umbukiso wemilingo
pontsho ya mehlolo
umboniso wemilingo
dipontsho tsa maselamose
towervertoning
pontšho ya maselamose

food stall
isitodlwana sokuthengisela ukudla
tafolana ya dijo
ivenkilana ekuthengiselwa kuyo ukutya
lebenkejana la dijo
kosstalletjie
lebenkejana la dijo

ghost train
isitimela sezipoki
terene ya dipoko
uloliwe owoyikisayo
terena ya dipoko
spooktrein
setimelasepoko

entrance fee
imali yokungena
tefo ya ho kena hekeng
intlawulo yokungena
madi a go tsena
ingangsfooi
tšhelete ya monyako

entrance gate
isango lokungena
heke
isango lokungena
kgoro ya matseno
ingangshek
keiti ya botsenelo

queue
uhele lwabantu
mola
ukrozo
mola
tou
molokoloko

cashier
umphathi wemali
molefisi
umtshintshi-mali
mmalamadi
kassier
mmalatšhelete

balloons
amabhaluni
dibalune
iibhaloni
dibalunu
ballonne
dipalune

spinning tea cups
izinkomishi ezipininizayo
kopi e potolohang
iikomityi ezijikelezayo
dikopitikologa
tolteekoppies
dikomoki tša go potologa

Our spare time • Sichitha isikhathi sethu • Nako ya rona ya boikgutso
Ixesha lokuzonwabisa • Nako ya rona ya boiketlo • Ons vrye tyd • Nako ya boikhutšo

carousel
idili nokuphuza utshwala
kharaosele
umthayi
kharaosele
mallemeule
karousele

ferris wheel
isondo eligitshwelwayo elizungeza kancane
lebidi le potolohang butle
isidlalisi esilivili elikhulu elijikelezayo
setshedisi
groot wiel
leotwana le le dikologelago godimo le fase

water ride
ukugibela uhambe emanzini
ho palama maqhubu
ukukhwela izikhitshana ezijikeleza emanzini
morelelometsing
waterrit
leeto lagodimo ga meetse

rocking boat
isikebhe sokuyendezela
sekepe se thekeselang
iphenyane eligungqayo
mokoro o o theekelang
skommelboot
sekepekgwara

ride
ukugibela
ho palama
ukukhwela
palama
rit
go namela

roller coaster
amawudlu okusheleleza
rolakhousetara
ukuhamba ngokutyibilika
kolotsanatikologa
tuimeltrein
rolakhousta

dodgem cars
imoto yokudlala
dikoloi tsa dojeme
iimotwana zedoji
dikolotsana tse di thulanang ka dibampara
stampkarretjies
dikoloi tša dojeme

Our spare time • Sichitha isikhathi sethu • Nako ya rona ya boikgutso
Ixesha lokuzonwabisa • Nako ya rona ya boiketlo • Ons vrye tyd • Nako ya boikhutšo

291

Phrases	Amabinzana	Dipolelwana	Amabinzana
How much is the entrance fee into the park?	Yimalini imali yokungena epaki?	Ho kenwa ka bokae pakeng?	Kungenwa ngamalini epakini?
R40 for adults and R20 for children.	Abadala ama-R40, izingane ama-R20.	Batho ba baholo ke R40 bana ke R20.	Ngama-R40 abadala nama-R20 abantwana.
What is the special exhibition about?	Umayelana nani umbukiso oyisipesheli?	Pontsho e ikgethileng e bontshang?	Umboniso owodwa ungantoni?
The exhibition is about the history of mining in South Africa.	Umbukiso umayelana nomlando wezimayini zaseNingizimu Afrika.	Pontsho e bontsha ka pale ya nalane Afrika Borwa.	Umboniso ungembali yemigodi yalapha eMzantsi Afrika.
Do you play a musical instrument?	Uyayidlala yini imfijoli yomculo?	Na ho na le seletsa sa mmino seo o se bapalang	Uyasidlala na isixhobo somculo?
Yes, I play the guitar and the flute.	Yebo, ngidlala isigingci nomntshingo.	Ee, ke bapala katara le fuluti.	Ewe, ndidlala isiginci nembande.
What is your favourite pop group?	Yiliphi iqembu lephopu olikhonzile?	Ke sehlopha sefe sa phopo seo o se ratang?	Leliphi elona qela ulithandayo lepopu?
I really like … .	Empeleni ngithanda … .	Bonnete ke rata … .	Ndiyithanda ngokwenene i… .
What is there to do and see in the city?	Yini ekhona, umuntu angayenza noma ayibuke edolobheni?	Nka etsa kapa ka bona eng toropong?	Yintoni ekhoyo onokuyenza nonokuyibona esixekweni?
You can go to the beach, visit the aquarium, climb the mountain and take a township tour.	Ungahamba uye ebhishi, uvakashele ithangi lamanzi lezilwane nezithombe, ucace intaba futhi uthathe uhambo oluya elokishini.	O ka ya lewatle, wa etela akhwariamo, wa hlwa thaba mme wa etela lekeisheneng.	Ungaya elwandle uhambele ne-akhwariyam, unyuke intaba, utyelele ilokishi.
Do you want to go on the Anaconda roller coaster?	Uyathanda yini ukuhamba ngamawudlu emishelelezo ye-Anakhonda?	Na o batla ho palama rolakhoustara ya Anaconda?	Uyafuna ukuhamba ngesityibilizi e Anakhonda?
Yes! Come on, let us go!	Yebo, asihambe!	Ee! Etlo, ha re ye!	Ewe! Masiye!
Do you play sport?	Uyayidlala imidlalo?	O bapala papadi efe?	Kukho umdlalo owudlalayo?
Yes, I play tennis and netball.	Yebo ngidlala ibhola lomphebezo nebhola lomnqakiswano.	Ee. Ke bapala tenese le bolo ya matsoho.	Ewe, ndidlala intenetya nebhola yomnyazi.

Dikapolelo	Frases	Dikafoko
Madi a go tsena mo phakeng ke bokae?	Wat is die ingangsfooi?	Go lefelwa bokae ge go tsenwa phakeng?
Bagolo ke R40 fa bana e le R20.	R40 vir volwassenes en R20 vir kinders.	Ba bagolo ke R40 mola bana e le R20.
Ke eng se se kgethegileng ka ga dipontsho tseno?	Waaroor handel die spesiale uitstalling?	A pontšho ye e sego ya mehleng e laetša eng?
Dipontsho tse ke tse di ka ga ditiragalo tsa meepo mo Aforika Borwa.	Die uitstalling gaan oor die geskiedenis van mynwese in Suid-Afrika.	Pontšho e mabapi le histori ya meepo mo Afrika Borwa.
A o tshameka seletswa sa mmino?	Speel jy 'n musiekinstrument?	A o raloka seletšo sa mmino?
Ee, ke tshameka katara le fulutu.	Ja, ek speel kitaar en fluit.	Ee, ke raloka katara le fulutu.
Ke setlhopha sefe sa mmino wa phopo se o se ratang?	Wie is jou gunsteling-popgroep?	Sehlopa sa gago sa mmamoratwa sa phopo ke sefe?
Tota ke rata …	Ek hou regtig van …	Ke tloga ke rata …
Ke eng se motho a ka se dirang kgotsa a se bona mo toropong?	Wat kan 'n mens in die stad sien en doen?	Ke eng seo se ka dirwago le go bonwa toropongkgolo?
O ka nna wa ya kwa lebopong, wa etela akhwariamo, wa palama dithaba kgotsa wa tsaya loeto go ya kwa motse-setoropong.	Jy kan strand toe gaan, die akwarium besoek, bergklim en 'n townshiptoer onderneem.	O ka ya lebopong la lewatle, wa etela akwariamo, wa namela thaba gomme wa etela motsesetoropo.
A o batla go ya kwa dikolotsaneng tse di thulanang ka dibampara tsa Anaconda?	Wil jy op die Anaconda-trein ry?	Naa o rata go namela rolakhoustara ya Anaconda?
Ee, tlaya, a re yeng!	Ja! Kom ons gaan!	Ee! Etlang, a re yeng!
A go na le motshameko o o tleng o o tshameke?	Neem jy aan enige sportsoorte deel?	O raloka papadi?
Ee, ke tshameka tenese le bolotlowa.	Ja, ek speel tennis en netbal.	Ee, ke raloka thenese le kgwele ya diatla.

Our spare time • Sichitha isikhathi sethu • Nako ya rona ya boikgutso
Ixesha lokuzonwabisa • Nako ya rona ya boiketlo • Ons vrye tyd • Nako ya boikhutšo

293

12

South Africa

INingizimu Afrika

Afrika Borwa

UMzantsi Afrika

Aforika Borwa

Suid-Afrika

Afrika Borwa

South Africans Abantu baseNingizimu Afrika
Baahi ba Afrika Borwa Abemi boMzantsi Afrika
Baagi ba Aforika Borwa Suid-Afrikaners Ma-Afrika Borwa

Pedi
umPedi
Mopedi
umPedi
Mopedi
Pedi
MoPedi

Venda
umVenda
LeVenda
umVenda
MoVenda
Venda
Movenda

Tsonga
umTsonga
LeTshakane
umTsonga
MoTsonga
Tsonga
Motsonga

Swazi
umSwazi
LeSwatsi
umSwazi
MoSwati
Swazi
MoSwati

Ndebele
umNdebele
LeTebele
umNdebele
MoNdebele
Ndebele
Motebele

Sotho
umSuthu
Mosotho
umSuthu
Mosotho
Sotho
Mosotho

Tswana
umTswana
Motswana
umTswana
Motswana
Tswana
Motswana

Zulu
umZulu
LeZulu
umZulu
MoZulu
Zoeloe
Mozulu

Xhosa
umXhosa
LeQhotsa
umXhosa
MoXhosa
Xhosa
Mothosa

San
umuThwa
Morwa
umThwa
MoSarwa
Sanmeisie
Mosene

Griqua
umGrikhwa
LeKgerikwa
umGrikwa
MoGriqua
Griekwa
MoKirikwa

Afrikaans man
iBhunu
Leburu
iBhulu
MoAforikanere
Afrikaanse man
Moafrikanere

English boy
iNgisi
Lenyesemane
iNgesi
Moesimane
Engelse seun
Moisemane

Malay
iMaleyi
LeMalei
umMaleyi
Molaysia
Maleier
Momeleyi

Indian
iNdiya
Le-India
um-Indiya
MoIndia
Indiër
MoIndia

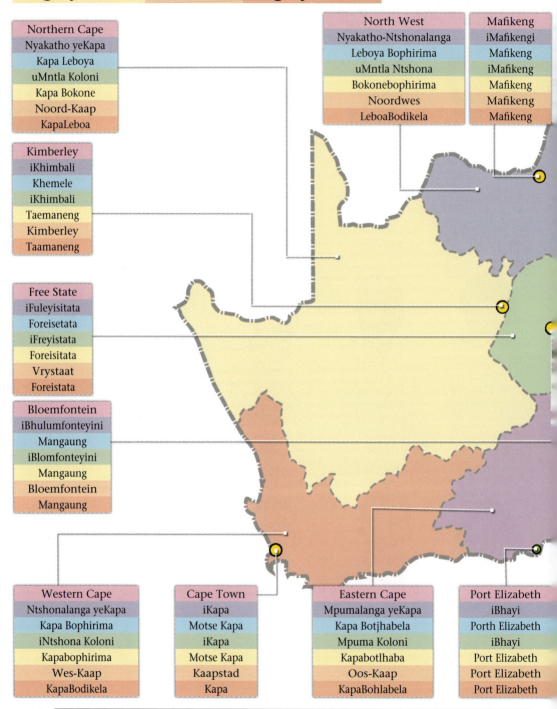

Our country **Izwe lakithi** **Naha ya rona** **Ilizwe lethu**
Naga ya rona **Ons land** **Naga ya rena**

Northern Cape
Nyakatho yeKapa
Kapa Leboya
uMntla Koloni
Kapa Bokone
Noord-Kaap
KapaLeboa

Kimberley
iKhimbali
Khemele
iKhimbali
Taemaneng
Kimberley
Taamaneng

Free State
iFuleyisitata
Foreisetata
iFreyistata
Foreisitata
Vrystaat
Foreistata

Bloemfontein
iBhulumfonteyini
Mangaung
iBlomfonteyini
Mangaung
Bloemfontein
Mangaung

North West
Nyakatho-Ntshonalanga
Leboya Bophirima
uMntla Ntshona
Bokonebophirima
Noordwes
LeboaBodikela

Mafikeng
iMafikengi
Mafikeng
iMafikeng
Mafikeng
Mafikeng
Mafikeng

Western Cape
Ntshonalanga yeKapa
Kapa Bophirima
iNtshona Koloni
Kapabophirima
Wes-Kaap
KapaBodikela

Cape Town
iKapa
Motse Kapa
iKapa
Motse Kapa
Kaapstad
Kapa

Eastern Cape
Mpumalanga yeKapa
Kapa Botjhabela
Mpuma Koloni
Kapabotlhaba
Oos-Kaap
KapaBohlabela

Port Elizabeth
iBhayi
Porth Elizabeth
iBhayi
Port Elizabeth
Port Elizabeth
Port Elizabeth

South Africa • INingizimu Afrika • Afrika Borwa • UMzantsi Afrika
Aforika Borwa • Suid-Afrika • Afrika Borwa

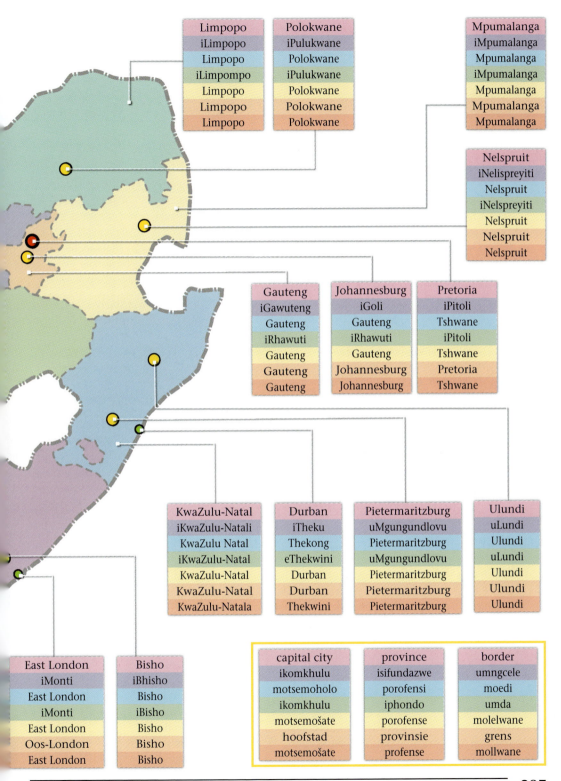

Limpopo
- Limpopo
- iLimpopo
- Limpopo
- iLimpompo
- Limpopo
- Limpopo
- Limpopo

Polokwane
- Polokwane
- iPulukwane
- Polokwane
- iPulukwane
- Polokwane
- Polokwane
- Polokwane

Mpumalanga
- Mpumalanga
- iMpumalanga
- Mpumalanga
- iMpumalanga
- Mpumalanga
- Mpumalanga
- Mpumalanga

Nelspruit
- Nelspruit
- iNelispreyiti
- Nelspruit
- iNelspreyiti
- Nelspruit
- Nelspruit
- Nelspruit

Gauteng
- Gauteng
- iGawuteng
- Gauteng
- iRhawuti
- Gauteng
- Gauteng
- Gauteng

Johannesburg
- Johannesburg
- iGoli
- Gauteng
- iRhawuti
- Gauteng
- Johannesburg
- Johannesburg

Pretoria
- Pretoria
- iPitoli
- Tshwane
- iPitoli
- Tshwane
- Pretoria
- Tshwane

KwaZulu-Natal
- KwaZulu-Natal
- iKwaZulu-Natali
- KwaZulu Natal
- iKwaZulu-Natali
- KwaZulu-Natal
- KwaZulu-Natal
- KwaZulu-Natala

Durban
- Durban
- iTheku
- Thekong
- eThekwini
- Durban
- Durban
- Thekwini

Pietermaritzburg
- Pietermaritzburg
- uMgungundlovu
- Pietermaritzburg
- uMgungundlovu
- Pietermaritzburg
- Pietermaritzburg
- Pietermaritzburg

Ulundi
- Ulundi
- uLundi
- Ulundi
- uLundi
- Ulundi
- Ulundi
- Ulundi

East London
- East London
- iMonti
- East London
- iMonti
- East London
- Oos-London
- East London

Bisho
- Bisho
- iBhisho
- Bisho
- iBisho
- Bisho
- Bisho
- Bisho

capital city
- capital city
- ikomkhulu
- motsemoholo
- ikomkhulu
- motsemošate
- hoofstad
- motsemošate

province
- province
- isifundazwe
- porofensi
- iphondo
- porofense
- provinsie
- profense

border
- border
- umngcele
- moedi
- umda
- molelwane
- grens
- mollwane

South Africa • INingizimu Afrika • Afrika Borwa • UMzantsi Afrika
Aforika Borwa • Suid-Afrika • Afrika Borwa

Government UHulumeni Mmuso URhulumente

national government
uhulumeni omkhulu
mmuso wa naha
urhulumente kazwelonke
mmuso wa bosetšhaba
nasionale regering
mmušo wa setšhaba

president
umongameli
moporesitente
umongameli
moporesidente
president
mopresitente

deputy president
iphini likamongameli
motlatsi wa moporesidente
usekela mongameli
motlatsaporesidente
adjunkpresident
motlatšamopresitente

cabinet
isigungu sikahulumeni
khabinete
isigqeba sombuso
kabinete
kabinet
kabinete

cabinet minister
ungqongqoshe wesigungu sikahulumeni
letona la khabinete
umphathiswa kwisigqeba sombuso
tona ya kabinete
kabinetsminister
tonakgolo ya kabinete

member of parliament
ilunga lephalamende
setho sa palamente
ilungu lepalamente
tokolo ya palamente
lid van die parlement
leloko la palamente

Parliament
iPhalamende
Palamente
iPalamente
Palamente
Parlement
Palamente

National Assembly
uMkhandlu kaZwelonke
Seboka sa Setjhaba
Undlunkulu wePalamente
Kokoanobosetšhaba
Nasionale Vergadering
Kopanotšhaba

politician
usopolitiki
radipolotiki
umpolitiki
radipolotiki
politikus
radipolotiki

National Council of Provinces
uMkhandlu weZifundazwe kaZwelonke
Lekgotla la Botjhaba la Diporofensi
iBhunga lamaPhondo kaZwelonke
Lekgotla la Bosetšhaba la Diporofense
Nasionale Raad van Provinsies
Khanselesetšhaba ya diprofense

Speaker
uSomlomo
Sebui
uSomlomo
Mmusakgotla
Speaker
Mmoledi

Government Gazette
iPhepha eliphethe izaziso zikaHulumeni
Koranta ya Mmuso
Iphepha ndaba loMbuso
Phasalatso ya mmuso
Staatskoerant
Kuranta ya mmušo

Law
Umthetho
Molao
Umthetho
Molao
Regte
Molao

Bill
Umthetho-sivivinywa
Molao o thehwang
Umthetho oyilwayo
Molaokakanngwa
Wetsontwerp
Molaokakanywa

Act
Umthetho osuphasile
Molao
Umthetho omiselweyo
Molao
Wet
Molao

official opposition
abaphikisayo ngokomthetho
mokgatlo o hanyetsang semmuso
abaphikisi abasemthethweni
lekokokganetso la semmuso
amptelike opposisie
lekgotlakganetšosemmušo

political party
iqembu lezombusazwe
mokgatlo wa dipolotiki
umbutho wezopolitiko
lekoko la sepolitiki
politieke party
mokgatlo wa dipolotiki

provincial government
uHulumeni wesifundazwe
mmuso wa diporofensi
urhulumente wephondo
mmuso wa porofense
provinsiale regering
mmušo wa profense

premier
uNdunankulu
tonakgolo
inKulumbuso
tonakgolo
premier
tonakgolo

Member of Executive Committee (MEC)
uNgqongqoshe wesifundazwe
Setho sa Lekgotla la Phethahatso
uMphathiswa wePhondo
Mokhuduthamaga
Lid van Uitvoerende Komitee (LUK)
Molekgotlaphethiši

local government
UHulumeni wasekhaya
Mmuso wa lehae
urhulumente wekhaya
mmuso wa selegae
plaaslike regering
pušo selegae

metropolitan council
Umkhandlu wedolobha elikhulu
Lekgotla la motse toropo
ibhunga lesixeko esikhulu
khansele ya lekgotlatoropo
metropolitaanse raad
lekgotlatoropokgolo

town council
uMkhandlu wedolobha
lekgotla la motse
ibhunga ledolophu
lekgotla
stadsraad
lekgotlatoropo

mayor
iMeya
ramotse
uSodolophu
ratoropo
burgemeester
ramotse

Mmuso   Regering   Mmušo

councillor	Constitutional Court	Supreme Court of Appeal	High Court
ikhansela	iNkantolo yoMthetho Siseko	iNkantolo yoKugcina	iNkantolo Enkulu
mokhanselara	Lekgotla la Molaotheo	Lekgotla le Phahameng la Dinyewe	Lekgotla le Phahameng
ilungu-lebhunga	iNkundla yoMgaqo-Siseko	iNkundla Ephakamileyo yeZikhalazo	iNkundla Ephakamileyo
mokhanselara	Kgotlatshekelokgolo ya Molaotheo	Kgotlatshekelokgolo ya boikuelo	Kgotlatshekelokgolo
raadslid	Konstitusionele Hof	Appèlhof	Hooggeregshof
mokhanselara	Kgorotsheko ya molaotheo	Kgorotsheko ya boipelaetšo	Kgorokgolo ya tsheko

Magistrate's Court	Constitution	Human Rights	election campaign
iNkantolo kaMantshi	uMthethosisekelo	Amalungelo Abantu	umkhankaso wokhetho
Lekgotla la mmaseterata	Molaotheo	Ditokelo tsa Batho	letsholo la dikgetho
iNkundla kaMantyi	uMgaqo-Siseko	Amalungelo Abantu	impembelelo yolonyulo
Kgotlatshekelo ya ga Magiseterata	Molaotheo	Ditshwanelo tsa Botho	letsholo la ditlhopho
Landdroshof	Grondwet	Menseregte	verkiesingsveldtog
Kgorotsheko ya maseterata	Molaotheo	Ditokelo tša Botho	lesolo la dikgetho

election	voter	voter's roll	polling booth	democracy
ukhetho	umvoti	uhlu lwabavoti	indawo yokuvota	umbuso wentando yeningi
dikgetho	mokgethi	lethathama la bakgethi	lebokoso la ho kgethela	taolo ya bongata
ulonyulo	umvoti	umqulu wabavoti	igunjana lokuvotela	urhulumente kawonke-wonke
ditlhopho	motlhophi	lenaane la batlhophi	sekhutlwana sa go tlhophela	temokerasi
verkiesing	kieser	kieserslys	stemhokkie	demokrasie
dikgetho	mokgethi	lenaneo la bakgethi	lepokisana la go boutela	temokrasi

---

Official Languages   Izilimi ezisemthethweni   Dipuo tsa semmuso
Iilwimi ezisemthethweni   Dipuo tsa semmuso   Amptelike tale   Maleme a semmušo

Afrikaans	English	IsiNdebele	IsiXhosa	IsiZulu	Sepedi	Sesotho
isiBhunu	isiNgisi	isiNdebele	isiXhosa	isiZulu	isiPedi	isiSuthu
Seafrikanse	Senyesemane	SeTebele	SeQhotsa	SeZulu	Sepedi	Sesotho
isiBhulu	isiNgesi	IsiNdebele	isiXhosa	IsiZulu	isiPedi	isiSuthu
Seburu	Seesimane	SeNdebele	SeXhosa	SeZulu	Sepedi	Sesotho
Afrikaans	Engels	Ndebele	Xhosa	Zoeloe/Zulu	Noord-Sotho	Suid-Sotho
Seafrikanse	Seisimane	Setebele	Sethosa	Sizulu	Sepedi	Sesotho

Setswana	SiSwati	Tshivenḓa	Xitsonga	Khoisan	Sign Language
isiTswana	isiSwazi	isiVenda	isiTsonga	isiKhoyisani	uLimi lweZandla
Setswana	SeSwatsi	SeVenda	SeTshakane	Khoisan	Puo ya Matshwao
isiTswana	isiSwazi	isiVenda	isiTsonga	umThwa/umKhoisani	uLwimi lweZandla
Setswana	SeSwati	SeVenda	SeTsonga	Khoisan	Puomatshwao
Tswana	Swati/Swazi	Venda	Tsonga	Khoisan	Gebaretaal
Setswana	Seswatsi	Sevenda	Setsonga	Khoisan	Polelomaswao

National symbols	Izimpawu zeSizwe	Matshwao a setjhaba	Imiqondiso kaZwelonke

Real Yellowwood
uMsonti
Sefate se se Sehla
Uqobo lomkhoba
Setlhare sa tota sa logong lo lo setlha
Opregte geelhout
Moserolwane

Giant/King Protea
iMbali iProthiya
Morena wa Diporotia
Isiqwene
Kgosi ya Diporothia
Reuse/Koningsprotea
Kgoši ya Diprotea

Springbuck
Insephe
Tshepe
Ibhadi
Tshepe
Springbok
Phuti

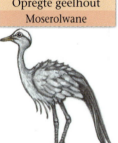

Blue Crane
uHlobo Lwendwandwe
Moholodi
Indwe
Mogolodi
Bloukraanvoël
Mogolodi

Galjoen
iGalijuni
Kgalejone
iGalyoni
Galejone
Galjoen
Kaljone

National flag
iFulegi lesizwe
Folakga ya naha
Iflegi kazwelonke
Folaga ya bosetšhaba
Nasionale vlag
Folaga ya bosetšhaba

Coat of Arms
Isiphandla
Kano
Umfuziselo
Sekano
Landswapen
Meeno

Motto: Diverse people unite
Isiqubulo esiwumgomo: Bantu abahlukahlukene hlanganani
Lepetjo: Kopano ya merabe e fapaneng
Isaci: Bantu abahlukeneyo manyanani
Moono: Batho ba merafe e e farologaneng ba kopane
Leuse: Eenheid in verskeidenheid
Moeno: Batho bao ba fapanego ba a kopana

Matshwao a sa bosetšhaba	Nasionale simbole	Dika tša bosetšhaba

National Anthem	Ihubo leSizwe	Pina ya Setjhaba	Umhobe weSizwe
Pina ya Bosetšhaba	Volkslied	Koša ya Setšhaba	

Nkosi sikelel' i-Afrika
Maluphakanyisw' uphondo lwayo,
Yizwa imithandazo yethu,
Nkosi sikelela, thina lusapho lwayo.

Morena boloka setjhaba sa heso,
O fedise dintwa le matshwenyeho,
O se boloke, o se boloke setjhaba sa heso,
Setjhaba sa South Afrika – South Afrika.

Uit die blou van onse hemel,
Uit die diepte van ons see,
Oor ons ewige gebergtes,
Waar die kranse antwoord gee,

Sounds the call to come together,
And united we shall stand,
Let us live and strive for freedom,
In South Africa our land.

13

Useful words

Amagama alusizo

Mabitso a molemo

Amagama aluncedo

Mafoko a a botlhokwa

Nuttige woorde

Mantšu a bohlokwa

Useful words • Amagama alusizo • Mabitso a molemo • Amagama aluncedo
Mafoko a a botlhokwa • Nuttige woorde • Mantšutirišo

yes	yebo	ee	ewe	ee	ja	ee
no	cha	tjhe	hayi	nnyaa	nee	aowa
please	ngicela	hle	nceda	tsweetswee	asseblief	hle
thank you	ngiyabonga	ke a leboha	enkosi	ke a leboga	dankie	ke a leboga
hello	sawubona	dumela	molo	dumela	hallo	thobela
goodbye	sala/hamba kahle	sala/tsamaya hantle	sala kakuhle	sala sentle	totsiens	gabotse
stop	yima	ema	yima	ema	stop	ema
help	siza	thusa	nceda	thusa	help	thuša

to be:	**yiba khona:**	**ho ba:**	**ukuba:**	**go nna:**	**om te wees:**	**go ba:**
I am	mina (ngi-)	ke	ndim-	ke nna	ek is	ke
you are	wena (u-)	o a	uya-	ke wena	jy is	o
he/she/it is	yena (u-)/yena (u-)/yona (i-)	o/o/e	Yena/Yena/Yona	ena/yona/ka yona	hy/sy/dit is	o/o/e
we are	thina (si-)	re a	sithi-	ke rona	ons is	re
you are	nina (ni-)	o a	uya-	ke wena	julle is	o
they are	bona (ba-)	ba a	baya-	ke bona	hulle is	ba

to have:	**yiba nakho:**	**ho ba le:**	**ukuba ne:**	**go nna:**	**om te hê:**	**go ba:**
I have	ngina-	ke na le	Ndine-	ke dirile	ek het	ke na
you have	una-	o na le	Une-	o dirile	jy het	o na
he/she/it has	una-/una-/ina-	o/o/e na le	Une-/Une-/Ine-	o/o/e dirile	hy/sy/dit het	o/o/e na
we have	sina-	re na le	Sine-	re dirile	ons het	re na
you have	nina-	o na le	Une-	o dirile/ke nale	julle het	o na
they have	bana-	ba na le	Bane-	ba dirile/ba nale	hulle het	ba na

Articles:	**Izakhi:**	**Dintho:**	**Izinto:**	**Athikele:**	**Lidwoorde:**	**Diathekele:**
a	u-/ulu-/isi-	—	i-	a	'n	—
an	u-/ulu-/isi-	—	i-	ka	'n	—
the	i-/isi-/uku-	—	i-	le-	die	—

Pronouns:	**Izabizwana:**	**Maemedi:**	**Izimelabizo:**	**Leemedi:**	**Voornaam-woorde:**	**Mainaina:**
I	(mina) ngi-	nna	ndi-	nna	ek	nna
you	(wena) u-	wena	wena/u-	wena	jy	wena
he/she/it	(yena) u-/(yena) u-/(yona) i-	yena/yena/yona	yena/yena/yona	ena/ena/yona	hy/sy/dit	yena/yena/yona
we	(thina) si-	re	si-	rona	ons	re
you	(nina) ni-	o	wena	wena	julle	le
they	(bona) ba-	ba	bona	bona	hulle	ba
me	mina	nna	mna	nna	ek	nna/ya ka
you	nawe	wena	wena	wena	jy/jou	wena
him/her/it	yena/yona	yena/yena/yona	yena/yena/yona	ena/ena/yona	hom/haar/dit	yena/yena/yona
us	thina	rona	thina/sithi	rona	ons	rena
you	wena	wena	wena/u-	wena	julle	wena
them	bona	bona	bona	bona	hulle	bona

Useful words • Amagama alusizo • Mabitso a molemo • Amagama aluncedo
Mafoko a a botlhokwa • Nuttige woorde • Mantšutirišo

my/mine	-mi	ya ka	yam/bam/sam/lam	ya me	myne	ya ka
your/yours	-kho	ya hao	yakho/bakho/sakho/lakho/owakho	ya gago	joune	ya gago
his/hers/its	-khe/-khe/-yo	yena/yena/yona	yakhe/yakhe/wayo/yayo	ya/ya/ gagwe/ ya yona	sy/haar/sy	ya gagwe/ya gawe/ya sona
his/hers	-khe/-khe	yena/yena	yakhe/yakhe	ya/ya/ gagwe	syne/hare	ya gagwe/ya gawe
ours	-lethu	ya rona	yethu	ya rona	ons s'n	tša rena
yours	enu	ya hao	yakho	ya lona	julle s'n	ya gago
theirs	-bo	ya bona	zabo	ya bona	hulle s'n	tša bona
myself	mina	nna	ngokwam	nna	myself	bonna
yourself	wena	wena	ngokwakho	wena	jouself	bowena
himself	yena	yena	ngokwakhe	ene-(botona)	homself	boyena
herself	yena	yena	ngokwakhe	ene-(bonamagatsana)	haarself	boyena
itself	yona	yona	ngokwayo	yona	self	bosona
ourselves	thina	rona	ngokwethu	rona	onsself	borena
yourselves	nina	lona	ngokwenu	lona	julself	bolena
themselves	bona	bona	ngokwabo	bona	hulself	bobona

Question words:	Amagama okubuza:	Mantswe a botsang:	Amagama okubuza:	Mafoko a dipotso:	Vraagwoorde:	Mantšupotšišo:
How?	Kanjani?	Jwang?	Njani?	Jang?	Hoe?	Bjang?
Why?	Kungani?	Hobaneng?	Kutheni?	Go reng?	Hoekom/waarom?	Ka lebaka la eng?
When?	Nini?	Neng?	Nini?	Leng?	Wanneer?	Neng?
What?	-ni?	Eng?	Yintoni?	Eng?	Wat?	Eng?
Where?	-phi?	Hokae?	Phi?	Kae?	Waar?	Kae?
Who?	-bani?	Mang?	Ubani?	Mang?	Wie?	Mang?
Which?	-phi?	Efe?	Yiphi?/Wuphi?	Efe?	Watter?	Efe?

Prepositions:	Izilandiso zendawo:	Mahokedi:	Imibekwaphambili:	Letlama:	Voorsetsels:	Mabopi:
about	nga-	ka	malunga	ka	oor	ka/ka ga
above	ngenhla	ka hodimo	(nga) phezulu	godimo	bokant	godimo/godimo ga
across	vundla	ka nqane	ngaphaya	go ralala	oorkant	ka kua
after	ngemuva	ka mora	emva	morago	na	morago
against	ncika	kgahlanong/mabapi le	chasene na-	kgatlhanong	teen	kgahlanong le
along	gudla	ithatikile	ecaleni kwa	le bapole	langs	bapilego/go ya le
around	zungeza	ho potoloha	kumacala onke	go dikologa	om	ka go dika/go dikologa
at	e-	ho	kwa-/e-	kwa	by	go
back	emuva	morao	(e)mva	e morago	terug	morago

304

before	ngaphambili	pele	phambi	pele	voor	pele
behind	ngemuva	ka mora	emva	morago	agter	morago
below	ngezansi	ka tlasa	ngaphantsi	kwa tlase	onder	fase/tlase
beneath	ngaphansi	ka tlase	ngaphantsi	botlase	onder(kant)	fase/tlase
beside	eceleni	ka thoko ho	ecaleni	mo thoko	langs	hleng ga/thoko/ ka ntle go
between	phakathi kwa-	mahareng	phakathi	magareng	tussen	gare ga/ makgatheng ga
by	ngase	ka	kufuphi	ka	by/met/deur/ teen	ka/ke/ga/fa go/ mo go
down	phansi	tlase	phantsi	tlase	af	tlase/fase
for	ka-	ho etsetsa	malunga na-/ loku-/woku-/ya-	ka	vir	ka baka la/ bakeng sa
from	vela/-phuma	ho tswa ho	ku-/se-/ ukusuka	go tswa	van	tswa go/go tloga ga
in	phakathi	ka hare	phakathi-/use-	teng	in	gare/teng
inside	phakathi	ka hara	-phakathi	mo gare	binne-in	ka gare
front	ngaphambili	ka pele	-phambili	pele	voor	pele/fa pele
near	eduze	haufi	-kufuphi	bapa	naby	kgauswi
next	eceleni	pela	ecaleni kwe-/ olandelayo	thoko	volgende	hleng ga
of	ka-/ya-	ya	ye-/yo-/ya-	ya	van	wa/ya/ba
off	a (ka)/a (zi)	ho tlohela	-cinyiwe/ -valiwe	tima	van … af	go tloga
out	phandle	ntle	-phandle	ntle	uit	ntle/ka ntle
outside	phandle	ka ntle	-phandle	kwa ntle	buite(kant)	ntle/ka ntle
over	ngale kwa-	ka hodima	ngaphaya	godimo	oor	godimo
since	selokhu	ho tloha	-sukela	fa e sale	sedert	e sa le/go tloga
through	phakathi kwa-	ho phunyeletsa/ka	(ngena)nge-	ralala	deur	ka/ke
till	kuze kube	ho fihlela	-de	go fitlhelela	tot(dat)	go fihla
to	-ya	ho	uku	kwa	tot/na	go
toward	-qonda	ho isa/ho ya ho	ngaku-	go ela	na … toe	go ya go
under	ngaphansi	tlasa	phantsi	tlase	onder	fase/tlase
up	phezulu	hodimo	-phezulu	godimo	op	godimo
with	na-/nga-	le	ne-/no-	ka	met	le/ka
Conjunctions:	**Izihlanganiso:**	**Makopanyi:**	**Izihlangisi:**	**Makopanyi:**	**Voegwoorde:**	**Makopanyi:**
and	(kanye) na-	le	no-/na-/ne-/ nee-/noo-	le	en	le
because	ngokuba/ngoba	hobane	kuba	ka gonne	omdat/want	ka lebaka la
but	kodwa	empa	kodwa	fela	maar	eupša/fela/upša
however	nokho-ke	le hoja	nangani	le gale	tog	le ge go le bjalo/fela
or	noma	kapa	okanye	kgotsa	of	goba
since	selokhu	ho tloha	kuba	fa e sale	aangesien	go tloga/e sa le
until	kuze kube	ho fihlela	de	ka go fitlhelela	totdat	go fihlela/go iša go/go fihla ge

Useful words • Amagama alusizo • Mabitso a molemo • Amagama aluncedo
Mafoko a a botlhokwa • Nuttige woorde • Mantšutirišo

305

Adverbs etc.:	Izichasiso nokunye:	Mahlalosi jwalojwalo:	Izihlomelo njalo-njalo:	Matlhalofi jalo jalo:	Bywoorde ens.:	Mahlathi bjalo bjalo:
this	lena	ena	le	seno	hierdie	se
these	lezi	tsena	ezi-	tseno	daardie	tše
that	leyo	eo	la-/loo/leyo	sele	dat	seo
those	lezo	tseo	ezo-	tsele	dié/daardie	tšeo
here	lapha	mona	apha	fano	hier	mo
there	lapho	mane	apho	fale	daar	moo
everywhere	yonke indawo	hohle	yonke indawo	gotlhe	oral	gohle
such	njeya, njenga	jwalo ka	kangaka	jaaka	so 'n/sulke	bjalo ka
some	-nje/-thile	tse ding	inxenye	dingwe	sommige	tše dingwe
few	ngcosana	mmalwa	iqaqobana	mokawanyana	'n paar	nene/nyane/sego kae
many	ningi	ngata	-ninzi	dintsi	baie	ntši
several	ningana	ngatanyana	iqela	mmalwa	vele	ntšinyana
sometimes	kwesinye isikhathi	mohlomong/nako tse ding	ngamanye amaxesha	dinako dingwe	soms	dinako tše dingwe
while	-sa-	le hoja/ha re ntse re	xa	fa	terwyl/hoewel	mola/ge/e tla re
very	kakhulu	haholo	eyona/elona/awona	tota	baie	gagolo/ruri/kudu
also	futhi	le	kwakhona	gape	ook	gape/ebile
too	-njalo	haholo	kwaye/kwaye-	le tota	ook	le/gape
always	njalo	jwalojwalo	lonke ixesha	dinako tsotlhe	altyd	ka mehla/matšatši ohle
never	ngeke	lekgale	ngaze/zange	le e seng/le goka	nooit	le gate e
ever	nanini nini	ho isa	-khe	e sale	ooit	ka mehla/kile
able	-azi	kgona ho	unga-	kgona/nonofa	kan	kgona

Adjectives:	Iziphawulo:	Lekgethi:	Iziphawuli:	Matlhaodi:	Byvoeglike naamwoorde:	Mahlaodi:
afraid	-esaba	tshaba	koyika	tshoga	bang	tšhoga
angry	-thukuthele	kwata	-qumba	ngala	kwaad	befelwa
awful	-bi kabi	makatsa	-oyikekayo(yo)	maswe	aaklig	boifišago/tšhabegago
bad	-bi	be	-mbi	maswe	sleg	mpe
beautiful	-hle	tle	-hle	bontle	pragtig	botse
big	-khulu	holo	-khulu	kgolo	groot	kgolo
blunt	-buthuntu	nthithi	-buthuntu	boboi	stomp	kubegile
bright	-khazimulayo	kganya/hlakile	-khanya/khazimla	galalela	helder	phadima/kganya
busy	-bambekile	qakehile	-xakekile(yo)	dira	besig	dira/itapiša
cheap	-shibhile	tjhiphile	-tshiphu/thoba ixabiso	tlhwatlhwa-tlase	goedkoop	tšhipile
clean	-hlanzekile	hlwekile	-coceka	phepa	skoon	hlwekiša
clear	-khanya bha	hlakile	-cacile(yo)	bonala-sentle	helder	sekilego
clever	-hlakaniphile	bohlale	-khalipha/krele-krele	botlhale	slim	hlalefile

Useful words • Amagama alusizo • Mabitso a molemo • Amagama aluncedo Mafoko a a botlhokwa • Nuttige woorde • Mantšutirišo

cold	-bandayo	bata	-banda	tsididi	koud	tonya
colourful	-mbalabala	mebalabala	-mbeje-mbeje	mebalabala	kleurvol	mebalabala
dark	-mnyama	fifetse	-mnyama	lefifi	donker	leswiswi
delicious	-mnandi kakhulu	monate	-mnandi	monate	heerlik	bose/mohlodi/monate
difficult	-lukhuni	boima	-nzima	bokete/thata	moeilik	thata/boima
early	-masinya	ka nako	ngethuba/kusasa	go sale mosong	vroeg	pele
easy	-lula	bonolo	-lula	bonolo	maklik	bonolo
enjoyable	-jabulisayo	thabisang	(i)mnandi/eyonwabisayo	jega	aangenaam/lekker	ipshinago
exciting	-sasisayo	tlotlisang	hlwabisa/nwabisa	kgatlhisa	opwindend	thabišago
expensive	-dulile/-biza	turang	-duru/-yabiza	tlhwatlhwa-godimo	duur	tura
far	-kude	hole	-kude	kgakala	ver	kgole
fast	-ngokushesha	ka pele	-khawuleza	bonako	vinnig	ka pele/ya lebelo
fat	-khuluphele	nonne	-tyebileyo	mafura	vet	makhura
flat	-yisicaba	pharameng	-caba	phaphathi	plat	phaphathi
fresh	-sha	ntjha	-ntsha	itekanetse	vars	nanana
fun	-ncokola	monate	(ubu)mnandi	boitumelo	prettig	lethabo/moswaso
funny	-ba ihlaya	qabolang	ngaqhelekanga	go sa tlwaelega	snaaks	e sa tlwaelegago
good	-hle	lokile	-lungile(yo)	sentle	goed	loka/botse
happy	-jabulile	thabile	-vuya	itumela	gelukkig	thabile/thakgetše
hard	-lukhuni	thata	-nzima/-qinile	thata	hard/moeilik	thata
heavy	-sindayo	boima	-nzima	bokete	swaar	boima/imela
horrible	-sabekayo	tshabeha	-oyikeka(yo)/-mbi	maswe	aaklig	boifišago/tšhabegago
hot	-shisayo	tjhesa	-shushu	bolelo	warm	borutho/fiša
huge	-khulukazi	kgolo	-nkulu	bogolo-thata	yslik	golo/tona/kgolokgolo
interesting	-hehayo	kgahlang	-mdla	go kgatlhisa	interessant	kgahlišago
juicy	-nompe	lero	nencindi	matute	sappig	bose
large	-banzi	kgolo	-nkulu	kgolo	groot	golo
late	-libele	morao ho nako/diehile	kade/emva kwexesha	thari	laat	morago ga nako
lazy	-vilapha	botswa	-nqena	botswa	lui	tšwafa
light	-khanyayo/-lula	kganya	-khanyisa/-khanya	botlhofo	lig	seetša
long	-de	telele	-nde	telele	lank	telele
loud	-nomsindo	hlodiya	-ngxola/-khwaza	godimo-modumo	hard/luid	hlabošago/dirago lešata
loving	-nothando	rateha	-thanda	rata	liefdevol	rategago
muddy	-kunodaka	seretse/sepetse	ubugxovu-gxovu	boretse	modderig	seretse/leraga
near	-duzane	haufi	ubufuphi/kufuphi	gaufi	naby	kgauswi

Useful words • Amagama alusizo • Mabitso a molemo • Amagama aluncedo
Mafoko a a botlhokwa • Nuttige woorde • Mantšutirišo

307

neat	-nobunono	hlwekile	-coceka	phepa	netjies	thakgegilego
noisy	-nomsindo	lerata	nengxolo	modungwana-tswelela	lawaaierig	dirago lešata
old	-dala	tsofetse	-ndala/-gugile	tsofetse	oud	tala/tšofetšego
painful	-buhlungu	bohloko	-buhlungu	ditlhabi	pynlik	bohloko/babago
peaceful	-thulile	kgutsitseng	-noxolo/-luxolo	kagiso	rustig	khuditšego
pleasant	-mnandi	monate	kamnandi	kgatlhisa	aangenaam	thabišago/kgahlišago
pretty	-bukekayo	ntlehadi	-hle/-ntle	bontle	mooi	botse
quiet	-thulile	thotse	cwaka	tidimalo	stil	homotšego
right	-lungile	nepahetse	-lungile	siame/moja	reg	nepagetše
ripe	-vuthiwe	butswitse	-vuthiwe	bodule	ryp	butšwitšego/budulego
rotten	-bolile	bodile	-bolile	bodile	vrot	bodilego
rough	-mahhadla-hhadla	kgahlafetsa	-rhabaxa	makgwakgwapa	rof/grof	makgwakgwa
round	-ndilinga	potapota	-sangqa	kgolokwe	rond	kgokolo/sediko
sad	-dumele	hloname	-khathazeka/-dakumba	hutsafetse	hartseer	manyami
safe	-phephile	bolokehile	-khuselekile	babalesega	veilig	bolokegilego/polokego
sharp	-cijile	motsu	-bukhali	bogale	skerp	bogale
short	-fushane	kgutshwane	-futshane	bokhutshwane	kort	kopana
slimy	-mincikayo	otileng/tshesane	-nciphile	bosesanenyane	slymerig	sesefetšego
slippery	-bushelelezi	thellang	-mtyibilizi	boreledi/reletsa	glibberig	boreledi/thelelago
slow	-nokozayo	monyebe	-cotha	bonya	stadig	nanya/nanakela
small	-ncane	nyenyane	-ncinane	-nnye	klein	nnyane
smart	-bukekayo/-hlakaniphile	ntle	-fanelekile(yo)	kgabileng	deftig/slim	tšhephile
smooth	-bukekayo/-colisekile	boreledi	-gudile(yo)	thelelo	glad	boreledi
soft	-thambile	thapileng	-thambile(yo)/ntofo-ntofo	botobe	sag	boleta
sore	-buhlungu	opang	-buhlungu	botlhoko/ntho	seer	sešo/bohloko
stale	-tshodile	tsofetse	-ndala	go sa itekanela	oud	utilego/bošula
strong	-namandla	matla	-namandla	maatla	sterk	tiilego/maatla
stupid	-nobuphuku-phuku	sethoto	-budenge	sematla	dom	sethoto/lešilo
tall	-de	telele	-nde	telele	lank/hoog	telele
tasty	-mnandi	latswehang	-nencasa	latswega	smaaklik	latswega/natefago
thick	-shubile/-minyene/-enile	tenya	-ngqindilili	sephara	dik	koto
thin	-hlambulukile/-gqalingene/-zacile	tshesane	-bhityileyo	tshesane	dun/maer	sese/otile

Useful words • Amagama alusizo • Mabitso a molemo • Amagama aluncedo
Mafoko a a botlhokwa • Nuttige woorde • Mantšutirišo

tidy	-nobunono	hlwekileng	-qoqosheka/-qoqosha	phepa	netjies	ka bothakga/hlwekilego
ugly	-bi	mpe	-bi	mpe	lelik	befa
unsafe	-ngaphephile	ho se bolokehe	-ngakhuseleki	tlhokapabalesego	onveilig	ya kotsi
untidy	-manyomfo-nyomfo	bohlaswa	-ngacocekanga/-mdaka	leswe/tlhaka-tlhakane	onnet/slordig	sa hlwekago
useful	-sizayo	molemo	-sebenziseka	mosola	nuttig/bruikbaar	nago le mohola/thušago
warm	-fudumele	futhumetse	shushu(beza)/-fudumala	bothito	warm	borutho/ruthufatša
weak	-ntengentenge/nteketeke	fokola	-buthathaka	bokowa	swak	fokolago
wonderful	-mangalisayo	babatsehang	mangalisa(yo)	kgatlhisang	wonderlik	tlabago/makatšago
wrong	-ngalungile	fosahetse	-ngalunganga	phoso	verkeerd	phošo
young	-sha	nyenyane	-ntsha/-ncinci	nnye/bobotlana	jonk	nnyane/nanana
Verbs:	**Izenzo:**	**Maetsi:**	**Izenzi:**	**Lediri:**	**Werkwoorde:**	**Madiri:**
act	-enza	tshwantshisa	-enza	dira	optree/toneelspeel	dira
argue	-qakulisa	phehisa	-xambulisa/-xoxa	ngangisana	redeneer/stry	phegiša
arrest	-bopha	tshwara	-bamba/-valela	tshwara	arresteer/in hegtenis neem	golega
arrive	-fika	fihla	-fika	goroga	aankom	goroga
bake	-bhaka	baka	-bhaka	baka	bak	paka
beat	-shaya	otla	-betha	betsa	slaan/klop	betha
believe	-kholwa	kgolwa	-kholelwa	dumela	glo	kgolwa
blow	-phephetha	butswela	-vuthela	gasa	blaas	budula
boil	-bilisa	bedisa	-bilisa	bela	kook	bediša
brush	-bhulasha	hlwekisa/borasha	-brasha	boratšhe	borsel	porosola
buy	-thenga	reka	-thenga	reka	koop	reka
call	-biza	bitsa	-biza	bitsa	roep	bitša
can	-azi	o ka	unoku-	kgonega	kan	kgona
carry	-thutha/-phatha/-thwala	jara	-thwala	rwala	dra	rwala
catch	-bamba/-nqaka	tshwara	-bamba	tshwara	vang	swara
chew	-hlafuna	hlafuna	-hlafuna	tlhafuna	kou	sohla
choose	-khetha	kgetha	-khetha	tlhopa	kies	kgetha
chop	-qoba	ratha	-gawula/-geca	rema	kap	phapha
clean	-hlanza	hlwekisa	-coca	phepafatsa	skoonmaak	hlwekiša
climb	-caca/-khwela/-gibela	hlwa	-khwela	palama	klim	namela
close	-vala	kwala	-vala/-kufutshane	tswala	toemaak	tswalela
collect	-qoqa/-butha	bokella	-qokelela	kokoanya	versamel	kgoboketša
cook	-pheka	pheha	-pheka	apaya	kook	apea
count	-bala	bala	-bala	bala	tel	bala

Useful words • Amagama alusizo • Mabitso a molemo • Amagama aluncedo
Mafoko a a botlhokwa • Nuttige woorde • Mantšutirišo

cry	-khala	lla	-khala/-lila	lela	huil	lla
cut	-sika	seha	-sika	sega	sny	ripa/sega
dance	-dansa	tantsha	-danisa	bina	dans	bina/tansa
depart	-suka	tloha	-mka/-suka	tloga	vertrek	tloga/sepela
dig	-mba	epa/tjheka	-grumba/-yimba	epa	grawe	epa
discuss	-xoxisana	buisana	-xoxa	buisana/tlotla	bespreek	rerišana
do	-enza	etsa	wenza-/yenza-	dira	doen	dira
draw	-dweba	taka	-krwela	tshwantsha	teken	thala
dress	-gqoka	tena	-nxiba	apara	aantrek	apara
drink	-phuza	nwa	-sela	nwa	drink	nwa
drive	-shayela	kganna	-qhuba	kgweetsa	bestuur	otlela
eat	-dla	ja	-tya	ja	eet	ja
feel	-zwa	utlwa	-yiva	utlwa	voel	kwa
fight	-lwa	lwana	-yilwa	lwa	baklei	lwa
find	-thola	fumana	-fumana	bona	vind/kry	hwetša
finish	-qeda	qeta	-gqiba/-gqibezela	fetsa	klaarmaak/afhandel	fetša
fold	-goqa	mena	-songa	menaganya	vou	phutha
forget	-khohlwa	lebala	-libala	lebala	vergeet	lebala
give	-nika	fa	-nika	go fa	gee	fa/nea
go	-hamba	tsamaya	-hamba	tsamaya	gaan	eya
grow	-khula	hola	-khula	gola	groei	mela
hear	-zwa	utlwa	-yiva	utlwa	hoor	theeletša
hide	-casha	pata	-fihla	fitlha	wegkruip	khuta/fihla
hit	-shaya	otla	-ngquba	betsa	slaan	betha
hug	-singatha/-gomothela	kopa	-xhaga	go haka	omhels	gokarela
hurt	-zwisa ubuhlungu	hlokofatsa	-nzakalisa	utlwisa botlhoko	seermaak	gobatša
jump	-gxuma	tlola	-tsiba	tlola	spring	taboga
kick	-khahlela	raha	-khaba	raga	skop	raga
kill	-bulala	bolaya	-bulala	bolaya	doodmaak	bolaya
know	-azi	tseba	-azi/-yazi	itse	weet	tseba
laugh	-hleka	tsheha	-hleka	tshega	lag	sega
leave	-shiya	tlohela	-shiya	tloga	los	tlogela
lick	-khotha	nyeka	-munca	gora	lek	latswa
lie	-lala/-qamba amanga	robala/thetsa	-lala/-xoka	robala/go bua maaka	lê/jok	aketša
listen	-lalela	mamela	-mamela	reetsa	luister	theeletša
live	-hlala/phila	dula	-phila	tshela	lewe	phela
look	-bheka	sheba	-jonga	leba	kyk	lebelela
make	-enza	etsa	-enza	dira	maak	dira
may	-nga-	o ka/nka	anga-	ka nna	mag	nka
meet	-hlangana na-	kopana	-dibana/-hlangana	kopana	ontmoet	hlakana/kopana
mix	-xuba	kopanya/tswaka	-xuba	tlhakanya	meng	hlakanya
move	-nyakaza	sutha	-shukuma/-hamba	suta	beweeg	šutha

Useful words • Amagama alusizo • Mabitso a molemo • Amagama aluncedo
Mafoko a a botlhokwa • Nuttige woorde • Mantšutirišo

must	kumele	tlameha	nyanzeleka-	tshwanetse	moet	swanetše
open	-vula	bula	-vula	bula	oopmaak	bula
pack	-pakisha	paka	-pakisha	phutha	pak	paka
pay	-khokha	lefa	-hlawula/-bhatala	duela	betaal	lefa
peel	-cwecwa	ebola	-xobula/-chuba	obola	skil	ebola
pick	-cosha	kgetha	-chola	tsaya	kies	topa
play	-dlala	bapala	-dlala	tshameka	speel	raloka
pray	-thandaza	rapela	-thandaza/bhedesha	rapela	bid	rapela
pull	-donsa	hula	-tsala	goga	trek	goga
push	-sunduza	sutumetsa	-tyhala	kgorometsa	stoot	kgorometša
read	-funda	bala	-funda	buisa	lees	bala
reap	-vuna	kotula	-vuna	roba	in(oes)	buna
receive	-mukela	fumana	-fumana/-yamkela	amogela	ontvang	amogela
remove	-susa	tlosa	-susa	ntsha	verwyder	tloša
repeat	-phinda	pheta	-phinda	boeletsa	herhaal	boeletša
reply	-phendula	araba	-phendula	araba	antwoord	fetola
rest	-phumula	phomola	-phumla	ikhutsa	rus	khutša
ride	-gibela	palama	-khwela	palama	ry	namela
rub	-hlikihla	pikitla/hohla	-hlikihla/-rhaba	sidila	vryf	šidila
run	-gijima	matha	-baleka	taboga	hardloop	kitima
save	-londoloza	boloka	-sindisa/-gcina	boloka	spaar	seketša
scream	-klabalasa	hoeletsa/tlerola	-khala/-tswina	goa	skreeu	goelela
see	-bona	bona	-bona	bona	sien	bona
sell	-thengisa	rekisa	-thengisa	rekisa	verkoop	rekiša
send	-thunga	romela	-thumela	romela	stuur	roma
sew	-thumela	roka	-thunga	roka	naaldwerk doen	roka
shake	-xukuza	sisinya	-shukumisa/-hlukuhla	kgotlhokgotsa/tshikinya	skud	šikinya
shoot	-dubula	thunya	-dubula	thuntsha	skiet	thunya
shop	-thenga	reka	-thenga	lebenkele	koop	reka
shout	-memeza	hoeletsa	-khwaza	goa	(uit)roep/skree(u)	hlaba lešata
shut	-vala	kwala	-vala	tswala	toemaak	tswalela
sing	-cula	bina	-cula/-hlabela	opela	sing	opela
sit	-hlala	dula	-hlala	dula	sit	dula
skip	-eqa	tlola/qhoma	-siba	tlola	huppel/spring	taboga/tshela
sleep	-lala	robala	-lala	robala	slaap	robala
smell	-nuka	nkgisa	-jojisa/-joja	nkga	ruik	dupa
sow	-tshala	jala	-hlwayela/-lima	jala	saai	gaša
speak	-khuluma	bua	-thetha	bua	praat	bolela
stand	-ma	ema	-phakama	ema	staan	ema
stay	-hlala	dula	-hlala	nna/dula	bly	dula
stop	-yima	ema	-yima	ema	stop	ema
strip	-yima/-khumula	hlobola	-khulula	apola	stroop	hlobola

Useful words • Amagama alusizo • Mabitso a molemo • Amagama aluncedo
Mafoko a a botlhokwa • Nuttige woorde • Mantšutirišo

311

surf	-hlamba emadlambini olwandle	sesa	-tyibiliza	lelesela	golfry	go namela lephoto
swallow	-gwinya	kwenya	-ginya	metsa	sluk	metša
swear	-thuka/-funga	hlapanya/hlapaola	-funga/-fungela/-thuka	rogana	vloek	ena
sweat	-juluka	fufulelwa	-bila	fufula	sweet	sethitho/sethokgothokgo
sweep	-shanyela	fiela	-tshayela	feela	vee	swiela
swim	-bhukuda	sesa	-dada/-qubha	thuma	swem	rutha
take	-thatha	nka	-thatha	tsaya	neem/vat	tšea
talk	-khuluma	bua	-thetha	bua	praat	bolela
taste	-nambitha	latswa	-ngcamla	tatso	proe	latswa
tear	-klebhula	tabola	-krazula	gagoga	skeur	kgeila
tell	-tshela	bolella	-chaza/-xela	bua	vertel	botša
throw	-phonsa	akgela	-gibisela	kolopa	gooi	foša
tie	-bopha	tlama	-bophela/-bopha	funela/bofa	vasmaak	bofa
travel	-hamba uhambo	eta	-hamba/-thabatha uhambo	tsamaya	reis	ralala
try	-zama	leka	-zama/-linga	lekeletsa	probeer	leka
turn	-jika	thinya	-jika	fapoga	(om)draai	fapoga
use	-sebenzisa	sebedisa	-sebenzisa	dirisa	gebruik	šomiša
visit	-vakasha	etela	-hambela	eta/jela nala	besoek	etela
vote	-vota	vouta	-votela/-vota	tlhopha	stem	bouta
wake up	-vuka	tsoha	-vuka	tsoga	wakker word	tsoga
walk	-hamba ngezinyawo	tsamaya	-hamba	tsamaya	loop	sepela
want	-funa	batla	funa-	batla	wil (hê)	nyaka
wash	-geza	hlatswa	-hlamba	tlhatswa	was	hlatswa
watch	-qapha	hlokomela	-buka/-bukela	bogela	kyk/dophou	lebelela/bogela
wear	-gqoka	tena	-nxiba	apara	dra	apara
whisper	-hlebeza	seba	-sebeza	seba	fluister	sebela
wish	-fisa	lakatsa	-nqwena	keletso	wens	lakaletša/kganyogela
work	-sebenza	sebetsa	-sebenza	tiro	werk	šoma
worry	-khathazeka	kgathatseha	-khathazeka	ngongorega	bekommer	belaela/hlobaela
worship	-dumisa	rapela	-nqula/-qubuda	rapela	aanbid	khunamela/rapela
write	-bhala	ngola	-bhala	kwala	skryf	ngwala

Useful words • Amagama alusizo • Mabitso a molemo • Amagama aluncedo
Mafoko a a botlhokwa • Nuttige woorde • Mantšutirišo

Index

Inkomba

IsiZulu

IsiZulu

IsiZulu

IsiZulu

Sesotho

Sesotho

Sesotho

Sesotho

Isalathiso

IsiXhosa

IsiXhosa

IsiXhosa

IsiXhosa

Dikaelo

Setswana

khukhwane 219
khuti 137
khutlonnetsepa 87
khutlonnetsepa ya
matlhakorema-
bapitekano 87
khutlotharo 87, 278
khutsafalo 24
khutsana 37
kidibatso 91
kinipitang 186
kiribane 77
kobo 54, 72
kofi 168, 254
koko 22, 30, 31, 34
Kokoanobosetšhaba
298
kokolohute 211
kolobe 202
kolobe ya naga 204,
206
kolobetso 39
kolofo 261
koloi 114
koloi ya mapodisi
96
koloikabole 282
kolojane 203
kolote 216
kolotsana 118
kolotsana ya dithoto
126
kolotsanatikologa
291
koma-koma 201
komelelo 201
komeletsane 248
konopo 44
konopo lebone 145
konopo ya go batla
seteišene 150
konopo ya go emisa
112
konopo ya go laola
modumo 150
konopo ya tshoga-
nyetso 90
konsarata 277
kontinente 195
konyana 203
kopaopa 213
kopelo ya ophera
149
kopi 68
kopore 198
korela 206
korong 224
kotlhao ya
boemisetso 106
kubu 205

kuku 243
kuku ya tshokolete
247
kukumaungo 246
kungo 172
kusuberi 230
kutlo 25
kutu 220, 221
kwa go leng diteng
sa tshimologo 147
kwa sefofane se yang
127
kwaba 230
kwaito 280
KwaZulu-Natal 297
kwena 209, 214
labenta 223
Labobedi 156
Labone 156
Laboraro 156
Labotlhano 156
laeborari 85, 99
lakane 72
Lamatlhatso 156
Latshipi 156
lebadi 22
lebala 263, 266, 269
lebala la bolotlowa
270
lebala la kgwele ya
dinao 264
lebala la kherikete
266
lebala la kolofo 273
lebala la metshame-
ko 86
lebala la rakibii 268
lebala la sekolo 86
lebala la sekwaše
273
lebala la thenese 271
lebanta 48, 55
lebanta la pabalesego
110, 130
lebanta la tsamaiso
ya dithoto 128
lebati 108, 130
lebati kgotsa kgoro
ya tshoganyetso
276
lebatitshipi 62
lebekejana la dijo
290
lebekere 68
lebelebele 224
lebelo la phefo 201
lebenkele 85, 164,
287
lebenkele la diaparo
170

lebenkele la dibuka
171
lebenkele la dikga-
bisa tsa botlhokwa
283
lebenkele la dikga-
bisa tsa segopotso
285
lebenkele la
dikwalelo 170
lebenkele la dilo tsa
kago 170
lebenkele la dilwana
tse di botlhokwa
166
lebenkele la
ditshamekisi 170
lebenkele la
fenitšhara 170
lebenkele la nnotagi
170
lebenkele la tsa
mmino 170
lebenkele le le reki-
sang kofi 165
lebenkele-nakwana
165, 169
lebodu 214
lebokoso la
diphensele 89
lebokoso la makwalo
99
lebokoso le le
tsidifatsang 289
lebolala 217
lebole 20
lebolobolo 215
lebone 66, 72, 94
lebone la bolao 72
lebone tshupopoelo-
morago 109
lebonekgolo 108
lebone-tsiboso 108
leborogo la botse-
nelofofane 126
lebota 62, 64
lebowa 233
lee 241, 244
lee le le bidisitsweng
244
lee le le gadikwang le
sa tlhakatlhangwa
244
leeba 212
leebarope 212
Lefatshe 193, 195
lefeelo 76
lefeelo la matlhokwa
76
lefela 158

lefelo la baoke-
lwantle 91
lefelo la boiki-
mololelo 101
lefelo la bothusetso
174
lefelo la dikungo tsa
mašwi 173
lefelo la ditlhare tsa
mofine 283
lefelo la ditshodi
135
lefelo la go betsa
269
lefelo la go bogela
282
lefelo la go latlhela
kgwele 268
lefelo la go phaka
120
lefelo la mminotetso
277
lefelo la nnotagi 179
lefelo la peelo ya
ditlhapi 173
lefelo la phenele
264, 269
lefelo la segopotso
285
lefelo la tshedi-
mosetso 174
lefelo le le beetsweng
sekepe 134
lefelo le le nang le
segagane 284
lefelo le le senang
metsi 135
lefeloboikhutso la
dikgakologo 282
lefelobotlogo 128
lefelobotshamekelo
84
lefeloitshidilo 273
lefelothekisetso la
hambeka 167
lefelothekisetso ya
boroso 166
lefetlho-sekepe 137
lefika 196, 288
lefuka 131
lefuka 210, 237
legadima 200
legae 64, 85
legakabe 211
legala 198
legapu 231
legetla 14, 18
legodi 212
legodu 249
legofi 20

legogo 242
legora 64
legotlo 207
lehututu 210
leiso 67
leitibolo 37
leitlho 16
lekadiba 197
lekakaie 216, 238
lekanyane 207
lekgolo 159
lekgotla 298
Lekgotla la bosetšha-
ba la diporofense
298
lekgwafo 23
lekhubu 288
lekoko la sepolitiki
298
lekokokganetso la
semmuso 298
lekwalo 99, 152
lekwalo le le kwadi-
sitsweng 98
lekwalodikgang 151
lekwati 221
lela 23, 25
lelana 95
leleme 17, 236
lemoneite 254
lenaane la batlhophi
299
lenaane la dijo tse
o tsamayang ka
tsona 171
lenaanemofine 171
lenaka 205
lenaka la metsotso
154
lenaka la metso-
tswana 154
lenaka la tshipi la
motlakase 122
lenaka la ura 155
lenaka lwa Sefora
279
lenala 211
lenanenjo 171
lenaneo 149, 277
lenaneo la imeile 147
lenaneo la
khomphiutha 145
lengau 204
lengena 49, 54
lengenana 21
lengole 19
lenong 211
lenongwatle 212
lentile 234
lentswe 196

lenyalo 38, 39
leoto 15
leotwana la go
kgweetsa 111
leotwana la kwa pele
130
lepara 97
lepele 219
lephoi le le nang le
matlho a masweu
213
lephutshe 234
lephutshe le le sweu
232
lepodisi la monna
96, 183
lepodisi la mosadi
183
lepothopo 145
lerago 19
lerama 16
lerapo 22
lerapo le le robe-
gileng 95
lere 187
lerete la tsebe 17
lero 202
leroba la nko 16
leru 197, 201
leruarua 216
lerwane 219
lesea 38
lesedi 67
lesela 76
lesimelo 253
lesufutsogo 18
leswana 69
leswana la logong
71
leswana la tee 68
letadi 95
letamo 196
letangwana la go
thumela 64, 179,
272
letheka 15, 19
lethombo la batima-
molelo 97
lethompo 77
lethoro 245
letlalo 22
letlapamotlhaba 199
letlha 156
letlhabaphefo 63,
130
letlhabula 201
letlhakore la sekepe
la moja 136
letlhalela 20
letlhare 220

Setswana

mpopi 274
Mpumalanga 297
naga 196
nako 154
nako e e oke-
    ditsweng 265
nako ya bosigo 155
nako ya go ikhutsa
    265, 277
nako ya motshegare
    155
nakokgaotso ya go
    nwa tee 244
nakotshameko 271
naledi 192
nama 237
nama e e senang
    marapo 237
nama le merogo 245
nama ya kalakune
    237
nama ya kgogo 246
nama ya kgomo 236
nama ya kolobe 236
nama ya kolobe e
    e botshe-botlha-
    nyana 251
nama ya legetla 237
nama ya nku 236
nama ya pidipidi 237
namagadi 203
namamorogo ya llili
    248
namane 203
namune 153, 231
nare 205
nawa 232, 235
nawaphatlo 234
nekeleise 49, 54
Nelspruit 297
Nepetšhunu 192
nete 219
ngaka 35, 90, 181
ngaka ya dikaro 91,
    185
ngaka ya dipholo-
    golo 185
ngaka ya meno 94
ngwaga 156
ngwaga e e latelang
    156
ngwagakgolo 156
ngwagasome 156
ngwana 36, 38
ngwanagare 37
Ngwanatsele 157
ngwedi 193
ngwetsi 35
njokaletso 171
njokgolo 171

nkale 217
nkgo 71
nkgodi 211
nkgonne-ka-nyalo
    36
nko 16
nku 202
nkwe 204, 208
nna 30
nnale 187
nnariki 231
nne 158
nngwe 158, 159
nno 264, 269
Nnyaa 303
noga 215
noga ya noka 216
noka 19, 197
noko 20, 207
nomoro ya mogala-
    tlhaeletsano 143
nomoro ya polate-
    fomo 123
nomoro ya sefofane
    129
nomoro ya sephiri
    175
nomoro ya tsho-
    ganyetso 143
nomorokonopo 142
nomoropolata 109
nonyane 202
nonyane e e tshelang
    ka tlhapi 212
notshe 219
ntlha 265
ntlha ya morago ga
    maleka 271
ntlo 60
ntlo ya baeng 285
ntlo ya manobonobo
    61
ntlo ya mo polaseng
    61
ntlo ya mopolanka
    60
ntlo ya segosi 61
ntlobobolokelo jwa
    dilwana 135
ntloborobalo kwa
    thabeng 283
ntlolohalahala ya
    baagi 85
ntlolohalahala ya
    kereke 100
ntlolohalahala ya
    sekolo 86
ntlwana 60
ntlwana ya go fetola
    diaparo 86

ntlwanabogorogelo
    129
ntlwanaboithusetso
    75, 86, 124
ntlwanataolo ya
    dikepe 135, 288
ntsha 149
ntshetswantle 267
ntshi 16,
ntshikgolo 218
ntsi 218
ntšhwe 210
ntšwa 202
ntšwanyana 203
ntsu 210
ntswanatshipi 199
nyala 205
nyenya 25
nyoba 225
nyumonia 95
obara 267
obotsweng 253
okotophase 216
oli 198, 252
oli e e apayang 168
omelete 244
omeletse 201
onorobaki 45
onoroko 46
ophale 199
ophera 277
ora-utang 209
orikanamo 235
Oseteralesia 195
otšhete 222
ouku 223
outshe 224
padi 151
pala ya seila 136
palama 291
Palamente 298
palamonwana 49
pale ya dino 264
pale ya dino 270
pampiri 89
pampiri e e gotlhang
    186
pampiri ya boithu-
    setso 75
pampiri ya fekese
    142
panana 230
pane 71
pane ya borotho 71
pane ya matlakala
    76
panekgadikelo 71
panekuku 246
papetlapolokelo
    (CD) 145

parafene 169, 198
paseporoto 128
pasetiri 243
patitšhoko 88
patlaka 274
pato 21
pedi 158
peelelo 39
peeletso 175
peke 77
pela 207
pelo 23
pene 89
peo 220
peolwane 211
pepere 233, 252
pere 231
perekisi 231
perelemune 238
peterolo 198
petsana 203
phae 243
phae ya apole 247
phage 204
phaka ya boita-
    poloso 284, 291
phaka ya dikhara-
    bane 284
phala 205
phamfolete 151
phantere 209
phaposi 62, 136
phaposi e e tsayang
    bobedi 179
phaposi e tsayang a
    le mongwe 179
phaposi ya balwetse
    90
phaposi ya bapagami
    131
phaposi ya bobo-
    lekelo 65
phaposi ya dikhonfe-
    rense 179
phaposi ya dikopano
    176
phaposi ya hotele
    178
phaposi ya poro-
    jeketara 276
phaposiboapeelo 65,
    70, 171, 178
phaposibodulo 124
phaposiboemelo 123
phaposiboitapoloso
    65, 67, 178
phaposibojelo 65,
    69, 179
phaposibojelo ya
    terena 125

phaposiborobalo 65,
    73, 179
phaposiborutelo
    86, 89
phaposibotlhapelo
    65, 75
phaposikaro 91
pharakano 121
phare 233
phasalatso ya
    mmuso 298
phasele 98
phaseli 235
phaseta 250
phasetapapetla 250
phatla 17
phatlaletseng 208
phatlha ya leino 94
phatlha ya konopo
    45
phatsimo 153
Phatwe 157
phefo 200
phefo e e tsididi ya
    borwa 200
phelehu 203
phelekene 210
phenele 265
phenkwine 212
phensele 89
phensi 222
phenti 47
phepheng 218
phepole 153
phetale 220
phikhene 241
phikoko 213
philo 23, 236
phini 187
phiri 206
phitlho 39
phitsa 250
phokojwe 206
pholitšhi 76
Pholuto 192
phopho 231
phopo 280
phorone 217
phororo 197
phorothia 222
phoso 265, 271
Phukwi 157
phuti 205
phuti ya metsi 204
phutshennye 233
piano 278
piano ya letsogo 280
pidipidi 213
Pietermaritzburg
    297

pilisi 93
pilisi ya ditlhabi 93
Pina ya Bosetšhaba
    301
pinki 153
pirinki 68
pitiki 219
pitsa ya tshipi 71
pitsa ya maoto a
    mararo 71
pitse 202
pitse e tilodi 205
platypus 209
podi 202
podile 20
polaka 74
polaka ya lobota 67
polamara 183
polanete 192
polanka 63
polantasi 225
polantere 119
polase 82
polasetera 92
polasetiki 52, 63
polata 61
polatefomo 123
polatinamo 198
poleite 69
poleitetlhakore 69
poletšhe ya dinala
    53
polokelomelaetsa e
    e rometsweng 146
polokelomelaetsa
    146
Polokwane 297
pomelo 230
pompo ya baesekele
    116
pompo ya go tima
    molelo 97
pompo ya peterolo
    110
pono 25
pontsho ya
    motshameko 149
poo 203
popegotaese 87
popi 223
poreimi 231
porofense 297
porojeketara ya
    filimi 276
porone 238
poroteine 253
Port Elizabeth 296
poso 85, 99
potata 234
potsane 203

Setswana

Setswana

Setswana

Indeks

Afrikaans

mantel 54
mantis 218
marathon 261
margarien 240
mark 165, 167
marmer 199
marog 248
Mars 193
mas 136
masels 95
maskara 53
mat 66, 72, 89
matras 72
matrone 90
matroos 136, 184
mayonnaise 252
Me. 35
medisyne 93
medisynekassie 75
meel 169
meer 196
meerkat 207
meganikus 182
Mei 157
Mej. 35
melk 168, 240, 254
melkpoeier 240
melkskommel 254
melktert 247, 248
Melkweg 192
meningitis 95
Meneer 35
Menseregte 299
ment 235
Mercurius 193
meringue 247
merrie 203
mes 69
metaal 63
metropolitaanse raad
   298
meubelwinkel 170
Mev. 35
Mevrou 35
meze 251
middag 155
middagete 244
middel 15, 19
middelkind 37
middelsirkel 265,
   270
middelvinger 20
middernag 155
mielie 224, 234
mieliemeel 169
mieliepap 248
mier 218
mikroligte vliegtuig
   133
miljard 159

miljoen 159
mimiekkunstenaar
   290
minaret 101
mineraal 253
minibustaxi 113
minuut 155
minuutwyser 154
mis 200
miskruier 219
MIV/vigs 95
Mnr. 35
modder 63
modem 145
modeontwerper 182
moeder 31
moersleutel 186
moesie 22
mond 16
monitor 144
monument 285
mop 70
mopaniewurms 249
môre 156
morsekode 152
moskee 84, 101
mossel 238
mossie 213
mosterd 252
mot 219
motor 109, 111, 114
motorfiets 114, 117
motorhuis 64
motorhuur 127
motorhuurtoonbank
   129
motorrenbaan 273
motorresies 261
motreën 201
mou 46
mousse 247
Mpumalanga 297
muesli 245
muffin 243
muggie 219
muis 144, 207
muismatjie 144
munt 175
munte 275
muntfoon 99
murgpampoentjie
   232
museum 284
musiekblyspel 277
musiekinstrument
   280
musiekwinkel 170
musikant 183, 278
muskiet 219
muur 62, 64

muurbal 261
muurbalbaan 273
muureenheid 67
muurkaart 88
muurprop 67
mynwerker 183
naaimasjien 187
naald 187
naaldekoker 218
nael 20
naelknipper 53
naelpolitoer 53
naelskêr 53
naelvyl 53
nag 155
nagapie 207
nagereg 171, 247
nagrok 47
narkose 91
narkotiseur 91
nartjie 231
Nasionale Raad van
   Provinsies 298
nasionale regering
   298
Nasionale
   Vergadering 298
Nasionale vlag 300
naslaanafdeling 99
naslaanboek 151
nat 201
natuurhoekie 89
natuurreservaat 283
Natuurwetenskappe
   87
navraagtoonbank
   174
naweek 156
Ndebele 295, 299
nee 303
neef 31
nege 158
negentien 158
negentig 159
nek 14, 18
nektarien 231
Nelspruit 297
Neptunus 192
net 264, 271
net links draai 121
net regs draai 121
netbal 260, 270
netbalbaan 270
netbalspeler 270
neus 16
neusgat 16
neushoringvoël 210
neute 241
niefiksie 99
nier 23

niertjie 236
niggie 30
njala 205
nommerplaat 109
nommers 159
noodgeval 91
noodnommer 143
noodhulptoerusting
   97
noodknoppie 90
nooduitgang 112,
   276
Noord 195
Noord-Amerika 195
Noordelike Halfrond
   194
Noord-Kaap 296
Noordpool 194
Noord-Sotho 299
Noordwes 296
noot 175
notebeurs 49
November 157
nul 158
nuusbulletin 149
nuusleser 183
oefeningboek 89
oeste 225
oester 238
oggend 155
okkerneut 241
Oktober 157
olie 198, 252
oliebol 243
olietenkskip 134
olifant 205
olifanttand 205
Olimpiese Spele 263
omelet 244
onderbaadjie 45
onderbroek 44
onderrok 46
onderstel 130
onderwyser 185
onderwyser se
   lessenaar 88
ongeval 91
onkant 265
onkruid 220
ontbyt 244
ontbytgraan 245
ontsmettingsmiddel
   93
onttrekkingstrokie
   174
ontvangs 178
ontvangspersoon
   176
ontwerper 181
oog 16

ooglid 16
oogskadu 53
ooi 203
ooievaar 211
oom 30, 31
oopdekbus 112
oor 17
oorbel 49, 54
oorlel 17
oorlogskip 137
Oos 195
Oos-Kaap 296
Oos-London 297
opaal 199
openbare telefoon
   99
openbare vakan-
   siedag 156
opera 277
operasanger 183
operasie 91
operasietafel 91
opgewonde 24
oplaai 147
opneem 149
Opregte geelhout
   300
oprit 64, 107
oprygskoen 51
opsigter 185
opstyg 126
opvoeding 39
opvoutafel 131
opwasbak 70
opwasmiddel 76
orangoetang 209
oranje 153
oreganum 235
orgidee 222
orkes 277, 278
orkesbak 277
oseaan 195, 196
oudste 37
ouer 36
ouma 30, 31, 34
oupa 30, 31, 35
outomatiese teller-
   masjien (OTM)
   175
ovasie 277
pa 30, 32
paalspring 262
paaltjie 267
paaltjiewagter 267
pad 107
padda 214, 216
paddavis 216
pajamas 45, 47
pak klere 45
pakhuis 135

pakkamer 65
pakker 172
pakkie 46, 98
pakkiestoonbank
   172
paling 217
palm 20
palmboom 223
pamflet 151
pampoen 234
pampoentjies 95
panda 208
paneelkassie 110
pannekoek 246
panter 209
pantoffel 50
pap 245
papaja 231
papawer 223
papegaai 202
papier 89
papierlaai 145
papiervoerder 145
paraffien 169, 198
paramedikus 97,
   183
park 84
parkeergarage 106,
   127, 165
parkeerkaartjie 106
parkeermeter 106
parkeerplek 106,
   120
Parlement 298
pasiënt 90
pasiënt se kaart 90
paspoort 128
passasier 122
passasiersboot 134
passasiersitplek 110
passer
pasta 250
pastei 243
pasteideeg 243
pastel 153
pedaal 116
Pedi 295
peer 231
peetouer 36
pekanneut 241
pelikaan 210
pen 89
pendeltrein 124
pens 236
peper 252
perd 202
perdeby 219
perdekar 118
perderesies 261
perdevlieg 219

Afrikaans

Afrikaans

362

Afrikaans

Afrikaans

Tšhupane

Sepedi

Sepedi